Brain, Vision and AI

Edited by
Cesare Rossi

Brain, Vision and AI
Edited by Cesare Rossi

Republished by InTech
Janeza Trdine 9, 51000 Rijeka, Croatia

Additional hard copies can be obtained from orders@intechopen.com

Brain, Vision and AI, Edited by Cesare Rossi
p. cm.
ISBN 978-953-7619-04-6

For EU product safety concerns :
IN TECH d . o . o . , Prolaz Marije Krucifikse Kozulić 3 , 51000 Rijeka , Croatia ,
info@intechopen . com or visit our website at intechopen . com .

Meet the editor

Cesare Rossi was born in Naples on 26 July1955. In 1973 was graduated at High School focusing on Humanities. In 1979 received the Mechanical Engineer Degree cum Laude at the University of Napoli - Federico II; in the same year the doctoral thesis received the Asmeccanica (Italian Mechanical Engineering Association) award. In the first years of his career he has worked at the Istituto di Meccanica Applicata alle Macchine (Applied Mechanics Institute) of the University of Napoli Federico II, attending researches on traction fluids for variable speed gearboxes and cooperating at several doctoral theses. In that period he was research fellow of the A.T.A. (Automobile Technicians Association) at the same University Institute. Then he has been the technical manager of a textile industry and later designer of tools for aircraft's tests and maintenance at an aerospace industry. In Dec.1983 he was appointed Ricercatore Universitario (Assistant Professor) at the Applied Mechanics Institute (then Department of Mechanical Engineering - D.I.M.E.) of the University of Napoli Federico II. In 1992 he has been appointed Associate Professor of Applied Mechanics and from 1 nov.1993 Associate Professor of Robot Mechanics. From those years he has established a Laboratory for experimental researches on Robot Mechanics at the D.I.M.E. and is a member of G.M.A (Italian Group for Mechanics of Machinery). From 1 nov.2000 has been appointed Full Professor of Applied Mechanics at the same University. Presently teaches Mechanics Fundamentals and Robot Mechanics both to Mechanical and Automation Engineering students. He is supervisor of Master and Ph.D. theses and professor at the Ph.D. coursed at the same University. He participated to many International Conferences, often with invited lectures and as Chairman. His research activities where carried on mainly in the topics of Tribology, Rotor Dynamics, Mechanical Vibrations, Chaotic Motions of Mechanical Systems, Robot Mechanics, Video Applications for Robotics. Since several years he is interested in studies and researches on the History of Engineering and presently he cooperates with researchers (also on the field) mainly in which the Classic Age is concerned. He is a member of the A.I.S.I (Italian Society for the History of Engineering).

Preface

There is no doubt that Brain, Vision and Artificial Intelligence are among the new frontiers of science and research; in addition these topics are particularly interesting both for the young scientists and for the less young ones. Moreover, this field of research is very multidisciplinary: the scientists that carry on researches on these topics belong to wide number of different academic education since different aspects of physics, engineering and also medicine are involved. It is really exciting to meet, at the conferences on this topic, such a number of different knowledge all together.

It is possible to affirm that the results of the researches on Vision and AI will lead up to considerable changes in many fields: researches on AI will improve, for instance, the interaction between man and computer; Vision involves the robotic vision and automation, the analysis of motion, the diagnostics, the cultural heritages conservation, security and surveillance. Recent applications already permit to machines and other devices to interact with man and with the environment; this had never happened in the history of man and, until few decades ago, it seemed just science fiction.

The scientists that have contributed to this book have studied different aspects of these disciplines, therefore it is also impossible to summarize the results of their researches. Briefly, the main field of research concerned vision models, visual perception of motion, neuron models, detection and restoration, models of cellular development, multiple image detection and processing, 3D vision, human movement analysis, artificial vision applications to robotics, AI application to prediction of trip generation and distribution, applications to the replication process of the CBSRSAS systems, MOPT, ranking and extraction of single words in a text.

The Authors that have contributed to this book work at Universities and Research Institutes, practically, all over the world and the results of their researches have been published on international journals and appreciated in many international conferences.

Editor

Cesare Rossi
Full Professor of Applied Mechanics
University of Naples "Federico II" ITALY

Contents

1

Visual Perception of Semi-transparent Blotches: Detection and Restoration

V. Bruni[1], A. J. Crawford[1], A. Kokaram[2] and D. Vitulano[1]
[1]*Istituto per le Applicazioni del Calcolo "M. Picone"- C.N.R.*
[2]*Electronic and Electrical Engineering Department, University of Dublin, Trinity College*
[1]*Italy,* [2]*Ireland*

1. Introduction

Digital image restoration has become a popular area of research (Gonzalez & Woods,2002). The increased demand for archived material and the increasing power of computers have led to a need for digital methods for the restoration of degradation. Common degradation includes noise, line-scratches, tear, moire, shake and flicker (see for instance (Bruni & Vitulano, 2004; Corrigan & Kokaram, 2004; Kokaram, 1998; Kokaram, 2004; Roosmalen et al., 1999)).
An important area in digital image processing, and in particular in digital restoration, is human visual perception (Winkler, 2005). Perception laws are crucial in several image processing models. They allow for the improvement of the visual quality of the result using adaptive and automatic methods. The visibility of a given object over a background depends on contrast sensitivity, luminance adaptation and contrast masking (Winkler, 2005; Damera-Venkata et al,2000; Gutiérrez et al., 2006; Barba & Barba, 2002; Pappas & Safranek, 2000). These measures are well defined for uniform objects over uniform backgrounds while they may fail in presence of sinusoidal stimuli, i.e. highly detailed regions (Damera-Venkata et al,2000; Nadenau et al., 2003). In this case, perception depends on the distance between the observer and the object, according to the width of the analysed region and the frequency of the stimulus. It turns out that point-wise contrast measures that do not take into account the global visibility of an object in a given image, can fail in the presence of complicated patterns.

Figure 1. Examples of semi-transparent blotches: Note the variation in intensity and colour while the underlying detail remains

This is the case for semi-transparent blotches which partially or completely obscure regions of images (see Fig. 1). They are usually caused by dirt or moisture on archived material and can be seen as complicated objects over more or less detailed patterns (Kokaram, 1998; Stanco et al. 2005). They appear as irregular regions with variable shape and size, having a slightly different colour from the original one. This is the reason why they can be easily confused with scene components. The additional difficulty is their semi-transparency since they do not completely hide the underlying original information. Classical restoration or inpainting methods (Gonzalez & Woods, 2002; Bertalmio et al. 2000; Criminisi et al. 2004) cannot be used as the original image content must be retained: this is an important issue from an historical point of view. It turns out that their recognition and restoration require the introduction of global measures, like the contrast of a region (group of pixels), instead of pixel-wise measures.

This chapter introduces a generalized perception based model that mainly exploits two global perception based measures oriented to the detection of the most visible object over a given context. In order to be significant, they must be evaluated over an image component (frequency, colour channel, etc.) where the blotches are more visible --- often the most visible part. This component is used both for detecting and for modelling the overall blotch shape. This is then used to guide the blotch removal in the remaining image components according to human perception. The choice of the best component can be inferred by the physical model that causes the degradation under study. The distortion measures account for the variation of the visibility of a set of pixels over a changing background and the variation of the visibility of a changing set of pixels over a fixed background. The 'changing' function can be modified with respect to the analysed case. In the simplest case the clipping operator can be used. Its aim is to separate two different regions, as is the case for the detection and restoration of semi-transparent blotches. The two measures are based on the hypothesis that blotches are detectable (by human observers) at a 'first glance' over the image, since they are recognized as "foreign" objects in different contexts over the same image. The two measures can be used for both a global detection and a local refinement of the result: the largest region where the blotch is the most visible object. The proposed approach has been tested on two very frequent examples: scratches on old films (Kokaram, 1998) and water blotches on archived documents (Stanco et al., 2005). Extensive experimental results have shown that the proposed model achieves high visual quality results in very delicate situations, in a completely automatic manner and with a low computational effort.

2. A perception based model

As already discussed in the previous section, semi-transparent blotches are very difficult to manage because of their structure: they show the same frequency properties of the affected image. Nonetheless, they are usually perceived by a human observer 'at first glance'. It is very difficult to understand the mechanics of this process because of the high variability of both the blotch appearance and the image context of the blotch. In fact, if on one hand their intrinsic structure produces a sort of masking, on the other this peculiarity enhances its visual detection by a human observer. The proposed model tries to exploit this contradictory aspect in order to write a mathematical model that may fit this very singular behaviour.

Figure 2. Original Pyramid image (*Left*) and its Saturation component (*Right*): blotches are more visible in the Saturation component and appear as bright regions

The model may be synthesized as follows. A degraded image I has to be projected, via an operator Π, into a new space where semi-transparent blotches become the most visible object in the scene. This step tries to simulate the human visual system that reacts in presence of this kind of defect. Π's structure will depend on both the physical model that produced the blotch and the resolution (or equivalently the scale) r at which the blotch shows its greatest visibility. Once the operator Π has been performed, a distortion measure that accounts for the visibility of the blotch has to be introduced. As already outlined, available contrast definitions generally account for pixel-wise measures. Moreover, an (opaque) object over a uniform or regular background is usually considered. But this is not our case: the blotch under investigation does not completely cover the background and very often preserves and inherits the background characteristics. In the following a new distortion *DET* that will account for this requirement will be introduced. The cascade of the two aforementioned operators completes the first phase whose objective is an automatic detection of the blotch. In order to achieve a restored image, the output of the cascade above will be the input of the restoration operator *RES*. It will depend, again, on the physical model that produced the blotch. Here this dependence plays a fundamental role, since it gives the 'a priori' knowledge that makes this phase somewhat independent of the context, and therefore, of the underlying image. It is obvious that the deeper the knowledge about the formation of degradation, the lower the dependence of the restoration on the original image. This aspect gives a noticeable advantage with respect to other classical image processing problems like, for instance, denoising. It is worth outlining the fact that the operator *RES* is not necessarily defined in the space produced by Π but also in its complementary (not necessarily orthogonal) one. Mathematically speaking, the detection phase can be written:

$$DET(\Pi(I), r, p) = B_{mask} \tag{1}$$

where the symbols have already been introduced apart from p that indicates the prior knowledge about the physical model producing the blotch. The restoration phase, then, results:

$$RES(B_{mask}, \Pi(I), p, r) = \hat{I} \tag{2}$$

where $\hat{I}$ is the restored image.

3. Optimal space for vision

The first step consists of introducing a suitable operator Π that projects the image I in a space that allows an improved detection. Such an operator can be built only with a deep knowledge of the physical process that generates the blotch. That is why this operation is probably the most delicate part of the whole detection process. It corresponds to a combination of two well known tasks in image processing: features extraction and image enhancement (Gonzalez & Woods, 2002). For instance, for particular blotches like those caused by the contact between water and paper, a possible space may be the saturation component in the HSV colour space, as shown in Fig. 2. The interesting aspect to outline is that this operation is not unique. In fact, in some cases the appearance of the blotch may present more than one peculiarity, such as luminance regularity or a particular colour. Hence, the projection operator can exploit just some or all of these characteristics to determine the best projection space. For this reason, the projection operator can also be enriched by further features that better characterize the blotch.

3.1 Optimal scale for perception

Even though blotches are usually non-homogeneous, they are perceived as uniform areas since the complex background masks its coarseness. A low pass filter simulates this effect: it removes the redundant frequencies that are not perceived by the HVS and therefore enhances those regions that are perceived as homogeneous. Key to this phase is to select the optimum level of resolution $\bar{r}$. It must be a good trade off between the enhancement of the degraded region, the preservation of the geometrical shape and location of the blotch. $\bar{r}$ can be automatically selected by computing the contrast between two successive low-pass filtered versions of the detection space. A moving average filter ϕ of size r can be then used to smooth the output $\Pi(I)$ of the projection operator. The definition of contrast given by Peli (Peli, 1990) can be employed.

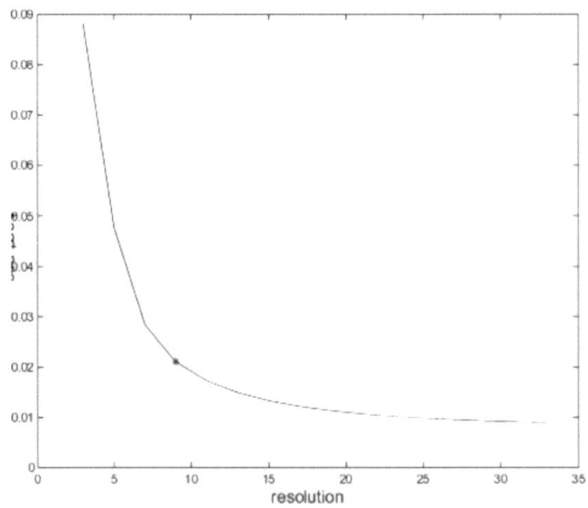

Figure 3. A typical contrast curve $C(r)$ (eq. (3)) versus resolution r. The star indicates the point where the contrast becomes less than Weber's threshold (0.02)

The rationale is that the best level of resolution $\bar{r}$ is that which measures the minimum perceivable contrast (i.e. 0.02) between two successive blurred images, i.e.

$$C(r)=\frac{1}{|\Omega|}\sum_{(x,y)\in\Omega}\frac{|(\Pi(I)*\phi_r)(x,y)-(\Pi(I)*\phi_{r-1})(x,y)|}{(\Pi(I)*\phi_r)(x,y)}, \tag{3}$$

where Ω is the image domain and $|\Omega|$ is its size. A typical behaviour of the contrast curve versus the level of resolution is depicted in Fig. 3. It is a decreasing function and the optimal point $\bar{r}$ coincides with the maximum inflection of the curve.

3.2 Contrast measures for detection

The major contribution of this part is the introduction of two new distortion measures. Their combination accounts for the global blotch visibility in the whole remaining image. Degraded regions are selected from the image $\Pi_{\bar{r}}(I)$ coming from the projection operator at the optimal scale, as shown above, i.e. $\Pi_{\bar{r}}(I)=\Pi(I)*\phi_{\bar{r}}$. A clipping operation with a perception based threshold value is then performed and a distortion measure is evaluated. The distortion metric accounts for the fact that non-uniform regions can be perceived as homogeneous. Thanks to the introduced distortion, clipping extracts the most visible regions by automatically selecting the correct threshold.
In particular, successive thresholds are applied to $\Pi_{\bar{r}}(I)$. They give different distortion values, whose maximum is achieved in correspondence to the most visible regions.
The clipping operator Θ is defined as follows:

$$\Theta(\Pi_{\bar{r}}(I),Th(t))=\begin{cases}\Pi_{\bar{r}}(I) & if \quad \Pi_{\bar{r}}(I)(x,y)\le Th(t)\\ Th(t) & otherwise\end{cases} \tag{4}$$

The threshold value $Th(t)\in[L_{\min,}L_{\max}]$, where $L_{\min}$ and $L_{\max}$ are the minimum and maximum admissible values for Th, i.e.

$$Th(t)=L_{\min}+t\ \Delta t \tag{5}$$

t is the time variable (t=0,1,2,...) while Δt is the time unit.
The distortion caused by the clipping operation can be defined as follows:

$$D(\Omega_t)=\frac{1}{|\Omega_t|}\sum_{(x,y)\in\Omega_t}D_1(x,y)D_2(x,y) \tag{6}$$

where Ω_t is the size of the region of the current blotch – i.e. detected through the actual threshold value Th(t). The first measure $D_1(x,y)$, gives the perceived distortion as the average contrast between the clipped regions of $\Pi_{\bar{r}}(I)$ and the clipping threshold value $Th(t)$ and it is defined as:

$$D_1(x,y)=\frac{\Pi_{\bar{r}}(I)(x,y)-Th(t)}{M}, \qquad \forall(x,y)\in\Omega_t \tag{7}$$

It measures the change in perception between the image with respect to the fixed background M (i.e. the mean of the degraded image), before and after clipping. In other words, it evaluates how an object of intensity $\Pi_{\bar{r}}(I)$ changes if it is substituted for the threshold value $Th(t)$. $D_1(x,y)$ is a decreasing function whose shape is depicted in Fig. 4 (left). Initially, for a decreasing threshold, it grows quickly as the clipping involves non-uniform regions with small areas. Subsequently, points with values close to the background are selected and the behaviour changes, as the threshold approaches M.

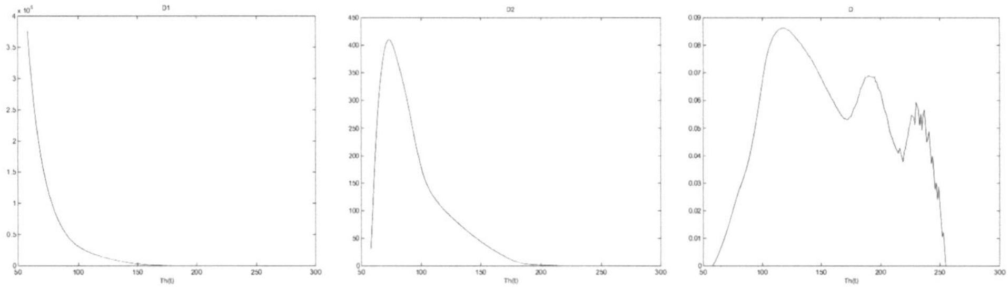

Figure 4. Distortion Curves for Pyramid image: Shown above are plot of the Distortion D_1 (Left), D_2 (Middle) and the total distortion D (Right) (using, $L_{\min} = M$, $L_{\max} = 255$ and $\Delta t=1$)

The distortion D_2 measures the change of the contrast of the same object $\Pi_{\bar{r}}(I)$ over different backgrounds (M_t and M):

$$D_2(x,y) = \frac{\Pi_{\bar{r}}(I)(x,y)(M_t - M)}{M_t M}, \qquad \forall (x,y) \in \Omega_t \tag{8}$$

Note that M_t is the background of the image after the clipping operation. It will be different from the initial M of the unclipped (original) degraded image. D_2 is the product of two different components: the first, $\Pi_{\bar{r}}(I)/\ M_t$, is a growing function with respect to the time t, i.e. as M_t decreases. The second, $(M_t - M)/M$, is a decreasing function converging to zero. As Fig. 4 (middle) shows, for larger threshold values, the term $(M_t - M)/M$ gives a minor contribution as the clipping operator selects few pixels and M_t does not change significantly. However, as the threshold decreases, M_t approaches M faster as more points close to the background are selected. Therefore, D_2 approaches zero for lower threshold values.
Combining D_1 and D_2, the maximum global distortion gives the detection threshold (see Fig. 4 (right)). As it can be observed, the distortion D achieves a trade off between the foreground and the background of the image at its maximum value. It represents the maximum contrast for the image, i.e. the maximum allowed distortion, which is able to separate different objects of the image without introducing artifacts. In fact, from that point on, pixels of the background are selected by the clipping operator, mixing the degradation and the original image. It is worth outlining that has been made the assumption that blotches are the brighter parts of the image $\Pi_{\bar{r}}(I)$. The blotch mask is found as all pixels greater than $Th(t_{\max})$, the threshold corresponding to the maximum value of $D(\Omega_t)$.

3.3 Local Detection Adjustment

For some types of degradation, it may be sometimes more useful to treat the whole image for detecting all the blotches on the image under study. However, this threshold does not

necessarily give the optimum value to detect all blotches accurately. It is therefore necessary to *fine-tune* the threshold for each blotch detected using the global method.
The distortion rate algorithm provides the optimum threshold when calculated on a segment of the image containing only the blotch and image background. When other objects are included in the segment, the threshold tends to rise. The optimum value is taken to be the minimum threshold for that blotch.

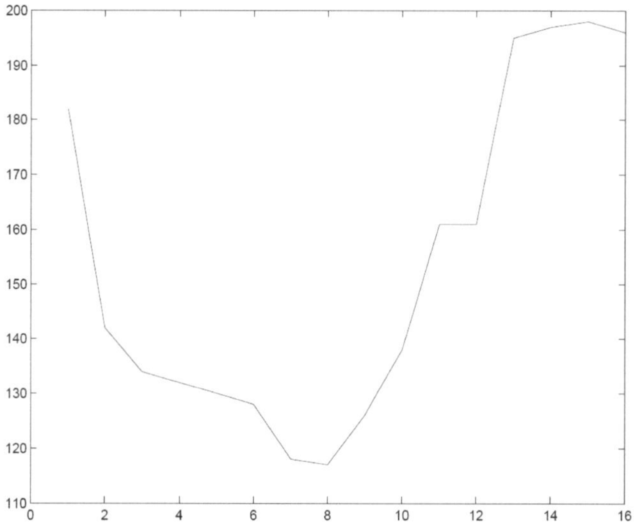

Figure 5. Fine Tuning: A plot of the threshold calculated, $Th(t_{max})$, on a square region around the blotch. As the region grows, the threshold reaches its minimum before increasing again as the region becomes too large

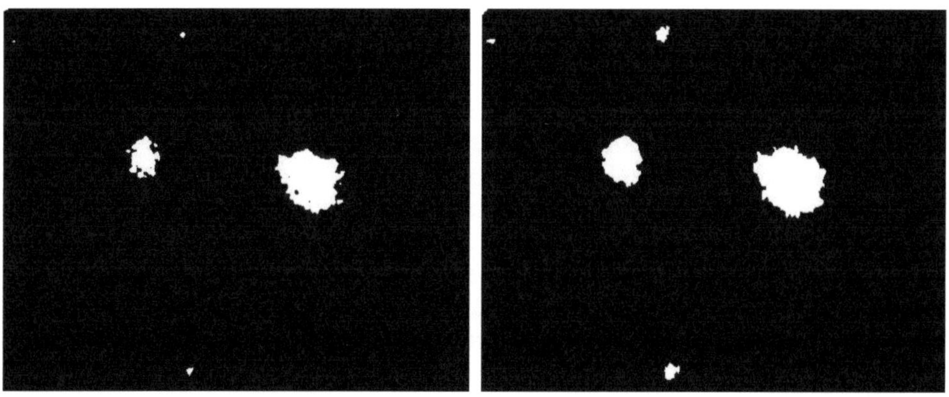

Figure 6. Detection: (Left) Image showing the blotches detected using the global detection algorithm and (Right) final detection mask after local adjustment

In order to find the optimum threshold, each connected region above the global threshold (i.e. each blotch) has its threshold re-evaluated. The Distortion Rate Algorithm is applied repeatedly to square regions around each blotch. Initially, the region is just large enough to contain the previous detection. The detection threshold is calculated for a growing region around the original detection. The threshold changes in agreement with the image content, increasing whenever new important components of the scene are included in the region. If the thresholds calculated for the increasing region are plotted, it is possible to see that it has a quite convex behaviour (see Fig. 5). More precisely, the curve monotonically decreases till the blotch is almost isolated in regions whose content does not significantly change. Therefore, in practice, the detection algorithm is applied to increasing regions surrounding the botch until the threshold reaches the local minimum. The minimum threshold calculated is taken as the optimum value. The size of the analysed regions increases along both the horizontal and vertical direction according to the optimal resolution $\bar{r}$. Fig. 6 shows an example of a global mask and a local refined mask.

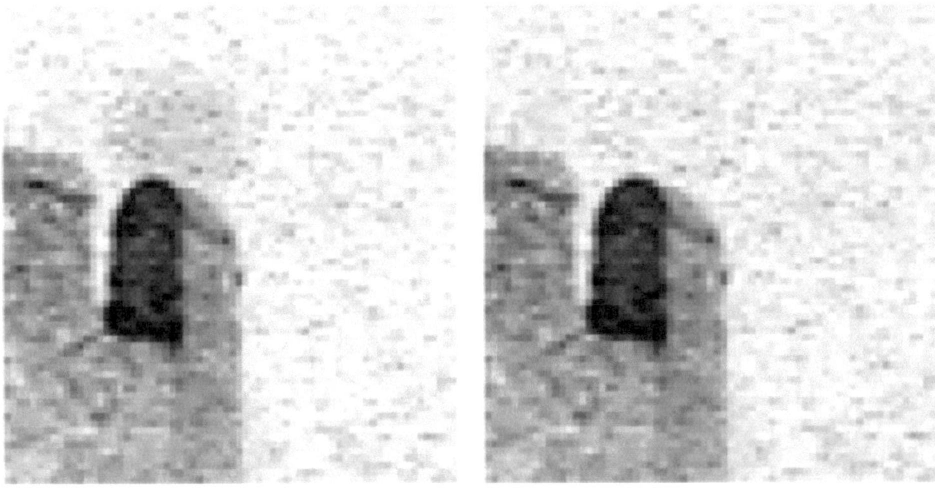

Figure 7. An example of blotch shrinking for achieving restoration: (Left) original, (Right) restored image

4. Perceptive Restoration

Restoration is another delicate step of the whole process. It may seem that after the detection step, restoration may require a minimal effort. On the contrary, it is the most difficult step if the primary objective is to recover the original image without visible artifacts. In order to achieve this goal it is often required, again, a deep knowledge of the physical model of the production of the defect. This usually suggests a possible shape or at least a sort of regularity of the shape of the blotch that should be subtracted from the degraded image. It is worth outlining that this is conceptually different from what generally happens in image processing. In the latter the properties or more specifically the regularity of the original image is assumed as 'a priori' knowledge. For instance, this is the case for denoising (Gonzalez & Woods, 2002; Mallat, 1998). In our case, as already outlined, the original image usually contains details that are still partially visible and that have to be recovered. Since a blotch frequently covers an area with a complicated background, it is not possible to adopt classical schemes for restoration. It is then more opportune a proper shape or regularity of the defect to be attenuated till it is not visible on the degraded image. An example of a restored image is shown in Fig. 7. Moreover, it is also important to highlight the fact that restoration is not necessarily performed in the same projection space adopted for detection. It often exploits the complementary space as well as different scale levels.

5. Algorithm

Shown below it is a sketch of the algorithm relative to the proposed scheme. The precise definition of the involved operators depends on the case study.

1. Define and perform the projection operator Π on the original RGB image
2. Find the best level of resolution $\bar{r}$ for the projection space, according to Section 3.1
3. Compute the mean value M of $\Pi_{\bar{r}}(I)$
4. Evaluate $D(\Omega_t)$ $\forall Th(t) \geq M$, as defined in Section 3.2
5. Find the maximum point for $D(\Omega_t)$. Let $Th(t_{max})$ be the selected threshold value
6. Produce the global detection mask (see Fig. 6 (left)) as follows:

$$Mask(x,y) = \begin{cases} 1 & if \quad \Pi_{\bar{r}}(I)(x,y) \geq Th(t_{\max}) \\ 0 & otherwise \end{cases}$$

7. Local adjustment performed to give final detection mask B_{mask} (see Fig. 6 (right)).
8. Define a shape or a regularity for the type of blotch under study, accounting for its physical model
9. Shrink the blotch until it is no longer visible – i.e. its contrast in the scene is not perceived

6. First example: scratches on old film

Line scratches are common defects on old film sequences. They appear as straight lines extending over much of the vertical extent of an image frame, as shown in Fig. 8. They can have a different colour and are of a limited width (Kokaram, 1998). They are often caused by mechanical stress during the projection of a film and occupy the same or a similar location in subsequent frames. For this reason, they cannot be classified as temporally impulsive defects.

Figure 8. Degraded frames (Knight, Sitdown and Man) having different kinds of scratch, respectively white, black and coloured

The main difficulty in detecting scratches is that they can be confused with other objects of the scene. Conventional detection methods exploit the vertical extension and the impulsive nature of the defect. For example, a suitable combination of the Hough transform for detecting vertical lines and a damped sinusoid model for the scratch horizontal projection is effectively exploited in (Kokaram, 1998), while in (Bretschneider et al., 2000), the scratch is detected in the vertical detail component of a wavelet decomposition, assuming a *sinc* shape for its horizontal projection. On the contrary, in (Joyeux et al. ,1999; Joyeux et al., 2000) scratches are characterized as temporal discontinuities of the degraded image sequence and the Kalman filter is used for their detection. As regards colour scratches, it is worth mentioning the work in (Maddalena & Petrosino, 2005): (intense) blue scratches are detected as maxima points of the horizontal projection of a suitable mask. The latter represents the enhanced vertical lines of the degraded image whose hue, saturation and value amplitudes fall into predefined ranges. With regard to restoration, most of the proposed approaches are based on the assumption that regions affected by scratches do not contain original information (Bertalmio et al., 2000; Bretschneider et al., 2000; Esedoglu & Sheno, 2002; Gulu et al., 2006; Haindl & Filip, 2002; Joyeux et al., 2000; Kokaram, 1998; Rosenthaler & Gschwind, 2001). Hence, they try to propagate neighbouring clean information into the degraded area. The neighbouring information can be found in the same frame (Bertalmio et al., 2000; Bretschneider et al., 2000; Esedoglu & Sheno, 2002; Kokaram, 1998) or also in the preceding and successive frame exploiting the temporal coherency, as done in (Gulu et al., 2006; Haindl & Filip, 2002; Joyeux et al., 2000). The propagation of information can be performed using inpainting methods, as in (Bertalmio et al., 2000; Esedoglu & Sheno, 2002), or interpolation schemes (Kincaid & Cheney, 2002). With regard to this point, different approaches have been presented. In (Kokaram, 1998), an autoregressive filter is used for predicting the original image value within the degraded area. On the other hand, a cubic interpolation is used in (Laccetti et al., 2004), by also taking into account the texture near the degraded area (see also (Rosenthaler et Gschwind, 2001) for a similar approach), while in (Bretschneider et al., 2000) low and high frequency components of the degradation are differently processed. Finally, in (Gulu et al., 2006) each restored pixel is obtained by a linear regression using the block in the image that better matches the neighbourhood of the degraded pixel. A second class of restoration approaches assumes that some of the original information is still contained in the degraded area. For that reason, in (Tenze & Ramponi, 2003) an additive multiplicative model is employed. It consists of a reduction of the image content in the degraded area until it has the same mean and variance of the surrounding information. With regard to blue scratches, in (Maddalena & Petrosino, 2005) removal is performed by comparing the scratch contribution in the blue and green colour channels with the contribution in the red channel; the assumption is that the contribution of scratches in the red channel is negligible.

In the following, after a short explanation of the physical model, a proposal for both detection and restoration is presented.

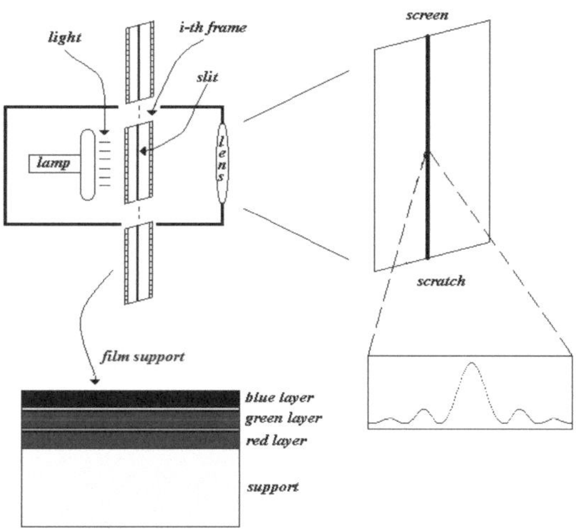

Figure 9. Scheme of the projection mechanism and the structure of the colour film support

6.1 The physical model for line scratches production

Scratches are slits on the film material. They are produced by the film transport mechanism that rubs the film material and removes a part of its content. During the projection or the scanning process, incident light passes through the slit causing diffraction (see Fig. 9). While the width of the slit regulates the width of the observed scratch, the strength (brightness of the observed scratch) of the diffraction effect depends on the depth of the scratch on the film material. In fact, if the projection mechanism does not crack the film, the incident light passes through the residual part of the film material causing the semi-transparency of the observed defect.

Hence, the scratch appears as an area of partially missing data (Bruni & Vitulano, 2004) and the horizontal section of the degraded image I can be modelled as follows

$$I(\bar{x},y)=(1-(1-\gamma)e^{-\frac{2}{m}|y-c_p|})\bar{I}(\bar{x},y)+(1-\gamma)L_{\bar{x}}(y), \quad \forall\ \bar{x} \tag{9}$$

where $\bar{I}$ is the original image, $L_{\bar{x}}(y)$ is the scratch shape function, $2m$ is its width, c_p its location and γ is a normalized parameter to be set according to the visibility of the defect on the whole image. It is tied to the depth of the scratch of the film material: the smaller γ the more perceptible the scratch (i.e. the deeper the slit). From the light diffraction, we have that the horizontal scratch shape is a $\sin c^2$ function (see Fig. 10), i.e.

$$L_{\bar{x}}(y)=b_p \sin c^2\left(\frac{y-c_p}{m}\right), \tag{10}$$

where b_p is the maximum brightness of the scratch on the image. It turns out that the most visible and less transparent part of the degraded region is the central part of the scratch ($y \in R = [c_p - m, c_p + m]$) while the transparency increases for pixels away from the centre.

The mechanical and physical formation of the defect also determines the colour of the observed scratch. In fact, the transport mechanism can impinge either on the side of the support material (negative side) or on the opposite side (positive side). This leads to black

and white scratches respectively, in case of monochromatic frames, or to differently coloured scratches on colour film. In fact, colour film is based on the subtractive synthesis, which filters colours from white light through three separate layers of sensitive (respectively to blue, green and red) emulsions (see Fig. 9). Hence, the colour of the scratch depends on how many (or which) layers have been removed during the stress of the film material.
Finally, not only the width of the slit but also the resolution of the acquisition influences the width of the observed scratch. In case of monochromatic images, this means that scratches can be 3-10 pixels wide, while for colour scratches (resolution 2K, i.e. 1828x1462 pixels) the width can vary from 3 to 30 pixels.

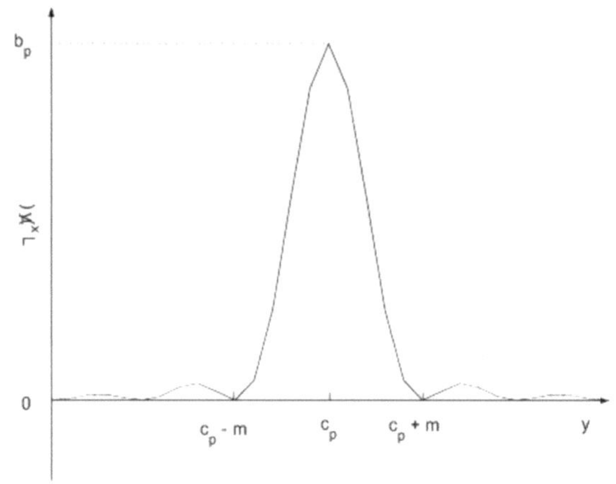

Figure 10. $Sinc^2$ shape of an ideal scratch on the horizontal cross-section of the degraded image, as in eq. (10)

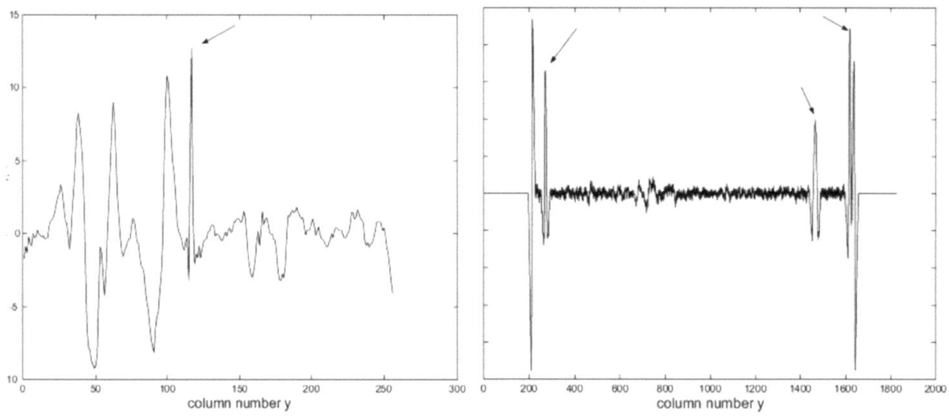

Figure 11. Horizontal cross sections of Knight and Man images in Fig. 8. Scratches are indicated by arrows. Their impulsive nature is evident

6.2. Detection

The main visible property of a scratch is its vertical extension and its horizontal impulsive nature: it is a long and thin line on the image. Hence, the optimal space for processing is that which emphasizes image high vertical frequencies. Moreover, thanks to this property, the detection of this defect can occur in a one dimensional space. Hence, the proper projection operator Π is the Radon transform of the degraded image I that is computed along the vertical direction, corrected by its local mean. This is the horizontal *cross-section* $\Pi(I)$. Scratches are then peaks of this signal, as show in Fig. 11. In fact, the Radon Transform emphasizes vertical lines while the local mean correction corresponds to a horizontal high pass filter[1].

The optimal scale for perception in this case determines the support of the high pass filter to use in the cross section computation. In our experiments, we observed that optimal scale selection algorithm in Section 3.2 gives $\bar{r} = 10$ for most of all the analysed black and white frames, corresponding to the maximum allowed width for a scratch. The same value has been obtained for colour frames, that have been subsampled by four for computational purposes.

As we have seen, scratches are peaks in the cross section. However, this condition is not sufficient to detect them without introducing false alarms. From the physical model we have some additional information: the observed scratch is caused by diffraction. It turns out that its horizontal shape can be modelled by a $sinc^2$. Hence, the detection algorithm has to extract the visible peaks of $\Pi_{\bar{r}}(I)$ that subtend a $sinc^2$ like shape, whose width is within a prefixed range. In Fig.ure 12 there are the detection results achieved on black and white frames. Scratches are the peaks of $\Pi_{\bar{r}}(I)$ that realize the maximum for the associated distortion in eq. (6). It is worth noticing that in the second picture of Fig.ure 12 the rope has also been detected. In fact, it has the same characteristics of a line scratch and it is highly visible in the image. To reject this kind of false alarms it is necessary to use a more specific procedure along the vertical direction.

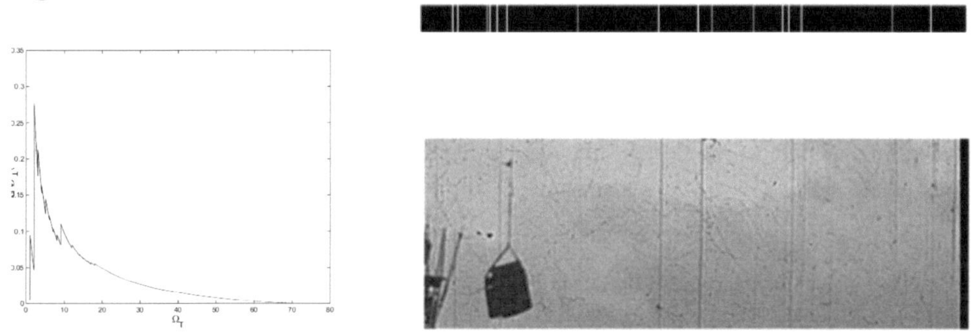

Figure 12. Detection results achieved on Sitdown image in Fig. 8. In the leftmost part of the figure there is the plot of the distortion measure D in eq. (6). The detected scratch locations are indicated in the picture on the right

7. Restoration

As we mentioned in Section 4, the restoration is performed in a domain different from that which is used for the restoration. In this case, we select the wavelet domain where only the low pass component and the vertical details are processed, according to the nature of the defect. The restoration is performed in the wavelet domain using biorthogonal symmetric filters H, G, H_r, G_r in an undecimated decomposition, using the 5/3 taps LeGall filters, as their

[1]In case of colour scratches, the operator Π is applied to the magenta component of the image where scratches are visible as white lines.

width well fits with that of the scratch . H and G respectively are the low pass and high pass analysis filters of the sub-band coding, while H_r and G_r are the corresponding low and high pass synthesis filters. This allows for a better removal of the scratch from the low pass component $I^A(x,y)$ of the degraded image. In fact, the shape of the scratch better fits the data, since it becomes more regular. Then the estimation of the scratch parameters, such as amplitude and width, is less sensitive to the local high frequencies. In the vertical high pass components $I_j^V(x,y)$ of the degraded image, the attenuation corresponds to a reduction of the contrast between the degraded region and the surrounding information at different resolutions, exploiting the semi-transparency model. The maximum level of resolution J for the decomposition is different for each scratch and it depends on its width m. More precisely, $J = \left\lceil \frac{m}{s_H} \right\rceil$, where s_H is the support of the low pass analysis filter H associated with the adopted wavelet. The shrinking coefficients are derived by inverting the equation model (9) and by embedding it in a Wiener filter like function, where the noise is the scratch, i.e.

$$w(\bar{x},y) = \frac{(I^A(\bar{x},y) - c_2 L_{\bar{x}}^A(y))^2}{\left((I^A(\bar{x},y) - c_2 L_{\bar{x}}^A(y))^2 + (\frac{c_2}{c_1} L_{\bar{x}}^A(y))^2\right)}, \quad \forall y \in R \tag{11}$$

where $L_{\bar{x}}^A(y)$ is the low pass component of the function in eq. (10), i.e. $L_{\bar{x}}^A(y) = \operatorname{sinc}^2\left(\frac{y-c_p}{m}\right) * H$, R is the scratch domain, i.e. $R = [c_p - m, c_p + m]$, $c_1 = (1-(1-\gamma)e^{-\frac{2}{m}|y-c_p|})$, and $c_2 = (1-\gamma)$. Notice that c_1 and c_2 are derived from eq. (9). The shrinking coefficients $w(\bar{x},y)$ depend on the signal to noise ratio, so that the scratch contribution is attenuated according to its local contrast. In order to make this measure more precise, the algorithm is adapted at each row of the analysed sub-band. In fact, the location c_p of the scratch could slightly change from one row to another, as well as the amplitude b_p and the width m. Therefore, the algorithm firstly corrects the global detection parameters (c_p, b_p, m) according to the local information: location of the maximum, width, asymmetry. In particular, the value of b_p is estimated from the data by minimizing the mean square error in the scratch domain R, i.e.

$$b_p = \min_{\alpha \in R} \sum_{y \in R} \left| I^A(\bar{x},y) - \alpha L_{\bar{x}}^A(y) \right|^2 \tag{12}$$

b_p is then the peak value of the *sinc*^{2} function that better matches, in the least squares sense, with the data at the considered resolution. The same procedure is repeated for the vertical detail bands $I_j^V(x,y)$ at scale j=1,…,J.

Some examples of restored images are depicted in Fig. 13. As it can be observed the visual quality of the restored image is satisfying. Scratches are removed without introducing blurring or artifacts both in the image content and in colour information, independently of the context. In particular, the underlying original information, texture or noise, is preserved thanks to the adaptivity of the attenuation filter in eq. (11) to the local image content, inside and outside the degraded region, even in presence of a diagonal edges – see the shoulder in the Knight figure, the see in Sitdown or the carpet in Man image. A Zoom of Man image is also depicted in Fig. 14.

Figure 13. Restored frames in Fig. 8 using the proposed algorithm

Figure 14. Zoom of the red scratch of Man frame in Fig. 8 (*left*) restored using the proposed algorithm (*right*)

8. Second example: water blotches on archive documents

The second example focuses on water blotches that are probably the most common defect on archived documents (Stanco et al., 2003; Bruni et al., 2004; Stanco et al., 2005). Such blotches are caused by water penetration into paper whose effect is a darker region on the document with variable shape, colour and intensity. Occasionally, dirt and dust are also present: This alters and complicates the blotch's structure.

Although an immediate detection by the human visual system on very complicated contexts, both digital detection and restoration are very difficult. Detection is difficult as the semi-transparent nature of the blotch leaves almost all high frequency information unchanged – see for instance (Bruni et al., 2006; Ramponi et al., 2005). But also the restoration phase is not trivial at all. In fact, for historical reasons the objective is to recover the document information as much as possible so that classical methods, those which synthesize information, cannot be used (Beltarmio et al, 2000; Beltarmio et al., 2003; Criminisi, 2004; Gonzalez & Woods, 2002; Kokaram, 2001). In order to reduce restoration costs, an automatic model that simulates the efficacy of the human visual system is required. In the following, after a short explanation of the physical model that causes their formation, a proposal for both detection and restoration is presented.

8.1 The physical model for water blotch production

The physical formation of a water blotch can be modelled by the spreading and penetration of water droplets into material (Clarke et al., 2002; Seveno et al., 2002). The evolution of a drop involves different parameters, such as the geometry of the original drop and the regularity of the surface of the paper. However, these parameters are unknown in real applications. The problem can be simplified by modelling the water drop as a semi-sphere (see Fig. 15) of radius R with a contact angle θ, assumed to be $\leq \pi/2$. During the spreading process, the radius grows to an equilibrium point which determines the contact angle. From this point on, the liquid is absorbed depending on the porosity of the considered medium. In ideal conditions, the central pores absorb more than the external pores, since they come in contact with the liquid earlier. This can be seen in most blotches, where the effects of the blotch are most evident towards its centre. In most cases, the spreading and absorption processes have been completed so that there is a small contact angle i.e. a smooth transition to the unaffected area.

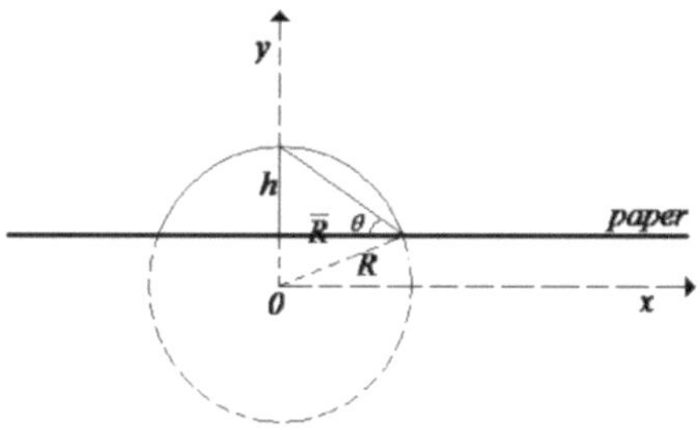

Figure 15. Model of a water drop's absorption into paper, causing a blotch

8.2 Detection

The detection phase has been performed on the Pyramid image shown in Fig. 2. left. Water blotches can be characterized by both a blurring of the degraded region and, typically, a redder colour – even though its intensity may change considerably. Hence, both the saturation component of the HSV space (that emphasizes the blurring) or an alternative component that emphasizes the redder regions can be employed. Here, the following component is proposed:

$$\Pi(I)(x,y) = Y(x,y) - Blue(x,y) \tag{13}$$

where

$$Y(x,y) = 0.3\, Red(x,y) + 0.59\, Greeen(x,y) + 0.11\, Blue(x,y) \tag{14}$$

and *Red*, *Green* and *Blue* are the colour channels in the RGB colour space.

Figure 16. (Left) Blotches appear as bright regions in the selected projection space $\Pi(I)$, as in eq. (13). (Right) Its smoothed version at scale level J=2

Fig. 16.Left shows the blue difference image $\Pi(I)$, based on contrast caused by opposed proportions of colours. In order to apply eq. (3) to select the optimal resolution, a suitable filter has to be employed. Here, the physical model plays a key role. In fact, the value of $\bar{r}$

reached via this process can be linked to a scale level J in a pyramidal decomposition (for instance a dyadic wavelet decomposition): $J = \log_2\left[\frac{\bar{r}}{s_H}\right]$, where s_H is the length of the low pass filter associated to the adopted wavelet. The *db2* (Daubechies with two vanishing moments (Mallat, 1998)) mother wavelet has been adopted as it has both minimum support and a reasonable regularity that are well adapted to the characteristic of the defect – blotches can also be regions containing 2 or 3 pixels. The computed scale level (in an undecimated dyadic decomposition) is the second one, i.e. J=2. The resulting image is shown in Fig. 16.Right.

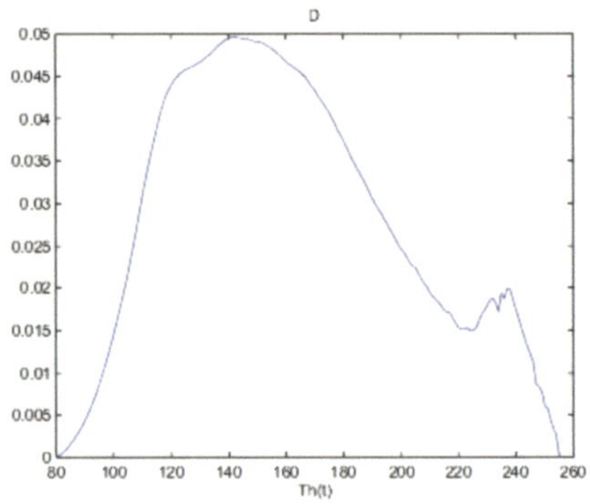

Figure 17. Distortion curve on the Pyramid image

Figure 18. (Left) Mask achieved by a global threshold. (Right) Mask after the local refinement

Figure 19. (Left) Original detail of Pyramid image. (Middle) Projection space image. (Right) Resulting final mask

At this point, the distortion introduced in section 3.2 can be performed. The plot of the distortion behaviour is shown in Fig. 17. The global detection mask, that is the output output of this phase is depicted in Fig. 18.Left. It can be observed that all blotches are automatically detected. However, if a more accurate localization is required, a local refinement has to be performed. The result of this operation is shown in Fig. 18. Right where it can be seen that blotch mask has been refined by filling holes or dilating smaller blotches. A zoom showing a small part of the sky and the castle with the relative mask is shown in Fig. 19.

8.3 Restoration

The restoration process can be performed as follows. The original (sepia) image is transformed to the HSV colour space. Each of the *H* (hue), *S* (saturation) and *V* (value) components are split into an over-complete wavelet basis until the optimal scale level, *J*. The approximation band of the intensity component V^A is restored according to the transparency model and perception laws yielding $\tilde{V}^A$. The wavelet details of the same colour component $\{V_j^D\}_{1\le j\le J}$ are left unchanged since such kind of blotch very often are smooth in agreement with the aforementioned physical model[2]. Finally, the inverse wavelet transform is performed to achieve $\tilde{V}$. The chroma components approximations H^A and S^A are subsequently processed yielding $\tilde{H}$ and $\tilde{S}$ after the inverse wavelet transform. The final restored image $\hat{I}$ is given when $\tilde{H}$, $\tilde{S}$ and $\tilde{V}$ are transformed in an RGB image.

As the blotch does not completely obscure the clean image, the luminance approximation band can be modelled as a multi-layer image similar to (Wang & Adelson, 1994), i.e. the luminance approximation band is modelled as a mixture between the clean image layer and the blotch layer (White et al., 2005). The layers mix is based on the following relationship:

$$V^A(\mathbf{x}) = \alpha(\mathbf{x})\tilde{V}^A(\mathbf{x}) + \varepsilon(\mathbf{x}) \tag{15}$$

where $V^A(x)$ is the observed luminance approximation band at point **x**, $\alpha(\mathbf{x})$ the distortion layer and $\tilde{V}^A(\mathbf{x})$ the clean luminance approximation band. Noise is represented by $\varepsilon(x) \sim N(0, \sigma_\varepsilon^2)$. Therefore, the restored luminance approximation will be:

$$\tilde{V}^A(\mathbf{x}) = V^A(\mathbf{x})\beta(\mathbf{x}) \tag{16}$$

where $\beta(x)$, the restoration function, equals: $\beta(x) = (\alpha(\mathbf{x}))^{-1}$.

The correct values of $\tilde{V}^A$ and α are those which maximise $p(\tilde{V}^A, \alpha \mid V^A, \sigma_\varepsilon^2)$. Bayes' law gives the following relationship

$$p(\tilde{V}^A, \alpha \mid V^A, \sigma_\varepsilon^2) \propto p(V^A \mid \tilde{V}^A, \alpha, \sigma_\varepsilon^2)\, p(\alpha \mid \overline{\alpha})\, p(\tilde{V}^A \mid \overline{\tilde{V}^A}) \tag{17}$$

where $\overline{\alpha}$ and $\overline{\tilde{V}^A}$ are α and $\tilde{V}^A$ in the neighbourhood of **x** respectively. It is now easier to compute the likelihoods on the right hand side of the previous equation in place of

[2]Cases where dirt causes a visible borderline of the blotch are not considered here.

$p(\tilde{V}^A, \alpha \mid V^A, \sigma_\varepsilon^2)$. The first two likelihoods on the right hand side ensure that alpha matches the behaviour of the blotch described, i.e. *i)* α must mix to give the observed data; *ii)* α must be smooth. The third term ensures that $\tilde{V}^A$ values are similar. The probabilities from expression (17) can be represented as follows:

$$p(V^A \mid \tilde{V}^A, \alpha, \sigma_\varepsilon^2) \propto \exp\left(\frac{-\left(V^A(x) - \alpha(x)\tilde{V}^A(x)\right)^2}{2\sigma_\varepsilon^2} \right) \tag{18}$$

$$p(\alpha \mid \overline{\alpha}) \propto \exp\left(-\sum_{k=0}^{n} \lambda_k (\alpha(x) - \alpha(x+q_k))^2 \right) \tag{19}$$

$$p(\tilde{V}^A \mid \overline{\tilde{V}^A}) \propto \exp\left(-\sum_{k=0}^{n} \lambda_k (\tilde{V}^A(x) - \tilde{V}^A(x+q_k))^2 \right) \tag{20}$$

where $\mathbf{x} + q_k$ is a neighbouring sample and λ_k is a weight based the distance to this sample. These expressions show that maximising $p(\tilde{V}^A, \alpha \mid V^A, \sigma_\varepsilon^2)$ is equivalent to minimising the following energy:

$$E = W_1 \frac{-\left(V^A(x) - \alpha(x)\tilde{V}^A(x)\right)^2}{2\sigma_\varepsilon^2} + W_2 \sum_{k=0}^{n} \lambda_k (\alpha(x) - \alpha(x+q_k))^2 + W_3 \sum_{k=0}^{n} \lambda_k (\tilde{V}^A(x) - \tilde{V}^A(x+q_k))^2 \tag{21}$$

Weights W_1, W_2 and W_3 regulate the emphasis on the different constraints modelled by the three terms of (21).

With regard to the algorithm, there are two main steps in the restoration process. The first step initialises each pixel inside the blotch. To each pixel is assigned a value chosen from the "clean" area close to the pixel. The next step uses the Iterative Conditional Mode (ICM) algorithm (Besag, 1986) to minimise the energy *E* from equation (21). The resulting images from these steps are shown in Fig. 20.

The initialisation step is a simple image synthesis method. For each pixel, its value is taken as a sample drawn from local "clean" pixels similar to the method used in (White et al., 2005). The local region is composed of all clean pixels contained within a circle, centred on the current pixel. The radius of the circle is proportional to the distance between the pixel and the nearest edge of the blotch. Specifically the radius is defined as: $\log(d(x)+1)+s_{\psi J}$where $d(\mathbf{x})$ is the distance to the edge and $s_{\psi J}$ is the wavelet support at the considered scale level *J*. The initialisation provides a reasonable solution for the blotch. However, it is void of the original underlying information clearly visible in the original image due to the semi-transparent properties of the blotch. To recover this information, *E* must be minimised using the original image. The initialisation gives the initial conditions for the minimisation process, $\tilde{V}_0^A$ and α_0. The minimisation is carried out using the ICM algorithm recursively improving estimates for $\tilde{V}_0^A$ and α as follows:

$$\tilde{V}_1^A \approx p(\tilde{V}^A \mid V^A, \alpha_0, \sigma_\varepsilon^2) \quad \alpha_1 \approx p(\alpha \mid V^A, \tilde{V}_1^A, \sigma_\varepsilon^2), \quad \tilde{V}_2^A \approx p(\tilde{V}^A \mid V^A, \alpha_1, \sigma_\varepsilon^2) \quad \alpha_2 \approx ...,$$

In practice, the value of α is fixed, and the E is calculated for a large range of $\widetilde{V}^A$ ([0,0.01,-0.02,0.03,…,0.99,1] for a normalised image). $\widetilde{V}^A$ is selected as that which gives the minimum value of E. The process is repeated fixing $\widetilde{V}^A$ and calculating E for a range of α. This is repeated until the whole blotch converges, i.e. the restored approximation band $\widetilde{V}^A$ is reached. The blotch is processed from the outside-in on the premise that values drawn from closer neighbourhoods are more likely to be accurate.

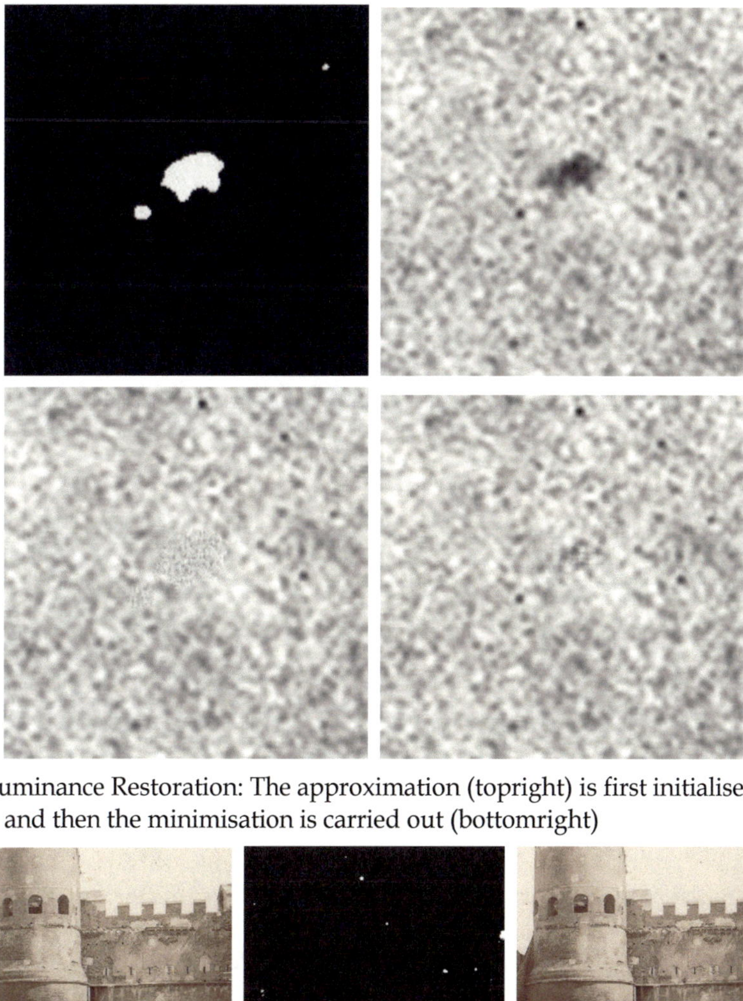

Figure 20. Luminance Restoration: The approximation (topright) is first initialised (bottomleft) and then the minimisation is carried out (bottomright)

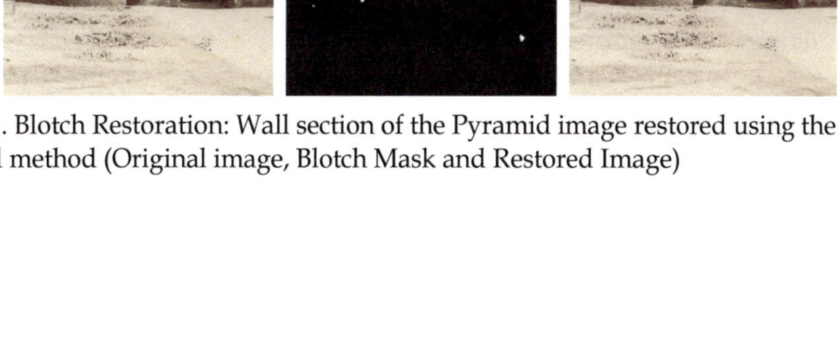

Figure 21. Blotch Restoration: Wall section of the Pyramid image restored using the proposed method (Original image, Blotch Mask and Restored Image)

Although colour images are being processed, the clean image is almost constant in colour. In the areas affected by the blotch, Hue and Saturation values are increased. However, there is no underlying colour detail as in the luminance channel. Therefore, the simple texture synthesis method adopted as the initialisation for the luminance process, applied to the approximations of H and S, is sufficient to remove the effects of the blotches from the chroma channels H and S. Finally, the restored H, S and V channels are combined to give the final restored RGB image. In order to better appreciate the proposed scheme on this kind of blotches, Figs. 21, 22, 23, show the intermediate steps as well as the final result on a zoom of the Pyramid image.

Original Luminance | Luminance Approximation | Initialisation

Minimisation | Alpha Function | Restored Luminance

Figure 22. Luminance Restoration: The four steps in Luminance restoration. Firstly, the wavelet approximation is calculated. The degraded regions are then initialised and minimisation is carried out. The Wavelet Transform is then inverted to give the restored Luminance

9. Conclusion

The two examples above show that the use of human visual perception can help in various fields of image processing and in particular in image restoration. Even though the model and the corresponding framework presented in this paper are just a first step in this direction, the achieved results show the huge potentiality of this approach. There are many cases, like those presented, that classical tools of image processing cannot manage in an efficacious manner. This is true both from the quality and from the automaticity point of view. In particular, visibility based techniques become a need for semitransparent blotches restoration. The examples of this contribution have been selected in order to present a case where image restoration shows its limits because of the difficulty in discerning the original information from the degradation one. Moreover, in cases like the aforementioned one, the line between a low level (strictly tied to the human visual system) and a high level perception (where also the brain with its classification functions is involved) becomes very subtle. We hope that this work can be a stimulus for a greater effort in investigating this interesting topic.

10. Acknowledgements

This paper has been partially supported by the FIRB project no.RBNE039LLC, "A knowledge-based model for digital restoration and enhancement of images concerning archaeological and monumental heritage of the Mediterranean coast".
The authors would like to thank Fratelli Alinari S.p.A and the Sacher Film s.r.l. for providing all the pictures and frames used in this paper.

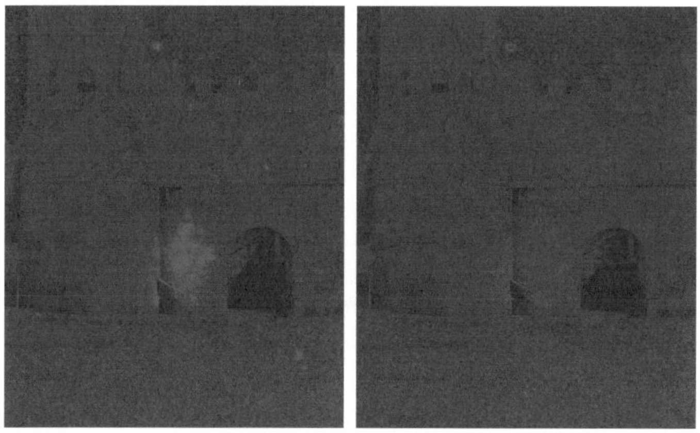

Original Hue Restored Hue

Original Saturation Restored Saturation

Figure 23. Degraded Hue and Saturation along with their restored version

11. References

Barba, M. & Barba, D. (2002). Simulating the human visual system: towards objective measurement of visual annoyance. *IEEE Transactions on Systems, Man and Cybernetics*, vol. 6, October 2002

Beltarmio, M.; Vese, L.; Sapiro, G.; Caselles, V. & Osher, S. (2003). Simultaneous structure and texture image inpainting. *IEEE Transactions on Image Processing*, vol. 12, August 2003, pp. 882 -889

Beltarmio, M; Sapiro, G.; Caselles, V. & Ballester, C. (2000). Image inpainting. *Computer Graphics, SIGGRAPH 2000*, July 2000

Besag, J. R. (1986). On the analysis of dirty pictures. *Journal of the Royal Statistical Society B*, vol. 48, pp. 259-302

Bretschneider, T.; Kao, O. & Bones, P.J. (2000). Removal of vertical scratches in digitised historical film sequences using wavelet decomposition. *Proc. of Image and Vision Computing New Zealand*, 2000, pp. 38–43

Bruni, V.; Crawford, A.; Stanco, F. & Vitulano, D. (2006) . Visibility based detection and removal of semi-transparent blotches on archived documents. *Proc. of Int. Conf. on Computer Vision Theory and Applications (VISAPP)*, Setùbal, Portugal, February 2006

Bruni, V. & Vitulano, D. (2004). A generalized model for scratch detection. *IEEE Transactions on Image Processing*, vol. 13, no. 1, January 2004, pp. 44 - 50

Clarke, A.; Blake, T.D.; Carruthers, K. & Woodward, A.(2002) . Spreading and imbibition of liquid droplets on porous surfaces. *Langmuir Letters 2002 American Chemical Society*, vol. 18, no. 8, pp. 2980–2984

Corrigan, D. & Kokaram, A. (2004). Automatic treatment of film tear in degraded archived media. *Proc. of Int. Conf. Image Processing (ICIP '04)*, Singapore, October 2004

Criminisi, A.; Perez, P. & Toyama, K. (2004). Region filling and object removal by exemplar-based image inpainting. *IEEE Transactions on Image Processing*, vol. 13, no. 9, September. 2004, pp. 1200–1212

Damera-Venkata, N.; Kite, T. D.; Evans B. L. & Bovik, A. C.(2000). Image quality assessment based on a degradation model. *IEEE Trans. on Image Processing*, vol. 9, no.4, April 2000, pp. 636–650

Esedoglu, S. & Sheno, J.. (2002). Digital inpainting based on the mumford-shah-euler image model. *European J. Appl. Math*, vol. 13, pp. 353–370.

Gonzalez, R. C. & Woods, R. E. (2002) *Digital Image Processing*. Prentice Hall, 2nd edition

Gulu, M.K. ; Urhan, O. & Erturk, S. (2006). Scratch detection via temporal coherency analysis and removal using edge priority based interpolation. *Proc. of IEEE International Symposium on Circuits and Systems, 2006*, May 2006.

Gutiérrez, J. ; Ferri, F. J. & Malo, J. (2006). Regularization operators for natural images based on nonlinear perception models. *IEEE Transactions on Image Processing*, vol. 15, no. 1, January 2006, pp. 189–200.

Haindl, M. & Filip, F. (2002). Fast restoration of colour movie scratches. *Proc. of ICPR 2002, Quebec, Canada*, August 2002, pp. 269–272.

Joyeux, L. ; Boukir, S. &Besserer, B. (2000). Film line removal using kalman filtering and bayesian restoration. *Proc. of IEEE WACV'2000, Palm Springs, California*, December 2000.

Joyeux, L. ; Buisson, O. ; Besserer, B.& Boukir, S.(1999). Detection and removal of line scratches in motion picture films. *Proc. of CVPR'99, Fort Collins, Colorado, USA*, June 1999.

Kincaid, D. & Cheney, W.(2002). *Numerical analysis*. Brooks/Cole, 2002.

Kokaram, A. C. (2001). Advances in the detection and reconstruction of blotches in archived film and video. *Proceedings of the IEE Seminar on Digital Restoration of Film and Video Archives*, London UK, January 2001.

Kokaram, A.C. (2004). On missing data treatment for degraded video and film archives: a survey and a new bayesian approach. *IEEE Transactions on Image Processing*, vol. 13, no. 3, March 2004, pp. 397 - 415.

Kokaram, A.C. (1998) *Motion Picture Restoration: Digital Algorithms for Artefact Suppression in Degraded Motion Picture Film and Video*. Springer Verlag

Laccetti, G. ; Maddalena, L. & Petrosino, A. (2004). Parallel/distributed film line scratch restoration by fusion techniques. *Lectures Notes in computer Science, Springer Berlin*, vol. 3044/2004, September 2004, pp. 525–535.

Maddalena, L. & Petrosino, A. (2005). Restoration of blue scratches in digital image sequences. *Technical Report ICAR-NA*, vol. 21, December 2005.

Mallat, S. (1998) *A Wavelet Tour of Signal Processing*. Academic Press

Nadenau, M. J.; Reichel, J. & Kunt, M. (2003) Wavelet-based color image compression: Exploiting the contrast sensitivity function. *IEEE Transactions on Image Processing*, vol. 12, no. 1, January 2003, pp. 58–70.

Pappas, T.N. & Safranek, R.J.(2000). Perceptual criteria for image quality evaluation. *Handbook of Image and Video Processing (A. C. Bovik, ed.)*, Academic Press 2000, pp. 669–684.

Peli, E. (1990). Contrast in complex images. *Journal of the Optical Society of America A*, vol. 7, October 1990, pp. 2032–2040.

Ramponi, G. ; Stanco, F. ; Dello Russo, W. ; Pelusi, S. & Mauro, P. (2005). Digital automated restoration of manuscripts and antique printed books. *Proc. of Electronic Imaging and the Visual Arts (EVA)*, Florence, Italy, March 2005.

Rosenthaler, L. & Gschwind, R. (2001). Restoration of movie films by digital image processing. *Proc. of IEE Seminar on Digital Restoration of Film and Video Archives 2001*, 2001.

Seveno, D.; Ledauphine, V.; Martic, G. & Voué, M. (2002). Spreading drop dynamics on porous surfaces. *Langmuir 2002 American Chemical Society*, vol. 18, no. 20, pp. 7496–7502.

Stanco,F., Ramponi, G. & De Polo, A.(2003). Towards the automated restoration of old photographic prints: A survey. In *IEEE EUROCON*, Ljubjana, Slovenia, Sept. 2003, pp. 370–374.

Stanco, F.; Tenze, L. & Ramponi, G. (2005). Virtual restoration of vintage photographic prints affected by foxing and water blotches. *Journal of Electronic Imaging*, vol 14, no. 4, December 2005.

Tenze, L. & Ramponi, G. (2003). Line scratch removal in vintage film based on an additive/multiplicative model. *Proc. of IEEE-EURASIP NSIP-03, Grado, Italy*, June 2003.

van Roosmalen, P.M.B.; Lagendijk, R.L. & Biemond, J. (1999). Correction of intensity flicker in old film sequences. *IEEE Transactions on Circuits and Systems for Video Technology*, vol. 9, no. 7, pp. 1013–1019.

Wang J.Y. A. & Adelson, E. H. (1994). Representing moving images with layers. *IEEE Transactions on Image Processing*, vol. 3, no. 5, September 1994, pp. 625–638.

White, P.R. ; Collis, W.B.; Robinson, S. & Kokaram, A.C. (2005). Inference matting. *Proc. of Conference on Visual Media Production (CVMP)*, November 2005.

Winkler, S. (2005) *Digital Video Quality - Vision Models and Metrics*. John Wiley and Sons

2

Computing the Vulnerable Phase in a 2D Discrete Model of the Hodgkin-Huxley Neuron

Dragos Calitoiu, B. John Oommen and Doron Nussbaum
Carleton University
Canada

1. Introduction

In several neurological diseases, like essential tremor, the functions of the brain are severely impaired by synchronized processes, in which the neurons fire in a synchronized periodical manner at a frequency closely related to that of the tremor. Stimulation techniques have been developed to desynchronize these neuronal populations. One such technique is the electrical Deep Brain Stimulation (DBS) (Luders, 2004), (Mayberg, 2005) which is performed by administering a permanent high frequency periodic pulse train to the brain by means of so-called *depth* electrodes. The DBS method was developed empirically, and its mechanism has not yet been understood.

Another stimulation technique is the perturbation with brief stimuli. Clinical results for this technique (some of them are briefly presented in this chapter) prove that a carefully chosen brief pulse applied at a specific time, denoted by the term "vulnerable phase", can *annihilate* the firing behaviour in the neuron. It is believed that by determining the vulnerable phase of a neuron, the result can be generalized to a population of neurons.

In this context, the first neural model analytically investigated in great detail was the Hodgkin-Huxley (HH) neuron, which exhibits stable periodic solutions for a certain range of constantly applied depolarizing currents.

To study the latter from a variety of perspectives, we shall first present, in Section 1.1, the dynamics of the HH neuron. Then, in Section 1.2, we informally describe its annihilation and stability properties and compare its characteristics with the properties of some of its close "relatives". Finally, in Section 1.3, we shall describe the HH model from the context of the works of Winfree and Guckenheimer.

1.1 Dynamics of the HH neuron

We present now a few considerations about the dynamical properties of the HH neuron. This neural model can be in one of two states: a resting state and a state that fires in response to certain forms of stimulation. Usually, the neuron is considered to be in a stable mode when it is in a resting state. However, this statement is not universal because there are two stable states associated with this neuron, namely a fixed point and the limit cycle, both of which are stable. One problem to be considered here is the switching of the neuron from one stable mode to the other, which is a phenomenon that can occur without modifying the number and the stability of the equilibria.

Put in a nutshell, we would like to determine if the HH neuron in 2D is controllable (i.e., if it can be driven from a quiescent state to a spiking state and vice versa). However, it turns out that the general system is unsolvable, the latter being a consequence of three well-known fundamental results, namely Hilbert 16-th Problem, the Poincare-Bendixon Theorem and the Hopf Bifurcation Theorem. These three results are cited to prove that an analytic analysis to obtain the exact representation of the separatrix is not feasible. Having achieved this, we proceed to tackle the problem of concern from a topological perspective, and show that the control is achievable by exciting the system with an appropriate pulse. Not only have we proved the existence of this pulse, but also described its characteristics (amplitude, duration etc.).

From a classical system theory point of view, the stable point of a nonlinear dynamical system may disappear or may lose its stability if a control parameter is changed, depending on the type of bifurcation displayed by the system. In our research, the HH neuron is considered to be a dynamical nonlinear system whose stable states are not to be radically changed with regard to its stability. We investigate the case when both stable states, namely the fixed point and the limit cycle, co-exist and remain stable. In addition to the fixed points and limit cycles, a 2D system can also possess homoclinic[1] points, which, in turn, imply the existence of a hyperbolic invariant set on which the 2D system is chaotic.

In this particular situation, the system is bi-stable, without homoclinic points, and, with a carefully chosen synaptic input, it is possible to switch the behaviour from being resting to one which demonstrates spiking, or from being spiking to a resting (spike annihilation) mode. The goal of this research is to describe the properties of the stimulus that can achieve this switching.

This above stimulus, chosen to be a brief pulse of current, is not a control parameter. Its behaviour affects neither the existence of the fixed points or limit cycles, nor their stability. The control parameter is the strength of the constantly applied current and, during our investigation, it is set to be constant. We argue that injecting a constant current into the axon is not equivalent to injecting a brief pulse of current. In the former, the system can go through a bifurcation of the stable state by changing the existence of the stable states or by affecting their stability. In the latter, however, the system can jump to an alternate location in the state space, which is achieved by the system resetting the initial condition. The neuron is driven to a state of "shock", and consequently, the membrane potential instantly switches

---

[1] It can be advantageous to clarify the concepts of points that are *homoclinic* and *heteroclinic*. We do this by invoking the following definitions essentially from (Devaney , 2003). Let p be a repelling fixed point, with $f'(p) > 1$, namely $|f(x)-p| > |x-p|$. We define a local unstable set at p, denoted as $W^u_{loc}(p)$, to be the maximal open interval in the neighbourhood of p. A point q is said to be *homoclinic* to p if $q \in W^u_{loc}(p)$ and if there exists $n>0$ such that $f^n(q)=p$ (where $f^n(x)$ is defined as $f(f^{n-1}(q))$). The point q is *heteroclinic* if $q \in W^u_{loc}(p)$ and if there exists $n> 0$ such that $f^n(q)$ lies on a different periodic orbit. If p has a homoclinic point q, p it is also so-called "snap-back repellor". Since q, by definition, lies in the local unstable set in the neighbourhood of p, it is possible to define a sequence of pre-images of q, each of which lies closer to p in the local unstable set. Thus, the homoclinic point, q, together with its backward orbit defined by the pre-images and its forward orbit, is called a homoclinic orbit. This orbit has the property that it tends to the fixed point, p, when a "backward iteration" is invoked, and it lands on the same fixed point if a "forward iteration" is invoked.

to a new value. The fixed point, corresponding to the resting state, co-exists with the limit cycle, which corresponds to the spiking state, and the system continues to be bistable. This leads us to the goals of this research: (i) to prove analytically the existence of such stimuli, and (ii) to describe the characteristics of these brief depolarizing shock-stimuli that, when inserted at the appropriate time, can switch the neuron from the spiking to the resting state.

1.2 The HH neuron: the annihilation perspective

The annihilation of the firing activity was predicted theoretically by Teorell (Teorell, 1971) for a two-variable model of a sensory pacemaker. He showed that the annihilation of the firing activity can be achieved by using a small brief test pulse injected into the refractory period, just prior to the system attaining to its firing level. Later, the annihilation of the spike train, by using a carefully chosen stimulus, was predicted by Rinzel[2] (Rinzel, 1980) and also independently by Best (Best, 1979). Rinzel calculated periodic solutions to the space-clamped HH equations when a depolarizing current was constantly applied. The computational analysis of Best stated that one could "shock" the HH neuron out of the repetitive mode by using a properly timed instantaneous current pulse. In addition, Guttman, Lewis, and Rinzel (Guttman, 1980) experimentally confirmed that repetitive firing in a space-clamped squid axon, merely stimulated by a suprathreshold step of current, can be annihilated by a brief depolarizing or hyperpolarizing pulse of the proper magnitude, applied at the proper phase. After the resting potential of the axon (whose central compartment was bathed in low *Ca* artificial seawater) had reached a steady state, the threshold for repetitive firing was established by a manually triggered stimulation with a step of current, 30 ms in duration, to avoid overstimulation of the axon. Thereafter, a slightly suprathreshold current step of approximately 30 ms duration, was used as a bias in order to initiate the repetitive firing. Upon being excited by this bias current, various magnitudes of brief 0.15 ms perturbations were added at various phases in the period of the response, to investigate the control of repetitive firing. In response to such perturbations, membrane potentials and ionic currents showed damped oscillations that converged towards a steady state. For the non-annihilating perturbations, the repetitive firing of the system resumed with an unaltered frequency, but with a modified phase.
Closely related to the Rinzel model for the HH neuron, is the model due to FitzHugh-Nagumo. Theoretical considerations relevant to the latter have also been derived by Baer and Erneux (Baer, 1986), who studied the phenomena of singular Hopf bifurcations from a basic state to that involving relaxation oscillations. For the model of the FitzHugh-Nagumo neuron, they analyzed the switching from a stable steady state to a stable periodic solution (spike generation) and the reverse situation (spike annihilation). They succeeded in formally explaining both these phenomena.

1.3 The HH neuron: the Winfree/Guckenheimer perspective

The annihilation problem that we have solved for a 2-dimension HH neuron can be viewed from an entirely different perspective. This point of view involves the control of the

[2] Although the Rinzel model that we have used is a few years old, we do not believe that it is outdated. As far as we know, the Rinzel model is probably the best reported 2-D model for the HH structure. Furthermore, is also well known that increasing the accuracy of the coefficients does not modify the fundamental dynamics of the neuron.

isochrones of a general dynamical system, and in particular, of networks involving neurons akin to the HH neuron. Historically, the origin of this perspective can be traced to "traditional biology", where Winfree, in his pioneering papers (Winfree, 1974) and (Winfree, 1977) anticipated the existence of a perturbing stimulus that could affect the dynamics of the system. This hypothesis actually resulted from his initial research on fibrillation, which involves the uncontrolled fluttering of the heart, possibly leading to sudden cardiac death. Later, Winfree applied topological concepts to investigate the effects of involving disturbing stimuli that could change the human biological clock expressed, for example, by alternating sleep-wake cycles at almost-regular intervals. He predicted that in order to generate an arrhythmic pattern, a stimulus should be applied at a specific point in the sleep-wake cycle. Winfree further suggested mathematical models for describing this family of behaviours related to biological clocks, and though these models were very pertinent, they also provided a fertile ground for further research because they raised unforeseen topological questions, that were related to phase resetting.

Winfree's research phenomena were subsequently investigated by Guckenheimer (Guckenheimer, 1975), who, on the other hand, described analytically, using the foundational theory of ordinary differential equations, many of the open problems proposed by the former. In particular, he concentrated on the existence and the properties of the above mentioned "isochrones". However, while Winfree's interest was related to biological clocks, Guckenheimer's intention was to establish a methodology for analyzing the stability of the limit cycle, which is a component of the dynamics of biological clocks. From this perspective, and based on the so-called assumption of nondegeneracy, Guckenheimer determined the condition for which two points could be isochrones. He concluded that the existence of isochrones is determined by the flow near the limit cycle, and more specifically, formulated the theorems that involve the intersections of the isochrones of a limit cycle and the neighborhood of its *frontiers*.

The followings are the three topics proposed by Winfree, and which Guckenheimer proved analytically in (Guckenheimer, 1975): 1. The properties of the isochrone lines: Guckenheimer showed that these are related to a stable manifold in a dynamical system, this being a special case of the Invariant Manifold Theorem. 2. The topology of a stable manifold of a stable limit cycle: Guckenheimer showed that this determines the dimension of its frontier. 3. The properties of points in the neighbourhood of the frontier that intersects the isochrones.

The last problem involves three distinct directions. The first direction introduced the concept of *open-dense sets* of vector fields. The second investigation included the concept of *generic*[3] *subsets*. The third theorem used the previous results and proved the existence of dense open subsets of vector fields with the property that every neighbourhood of every point in the frontier meets each isochrone of the limit cycles. Guckenheimer also tested his results experimentally. He stated that the results displayed one of the following two phenomena: (i) The destruction of the oscillation entirely, or (ii) The fact that points arbitrarily close to each another lay on isochrones of every point of a limit cycle. In summary, Guckenheimer's work was conducted so as to analytically characterize the second scenario.

To present our work in this perspective, we, first of all, mention that in our research, we analytically investigate the first scenario. Also, we can formally describe the relation between our work and the Winfree-Guckenheimer research, as follows:

---

[3] A subset of a topological space is *generic* if it is a countable intersection of open-dense sets.

Similarity: Both of approaches investigate the stability of a dynamical system, with the goal of controlling it in the neighbourhood of a limit cycle. The control is achievable by exciting the system with an appropriate pulse, which is invoked when the system is in the neighborhood of the limit cycle. Finally, both Guckenheimer and we demonstrate that the characteristics of the limit cycle determine the effect of the excitation.
Difference: Although the similarities between the works exist, it is prudent for us to highlight the dissimilarities. Our first intention is to prove the existence of the stimulus that is able to entirely *destroy* the oscillation -- which is an issue that Guckenheimer has not analyzed. To achieve this, we have used the bi-stability property of the HH neuron, with the goal of annihilating the oscillation, and of forcing the system to move through the stable fixed point. Consequently, we have also investigated analytically the first scenario unearthed by the simulations that Guckenheimer reported. From an analytical point of view, Guckenheimer's work investigated the conditions that maintain the limit cycle to be unaffected by the stimuli. His work is related only to the neighbourhood of the stable limit cycle without investigating a model which contains both a stable limit cycle, a fixed point *and* a region separating them which includes a separatrix - an *unstable* limit cycle. Thus, Guckenheimer has not investigated the effect of adding a stimulus with a goal of forcing the system through separatrix so as to reach the fixed point.
In contrast to the previous pieces of work cited above, which validated experimentally or anticipated theoretically that annihilation is possible, we achieve the following:

1. We formally prove that the problem of spike annihilation has a well defined solution.
2. We formally derive the characteristics of the proposed solution.
3. We demonstrate experimentally the validity of the solution (i.e., by numerical simulations).

All of the results are novel, and we thus believe that our analysis of the HH neuron has practical implications in clinical applications[4], especially in the case of the desynchronization of neuronal populations.

1.3 Format of the chapter

Section 1 presents an overview of the clinical research related to the problem of spike annihilation in HH neurons. Section 2 contains the dynamical formulation of the problem, namely the bistable neuron, the equations of the system, and its stable and unstable limit cycles. Section 3 investigates the problem of annihilation and presents a formal proof of the existence of the stimulus, and the suggested numerical approach for computing the bifurcation point. Section 4 describes the experiments conducted for determining the properties of the annihilation stimulus, and Section 5 concludes the chapter.

---

[4] A few investigations which are applicable to optimizing the characteristics of the stimuli used to annihilate real NNs have been reported. Two renowned investigators, in this field are Dr. Osorio from University of Kansas - Kansas Medical Center, and Dr. McIntyre from Carleton University, in Ottawa, Canada. The former has been praised for his work in the project titled "Safety, tolerability and efficacy of high-frequency periodic thalamic stimulation in inoperable mesial temporal epilepsy" (Osorio et al., 2005), and the latter is well known for his work in low frequency brain stimulations against kindled seizures (Carrington et al., 2007) and (McIntyre et al., 2005). Unfortunately, their more recent results are not published yet.

2. The bistabile HH neuron

In this section we investigate the stability-related characteristics of the HH neuron. In the previous section, we stated that the HH neuron can be perceived as a dynamical nonlinear system with two stable equilibria. This is formalized below.
Consider a two-dimensional dynamical system:

$$\frac{dV}{dt}=P(V,R) \tag{1}$$

$$\frac{dR}{dt}=Q(V,R) \tag{2}$$

where $P(V,R)$ and $Q(V,R)$ are polynomials of real variables V and R, and where the corresponding coefficients are real. The fundamental problem associated with the qualitative theory of such systems seems to be the second part of Hilbert's Sixteenth Problem (Gray, 2000), stated as follows:

> *Specify the configuration and the maximum number of limit cycles that a planar polynomial differential system can have as a function of its degree.*

This problem remains unsolved.
It should be mentioned that there are many methods which yield *specific* results related to the study of limit cycles. However, the above general problem has not been solved,[5] even for the quadratic systems. Rather, we intend to explore, *numerically*, the less general system defined by Equations (3) and (4) proposed by Wilson (Wilson, 1999), which, indeed, approximate the Hodgkin-Huxley neuron:

$$\frac{dV}{dt}=\frac{1}{\tau}\left[-(a_1+b_1V+c_1V^2)(V-d_1)-e_1R(V+f_1)+B+\sigma\right] \tag{3}$$

$$\frac{dR}{dt}=\frac{1}{\tau_R}(-R+a_2V+b_2) \tag{4}$$

where $a_1, a_2, b_1, b_2, c_1, d_1, e_1, f_1, \tau$ and τ_R are constants[6], B is the background activity[7], and σ is an excitation stimulus. Apart from deriving certain specific analytic results, we propose to discover, *numerically*, the number and the positions of the limit cycles.
By introducing Hilbert's Sixteenth Problem as a motivation for the solutions of the system, we argue that the numerical approach to yield the number and the relative positions of the

[5] Solutions for specific cases of classes of planar differential equations, such as the Lienard equations, systems having homogeneous components of different degree, homogeneous systems perturbed by a constant system, etc. have been reported. Even in these cases, the solutions only yield the number of limit cycles, but not their specific forms.
[6] In their experiments, Wilson (Wilson,1999) set the constants as: a_1=17.81, b_1=47.71, c_1=32.63, d_1=0.55, e_1=0.55, f_1=0.92, a_2=1.35, b_2=1.03, τ=0.8 ms and τ_R =1.9 ms. The stimulus σ was expressed in μA/100, and V was measured in deci-volts. All these values were assigned to mimic real-life brain phenomena.
[7] The background activity generates limit cycles in the system. Without this value, the system will converge through the stable spiral point.

limit cycles of the system, described by Equations (3) and (4), is the only reasonable strategy (instead of an analytical one) to tackle the problem.

It is true that there are some theoretical results (Gray, 2000), which can be postulated as theorems, that can be applied for two-dimensional nonlinear systems. But their contributions are only qualitative without being capable of describing the *complete* picture of the number and the relative positions of the limit cycles. Thus, in the interest of completeness we mention these formal results that can be used to prove that a system described by Equations (3) and (4) has a limit cycle and a bifurcation point.

In our analytical approach, we propose the following:

1. To identify if in the space of the trajectories of the HH neurons there is only a single area corresponding to the spiking behaviour, and only a single area corresponding to the quiescent behaviour.
2. To identify the curve that separates these two areas - also known as the "separatrix". Observe that the knowledge of the equations of the curve can lead us to determine a stimulus that crosses the boundary, from the spiking state area into the quiescent state area. Since the explicit form of the separatrix is not available (and cannot be determined), we intend to use topological arguments to demonstrate the existence of the excitation sought for.

In this vein, after computing the fixed points and analyzing their stability, we shall further investigate the computation of the limit cycles. The first hurdle encountered is the fact that the stable limit cycle that corresponds to the spiking behaviour has a set of equations that cannot be determined analytically. In addition, the curve that separates the two areas is itself a limit cycle, *albeit* an unstable one, that also can not be computed analytically. Thus, as mentioned earlier, we have opted to prove the existence of the curve that separates the two areas by using only topological arguments. Having achieved this, we shall proceed to solve the original problem, i.e., to prove the existence of the stimulus by using only qualitative aspects of the system. Thus, we shall answer the following: (i) When do the limit cycles occur? and (ii) When is a limit cycle stable or unstable?

To aid us in this endeavour, we shall use the results of the following theorems, first explained informally, and then more formally.

1. **The Poincare-Bendixon Theorem**. This theorem states that if a system has a long-term trajectory in a two dimensional state space limited to some finite-size region, called its *invariant* set[8], the system has a fixed point or a limit cycle. This theorem works only in two dimensions because only in a two-dimensional domain a closed curve separates the space into a region "inside" the curve and a region "outside". Thus, a trajectory starting inside a limit cycle can never get out of it, and a trajectory starting outside can never enter into it.
2. **The Hopf Bifurcation Theorem**. This theorem describes the birth and the death of a limit cycle. We resort to this result because our task is to prove the existence of an unstable limit cycle (i.e., the separatrix) between the basin of attraction of the attracting fixed point and the basin of attraction of the attracting stable limit cycle. Fortunately, this separatrix, which can only be proven to exist using the Hopf Bifurcation Theorem, is the curve that separates the area that corresponds to the spiking behaviour and the second area that corresponds to the quiescent behaviour.

---

[8] Any trajectory starting from a point in this region will stay there for all time.

The reader will observe that as a consequence of these theorems, we can conclude that it is not possible to find the analytical representation of the separatrix, although we can prove its existence.

2.1 Related Theoretical Foundation

The first useful Theorem, due to Poincare and Bendixon (Hilborn, 2000), defines the conditions for the existence of a limit cycle.

The Poincare-Bendixon Theorem

1. *Consider a system whose long-term motion of a state point in a two-dimensional state space is limited to some finite-size region;*
2. *Suppose that this region, say R, is such that any trajectory starting within R stays within R for all time*[9].
3. *Consider a particular trajectory starting in R. There are only two possibilities for that trajectory:*
   a. *The trajectory approaches a fixed point of the system as $t \to \infty$.*
   b. *The trajectory approaches a limit cycle as $t \to \infty$.*

The *Hopf Bifurcation Theorem* and a supporting result (referred to as *Theorem 0*) (Devaney, 2003) presented below, define the conditions for the existence of a stable or unstable limit cycle. The following theorems[10] are essentially taken from (Devaney, 2003).

Theorem 0 *Consider the family of maps $F_\mu(z)=\mu z+O(2)$ where μ is not a kth root of unity for $k=1,\ldots,5$. Then there is a neighborhood U of 0 and a diffeomorphism L on U such that the map $L^{-1} \circ F_\mu \circ L$ assumes the form $z_1=\mu z + \beta(\mu) z^2 z' + O(5)$.*

Hopf Bifurcation Theorem *Suppose F_λ is a family of maps depending on a parameter λ and satisfying:*

i. $F_\lambda(0)=0$ *for all* λ.

ii. $DF_\lambda(0)$ *has complex conjugate eigenvalues* $\{\mu(\lambda), \mu'(\lambda)\}$ *with* $|\mu(0)|=1$ *and* $\mu(0) \neq k^{th}$ *root of unity for* $k=1,\ldots,5$.

iii. $\dfrac{d}{d\lambda}|\mu(\lambda)| > 0$ *when* $\lambda=0$.

iv. In the normal form given by Theorem 0, the term $\beta(\mu(0))<0$.

Then there is an $\varepsilon > 0$ and a closed curve ζ_λ in the form $r=r_\lambda(\theta)$, defined for $0 < \lambda < \varepsilon$ and invariant under F_λ. Moreover, ζ_λ is attracting in a neighborhood of 0 and $\zeta_\lambda \to 0$ as $\lambda \to 0$.

It is necessary to mention the following two relevant remarks, taken from (Devaney, 2003):

1. The assumption that $\dfrac{d}{d\lambda}|\mu(\lambda)| > 0$ when $\lambda=0$ means that the eigenvalues cross from the inside of the unit circle to the outside as λ increases.
2. If we reverse the inequalities (ii), (iii) and (iv) above, the *Hopf Bifurcation Theorem* still remains valid. However, after the bifurcation, the invariant circle is repelling while the origin is attracting.

The *Hopf Bifurcation Theorem* indicates that in the parameter space there is a limit cycle. It does not tell us whether this is an unstable limit cycle or an asymptotically stable limit cycle. However, the theorem specifies where in the parameter space we can search to locate a limit cycle behaviour. Thus, although we are not able to provide the equation that describes the limit cycle, we can qualitatively describe it.

---

[9] R is called an "invariant set" for the system.

[10] The notation *O(k)* means terms of degree *k* or more.

To render our theoretical consideration meaningful, in the following, we shall derive:
1. The fixed points of the HH neuron by solving the system of equations described by the isoclines,
2. The Jacobian corresponding to the system described by Equations (3) and (4), at the fixed points,
3. The eigenvalues of the Jacobian, by solving the characteristic equation associated with the Jacobian, and
4. The requirements on the eigenvalues as specified by the *Hopf Bifurcation Theorem* for identifying the limit cycle.

2.2 Computing the fixed points

Consider a system described by Equations (3) and (4). We compute the fixed points by solving the system of equations described by their isoclines. This is formalized in the following Lemma.

Lemma 1 *The fixed points of the HH neuron can be obtained by solving a cubic polynomial equation:*

$$x_3V^3+x_2V^2+x_1V+x_0=0, \tag{5}$$

where: $x_3=-c_1$, $x_2=-(b_1+a_2e_1-c_1d_1)$, $x_1=-(a_1-b_1d_1+a_2e_1f_1+b_2e_1)$, $x_0=a_1d_1-b_2e_1f_1+B$.

Proof From Equations (3) and (4), we see that the system has two isoclines, specified by the contours: $\frac{dV}{dt}=0$ and $\frac{dR}{dt}=0$, which can be written as:

$$\frac{1}{\tau}[-(a_1+b_1V+c_1V^2)(V-d_1)-e_1R(V+f_1)+B]=0, \tag{6}$$

$$\frac{1}{\tau_R}(-R+a_2V+b_2)=0. \tag{7}$$

The background activity B is the control parameter β specified in the *Hopf Bifurcation Theorem*.

The fixed points can be computed as solutions of Equations (6) and (7). By substituting R from Equation (7) as $R=a_2V+b_2$, and utilizing this value in Equation (6), we obtain the equation:

$$x_3V^3+x_2V^2+x_1V+x_0=0, \tag{8}$$

where the coefficients x_3, x_2, x_1 and x_0 are as defined in the Lemma statement. Hence the Lemma.

Remarks:
1. The roots for the variable V in Equation (5) can be computed for specific values of B, the background stimulus, which is constantly applied to obtain a bistable neuron.
2. Using the settings of Rinzel and Wilson (Wilson, 1999), assigned to mimic real-life brain phenomena, Equations (6) and (7) become:

$$\frac{1}{\tau}[-(17.81+47.71V+32.63V^2)(V-0.55)-26R(V+0.92)+B]=0 \qquad (9)$$

and

$$\frac{1}{\tau_R}(-R+1.35V+1.03)=0. \qquad (10)$$

The fixed points can thus be computed as solutions of Equations (9) and (10), leading to the resulting cubic polynomial equation:

$$-32.6304V^3-64.8632V^2-50.6416V+B-14.8424=0 \qquad (11)$$

The roots of the Equation (11) are computed for specific values of *B*, and tabulated in Table 1.

B	Root1	Root2	Root3
0	-0.6979	-0.6449+0.4856i	-0.6449-0.4856i
0.025	-0.6947	-0.6465+0.4854i	-0.6465-0.4854i
0.05	-0.6915	-0.6482+0.4852i	-0.6482-0.4852i
0.06	-0.6902	-0.6488+0.4852i	-0.6488-0.4852i
0.065	-0.6896	-0.6491+0.4852i	-0.6491-0.4852i
0.07	-0.6889	-0.6494+0.4851i	-0.6494-0.4851i
0.075	-0.6883	-0.6498+0.4851i	-0.6498-0.4851i
0.08	-0.6876	-0.6501+0.4851i	-0.6501-0.4851i
0.085	-0.6870	-0.6504+0.4851i	-0.6504-0.4851i
0.1	-0.6850	-0.6514+0.4850i	-0.6514-0.4850i
0.125	-0.6818	-0.6530+0.4849i	-0.6530-0.4849i
0.15	-0.6785	-0.6546+0.4848i	-0.6546-0.4848i
0.2	-0.6720	-0.6579+0.4847i	-0.6579-0.4847i
0.25	-0.6655	-0.6612+0.4846i	-0.6612-0.4846i

Table 1. The roots of the value *V* variable for the fixed points equation of the HH neuron as a function of *B*, the background stimulus. The parameters of the neuron are as advocated in (Wilson, 1999)

3. To consider the real-life settings, we have also computed the corresponding value of *R* for all the real values of the roots, *V*, namely for *Root1* from Table 2. From this Table, we can deduce the range of values for *R* that is useful in simulating brain-like phenomena. These values will be used later in this paper.

B	Root1(V)	R=R(V)
0	-0.6979	0.0878
0.025	-0.6947	0.0922
0.05	-0.6915	0.0965
0.06	-0.6902	0.0982
0.065	-0.6896	0.0958
0.07	-0.6889	0.1000
0.075	-0.6883	0.1008
0.08	-0.6876	0.1017
0.085	-0.6870	0.1025
0.1	-0.6850	0.1052
0.125	-0.6818	0.1096
0.15	-0.6785	0.1046
0.2	-0.6720	0.1140
0.25	-0.6655	0.1228

Table 2. The values of R obtained for a real root of the fixed points as computed for a particular value of B. The parameters of the neuron are as advocated in (Wilson, 1999)

2.3 Computing the Jacobian

We now consider a Jacobian-based analysis of the HH neuron, formalized in the following Lemma.

Lemma 2 *The Jacobian matrix of the system representing the HH neuron is given by:*

$$J(V,R)=\begin{pmatrix} y_{12}V^2+y_{11}V+y_{10} & y_{21}V+y_{20} \\ y_{30} & y_{40} \end{pmatrix},$$

where $y_{12}=-\frac{1}{\tau}3c_1$, $y_{11}=-\frac{1}{\tau}(2b_1+2c_1d_1+a_2e_1)$, $y_{10}=-\frac{1}{\tau}(a_1+b_1d_1+e_1b_2)$, $y_{21}=-\frac{1}{\tau}e_1$, $y_{20}=-\frac{1}{\tau}f_1$, $y_{30}=-\frac{1}{\tau_R}a_2$, *and* $y_{40}=-\frac{1}{\tau_R}$.

Proof We know from the theory of dynamical systems that the Jacobian matrix of the system is :

$$J(V,R)=\begin{pmatrix} \frac{\partial V(V,R)}{\partial V} & \frac{\partial V(V,R)}{\partial R} \\ \frac{\partial R(V,R)}{\partial V} & \frac{\partial R(V,R)}{\partial R} \end{pmatrix}$$. Evaluating each of these components yields:

$$\frac{\partial V(V,R)}{\partial V}=\frac{\partial\left[\frac{1}{\tau}\left[-(a_1+b_1V+c_1V^2)(V-d_1)-e_1R(V+f_1)+B\right]\right]}{\partial V}=$$

$$=\frac{1}{\tau}\,[-3c_1V^2-(2b_1+2c_1d_1)V-(a_1+b_1d_1)-e_1R],$$

$$\frac{\partial V(V,R)}{\partial R}=\frac{\partial\left[\frac{1}{\tau}\left[-(a_1+b_1V+c_1V^2)(V-d_1)-e_1R(V+f_1)+B\right]\right]}{\partial R}=-\frac{1}{\tau}\,e_1(V+f_1),$$

$$\frac{\partial R(V,R)}{\partial V}=\frac{\partial\left[\frac{1}{\tau_R}\left(-R+a_2V+b_2\right)\right]}{\partial V}=\frac{1}{\tau_R}\,a_2,$$

$$\frac{\partial R(V,R)}{\partial R}=\frac{\partial\left[\frac{1}{\tau_R}\left(-R+a_2V+b_2\right)\right]}{\partial R}=-\frac{1}{\tau_R}.$$

However, Equation (7) can be used to eliminate R from the partial derivatives. By achieving this, and omitting the laborious algebraic steps, the result follows.

Remarks:

1. Observe that the Jacobian J is not dependent on B. However, it is clear that J can be evaluated at each fixed point, which, in turn, is dependent on B.
2. Using the same settings of Rinzel and Wilson (Wilson, 1999), the Jacobian matrix of the "real-life" HH neural system becomes:

$$J(V,R)=\begin{pmatrix}\frac{\partial V(V,R)}{\partial V} & \frac{\partial V(V,R)}{\partial R}\\ \frac{\partial R(V,R)}{\partial V} & \frac{\partial R(V,R)}{\partial R}\end{pmatrix},\quad \frac{\partial V(V,R)}{\partial V}=-122.36V^2-74.40V+10.55-32.5R;$$

$$\frac{\partial V(V,R)}{\partial R}=-32.5V-29.9;\quad \frac{\partial R(V,R)}{\partial V}=0.71053;\quad \frac{\partial R(V,R)}{\partial R}=-0.52632.$$

As mentioned in the proof of the Lemma, Equation (10) can be used to eliminate R from the partial derivatives and thus, the Jacobian becomes:

$$J(V)=\begin{pmatrix}-122.36V^2-118.28V-22.937 & -32.5V-29.9\\ 0.71053 & -0.52632\end{pmatrix}.$$

2.4 Finding the bifurcation point

We shall now consider the problem of finding the neuron's bifurcation point by using the dynamical matrix of the system. This value of the bifurcation point is used to "set" the neuron so as to render it to be bi-stable.

Theorem 1 *A HH neuron obeying the Equations (3) and (4) has a bifurcation point if and only if a root of the equation*

$$\frac{1}{\tau}[-3c_1V^2-(2b_1+2c_1d_1)V-(a_1+b_1d_1)-e_1R]-\frac{1}{\tau_R}=0 \text{ satisfies the inequality } V>-f_1-\frac{1}{e_1}\frac{1}{\tau_R}.$$

Proof It is well known that for the bifurcation point, the roots of the characteristic equation, computed from the Jacobian, are purely imaginary. It is also well known that a quadratic equation $x^2-Sx+P=0$ has imaginary roots if:

Condition 1: $S = 0$,

Condition 2: $P > 0$,

where S and P are the sum and the product of the roots, respectively.

Consider the Jacobian of the HH neuron as given by *Lemma 2*. Applying *Condition 1* to this Jacobian generates the equation:

$$\frac{1}{\tau}[-3c_1V^2-(2b_1+2c_1d_1)V-(a_1+b_1d_1)-e_1R]-\frac{1}{\tau_R}=0.$$

This equation has two roots, say V_1 and V_2. The problem now is one of verifying whether V_1 and V_2 satisfy *Condition 2*. This in turn implies that for V_1 and V_2:

$$\frac{1}{\tau_R}\frac{1}{\tau}[-3c_1V^2-(2b_1+2c_1d_1)V-(a_1+b_1d_1)-e_1R]+\frac{1}{\tau_R}\frac{1}{\tau}e_1(V+f_1)>0.$$

We can rewrite this inequality using the observation that V_1 and V_2 are solutions to the equation corresponding to *Condition 1*, namely: $\frac{1}{\tau}[-3c_1V^2-(2b_1+2c_1d_1)V-(a_1+b_1d_1)-e_1R]=\frac{1}{\tau_R}$.

Using this relation, *Condition* 2 becomes: $\frac{1}{\tau}+\frac{1}{\tau_R}\frac{1}{\tau}e_1(V+f_1)>0.$

We know that τ and τ_R are time constants, being positive. We make a convention that e_1 is also a positive constant. With these considerations, *Condition* 2 can be rewritten in a new form as: $V>-f_1-\frac{1}{e_1}\frac{\tau}{\tau_R}$. The theorem follows since whenever these constraints are satisfied, we obtain purely imaginary roots.

Remarks:

1. As before, using the same settings of Rinzel and Wilson (Wilson, 1999), *Condition 1* applied to the Jacobian generates the equation $-122.36V^2-118.28V-22.937-0.52632=0$, whose roots are -0.6879 and -0.2788. It is easy to verify whether either of these roots satisfy the constraint specified by *Theorem 1*. Observe that the first root, V=-0.6879,

satisfies the *Condition 2* that is equivalent to $V > -0.9361$, implying that the HH neuron has a bifurcation point.

2. From Equation (11), we can compute the value of B that corresponds to the root V=0.6879. This value[11], of B=0.0777, generates a bifurcation in the system.
3. The second root, -0.2788, does not have any biological significance, being distant from the resting potential of the neuron.
4. The values of the roots (and the corresponding stability consequences) are tabulated in Table 3 as a function of B. Examining this table, we can conclude (using the notation of the *Hopf Bifurcation Theorem*) that α=0.0777. Thus, if B<0.0777 (namely, $\beta < \alpha$) the system has an stable spiral point. If $B > 0.0777$, the stable spiral point becomes unstable and the system has a stable limit cycle. The value $B = 0.0777$ is a subcritical or hard Hopf bifurcation point. The system has an unstable limit cycle for $B < 0.0777$, and this is a point that is not observable in the real world due to its instability. It is only possible to *detect* the *consequences* of its presence.

B	$V_{equilib}$	λ_1	λ_2	
0	-0.6979	- 0.2565+2.2485i	- 0.2565-2.2485i	S
0.025	-0.6947	- 0.1731+2.2534i	- 0.1731-2.2534i	S
0.05	-0.6915	- 0.0909+2.2554i	- 0.0909-2.2554i	S
0.06	-0.6902	- 0.0579+2.2555i	- 0.0579-2.2555i	S
0.065	-0.6896	- 0.0909+2.2554i	- 0.0909-2.2554i	S
0.07	-0.6889	- 0.0909+2.2554i	- 0.0909-2.2554i	S
0.075	-0.6883	- 0.0100+2.2548i	- 0.0100-2.2548i	S
0.08	-0.6876	+0.0075+2.2543i	+0.0075-2.2543i	U
0.085	-0.6870	+0.0225+2.2537i	+0.0225-2.2537i	U
0.1	-0.6850	+0.0721+2.2514i	+0.0721-2.2514i	U
0.125	-0.6818	+0.1504+2.2456i	+0.1504-2.2456i	U
0.15	-0.6785	+0.2299+2.2372i	+0.2299-2.2372i	U
0.2	-0.6720	+0.3825+2.2138i	+0.3825-2.2138i	U
0.25	-0.6655	+0.5300+2.1820i	+0.5300-2.1820i	U

Table 3. Eigenvalues of the Jacobian computed from the real root of the fixed point equation obtained with particular values of the background stimulus B. Last column describes the stability of the fixed points, namely S (stable) and U (unstable)

[11] The more exact value is 0.07773267 and it is obtained for V=-0.687930 and R=0.101295. The Largest Lyapunov exponent for this Hopf bifurcation is 1.000287e-002. For his neural model, Cooley et al. (Cooley et al., 1965) found a value of 0.0765 (7.65 μA) for the value of B. By increasing the stimulus further, he obtained finite trains of shortening duration, and finally, at higher intensities, claimed to obtain the annihilation.

2.5 The Stable and Unstable Limit Cycles

If we consider B to be a control parameter, we can analytically compute the fixed point, which, for certain values of σ, leads to a *spiral stable point* and, for other values of σ, leads to an *unstable spiral point*. The behaviour around a specific value, namely the change of the stability of the fixed point, induces the concept of a *subcritical (hard) Hopf bifurcation*.

Let us focus on the issue of the limit cycles themselves. By plotting the evolutions of the numerical solutions of the system (Equations (3) and (4)), we discover that for the settings of Rinzel and Wilson (Wilson, 1999), there is a stable limit cycle to the right of the bifurcation point. To identify a hypothetical unstable limit cycle, we can modify the system's equations to make time run "backwards". The modification, which consists of rendering the sign of the two constants, τ and τ_R, to be negative, changes the unstable limit cycle to become asymptotically stable. In this way, by using a numerical method, we can identify the position of a second limit cycle, which happens to be unstable. The stable spiral point is surrounded by this unstable limit cycle which, in turn, acts as a *separatrix* defining a basin of attraction for the stable point.

In Figures 1 and 2 we present the stable and unstable limit cycles, together with the isoclines $\frac{dV}{dt}=0$ and $\frac{dR}{dt}=0$. The trajectory starts at the point indicated by '1' and follows the arrowed curves. Observe that in the case of Figure 1, the trajectory of the HH neuron follows the stable limit cycle, and in Figure 2, the trajectory follows the unstable limit cycle. Figure 3 depicts the bifurcation diagram. When B is increased from the resting value, the steady state remains asymptotically stable and the spikes are generated only after the bifurcation point is reached by increasing the value of B. In other words, the HH neuron indicates spiking at B = 0.0777, and the spiking process continues for all values of B > 0.0777.

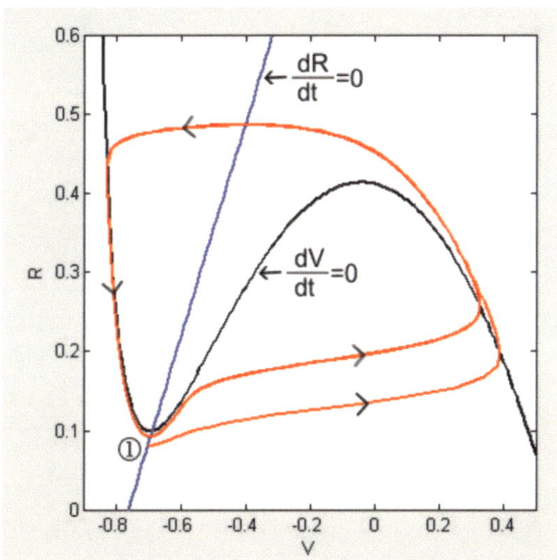

Figure 1. The phase space representing the *stable* limit cycle and the resulting isoclines ($\frac{dV}{dt}=0$ and $\frac{dR}{dt}=0$) obtained by using Rinzel and Wilson settings for the HH neuron. The starting point, (represented by '1') is V_0=-0.7, and R_0=0.08. In addition, B=0.08

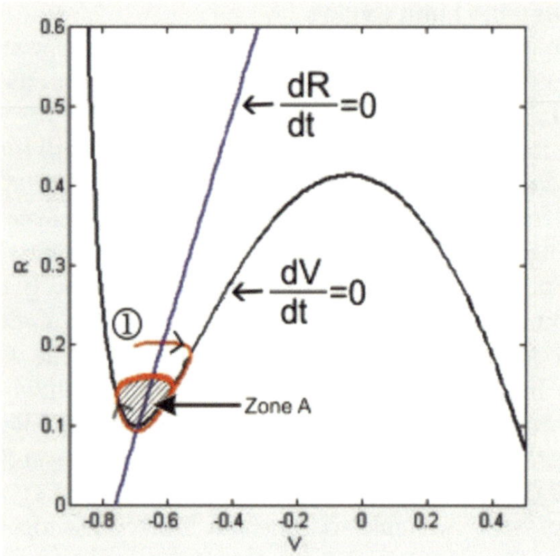

Figure 2. The phase space representing the *unstable* limit cycle and the resulting isoclines ($\frac{dV}{dt}$=0 and $\frac{dR}{dt}$=0) obtained by using Rinzel and Wilson settings for the HH neuron. The starting point, (represented by '1') is V_0=-0.7, and R_0=0.2. In addition, B=0.08

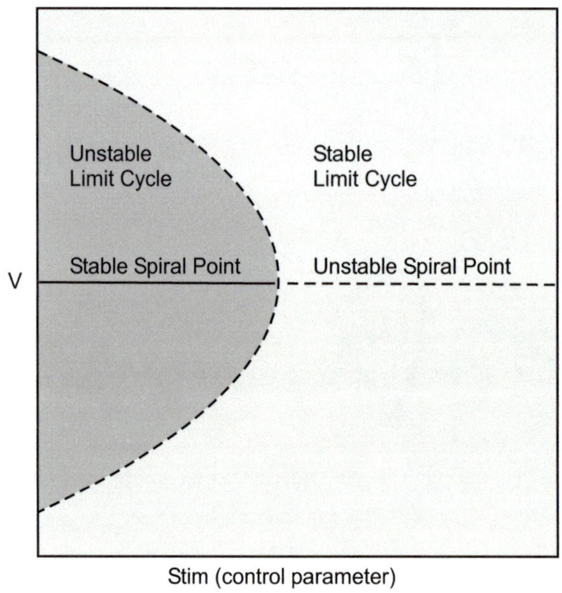

Figure 3. The bifurcation diagram for the system specified in Figures 1 and 2. The variable B is the control parameter. We consider B as a background stimulus that generates a bi-stable neuron

3. The problem of annihilation

The problem of the annihilation of spikes for the HH neuron involves moving the state of the system, by using a pulse stimulus, from outside a particular zone (denoted as $Zone_A$) to being inside $Zone_A$, where $Zone_A$ is a basin of attraction of the stable spiral point which is described by an unstable limit cycle. For example, if the system is characterized by the settings specified by Rinzel and Wilson (Wilson, 1999), $Zone_A$ is contained in the region given by $V\in[-0.6, -0.8]$ and $R\in[0.1, 0.15]$, as depicted in Figure 2. Figure 4 contains all the steady states of the system, including the stable spiral point, and the stable and unstable limit cycles.
The success of the annihilation process depends on four crucial issues:

1. What should be the initial point *(V,R)* for the system to exhibit annihilation?
2. When should the pulse stimulus, σ, be applied to the system to annihilate it?
3. What should the amplitude of the pulse stimulus be for the annihilation to be achieved?
4. What should the duration of the pulse stimulus be for the annihilation to be achieved?

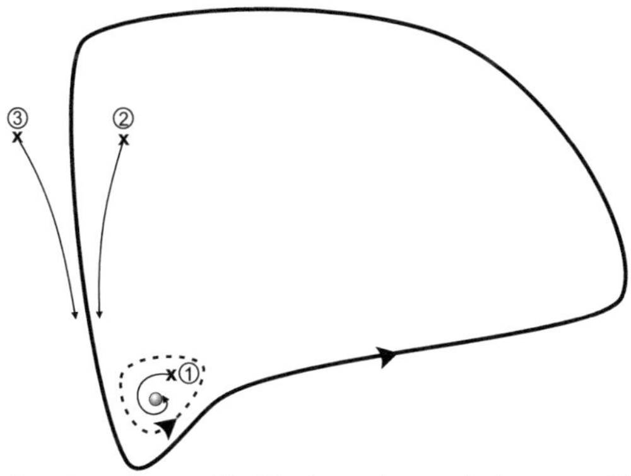

Figure 4. The stable fixed point, the stable limit cycle, and the unstable limit cycle (the *separatrix* given by the dashed line) are represented together. If the system starts in State 1, it will move towards the stable fixed point. If it starts in State 2 or State 3, it will converge to the stable limit cycle

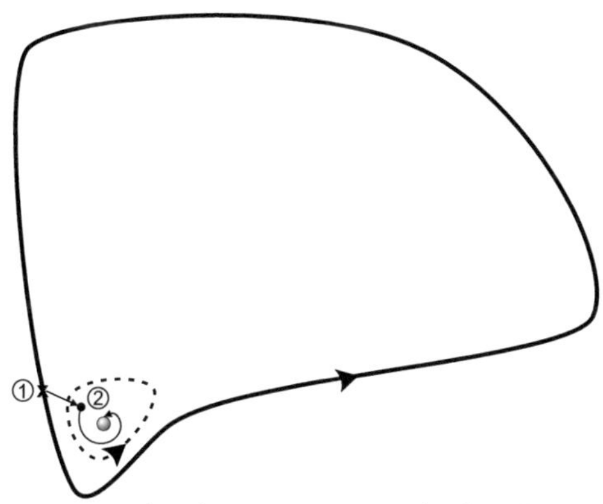

Figure 5. The annihilation process for the system specified in Figures 1 and 2. If the system starts in a carefully chosen configuration at State 1 on the stable limit cycle, the system can be driven to State 2 by applying a carefully chosen stimulus. From this state, it will then go to the stable fixed point

The solution of the annihilation problem consists of determining a stimulus which adequately responds to all the above questions.
We now formally prove that the problem of spike annihilation is well-defined, and propose an algorithm for finding a solution to it. In addition, we also study the solution of annihilating the spikes by using multi-stimuli. Finally, we investigate the inverse problem, namely that of spike generation (see Figure 6).

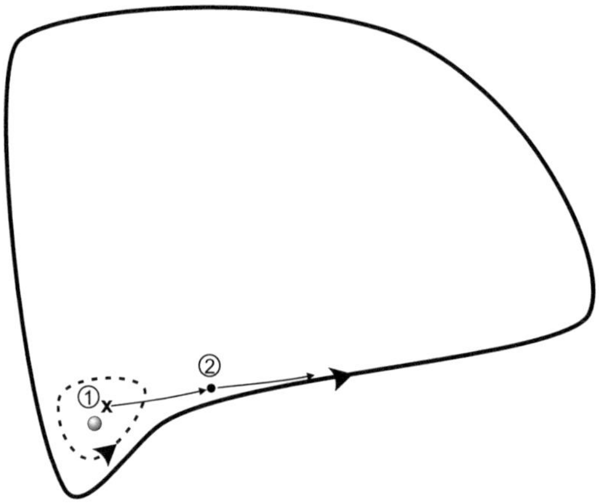

Figure 6. The spike generation process for the system specified in Figures 1 and 2. If the system starts in a stable fixed point or at State 1, in the close neighborhood of the stable fixed point, the system can be driven to State 2, by applying a specific stimulus, and, from this state, it will go further toward the stable fixed point

The two problems are clarified in Figures 5 and 6. In Figure 5 we present the annihilation process. If the system starts in a carefully chosen configuration at State 1 on the stable limit cycle, the system can be driven to State 2 by applying a carefully chosen stimulus. From this state, it will then go to the stable fixed point. Similarly, in Figure 6, we depict the spike generation process. If the system starts in a stable fixed point or in State 1, in the close neighborhood of the stable fixed point, the system can be driven to State 2 by applying a specific stimulus, and, from this state, it will go further toward the stable fixed point.
We propose to solve the problem of annihilation from two perspectives:
Problem 1 We plan to analytically demonstrate that the spike annihilation problem has a well-defined solution.
The strategy of solving *Problem 1* consists of:

a. Computing the steady states.
b. Analyzing the stability of the steady states.
c. Computing the bifurcation points and the bifurcation diagram.
d. Computing the stable and unstable limit cycles.
e. Analyzing the existence of the stimulus that can annihilate the system.

Problem 2 We intend to numerically compute the characteristics of the stimuli that achieve annihilation, for the settings of Rinzel and Wilson (Wilson, 1999).
The strategy of solving *Problem 2* consists of:

a. Proposing an algorithm for computing the moment of insertion, the magnitude, and the duration of the stimulus used to annihilate the system.
b. Analyzing the problem for the case when there are multiple stimuli.

3.1 The NN Neuron Annihilation Theorem

Since we are interested in annihilating the spikes, we shall demonstrate that this can be done by invoking a discretized[12] time model. To achieve this, first of all, we rewrite the dynamical system of equations for a bi-stable model of the HH neuron in a discrete-time manner as:

$$V[n+1]=V[n]+\frac{1}{\tau}[-(a_1+b_1V[n]+c_1V^2[n])(V[n]-d_1)-e_1R[n](V[n]+f_1)+B+\sigma], \quad (12)$$

$$R[n+1]=R[n]+\frac{1}{\tau_R}(-R[n]+a_2V[n]+b_2) \quad (13)$$

The general Theorem of Annihilation is formally written below.

Theorem 2 (HH Neuron Annihilation) *Consider a system described by its discretized dynamical equations:*

$$\begin{pmatrix} V[n+1] \\ R[n+1] \end{pmatrix} = \begin{pmatrix} V[n] \\ R[n] \end{pmatrix} + \begin{pmatrix} f_1(V[n],R[n]) \\ f_2(V[n],R[n]) \end{pmatrix} + \underline{S}[n], n=0,1,... \quad (14)$$

where f_1 and f_2 specify the unexcited dynamics, and $\underline{S}[n]$ is the excitation applied to the system. If the system has a stable limit cycle, a stable spiral point and an unstable limit cycle which separates the fixed point and the stable limit cycle, then, there exists an excitation function $\underline{S}[n]$, which equals 0 everywhere except at a specific point $(V[0],R[0])$ on the stable limit cycle, at which point $S[0]$ has the value $[A, 0]^T$ for a duration of one iteration, and which when applied to the system, forces it from the stable limit cycle to the stable spiral point.

Proof Consider the system defined by Equation (14), which has the excitation $\underline{S}[n]$. Analyzing the Jacobian of the system, we observe that it has the same form[13] as the one corresponding to the continuous case. Thus, all the qualitative results obtained in the previous Section are also applicable for the discrete time approach, and thus, the system has a stable fixed point, a stable limit cycle and an unstable limit cycle (also known as a *separatrix*).

---

[12] A continuous-time approach cannot be invoked to prove this theorem because, by virtue of its relation to Hilbert's Sixteenth Problem, it is not known how we can compute the explicit solutions for the system of equations.

[13] The Jacobian of the system is obtained by computing the partial derivative with respect to the state variables without involving time (continuous or discrete). If the system variable u is expanded infinitesimally around a quiescent point u_0 as $u=u_0+\Delta u$, the continuous system will lead to $\frac{du}{dt}=F(u)$ and the discrete system will lead to $u_{n+1}=F(u_n)$. By dropping the quadratic and higher order terms in Δu, we can obtain for each of these two systems: $\frac{d\Delta u}{dt}=DF(u_0)\Delta u$ and $\Delta u_{n+1}=DF(u_0)\Delta u_n$, respectively. Observe that the Jacobian in both cases has the same form.

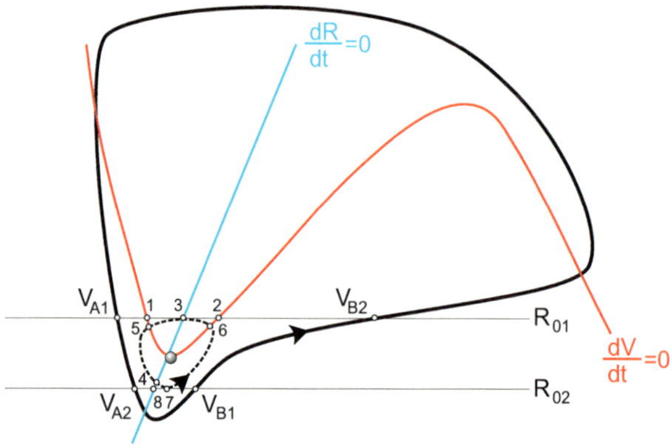

Figure 7. The stable spiral point, the stable and the unstable limit cycle for the bi-stable HH neuron

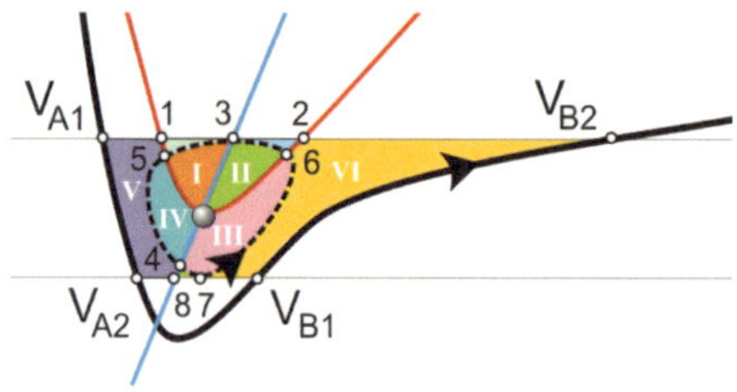

Figure 8. A zoom-in of the Figure (7), namely the phase space of the bi-stable HH neuron. The regions $A_{Out,1}$ and $A_{Out,2}$ correspond to *Area V* and *Area VI*, respectively. The regions $A_{In,1}$, $A_{In,2}$, $A_{In,3}$, and $A_{In,4}$ correspond to *Area I*, *Area II*, *Area III*, and *Area IV*, respectively

For the purpose of proof, we define three distinct areas in the state space, as depicted by Figure 8:

1. We denote A_{In} as the region corresponding to the basin of attraction of the stable fixed point, bordered by the separatrix.
2. We observe two regions outside the separatrix, that can have as their boundaries the tangents in the maximum and minimum 'R' points on the separatrix, the stable limit cycle and the isoclines. We denote them as:
   a) $A_{Out,1}$: The region where $V[n+1] > V[n]$ and $R[n+1] < R[n]$, and
   b) $A_{Out,2}$: The region where $V[n+1] > V[n]$ and $R[n+1] > R[n]$.

Let us denote the intersection between the tangents in the maximum and minimum 'R' points on the separatrix, and the stable limit cycle (see Figure 8) as $V_{A1}, V_{A2}, V_{B1}, V_{B2}$. The sequence of these points corresponds to the time evolution on the stable limit cycle.

Within the discrete-time model of computation, the problem of annihilation involves proving that there exists a stimulus A which, when applied between V_{A1} and V_{A2} or between V_{B1} and V_{B2}, moves the system into the basin of attraction of the stable fixed point, namely within A_{In}. Observe that if the system is within this region, it is inside the separatrix, and it will thus converge to the fixed point. Indeed, it suffices to show that this input can be applied for a single time unit.

Consider the scenario in which the system is on an initial point $V[0]$ between V_{A1} and V_{A2}. Since the stable limit cycle and the separatrix are non-intersecting, there exists a positive "distance" d_0 between $V[0]$ and the separatrix. We intend to determine a value of A that moves the system from ($V[0]$,$R[0]$) to an arbitrary point in A_{In}. Clearly, the magnitude A has to satisfy the condition :

$$(V[1]-V[0]) > d_0 \tag{15}$$

Computing $V[1]$ as a function of $V[0]$ we have: $V[1]=V[0]+f_1(V[0])+A$.
The condition (15) becomes:

$$(V[0]+f_1(V[0])+A-V[0]) > d_0 \Rightarrow (f_1(V[0])+A) > d_0 \Rightarrow A > d_0 - f_1(V[0]) \tag{16}$$

We now invoke the monotonic property of the function V[n], that corresponds to the portion of the state space below the isocline, where $V[n+1] > V[n]$, namely in A_{In}. Here, the term $f_1(V[n])=V[n+1]-V[n]$ is positive. We thus see that there exists a value of A, satisfying the condition (16), that moves the initial point of the system between V_{A1} and V_{A2}, to be in A_{In}. We have now to evaluate the sign of the expression $[d_0 - f_1(V[0])]$. Starting from ($V[0]$,$R[0]$) on the stable limit cycle, with $V[0]$ between V_{A1} and V_{A2}, we know that, without adding the A stimulus, the next point ($V[1]$,$R[1]$) will also be on the stable limit cycle. The difference between $V[1]$ and $V[0]$ is exactly $f_1(V[0])$. In this context, $f_1(V[0])$ will satisfy the condition $f_1(V[0]) < d_0$, because there is no intersection between the limit cycle and the unstable limit cycle (described by the separatrix). We have now thus proved that $[d_0 - f_1(V[0])] > 0$. Thus, A is a positive value satisfying $A > d_0 - f_1(V[0])$.
The analogous rationale can be used if the initial point $V[0]$ is between V_{B1} and V_{B2}. In this case, there exists a distance d_1 (a positive value) between $V[0]$ and the separatrix. We intend again to find a value of A that moves the system into region A_{In}. The magnitude A has to satisfy the condition:

$$(V[0]-V[1]) > d_1 \tag{17}$$

Observe also that this part of the state space, (also below the isocline), corresponds to $V[n+1]>V[n]$, and, thus, the term $f_1(V[n])=V[n+1]-V[n]$ is also positive.
Computing $V[1]$ and $R[1]$ as a function of $V[0]$ and $R[0]$ we have: $V[1]=V[0]+f_1(V[0])+A$.
The condition (17) thus becomes:

$$(V[0]-V[0]-f_1(V[0])-A > d_1 \Rightarrow A < -d_1 - f_1(V[0]) \tag{17}$$

Observe that both d_1 and $f_1(V[0])$ are positive quantities, and thus the term $[-d_1 - f_1(V[1])]$ is a negative value. We have thus proved that there exists a value of A that moves the initial point of the system from being between V_{B1} and V_{B2}, to be within A_{In}.
Since both these cases are exhaustive, the theorem is proved.
Comments:

1. For each interval $[V_{A1}, V_{A2}]$ or $[V_{B1}, V_{B2}]$ it is possible to choose a value $V[0]$ that corresponds to a particular time instant in the phase space. This time instant can be described as a percentage of the total period of time of the spike. For each chosen $V[0]$, there is a value d_0 with a corresponding magnitude A of a unit time stimulus, determined by the conditions (16) or (18).
2. The above proof shows that for any neuron described by Equation (14), there exists an unit time stimulus with the magnitude A satisfying the property that, if it is applied in any place on the limit cycle between V_{A1} and V_{A2} or between V_{B1} and V_{B2}, it will annihilate the spiking behaviour. The problem of annihilation has also a solution for the case when the stimulus is longer then the unit of time. In this case, we need to define in

the state space four regions inside the separatrix (see Fig. 8), that can be bordered by the isoclines of the system, namely :
a) $A_{In,1}$ with the property $V[n+1] < V[n]$ and $R[n+1] < R[n]$;
b) $A_{In,2}$ with the property $V[n+1] < V[n]$ and $R[n+1] > R[n]$;
c) $A_{In,3}$ with the property $V[n+1] > V[n]$ and $R[n+1] > R[n]$;
d) $A_{In,4}$ with the property $V[n+1] > V[n]$ and $R[n+1] < R[n]$.

The duration of the stimulus and its magnitude will determine if the system will move from the stable limit cycle, namely from a point in $[V_{A1}, V_{A2}]$ to $A_{In,1}$ or to $A_{In,4}$, both of them *via* $A_{Out,1}$. The same determination has to be made if the system has to move from a point in $[V_{B1}, V_{B2}]$ to $A_{In,2}$ or to $A_{In,3}$ *via* $A_{Out,2}$.

3.5 The numerical approach

In order to discover the properties of the stimulus which achieves the spikes annihilation, we have also opted to simulate this numerically. To do this, we have to work towards controling the model, namely, to move the system to a bi-stable state, in the neighborhood of the bifurcation point. All these steps will be discussed in the next Section.

4. Experiments

In this Section, the analytical results described in Section 3 are experimentally evaluated to verify their validity, and to explore the state space characteristics for each parameter of the annihilation stimulus. If a background stimulus B is applied to create a train of spikes, we demonstrate that it is possible to annihilate the limit cycle with an additional *brief* stimulus, and to move the system from a stable limit circle to an unstable spiral point.

The solution to this problem has to respond to the following questions:

1. What is the amplitude of the stimulus?
2. What is the suitable phase when the stimulus should be applied?
3. How long should the stimulus be?
4. Is it possible to apply two successive pulses instead of only a single one, in which the phase specification is not so precise? Would this pair of two successive pulses possess the property that they would together be able to annihilate the spikes if the first one, by itself, could not?

In order to analyze the effect of the stimulus, we have to choose initial values for V and R. We have studied this for various numerical settings, but present only one scenario here, in the interest of brevity. In Figure 9, we present an example of train spikes that we propose to annihilate with a stimulus. This train of spikes started from V=-0.7043 and R=0, and was generated with B=0.08. In addition, Figure 10 illustrates the corresponding Phase Space of the bi-stable neuron.

In Figure 11, we observe an example of annihilation, where the duration of the train of spikes is 100 ms. In Figure 12, we present the phase space for the bi-stable neuron. Figure 13 is an example of an unsuccessful annihilation observed using a stimulus σ=0.2, applied at the time instant 3.4 ms from the beginning of the simulation.

From the bifurcation diagram, we chose the background stimuli B to be between 0.68 and 0.7. These stimuli generate a spike train. We here chose V=-0.7043 and R=0 as initial values for the subsequent simulations.

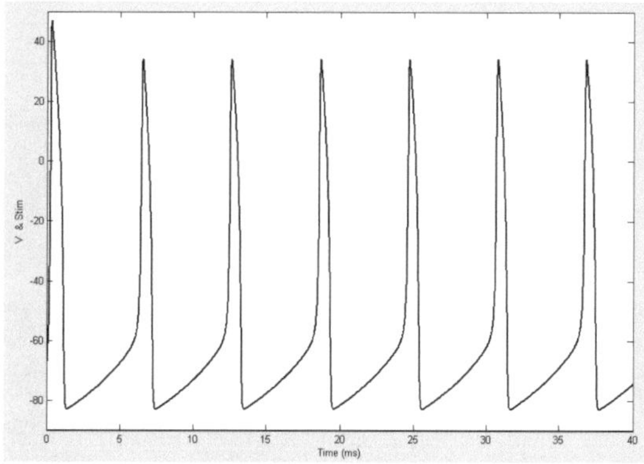

Figure 9. The train of the spikes generated with B=0.08

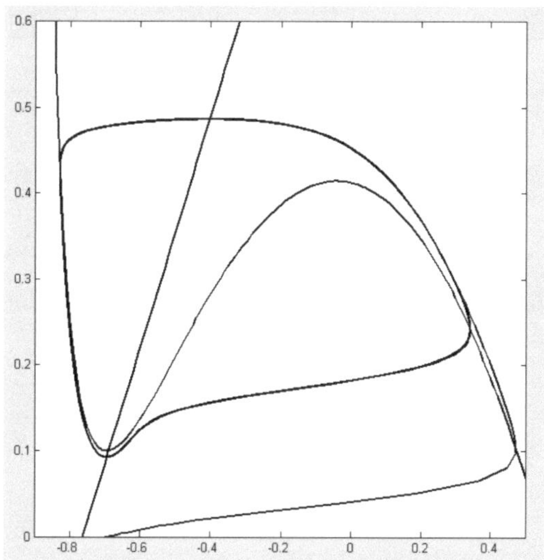

Figure 10. The phase space of the train of the spikes generated with B=0.08

For an additional stimulus σ, namely, a pulse of 0.1 ms duration[14], we identified its position of insertion and its amplitude. In Table 4, we present the range of values for σ (the minimum and the maximum values) for which we can annihilate the spikes. Each range is computed for different times of insertion of the stimulus (from 3.0 ms to 4.4 ms) and for different values of the quantity B. The neuron exhibited spikes only for a range of B, which spanned values from 0.68 to 0.70 μA/100. The results from Table 4 are depicted in Figure 14. From this simulation we can conclude that:

1. The neuron spikes only for a specific range of values of B;
2. If the neuron generates spikes, these can be annihilated with particular stimuli found in the area plotted in Figure 14.

[14] We will analyze later the effect of the duration of the pulse.

ms	B(0.68)		B(0.69)		B(0.70)	
	σ_{min}	σ_{max}	σ_{min}	σ_{max}	σ_{min}	σ_{max}
3.0	0.4	1.54				
3.1	0.14	1.57				
3.2	0.06	1.47	0.47	1.15		
3.3	0.28	1.34	0.19	1.23	0.50	0.97
3.4	0.014	1.21	0.09	1.17	0.21	1.08
3.5	0.008	1.09	0.05	1.06	0.11	1.02
3.6	0.005	0.97	0.03	0.95	0.062	0.93
3.7	0.003	0.85	0.018	0.84	0.03	0.83
3.8	0.002	0.74	0.016	0.73	0.027	0.72
3.9	0.002	0.63	0.01	0.63	0.02	0.62
4.0	0.002	0.53	0.008	0.53	0.016	0.52
4.1	0.002	0.45	0.007	0.44	0.015	0.43
4.2	0.002	0.35	0.007	0.34	0.015	0.33
4.3	0.002	0.25	0.008	0.25	0.017	0.25
4.4	0.002	0.16	0.011	0.15	0.024	0.14

Table 4. The amplitude and the moment of insertion of the stimulus σ in order to annihilate the spikes

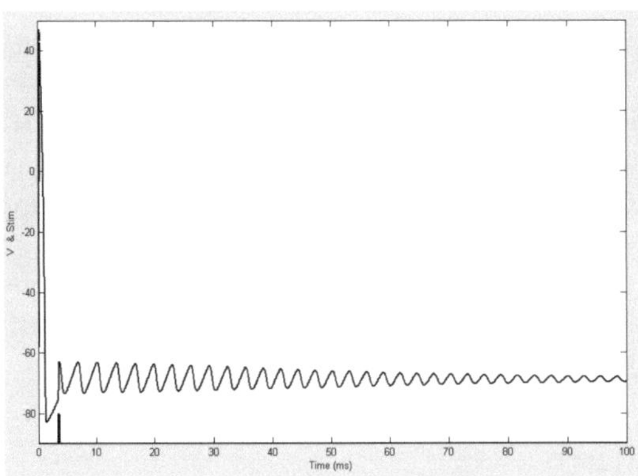

Figure 11. The annihilation of the train of spikes. The presentation is made for 100 ms

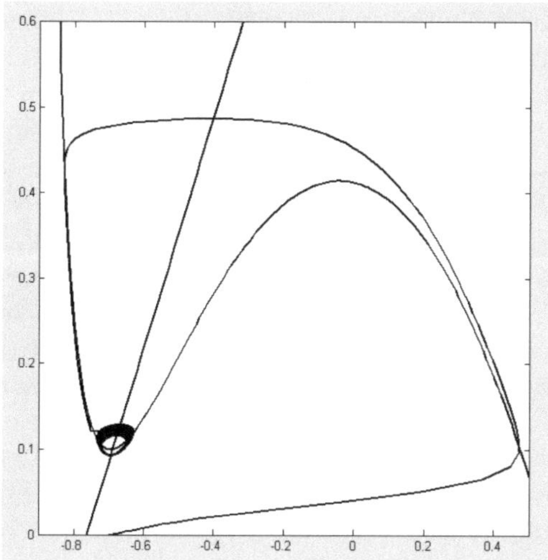

Figure 12. The phase space of a system with the train of spikes annihilated by a stimulus σ. The presentation is made for 40 ms

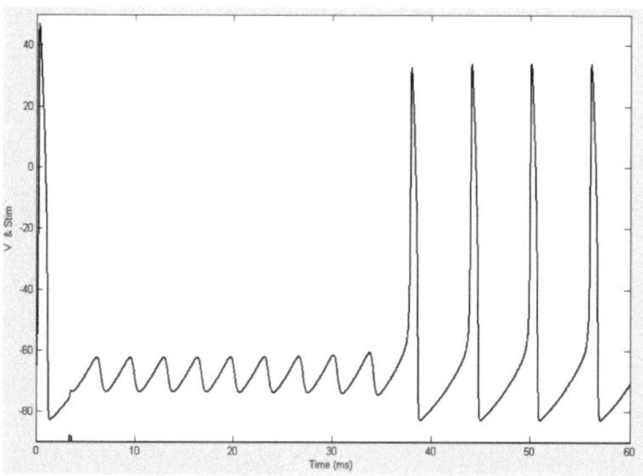

Figure 13. An example of an unsuccessful attempt to annihilate the spikes by using a stimulus σ applied at a time instant of 3.4 ms

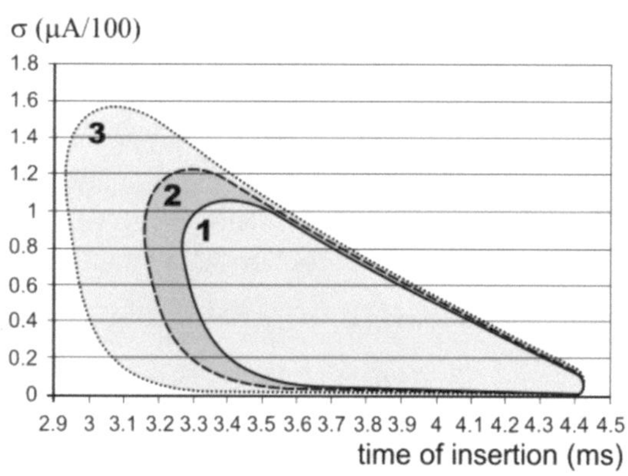

Figure 14. The three areas for the three different values for the background, *B*, namely 0.70 (*Area 1*), 0.69 (*Area 2*), and 0.68 (*Area 3*)

Consider now the problem of finding the vulnerable phase of the neuron, namely the duration of the period of the signal when the stimulus can be inserted in order to annihilate spikes.
For a value of σ= 0.7, we see from Figure 14 that the length of the vulnerable phase is between 3 ms to 4.4 ms. Since the period is 6 ms, the neuron has an interval of 23.33% of its period where one can insert a proper stimulus to achieve this annihilation.
The reader can observe that for the experimental results reported, we conducted experiments with three different background stimuli in order to generate a bi-stable neuron, namely with B=0.68, B=0.69, and B=0.70. For all these values, we present in Figure 14 three areas, namely those depicted by *Area 1*, *Area 2*, and *Area 3*. Fortunately, there seems to be an inclusion relationship between these three areas, namely *Area 1* is included in *Area 2* and *Area 3*. Consider now the scenario when a population of neurons from the brain receives a constant stimulus with the magnitude having a minimum value of 0.68 for an interval of time. If the task is to annihilate the spiking behaviour of this population of neurons, the imprecision of determining the background stimulus will not affect our selection of the annihilation stimulus. Choosing one with a magnitude corresponding to the minimum background is successful because such a stimulus is common for all background stimuli greater than this minimum one. For example, the area corresponding to B=1 includes the area corresponding to the minimum B=0.68. This observation makes the choice of a successful annihilation stimulus easier and independent from the precision of determining B.

4.1 The duration of the stimulus

A brief analysis of the *duration* of the stimulus would be beneficial. Such a study would help the reader to decide on the best stimulus to be used to achieve the annihilation. To do this, we explore numerically the range of the duration for a stimulus with magnitude equal to unity. For example, if the time of insertion is set to be at 3.5 ms, the range of the duration of the stimulus can be between 0.0099 ms and 0.1095 ms, independent of the value of B whose value lies between 0.68 and 0.7.
We mention that this numerical determination was made in a scenario with an *a priori* setting of the amplitude of the stimulus. In the general case, we want to apply a stimulus with the duration δ_1, smaller than the period of firing of the HH neuron, for example 6 ms. One possible approach to determine the magnitude of the stimulus is by using a heuristic search. An algorithm for computing a solution contains, first of all, the determination of the number of iterations corresponding to the duration of the stimulus, namely k=$\frac{\delta_1}{\delta_2}$, where δ_0 is the numerical time unit, typically chosen to be very small.
Next, we have to determine, by a heuristic search, the magnitude, A, of the stimulus, by estimating the pairs (V_0, R_0) and (V_{new},R_{new}). This involves using k and the rule of computing the new initial point, proposed in Section 3.1, namely:

$$V_{new}=V_0+f_1(V_k)+ ...+ f_1(V_0)+ k^*A ,$$

$$R_{new}=R_0+f_2(R_k)+...+f_2(R_0).$$

The reader should observe that we have presented here the difficult scenario of achieving the spike annihilation with a pulse of duration k* δ_0. In a clinical application, the solution to the problem of annihilation can be reduced to the computation of the magnitude of a brief pulse, where it is sufficient to set k=1.

4.2 How many stimuli?

We analyze now the problem of using two successive stimuli to annihilate the spike train. This pair of successive pulses has the property that the first pulse is not able to annihilate the spike train by itself. However, in order to cumulate the effects of the stimuli, we have to apply a second pulse so as to have the distance in time between stimuli less than the period of firing of the HH neuron. Intuitively, if the distance between the stimuli is more than a period, the neuron does not memorize the effect of the first stimulus, which we can also verify.

To simulate this in a realistic setting, we assume that we don't know exactly the juncture in time where we can insert the single stimulus in order to annihilate the spikes, namely the range $[\theta_1, \theta_2]$. Thus, we intend to insert two stimuli, having the same amplitude and a temporary distance between them, δ_2.

Consider the general problem of inserting the first stimulus anywhere in the range of $[\theta_1\text{-}\varepsilon, \theta_1 +\varepsilon]$. By proposing δ_2, the temporary distance between them, we intend to devise an algorithm for the heuristic search of the magnitude of the stimuli.

We set the initial magnitude to a small value. The proposed algorithm, then, has three phases:

i. The first step consists of the computation of the pair (V^1_{new}, R^1_{new}), after the insertion of the first stimulus;
ii. The second step consists of the computation of the pair (V,R), knowing the pair (V^1_{new}, R^1_{new}), and the number of iterations required by dividing δ_2 by the integration time unit.
iii. The third step consists of the computation of the (V^2_{new}, R^2_{new}), after the insertion of the second stimulus.

If, after this computation, the new point, namely (V^2_{new}, R^2_{new}), is not a point inside the unstable limit cycle, we increase the initial magnitude with a quantity ΔA, and we repeat all the above three steps. Clearly, it is a straightforward "Hypothesize and Test" heuristic search scheme for the amplitude of the stimuli. The problem will lead to (or not lead to) a solution, depending on the values of ε and δ_2.

In this way, a pair of stimuli with a carefully chosen amplitude and a fixed temporal distance between them can annihilate a train of spikes by decreasing the accuracy of the place of insertion. The first stimulus is chosen with a random magnitude and is inserted into the neuron. At his juncture, we will not know if this stimulus is successful or not in annihilating the spikes. By taking into consideration *a posteriori* its magnitude and its moment of insertion, we want to be able to set the properties of the second stimulus so as to annihilate the neuron, if the first stimulus was not successful. In this way, we can extrapolate the problem of applying, in a range of time $[\theta_1\text{-}\varepsilon_1, \theta_2 +\varepsilon_2]$, a pair of two stimuli with the same amplitude A, with a duration equal to unity and a temporary distance between them of δ_2 .This leads us to a scheme for computing the properties of the second stimulus when the first stimulus is given. However, the problem of determining A, ε_1 and ε_2, having only δ_2 is still open.

By simulations, for the setting described in (Wilson, 1999), we showed that, for a *Background* of 0.7, the range $[\theta_1, \theta_2]$ is 3.3 ms - 4.4 ms (see Table 4). We have tested the effect of a pair of two successive stimuli, the first being applied too early, at 3.2 ms, and the second one, at 4.2 ms. Both stimuli have the same amplitude, 0.7. From Table 4, we observe that the successful annihilation can be achieved with a stimulus having the amplitude between 0.015 and 0.33.

In the scenario with the first stimulus being inserted too early, the second one was successful in annihilating the spikes at an amplitude of 0.7. Thus, the presence of the first stimulus in a zone outside of *Area 1* (see Figure 14) has a positive effect, allowing the second stimulus to achieve annihilation, also from a zone outside of *Area 1*.

In Figure 15, we present an example of a successful annihilation by using two stimuli with amplitude of 0.7, the first one being applied at 3.2 ms, and the second one at 4.2 ms, where the neuron has a background stimulus, *B*, equal to 0.7.

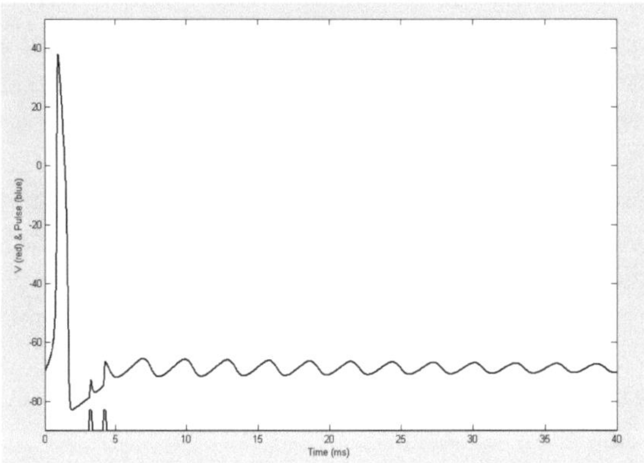

Figure 15. The annihilation using two stimuli with amplitude 0.7, the first applied at 3.2 ms and the second applied at 4.2 ms

4.3 Spike Generation

We present here, for sake of the completeness of the modeling approach, a particular case involving spike generation. In Section 2, we stated that the HH neuron has two equilibria, a fixed point and the limit cycle, both of them co-existing and being stable. Thus, the HH neuron is bi-stable and, with a carefully chosen synaptic input, it is possible to switch its behaviour from a resting state to a spiking (spike generation) state or from a spiking state to a resting state (which is the spike annihilation phenomenon). The spike annihilation problem was solved in Section 3. Here, we study the generation of the spiking behaviour.

If the neuron is in the resting state, namely in the stable fixed point, there are no changes in time. Thus, there is no preference for the moment when one can insert a stimulus in order to move the point (*V,R*) to be outside of the unstable limit cycle. The stimulus will modify only the *V* component of the pair (*V,R*). Observe that in this case there are two limit values for this problem: a positive minimum value that moves the system to the left side of the fixed point and outside of the unstable limit cycle, and a negative maximum value that moves the system to the right side of the fixed point while being outside of the unstable limit cycle.

Again, to demonstrate that this can be achieved, we tested by simulations the scenario when the system is in an fixed point (V=0.6889, R=0.1), for B=0.7. In this situation, the system remains in this fixed point forever. If, however, at anytime we excited the system with a single pulse, for example one with the amplitude equal to unity, the system started to oscillate *forever*. This phenomenon is portrayed in Figure 16. We observe here that, without any background activity, namely with B=0.0, the system cannot oscillate, because it is not bi-stable.

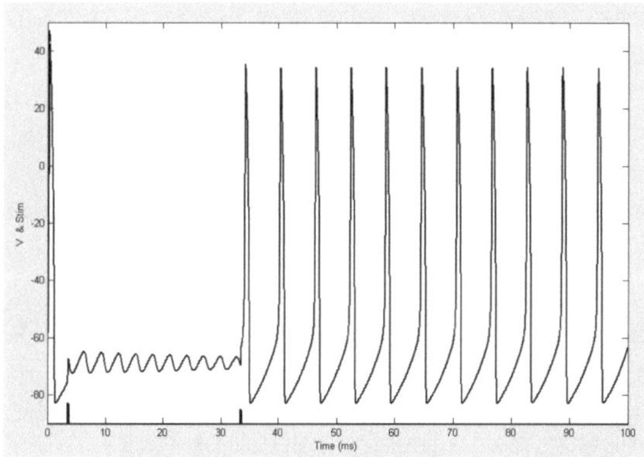

Figure 16. The annihilation and the generation of a new train of spikes. The first stimulus has an amplitude of 0.7 and is applied at 3.5 ms. The second stimulus has an amplitude of 0.5 and is applied at 33.5 ms. The value of *B* is 0.7

4. Discussion and Conclusions

This chapter discussed the HH neuron and formally derived various properties of its stability. It also described the first (to the best of our knowledge) reported formal proof that the problem of spike annihilation has a well defined solution, and presented an algorithm for computing the properties of the stimulus. We elaborated, in Sections 3 and 4, all the details of this algorithm. We add that the method of perturbation with brief stimuli differs from the classical approach of modifying the control parameter and changing the Jacobian of the system. In our approach, we keep the system bi-stable all the time, and our task is to switch between these two states without modifying their stability.

To conclude, in this chapter we have analytically proved the existence of the brief current pulse that annihilates the spikes of the HH neuron, when delivered to its repetitively firing state, and have also analyzed the properties of this pulse, namely, the range of time when it can be inserted, its magnitude, and its duration. In addition, we have also studied the solution of annihilating the spikes by using two successive stimuli, where the first one is unable to annihilate the spikes by itself. We have also briefly investigated the inverse problem to annihilation, namely, the spike generation problem, and proposed a straightforward numerical solution.

8. References

Baer, S.M. & Erneux, T. (1986). Singular Hopf bifurcation to relaxation oscillations, *SIAM Journal of Applied Mathematics,* 46:1986, pp. 721-739, ISSN 0036-1399

Best, E.N. (1979). Null space in the Hodgkin-Huxley equations. *Biophysical Journal,* 27:1979, pp. 87-104, ISSN 0006-3495

Carrington, C.; Gilby, K.L., & McIntyre, D.C. (2007). Effect of low frequency stimulation on amygdala kindled afterdischarge thresholds and seizure profile in Fast and Slow kindling rat strains. *Epilepsia,* 48:2007, pp. 1604-1613 (2007) ISSN 0013-9580

Cooley, J.; Dodge, F., & Cohen, H. (1965). Digital computer solutions for excitable membrane models. *Journal of Cellular and Comparative Physiology,* 66:1965, pp. 99-108, ISSN 0021-9541

Devaney, R.L (2003). *An Introduction to Chaotic Dynamical Systems* (second edition). Westview Press, ISBN-10: 0813340853, Colorado

Gray, J.J. (2000). *The Hilbert Challange.* Oxford University Press, ISBN-10: 0198506511, USA

Guckenheimer, J. (1975). Isochrons and phaseless sets. *Journal of Mathematical Biology,* 1:1975, pp. 259-273, ISSN 0303-6812

Guttman, S.L. & Rinzel, J. (1980). Control of repetitive firing in squid axon membrane as a model for a neuron-oscillator, *Journal of Physiology,* 305:1980, pp.377-395, ISSN 0022-3751

Hilborn, R.C. (2000). *Chaos and nonlinear dynamics* (second edition), Oxford University Press, ISBN-10: 0198507232, USA

Luders, H.O. (ed.) (2004). *Deep brain stimulation and epilepsy.* Martin Dunitz, an imprint of the Taylor and Francis Group, ISBN-10: 1841842591, USA

Mayberg, H.S.; Lozano, A.M., Voon, V., McNeely, H.E., Seminowicz, D., C, Hamani, J. M. & Schwalb, S.H.K.(2005): Deep brain stimulation for treatment-rezistant depression, *Neuron*, 45:2005, pp. 651-660 ISSN 0896-6273

McIntyre, D.C.; Carrington, C., & Gilby, K.L. (2005). The ying-yang of low frequency sinewave stimulation in amygdalia kindled rats, *American Epilespy Society Abstr.* 2005, ISSN 15357957

Osorio, I., Frei, M.G., Wilkinson, S.B., Sunderam, S., Bhavaraju, N.C., Graves, N., Schaffner, S.F., Peters, T., Johnson, A.M., DiTeresi, C.A., Ingram, J., Nagaraddi, V., Overman, J., Kavalir, M.A., & Turnbull, M. (2001) Seizure Blockage with Automated Closed-Loop Electrical Stimulation: A Pilot Study. *Epilepsia,* 42:2001, ISSN 0013-9580

Rinzel, J. (1980). Numerical calculation of stable and unstable periodic solutions to the Hodgkin-Huxley equations, *Mathematical Biosciences,* 49:1980, pp. 27-59, ISSN 0025-5564

Teorell, T. (1071). A biophysical analysis of mechano-electrical transduction, in *Handbook of Sensory Physiology*, vol 1, 1971, pp. 291-339 W.R.Loeswenstein ed, Springer Verlag, ISBN 35400514449, Berlin

Wilson, H. (1999). Spikes decisions and actions: Dynamical foundations of Neuroscience, Oxford University Press, ISBN-13:9780198524304, USA

Winfree, A. (1974). A Patterns of Phase Compromise in Biological Cycles. *Journal of Mathematical Biology*, 1:1974, pp.73-95, ISSN 0303-6812

Winfree, A. (1977): Phase Control of Neural Pacemakers, *Science*, 197:1977, pp. 761-763, ISSN 0036-8075

3

Bio-inspired Connectionist Modelling: An Application to Visual Perception of Motion

Claudio Castellanos Sánchez and Pedro Luis Sánchez Orellana
Laboratory of Information Technologies (LIT) of Cinvestav - Tamaulipas
México

1. Introduction

The visual system of human beings has been optimised through millions of years by natural selection. This helps us to detect the pattern of 3D moving objects, its depth, speed and direction estimation, etc. The research in connectionism is inspired by complexity of neural interactions and their organisation in the brain that can allow us to propose a feasible neuromimetic model to imitate the capacities of human brain.

Although visual perception of motion has been an active research field for the scientific community (since motion is fundamental for most machine perception tasks) [McCane, 2001], recent research on computational neuroscience has provided an improved understanding of human brain functionality. In the human brain, the motion is perceived as an interaction between several cortical areas and in two main pathways : the dorsal pathway formed by primary visual area (V1), middel temporal area (MT), middel superior area (MST), etc., specialized on the detection of motion. The ventral pathway, formed by primary visual area (V1), secondary visual area (V2), third visual area (V3), inferotemporal area (IT), etc., which processes characteristics related to the form of the visual information.

This visual information has been taken to create the so called bio-inspired algorithms, which are based on or inspired by functions of some areas in the brain. This bio-inspired algorithms have been proposed to mimic the abilities of the brain for motion perception and understanding [Castellanos-Sánchez, 2005]. There are several bio-inspired models for visual perception of motion, some of them inspired by V1 neurons with a strong neural cooperative-competitive interactions that converge to a local, distributed and oriented auto-organisation [Fellez & Taylor, 2002; Moga, 2000]. Some others are inspired by MT neurons with cooperative-competitive interactions between V1 and MT and an influence range [Derrington & Henning, 1993; Mingolla, 2003]. And the others are inspired by MST for coherent motion and egomotion detection [Pack et al., 2000; Zemel & Sejnowski, 1998], see [Castellanos-Sánchez, 2005] for a more detailed explanation.

All these works are based on a specific cortical area. However, for our proposal we considered that all these specializations might be integrated to make a more robust process. Here we present a bio-inspired connectionist approach, called CONEPVIM model (Neuromimetical Coneccionist Model for the Visual Perception of Motion), which not only considers the higher areas of processing, but also the information from V1, since it might add descriptors for the motion detection problem, based on a particular adaptation of the

spatiotemporal Gabor filters. Also it takes advantage of a modular and strongly localized approach for the visual perception of motion that handles a shunting inhibition mechanism (based on MT and MTS). Due to the methodology used in the model three neuromimetic indicators emerged for visual perception of motion (proposed [Castellanos-Sánchez, 2005; Castellanos-Sánchez et al., 2004]), they allowed us to identify: null motion in objects, whether the motion in the scene is caused by moving objects or ego-motion, and also the speed and direction of the motion.
In this chapter we discuss about some neurobiological principles, next we mention the foundations for the CONEPVIM model, then we continue with the manipulation of several parameters obtained in the antagonist interaction mechanism and three neuromimetic indicators for motion estimation are shown, these indicators emerge from the interactions between the neurons of V1, MT and MST mainly. A series of experiments with real image sequences are described. Finally, we make some conclusions about the proposed methodology and the results.

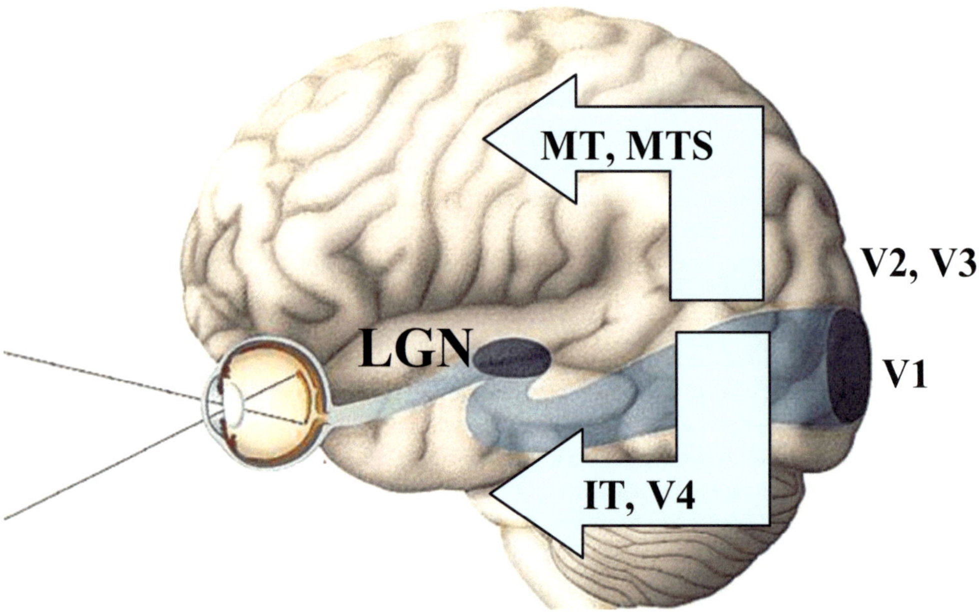

Figure 1. The visual pathway. The information comes in from the retina, after it is integrated in LGN, treated in V1, and finally processed in two different pathways : dorsal (MT, MTS, etc.) and ventral (V4, IT, etc.)

2. Biological foundations

In order to understand better how the bio-inspired model that we propose as well as the existing model work it is necessary to describe some biological bases that sustain them. We separated these foundations in two subsections mentioned in the following: the course of the light signals in the human brain, and the bio-inspiration modelling from the visual pathway.

2.1 The course of the light signals in the human brain

From the retina up to the cerebral cortex of a human being, seventeen different areas take part in vision processing [Sunaert, 1999]. The main areas may be organized in four major stages: acquisition and compression of light signals in the retina; their relaying in the lateral geniculate nucleus (LGN); their cortical analysis in V1, and their secondary treatment in areas MT and MTS of the temporal cerebral cortex in the areas IT and V4 of the parietal cerebral cortex (see figure 1).

a) Acquisition and compression of the light signals in the retina.

In the eye the information from the world is received by photoreceptors, they are called the cones and rods cells. It is from this acquisition that the integration starts by means of the interactions between horizontal and bipolar cells. Finally the information is compressed in a proportion of 160:1 in the ganglional cells [Imbert, 19883].

b) Integration in LGN.

The information comes out from the retina through the optical nerve (formed by the ganglional cells) and receives the next treatments:

- A binocular selection at a optical chiasm, it shares partial information from both eyes.
- A temporal integration in the LGN, which acts as a relay.

80% of the information received in LGN comes from the feedback from the higher areas, and only 20% arrives from the retina [Castellanos-Sánchez, 2005].

c) Analyse in V1.

After the relay in LGN the information of luminal signals is concentreted in the primary visual area (V1), and receives its first cortical treatment by means of the cells sensitive to the contrast (simple cells). These cells have been modelled by local motion energy filters (Gabor filters) [Adelson & Bergen, 1985; Heeger, 1987].

d) Secondary treatment.

Here two pathways may be discovered in this course of visual signals [Hengyi, 2003]: the ventral or occipito-temporal pathway and the dorsal for occipito-parietal pathway. The first one mostly consists of parvocellular cells and it is responsible for the perception of the objects and of their shape, and the second one mostly consists of magnocellular cells and it is responsible for motion and space perception. In the present study, we are particularly interested in the dorsal pathway and in areas specialized in motion analysis.

The processing of the visual signals in the brain might be summariezed in the figure 2.

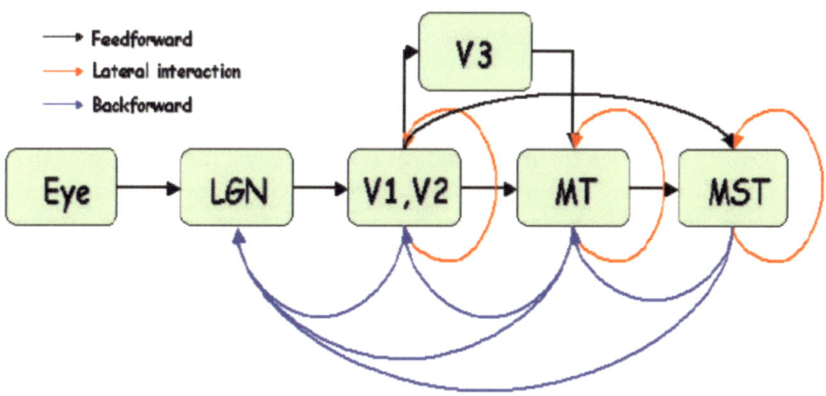

Figure 2. Simplified description of the visual pathway for motion treatment, starting from the eye and ending with the processing in the MST

2.2 Bio-inspired modelling from vision

An important fact is that all the processes mentioned before might be integrated to comform the so called bio-inspired computational models for motion detection, by using local detections and integrating various directions for various scales and spaces to end in a global answer [Van Santen, 1985; Adelson, 1985]. Motion detection, spatiotemporal local inhibition, and integration are the main ideas of neurosciences research that will inspire our connectionist conception. From a biological point of view it is known that motion detection and analysis are achieved by means of a cascade of neural operations [Sekuler, 2002], called: the detection of local motion signals within restricted regions of the visual field and their integration into more global descriptions of the direction and speed of object motion.

The main areas that we are considering in this paper are the human brain areas specialized in motion perception are [Sekuler, 2002]: V1, MT, MST, the kinetic occipital area (KO), and finally the superior temporal sulcus (STS).

The first cortical analysis is performed in V1 by ensuring contrast sensitivity thanks to extended receptive fields. These neurons mainly send their extensions in the vertical direction and they are tuned to a preferred direction of motion [Hubel, 1962] so they perform a local analysis of motion energy that is called filtering. These orientation-selective cells may be modelled as spatiotemporal filters [Adelson, 1985; van Santen, 1984] and their receptive fields may be modelled as a product of inhibitory and excitatory interactions in space and time. On the other hand, contrast detection is sufficient for the identification of motion direction, so that the visual mechanisms that extract motion are built from direction-selective primitives [Derrington, 1993].

Summarizing, the process starts from the local motion of a retinal image that is extracted by neurons in V1 that have a receptive field similar to a small spatially bounded window where they can detect the presence of movement in a specific direction. This strongly localized processing based on lateral interactions is our first source of inspiration for motion detection and estimation. However, the visual perception of motion is not completely determined by the local responses in the neural receptive fields. These responses are also handled to obtain speed information after having collected and combined them from V1 and after having grouped them together in MT. The ambiguity of individual neural responses is solved by this combination of signals.

In the next section we make wider description of the functioning of the stages in the CONEPVIM model, starting from the Casual spatial-temporal Gabor-like filters to finish with the Antagonist interaction mechanism.

3. CONEPVIM model

This section broadly describes the mathematical and biological foundations of the proposed bio-inspired model for visual perception of motion based on the neuromimetic connectionist model reported in [Castellanos-Sánchez, 2005; Castellanos-Sánchez, 2004]. The first stage of this neuromimetic model is mainly based on the causal spatiotemporal Gabor-like filtering and the second stage is a local and massively distributed processing defined in [Castellanos-Sánchez, 2004], where they have proposed a retinotopically organised model of the following perception principle: local motion information of a retinal image is extracted by neurons in the primary visual cortex, V1, with local receptive fields restricted to small areas of spatial interactions (first stage: causal spatio-temporal filtering, CSTF); these neurons are densely interconnected for excitatory-inhibitory interactions (second stage: antagonist interaction mechanism, AIM).

We will describe in this section the stages of the CONEPVIM model: the spatial processing to model the orientation-selective neurons of V1, temporal processing to model the speed selectiveness of neurons in the medium temporal area, MT, connectionist processing to mimic the excitatory-inhibitory local interactions in the cerebral cortex of human beings, and self-organising mechanisms for coherent motion estimation.

3.1 Casual spatial-temporal Gabor-like filtering (CSTF)

Receptive fields modeled by bidimensional spatial Gabor filters were proposed by Marcelja [Marcelja, 1982] and they were discovered in biological vision systems [Pollen, 1981]. The spatial part of a standard Gabor function approximates well the spatial profile of receptive fields in the cerebral cortex [Jones, 1987]. But its temporal part is non-causal (negative weights are assigned to immediate past images). Several more causal approaches have been proposed. Adelson and Bergen used an asymmetric spatial distribution [Adelson, 1985] and Gzrywacz and Yuille made it with Gabor functions in spatiotemporal co-dependence [Grzywacz, 1990; Grzywacz, 1991]. They concluded that directional selectiveness is equal to orientation in space-time. Our approach handles causality in a simple and local way with a strong hypothesis that ensures the ability to detect local motions.

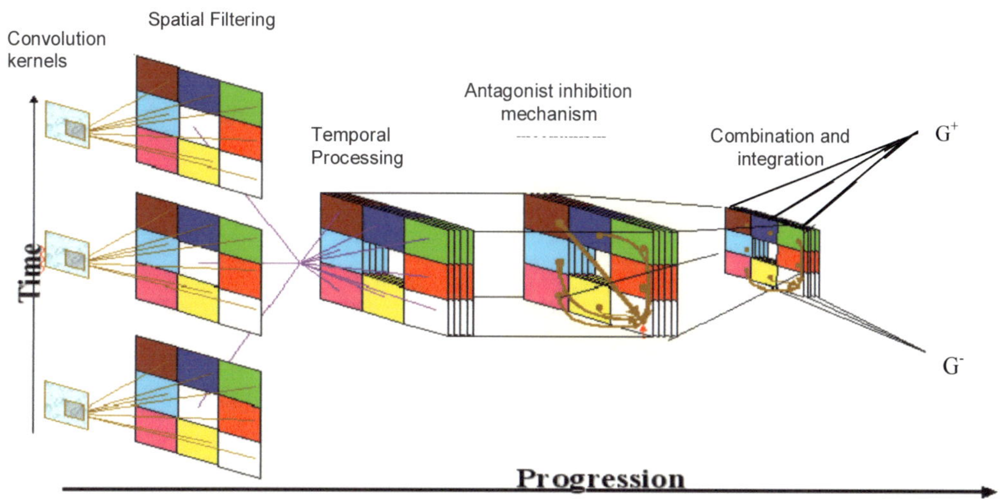

Figure 3. CONEPVIM model. It is divided in four stages: the spatial treatment of the images, the temporal processing of the information (these both stages are grouped in CSTF), the antagonist interaction mechanism (AIM) and the combination and integration of the information

Let *I(x, y, t)* be an image sequence representing the shape of intensity in the time-varying image, assuming that every point has an invariant brightness.

Let us assume that $I(x, y,t) = I(x-ut, y-vt)$ where *(u, v)* is the motion vector of a small region f the image, and where *I(x, y)* is the frame of the image sampling the time $t = 0$.

Thanks to the hypothesis of a high enough sampling frequency to ensure local motion detection, we may assume an immediate constant local speed. Therefore, for a given supposed motion direction and speed, we expect to identify a local motion by finding a spatial contrast at expected places and times.
By applying the oriented Gabor filter, $G_\theta(x,y)$ with $0 \le \theta \ge \pi$, in $I(x, y)$ we obtain (intensity consevation principle):

$$D_\Theta(t) = \iint_{t=0} \frac{dI(x,y,t)}{dt} * G_\Theta(\hat{x}-\hat{u},\hat{y}-\hat{v})dxdy$$
$$= d\iint_{t=0} \frac{I(x,y,t) * G_\Theta(\hat{x}-\hat{u},\hat{y}-\hat{v})dxdy}{dt} \quad (1)$$

Where the rotational equations are given by:

$$\hat{x} = (x-\xi)\cos\Theta - (y-\eta)\sin\Theta$$
$$\hat{y} = (x-\xi)\sin\Theta - (y-\eta)\cos\Theta \quad (2)$$

where $(\xi,\eta) \in \Upsilon$ is a small neighbourhood around (x,y) and:

$$\hat{u} = \frac{t-t'}{\mathrm{T}-1} v\cos\Theta$$
$$\hat{v} = \frac{t-t'}{\mathrm{T}-1} v\sin\Theta \quad (3)$$

for T consecutive images, $t' \le t$, and the supposed velocity v that ranges from $-w$ to w, where w is the number of supposed absolute speeds.
$(\hat{x},\hat{y})$ is the place where the oriented Gabor signal is going to be computed in a standard way:

$$G_\Theta(\hat{x},\hat{y}) = \frac{1}{2\pi\sigma_x\sigma_y} \exp\left(-\frac{\hat{x}^2}{2\sigma_x^2} - \frac{\gamma\hat{y}^2}{2\sigma_y^2}\right) \exp(2\pi_i \frac{\hat{x}}{\lambda} + \phi) \quad (4)$$

Is the response function to the impulse of the Gabor filter that models the function of the ganglion magnocellular cells, where γ is the eccentricity of the receptive field and σ_x, σ_y the dimensions, λ is the wavelength and ϕ is the phase Y. Discretizing the equation 4, we finally compute the following spatial-temporal filter:

$$f_{\mathrm{T},\Theta,v}(x,y,t) = \sum_{t'=0} \sum_{\hat{x},\hat{y}} G_\Theta\left(\hat{x} - \frac{t-t'}{\mathrm{T}-1} v\cos\Theta, \hat{y} - \frac{t-t'}{\mathrm{T}-1} v\sin\Theta\right) \quad (5)$$

However, the measure obtained by a single filter is not ale to determine the 2D motion vector. It is necessary to use a set of filters that differ only in moition. Then they are gathered in a vector called motion sensor vector where every orientation is a motion sensor.

3.2 Antagonist interactions mechanism (AIM)

The second stage of model describe in [Castellanos-Sánchez et al., 2004] (depticted in the centre of figure 3) emulates an antagonist interaction mechanism by means of excitatory-inhibitory local interactions in the different oriented cortical columns of V1.

In this mechanism each neuron receives both excitation and inhibition signals from neurons in a neighbourhood or influence range to regulate its activity. The figure 3 shows the excitatory and inhibitory local interactions where neurons interact with their close neighbours in this mechanism that change the internal state of neurons and, consequently, their influence range, which generate a dynamic adaptive process. The exitatory and inhibitory influence ratios are defined as $\Omega^{\Theta_E}_{(x,y)} = \{(\xi_e,\eta_e) \mid |x-\xi_e| \leq \xi_E, |y-\eta_e| \leq \eta_E, \xi_e,\eta_e \in Z\}$, where ξ_E and η_E are the superior limits of the exitatory influence ratio. And the inhibitory influece ration given by $\Omega^{\Theta_I}_{(x,y)} = \{(\xi_i,\eta_i) \mid |x-\xi_i| \leq \xi_I, |y-\eta_i| \leq \eta_I, \xi_i,\eta_i \in Z\}$, where ξ_I and η_I are the superior limits of the inhibitory influence ratio. This is done for each one of the orientations.

Usually in excitatory-inhibitory neural models, the weighted connections to and from neurons have modulated strength according to the distance from one another. Nevertheless, we call it an interaction mechanism because the inhibitory connections among neurons regulate downwards the activity of opposing or antagonist neurons, i.e. neurons that do not share a common or similar orientation and speed. On the other hand, excitatory connections increase the neuron activity towards the emergence of coherent responses, i.e. grouping neuron responses to similar orientations and speeds through an interactive process.

Then the updaiting of the of the internal state of a neuron is given by:

$$\begin{aligned} \eta \frac{\partial H(x,y,T)}{\partial T} &= -A \cdot H(x,y,T) \\ &+ (B - H(x,y,T)) \cdot Exc(x,y,T) \\ &- (C + H(x,y,T)) \cdot Inh(x,y,T) \end{aligned} \quad (6)$$

Where $-A \cdot H(\cdot)$ is the passive decay, $(B - H(\cdot)) \cdot Exc(\cdot)$ the feedback excitation and, $(C + H(\cdot)) \cdot Inh(\cdot)$ the feedback inhibition. Each feedback term includes a state-dependent nonlinear signal, $(Exc(x,y,T)$ and $Inh(x,y,T))$ and an automatic gain control term ($B - H(\cdot)$ and $C + H(\cdot)$, respectively). $H(x,y,T)$ is the internal state of the neuron localised in (x,y) at time T, $Exc(x,y,T)$ is the activity due to the contribution of excitatory interaction in the neighbourhood $\Omega^{\Omega_E}_{(x,y)}$ and $Inh(x,y,T)$ is the activity due to the contribution of inhibitory interactions in the neighbourhood $\Omega^{\Omega_I}_{(x,y)}$. Both neighbourhoods depend on the activity level of the chosen neuron in each direction. A, B and C are the real constant values and η is the learning rate. For more details on the excitation and inhibition areas see [Castellanos-Sánchez et al., 2004; Castellanos-Sánchez, 2005].

The excitation is defined as follows:

$$Exc(x,y,T) = H(x,y,T) + \sum_{\Omega^{\Theta_E}_{(x,y)}} W_{\Theta_E}(x,y) L(x,y) \quad (7)$$

and the inhibition is calculated by

$$Inh(x,y,T) = \sum_{\Omega^{\Theta_I}_{(x,y)}} W_{\Theta_I}(x,y)L(x,y) \tag{8}$$

and where

$$W_{\Theta_{E,I}}(x,y) = \begin{cases} g(d(x,y,\xi_e,\eta_e),R(x,y,t),\mu,\sigma) & \text{if } d(\cdot) < R(\cdot) \\ 0 & \text{otherwise} \end{cases} \tag{9}$$

with $g(d(\cdot),R(\cdot),\mu,\sigma)$ as a gaussian centered in (x, y) with mean μ and standar deviation σ. Let $R(x,y,t)$ be the influence ratio of neuron (x,y) defined as $\Gamma \mid H(x,y,t)/saturation$, where Γ is the proposed influence ration and $saturation = 2\max_{(x,y,t,\theta,\upsilon)}(H(x,y,t))$. This neuron receives at most $R(x,y,t)^2$ excitatory connections from neurons with the same direction and speed and at most $(V\cdot\Theta-1)\cdot R(x,y,t)^2$ inhibitory connections from other close neurons. At this level, each pixel correspond to $\Theta\cdot V$ different neurons that encode information of directions and speeds. Finally $L(x,y)$ is the algebraic sum on the all speeds, for each orientation.

The computations described in this subsection analysing its neural and synaptic parallelism have been implemented on FPGA circuits [Girau et al., 2005].

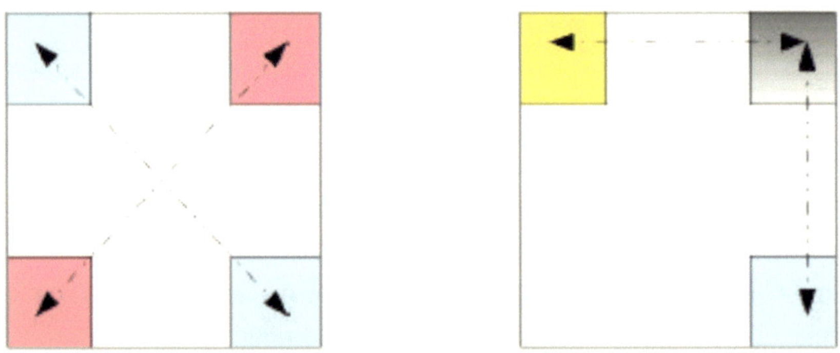

Figure 4. Different directions of controlled sub sequences of real images generated for each supposed speed

4. Neuromimetic indicators

The visual perception of motion is not totally determined in the local responses of the V1 neurons. They are processed to obtain the speed after being collected and combined from V1 and being integrated in MT. It is this combination of signals that resolve the local ambiguity of responses of neurons in V1 [Castellanos-Sánchez, 2005]. This activity is the inspiration of the last part of figure 3 (directions and speeds combination and integration).

4.1 Controlled generation of sequences of real images

The model described here has several parameters to be fixed. The results shown are the product of several experiments. To begin with, we analysed the active neurons in each direction and speed, the frequencies of active neurons after updating (ANaU) and the negative updating increase (NUI) through m different sequences of real images about 384x288 pixels per image.

Next, to analyse ego-motion, we selected n images of each sequence of real images and for each selected image we generated $\Theta \times V$ controlled sub-sequences (Θ are different directions and V different speeds) indicated in the figure 4.

Finally for motion classification, we took a subsequence of each sequence of real images too where : a) the motion does not exist, b) one object moves, c) two or more objects move simultaneously. The interpretation of the different obtained values are shown in the next subsections.

4.2 Motion type

It is important to mention that this neuromimetic indicator is purely based on the interactions between cells of the orientation columns in V1 and integration and treatment of the proposed velocities in the MST cells.

The equation 6 shows the actualisation rule in the AIM for the active neurons. Let S be a real image sequence and let $R \subset S$ be a subsequence with $Card(R) = \tau$ the subsequence size and let p be the percentage of the neurons to update.

The AIM mechanism updates $p\%$ of active neurons and we obtain in it two frequency percentages : the active neurons after updating (*ANaU*) and negative updating increase (*NUI*, see the right side in the equation 6).

The frequencies of the products between *ANaU* and *NUI* indicators in all the different controlled sub-sequences (see last section) inspire us to propose our first neuromimetic indicator: **neuromimetic motion indicator**, $NMI = ANaU * NUI$. The experimented ranges of NMI obtained are shown in table 1.

4.3 Speed and direction

Once the orientations have been estimated by the V1 cells the information must be collected, integrated and homogenized in MT, following a hierarchical principle (grouped by orientation columns). Achieving this way a disambiguation of the orientation (caused by the local treatment in V1 cells) of the moving objects, and so forth, it solves the local aperture problem and homogenates the orientations. In the case of the speed the neurons in MST group the information from the different speeds, using a extended-type of receptive fields, to offer an estimation of the velocity.

The equation 6 shows the actualisation rule in the AIM for the active neurons. Let S be a MT neurons sum the responses of V1 neurons with receptive field positions inside a local spatial neighbourhood that is defined through time and generates a response according to the speed of the visual stimulus [Castellanos-Sánchez, 2005]. This locality of the AIM mechanism on all the several considered motion directions in V1 bring an emerging answer corresponding to the global direction [Castellanos-Sánchez et al., 2004; Castellanos-Sánchez, 2005].

Condition	Description
NMI < 0.10	Null motion
NMI < 1.00	Small movin objects or bruit
NMI < 5.00	One or two moving objects
NMI < 10.00	Three to five moving objects
NMI < 40.00	Six or more moving objects, or ego-motion
NMI < 250.00	Ego-motion or big moving objects
NMI < 400.00	Ego-motion
NMI ≥ 400.00	Strong Ego-motion

Table 1. Experimental ranges for neuromimetic motion indicator (NMI)

On the other hand, neurophysiological studies roughly indicate that neurons in MT of the visual cortex of primate brains are selective to speed of visual stimuli; which implies that neurons respond strongly in a preferred direction and with a preferred speed [Simoncelli, 1998].

For each real subsequence R and for the filtering images generated in the equation 1 we define

$$sat^{+} = \max_{t,\Theta,v}(H_{t,\Theta,v}(x,y)), sat^{-} = \min_{t,\Theta,v}(H_{t,\Theta,v}(x,y)) \tag{10}$$

where sat^{+} and sat^{-} are the positive and negative saturation respectively.

For each direction and speed of each neuron, we count the neurons with a response greater than *at*. This parameter is the average of positive and negative saturations. The equation 12 shows its behaviour and the equation 11 computes this frequency in direction θ with speed v.

$$C(\Theta,v) = \sum_{x,y} D(at, H_{t,\Theta,v}(x,y)) \tag{11}$$

with

$$D(at, H_{t,\Theta,v}(x,y)) = \begin{cases} 1 \text{ if } H_{t,\Theta,v}(x,y) > at \\ 0 \text{ otherwise} \end{cases} \tag{12}$$

where $D(\cdot,\cdot)$ is the threshold of the CSTF filtering.The collection and combination in MT for direction estimation is computed by:

$$E(\Theta,v) = 3\cdot C(\Theta,v) + 2\cdot(C(\Theta-\phi,v)) + C(\Theta+\phi,v)) + C(\Theta-2\phi,v) + C(\Theta+2\phi,v) \tag{13}$$

where $\phi = 2\pi/\Theta$ is the separation in degrees between each oriented column and $E(\cdot,\cdot)$ is the sum of several oriented responses of V1 that activate a neuron in MT. Finally we computed the frequencies for negative and positive supposed speeds by the following equations:

$$G^{+} = \sum_{v>0,\Theta} C(\Theta,v), \qquad G^{-} = \sum_{v<0,\Theta} C(\Theta,v) \tag{14}$$

Then we arranged $E(\Theta,v)$ in a direction according to each speed and arranged G^{+} and G^{-} too for processing them to obtain speed and direction indicators. These indicators will be describe in the next two paragraphs.

4.3.1 Speed

To obtain the winner speed, we propose the **neuromimetic speed indicator (NSI)** defined by following equation:

$$NSI = \frac{100 \cdot \min(G^+, G^-)}{\max(G^+, G^-)} \tag{15}$$

With this indicator we compute the relative speed (*rs*) that compares the different speed frequencies and their proportion. The table 2 shows our experimental values for *V*=5. Then *v_i={-2,-1,0,1,2}*, with *v1* is the frequency of |*v_i*|=*1* and *v2* is the frequency of |*v_i*|=2.

4.3.2 Direction

Finally, for an interpretation of integration of directions for each neuron in MT, we compute the equation 10 for each direction and speed. Next, we arrange their values from major to minor and we take the first three. If these candidates are contiguous in direction, the winner will be at the centre of the three candidates' directions. This is our **neuromimetic direction indicator *NDI***.

Finally, if the maximum of the two computed speeds in the equation is the negative one, the winner direction will be its antagonist, ei, $\Theta = \Theta - 180^o$.

Type	Condition Relative speed	Prototype speed
Weak if *v1* > *v2*	NSI > 70.0 rs = (100.00-NSI)/29.0	0
	NSI > 12.0 rs = (71-NSI)/59 + 1	1
	otherwise rs = (12-NSI) * 0.3529 / 12 + 1	2
Strong if *v1* < *v2*	NSI > 22.0 rs = (NSI * 0.6470)/22 + 2.3530	3
	NSI > 39.0 rs = (NSI - 22) / 10 + 3	4
	Otherwise Speed not processed	≥ 5

Table 2. Experimental ranges for neuromimetic speed indicator (NSI)

5. Results

The free parameters of our model were set according to the suggestions in [Castellanos, 2004]. We chose only three sequences of images among m = 50 analysed sequences : the Yosemite Fly-Through (sequence of synthetic images), the Hamburg Taxi, the Karl-Wilhelm (DKW, traffic video surveillance) and the BrowseB (issue of a surveillance camera). They include various numbers of RGB images (15, 42, 1035 and 875 images, respectively) and of sizes of : 316×252, 256×191, 702×566, 384×288, respectively, and they are first gray-scaled.

The figure 5 and 6 shows four images of these sequences and their graph of the proposed neuromimetic indicators. The values of NMI are between 0 (null motion) and 1000 (ego-motion), of NSI between 0 and 6, and NDI is in {1, 2, 3, 4, 5, 6, 7, 8} (0°,45°,...,315°).

The real Hamburg Taxi sequence shows three moving cars and a pedestrian. The NMI is between 6 and 18, then according to the table 1 there are about three moving objects and the global speed is 2 pixels per image moving at approximately 180° and end at around 135°.

The BrowseB sequence issue of video surveillance in the hall of INRIA laboratory, Grenoble, France, may be split into three parts : (1) a person walks to the centre, stops and returns; (2) there is no motion; (3) another person walks in, stops and goes farther.

The Hamburg Taxi Sequence.

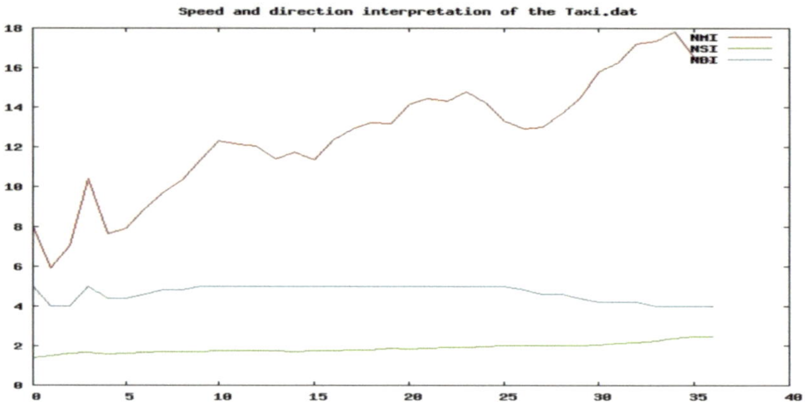

The BrowseB sequence.

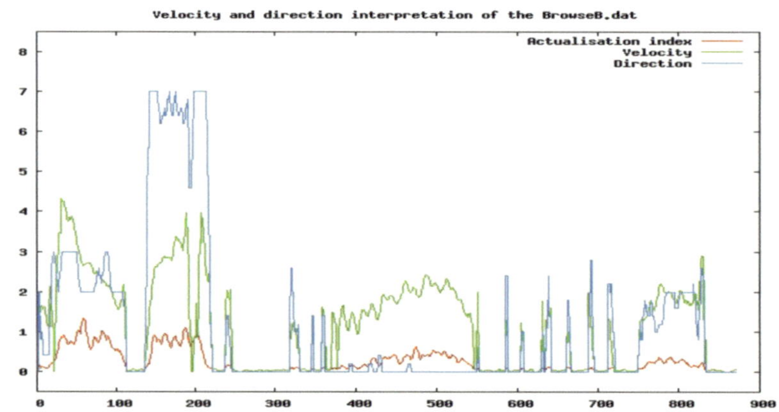

Figure 5. Two natural sequences, showing the sequence contents. In the first line and down of each one the graphic describing its motion behaviour (decomposed in the three neuromimetics indicators)

The DKW sequence

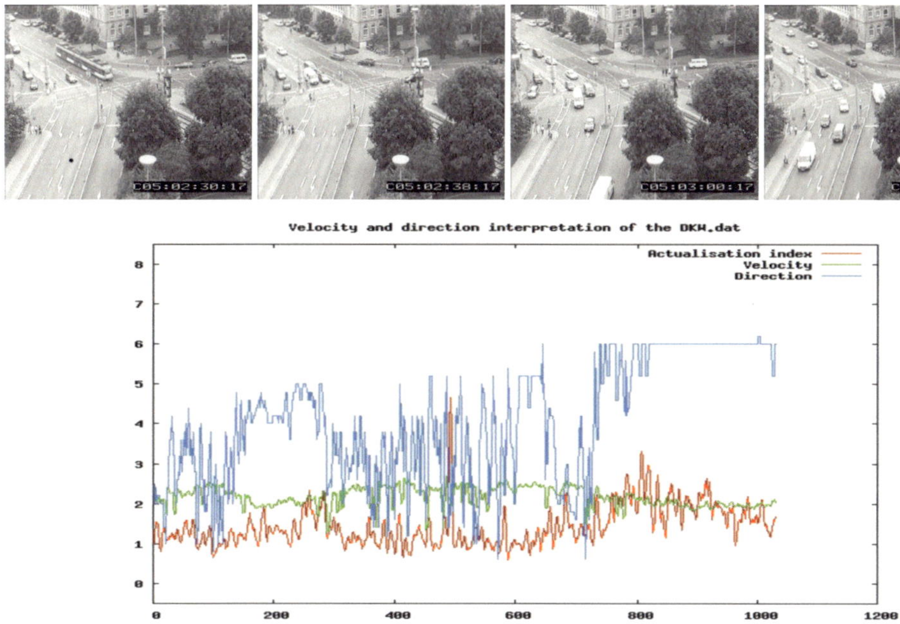

The Yosemite Sequence

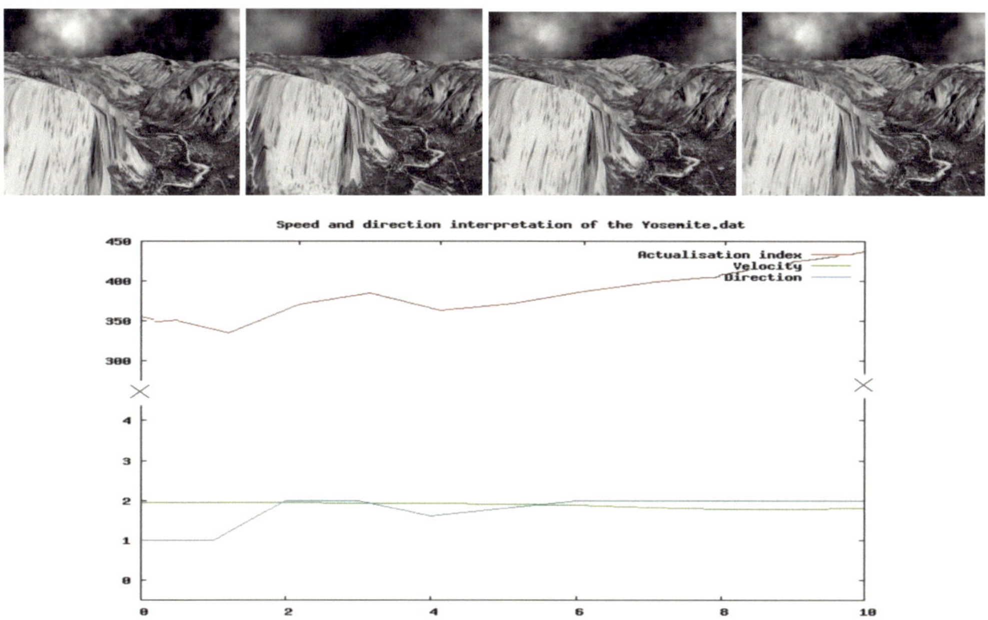

Figure 6. Sequences of real and synthetic images, Yosemite and DKW sequence below each one the graphic describing its motion behaviour (decomposed in the three neuromimetics indicators)

For the case of the BrowseB sequence in figure 5. The first part (images 0 to 220) may be split into three parts according to NMI : two parts with motion and the other part with null motion that correspond to the first person walking between 90° and 135° and with a speed of 4 to 2 pixels per image, stops and returns between 270° and 315° and with a speed of 2 to 4 pixels per image. For the second part (images 221 to 325) there is null motion. The last part may be split too into three parts according to NMI : (1) motion, (2) generally null motion and (3) motion, respectively to describe this part of the BrowseB sequence. The person walks approximately at 0° with a speed of 1-2 pixels per image. Next, a period of null motion with very weak motions (see pics in the graph between image 550 and 750). Finally, the person moves to about 90° with a speed of about 2 pixels per image.

The DKW sequence shows the images taken with a surveillance camera. In the first part (images around the 230) describe an increment in the motion due to the amount of objects moving in the scene. This kind of increments are accented in images around the 700, where after a period of low motion (images from 580 to 600). Besides the speed tends to remain stable during the whole sequence, this because the combination of objects in motion is almost the same for the whole sequence. Besides, in this last sequence it is important to mention that the obtained results of the direction are due to the combination of the objects that are moving in multiple direction (south or north, east or west).

Finally, the synthetic Yosemite Fly-Through sequence shows an aeroplane flying on the mountains, and mainly presents an ego-motion with a speed of five pixels (down image) that diverge and two pixels for the moving clouds to the right (top image). The NMI is between 300 and 450, then according to the table 1 it proposes an ego-motion with 2 pixels per image moving at around 45°.

In the figure 7, we show the average of direction and speed of optical real flow of Yosemite sequence and the experimental results obtained by our model. Our model presents a conceptual error about 22.5°, despite which it is sufficient to describe the real movement towards the North-East. Finally, the speed is not numerically exact, but our estimation is very similar to the real one. Then, the global motion obtained here is very similar to the Yosemite Fly-Through data.

6. Conclusions and Perspectives

This work is based on the CONEPVIM model [Castellanos-Sánchez et al., 2004]: a neuromimetic connectionist model for visual perception of motion. A model fully inspired by the visual cortex system, the superior areas and their relations.

In this paper we took advantage of the low-level analysis to detect local motions to obtain the global speed and direction. They are determined by the neuromimetic motion indicator issued by AIM mechanism.

Our first experiments show that this model is capable of estimating the null motion, simple motion and ego-motion with an estimation of global speed and direction in an environment where other persons or objects move. The estimation of motion is robust in quite complex scenes without any predefined information. Nevertheless, the estimation of NMI is fastidious. The experimental values are correct for the sequence of real images of ±33% the size of 384 × 288.

Besides, it has been seen that the proposed model gives good results, it has do basically with two characteristics, the first one is the local and distributed treatment of the information used for the analyse of the sequences. The second is the integration of these stages of processing, the last one is very important due to it is strongly linked to the methodology proposed to overcome the task.

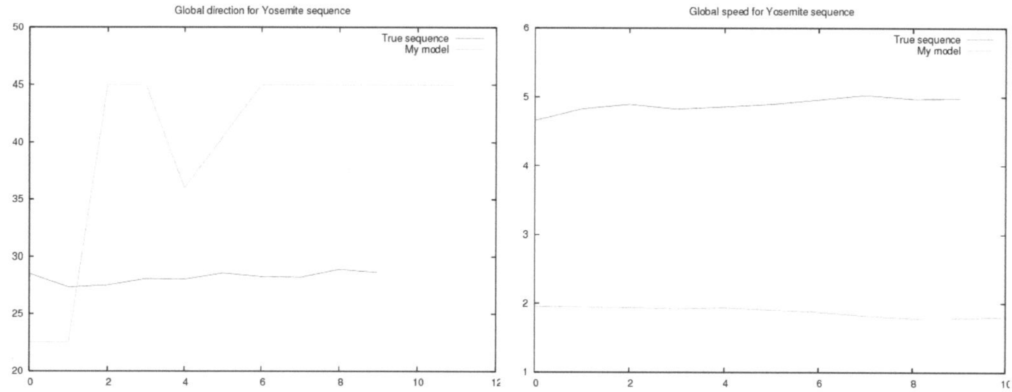

Figure 7. Comparison between the optical real flow of Yosemite sequence and the experimental results obtained by our model. In this case, both the speed and direction estimated are very similar to the results that are taken as the true. In the case of the direction the precision we are handling (the separation of the groups of neurons in 45° sets) gives a range of error

In this sense we have some perspectives about the methodology:

1. Following this methodology it is possible to understand not only the type of motion that is perceived but also to understand what is moving in the scene, since this processing belongs to the Ventral Pathway and in theory it works very similar to the Dorsal Pathway. This because it might be inferred that the processing in this path might also have strong interactions with the Dorsal Pathway, which help us to depict the information perceived.
2. Assuming that the information from other senses (auditory or sensitive) in the brain is processed by groups of neurons (just like it happens in the case of the visual processing) so this methodology will be helpful to understand how these arrangements of neurons work and how the information is combined with the information from other senses to interact with the environment.

8. Acknowledgment

This research was partially funded by project number 51623 from "Fondo Mixto Conacyt-Gobierno del Estado de Tamaulipas".

8. References

Adelson E. H., Bergen J. (1985). Spatiotemporal energy models for the perception of motion. *Journal of the Optical Society of America A*, 2(7):284-299.

Castellanos-Sánchez C. (2005), Neuromimetic connectionist model for embedded visual perception of motion. *PhD hesis*, Université Henri Poincaré (Nancy I), Nancy, France, Biblioth`eque des Sciences et Techniques.

Castellanos-Sánchez C., Girau B., Alexandre F. (2004). A connectionist approach for visual perception of motion. In Smith, L., Hussain, A., Aleksander, I., eds.: *Brain Inspired Cognitive Systems* (BICS 2004). BIS3-1:1-7.

Derrington A. M.,Henning. G. B.(1993). Detecting and discriminating the direction of motion of luminance and colour grattings. *Visual Research*, 33:799-811.

Fellez, W.A., Taylor, J.G. (2002). Establishing retinotopy by lateral-inhibition type homogeneous neural fields. *Neurocomputing* 48. 313–322.

Huitzil-Torres C., Girau B., Castellanos-Sánchez C. (2005). On-chip visual perception of motion: A bio-inspired connectionist model on fpga. Pages 557-565.

Grzywacz N. M., Yuille A. L. (1990). A model for the estimate of local image velocity by cells in the visual cortex. In *Proceedings Royal society London* B, volume 239, pages 129–161.

Grzywacz N. M., Yuille A. L. (1991). Theories for the visual perception of local velocity and coherent motion. In *Computational models of visual processing*, pages 231–252. M. I. T.

Heguer D. (1987). Model for the extraction of the image flow. *Journal of the Optical society of America*. 1455-1471.

Hengyi R., Tiangang Z., Yan Z., Silu F., and Lin C.(2003). Spatiotemporal Activation of the Two Visual Pathways in Form Discrimination and Spatial Location: A Brain Mapping Study. *Human Brain Mapping*, 18:79–89.

Hubel D. H., Weisel T. N.. (1962). Receptive fields, binocular interaction and functional architecture in the cats visual cortex. Journal Physiology, 160:106–154,.

Imbert M. (1983). Neurobiology of the Image. *La Recherche*, 144:600-613.

Jones J. and Palmer L. (1987). An evaluation on the two dimensional Gabor filter model of simple receptive fields in cat striate cortex. *Journal of Neurophysiology*, 58:1233–1258.

Marcelja S. (1980). Mathematical description of the responses of simple cortical cells. *Journal of the Optical Society of America* A, 70/11:1297–1300.

McCane, B., Novins, K., Grannitch, D., Galvin, B. (2001). On benchmarking optical flow. *Computer Vision and Image Undestanding*.126–143.

Mingolla, E. (2003). Neural models of motion integration and segmentation. *Neural Networks* 16. 939–945.

Moga, S. (2000). Apprendre par imitation: une nouvelle voie d'apprentissage pour les robots autonomes. *PhD thesis*, Université de Cergy-Pontoise, Cergy-Pontoise,France.

Pack, C., Grossberg, S., Mingolla, E. (2000). A neural model of smooth pursuit control and motion perception by cortical area MST. *Technical Report* CAS/CNR-TR-99-023, Department of Cognitive and Neural Systems and Center for Adaptive Systems, 677 Beacon St, Boston, MA 02215.

Pollen D., Ronner S. (1981). Phase relationships between adjacent simple cells in the visual cortex. *Science*, 212:1409- 1411, 1981.

Sekuler R., Watamaniuk S. N. J., Blake R. (2002). Motion Perception. *Steven's Handbook of Experimental Psychology*, 1:121–176.

Simoncelli, E.P., Heeger, D.J. (1998). A model of neural responses in visual area MT. *Vision Research* 38. 743–761.

Van Santen J. P. H., Sperling G. (1984). Temporal covariance model of human motion perception. *Journal of the Optical Society of America* A, 1:451, 1984.

Van Santen J. P. H., Sperling G. (1985). Elaborated Richardt detectors. *Journal of the Optical Society of America* A, 2:300- 321, 1985.

Zemel, R.S., Sejnowski, T.J. (1998). A model for encoding multiple object motions and self-motion in area MST of primate visual cortex. *The Journal of Neurosciences* 18. 531–547.

4

Cell Pattern Generation in Artificial Development

Arturo Chavoya
Universidad de Guadalajara
Mexico

1. Introduction

In biological systems, development is a fascinating and very complex process that involves following an extremely intricate program coded in the organism's genome. One of the crucial stages in the development of an organism is that of pattern formation, where the fundamental body axes of the individual are outlined. It is now evident that gene regulatory networks play a central role in the development and metabolism of living organisms. Moreover, it has been discovered in recent years that the diverse cell patterns created during the developmental stages are mainly due to the selective activation and inhibition of very specific regulatory genes.

Over the years, artificial models of cellular development have been proposed with the objective of understanding how complex structures and patterns can emerge from one or a small group of initial undifferentiated cells. An artificial development model that generates cell patterns by means of the selective activation and inhibition of development genes under the constraints of morphogenetic gradients is proposed here. Cellular growth is achieved through the expression of structural genes, which are in turn controlled by an Artificial Regulatory Network (ARN) evolved by a Genetic Algorithm (GA). The ARN determines when cells are allowed to grow and which gene to use for reproduction, while morphogenetic gradients constrain the position at which cells can replicate. Both the ARN and the structural genes constitute the artificial cell's genome. In order to test the functionality of the development program found by the GA, the evolved genome was applied to a cellular growth testbed that has been successfully used in the past to develop simple 2D and 3D geometrical shapes (Chavoya & Duthen, 2006b).

The artificial development model for cell pattern generation was based on the cellular automata (CA) paradigm. CA have previously been used to study form generation, as they provide an excellent framework for modelling local interactions that give rise to emergent properties in complex systems. Morphogenetic gradients were used to provide cells with positional information that constrained cellular replication. After a genome was evolved, a single cell in the middle of the CA lattice was allowed to reproduce until a cell pattern was formed. The model was applied to the canonical problem in cellular development of growing a French flag pattern.

2. Artificial Development

This section covers the main research areas pertaining to artificial development with special emphasis on the work more directly related to the model presented in Section 4.

2.1 Reaction-Diffusion Systems

It is usually attributed to Turing the founding of modern research on artificial development. He suggested in his seminal article on the chemical basis of morphogenesis (Turing, 1952) that an initially homogeneous medium might develop a structured pattern due to an instability of the homogeneous equilibrium, triggered by small random perturbations.
Using a set of differential equations, Turing proposed a reaction-diffusion model where substances called morphogens, or form generators, would react together and diffuse through a medium, which could be a tissue. The system can be fine-tuned with the proper parameters such that at some point the slightest disruption in the equilibrium can be amplified and propagated through the medium generating unpredictable patterns.
Even though his model was based on an oversimplification of natural conditions, Turing succeeded in demonstrating how the emergence of a complex pattern could be explained in terms of a simple reaction and diffusion mechanism using well-known physical and chemical principles.

2.2 Self-Activation and Lateral Inhibition Model

Experiments with biological specimens have demonstrated that development is a very robust process. Development can continue normally even after a substantial amount of tissue from certain parts has been removed from an embryo. However, there are small specialized regions that play a crucial role in the organization of the development process.
In order to explain the long range effect of these small organizing regions on the larger surrounding tissue and the robustness of their influence even after induced interferences, Wolpert introduced the concept of "positional information", whereby a local source region produces a signalling chemical (Wolpert, 1969). This theoretical substance was supposed to diffuse and decay creating a concentration gradient that provided cells with information regarding their position in the tissue.
Nevertheless, the problem remained as to how a local differentiated source region could be generated from a seemingly homogeneous initial cluster of developing cells. Even though many eggs have some predefined structure, all the patterns developed after a number of cell divisions cannot initially be present in the egg. A mechanism must exist that allows the emergence of heterogeneous structures starting with a more or less homogeneous egg.
Gierer and Meinhardt proposed that pattern formation was the result of local self-activation coupled with lateral inhibition (Gierer & Meinhardt, 1972; Gierer, 1981; Meinhardt, 1982). In this model, which has some resemblance to Turing's model, a substance that diffuses slowly, called the activator, induces its own production (autocatalysis or self-activation) as well as that of a faster diffusing antagonist, the inhibitor. These authors suggest that pattern formation requires both a strong positive feedback (autocatalysis) and a long-ranging inhibitor to stop positive feedback from spreading indefinitely (lateral inhibition).
Their results suggest how a relatively simple mechanism of coupled biochemical interactions can account for the generation of very complex patterns. The components of the model are based on reasonable assumptions, since mutual activation and inhibition of

biochemical substances and molecular diffusion actually exist in the real world. In recent years, molecular biology and genetics experiments have given support to many elements of the model.

2.3 Lindenmayer Systems

Lindenmayer systems, or L-systems, were originally introduced as a mathematical formalism for modelling development of simple multicellular organisms (Lindenmayer, 1968). The organism is abstracted as an assembly of repeating discrete structures or modules. The formalism is independent of the nature of the module, which can be an individual cell or a whole functional structure such as a plant branch. An L-system is a formal grammar with a set of symbols and a set of rewriting rules. The rules are applied iteratively starting with the initial symbol. Unlike traditional formal grammars, rewriting rules are applied in parallel to simulate the simultaneous development of component parts of an organism.

One of the main applications of L-systems has been in the modelling of the development of higher plants (Prusinkiewicz & Lindenmayer, 1990). The modelling does not take place at the cellular level. Instead, it is based on a modular construction of discrete structural units that are repeated during the development of plants, such as branches, leaves and petals (Prusinkiewicz, 1993). Initial models did not consider the influence of the environment on development. However, as organisms in nature are an integral part of an ecosystem, an extension to the modelling framework that considered interaction with the environment was introduced (Mech & Prusinkiewicz, 1996).

The use of L-Systems has been extremely fruitful in modelling the development of organisms at a high structural level. Implemented models of plant development that use L-systems are visually striking because of their resemblance to growth seen in real-life plants and trees.

2.4 Biomorphs

Richard Dawkins' well-known Biomorphs were first introduced in his famous book "The Blind Watchmaker" to illustrate how evolution might induce the creation of complex designs by means of micro-mutations and cumulative selection (Dawkins, 1996). Dawkins intended to find a model to counteract the old argument in biology that a finished complex structure such as the human eye could not be accounted for by Darwin's evolution theory.

Biomorphs are the visible result of the instructions coded in a genome that can undergo evolution. Dawkins introduced a constraint of symmetry around an axis so that the resulting forms would show bilateral symmetry, as in many biological organisms. Initially Dawkins thought that the forms produced would be limited to tree-like structures. However, to his surprise, the forms generated were extremely varied in shape and detail. There were biomorphs that roughly resembled insects, crustaceans or even mammals.

This author proposed next an "interactive" evolutionary algorithm, where the user played the part of the selection force. Initially the user has to decide which form he/she wants to evolve, such as a spider or a pine tree, and in each step of the algorithm he/she chooses the biomorph that best resembles the target form (cumulative selection).

Dawkins showed with his models that the evolution of complex structures was indeed feasible in a step by step manner by means of the cumulative selection of the individual that best approached the final structure.

2.5 Artificial Embryogenesis

Hugo de Garis worked on the creation of a self-assembly process that he called "artificial embryogenesis". His motivation was that he believed that in the future, machines would have so many components that a sequential mechanical assembly would not be feasible. He theorized that highly complex machines should be self-assembled in a similar way as biological organisms are developed.

He worked on artificial "embryos" as 2D shapes formed by a colony of cells using the CA paradigm (de Garis, 1991). He developed a model that evolved reproduction rules for CA, with the goal that the final shape of a colony of cells was as close as possible to a predefined simple shape such as a square or a triangle (de Garis, 1992). In this model, cells can only reproduce if there is at least one adjacent empty cell, i.e. only edge cells are allowed to reproduce. Several target shapes, both convex and non-convex were tested. Results showed that convex shapes could be obtained with a fitness value around 95%, but non-convex shapes evolved poorly, with low fitness values.

After these initial results, de Garis concluded that evolving an artificial embryo implies a type of sequential, synchronized unfolding of shapes. For example, after the main body is grown, then the head and limbs can be grown, followed by the emergence of more detailed shapes, such as those corresponding to fingers and toes (de Garis, 1992).

Even though the approach used by de Garis proved the potential of the application of evolutionary techniques to the growth of artificial cells in order to generate desired shapes, his results were of limited success. However, he was one of the first researchers to use the concept of sequential gene activation for the production of artificial cellular structures using the CA paradigm.

2.6 Evolutionary Neurogenesis and Cell Differentiation

Kitano (1990) was another of the first researchers that conducted experiments towards evolving an artificial development system. This author was successful at evolving large neural networks using GAs. He encoded into the GA chromosome the neural network connectivity matrix using a graph generating grammar. Instead of using a direct encoding of the connectivity matrix, a set of rules was created by a grammar overcoming the scalability problem on the cases tested. Previous attempts saw how convergence performance was greatly degraded as the size of the neural network grew larger. The grammar used was an augmented version of Lindenmayer's L-System and used matrices as symbols.

Kitano (1994) later developed a model of neurogenesis and cell differentiation based on a simulation of metabolism. The idea was to see if artificial multicellular organisms could be created using GAs evolving the metabolic rules in the cell genome. Although all cells carry the same set of rules, individual cells can express different rules because of differences in their local environment, thus producing a sort of cell differentiation. Metabolic rules define which kind of metabolite can be transformed into another kind and under what conditions of metabolite concentration and enzyme presence.

2.7 Evolutionary 2D/3D Morphogenesis

Fleischer & Barr (1992) presented a simulation framework and computational testbed for the study of 2D multicellular pattern formation. Their initial motivation was the generation of neural networks using a developmental approach, but their interest soon shifted towards the study of the multiple mechanisms involved in morphogenesis.

Their approach combined several developmental mechanisms that they considered important for biological pattern formation. Previous work from other researchers had individually considered chemical factors, mechanical forces, and cell-lineage control of cell division to account for some aspects of morphogenesis. These authors decided to combine these factors into one modelling system in order to determine how the interactions between these components could affect cell pattern development. They emphasized that it was the interactions between the developmental mechanisms that were at the core of the determination of multicellular and developmental patterns, and not the individual elements of the model.
On the other hand, Eggenberger used an evolutionary approach for studying the creation of neural network and the simulated morphogenesis of 3D organisms based on differential gene expression (Eggenberger, 1997a; Eggenberger, 1997b). His model for simulating morphogenesis includes a genome with two types of elements: regulatory units and structural genes. The regulatory units act as switches to turn genes on and off, while structural genes code for specific substances that are used to modulate developmental processes. Eggenberger's models showed that a number of mechanisms central to development such as cellular growth, cell differentiation, axis definition, and dynamical changes in shape could be simulated using a framework not based on a direct mapping between a genome and the resulting cellular structure. The shapes that emerge in the models are the result of the interaction among cells and their environment.

2.8 METAMorph

METAMorph, which stands for *Model for Experimentation and Teaching in Artificial Morphogenesis*, is an open source software platform for the simulation of cellular development processes using genomes encoded as gene regulatory networks. The design is made by hand and it allows visualization of the resulting morphological cellular growth process (Stewart et al., 2005). As in higher organisms, cellular growth starts in METAMorph with a single cell (the zygote) and is regulated by gene regulatory networks in interaction with proteins. All cells have the same genome consisting of a series of genes. Each gene can produce exactly one protein, although the same protein can be produced by different genes.
The main disadvantage of this simulation platform is that the cellular development model has to be designed through a trial and error process that is limited by the designer's ability to introduce the appropriate parameter values. By the authors' account, this trial and error process typically involves a considerable amount of time, since simulation times are usually high due to the parallel nature of the morphogenetic process. To compound the problem, small changes in design can have substantial consequences on the final shape caused by "the butterfly effect."

2.9 Random Boolean Networks

Random Boolean Networks (RBNs) are a type of discrete dynamical networks that consist of a set of Boolean variables whose state depends on other variables in the network. In RBNs, time and state values take only integer values. The first Boolean networks were proposed by Kauffman (1969) as a randomized model of a gene regulatory network. The connections between nodes are randomly selected and remain fixed thereafter. The dynamics of the RBN is determined by the particular network configuration and by a randomly generated binary function, defined as a lookup table for each node.

Depending on the behaviour of the network dynamics, three different phases or regimes can be distinguished: ordered, chaotic and critical (Kauffman, 2004). The critical type of behaviour is usually considered by researchers as the most interesting of the three types. The ordered type is too static to derive useful observations applicable to dynamic systems, whereas the chaotic type is too random to study any kind of reproducible property.

Kauffman suggested that biological entities could have originally been generated from random elements, with no absolute need of precisely programmed elements (Kauffman, 1969). This conjecture was derived from his observations of the complex behaviour of some of these randomly generated networks and the inherent robustness he found in them.

2.10 Artificial Regulatory Networks

Over the years, many models of ARNs have emerged in an attempt to emulate the gene networks found in nature. Reil (1999) was one of the first researchers to propose an artificial genome with biologically plausible properties based on template matching on a nucleotide-like sequence. The genome is defined as a string of digits and is randomly created. Genes in the genome are not predefined, but are identified by a "promoter" sequence that precedes them. As with RBNs and other dynamical systems, three basic types of behaviour were identified: ordered, chaotic, and complex. Gene expression was called ordered if genes were continuously active or inactive throughout the run. If gene expression seemed to be random with no apparent emerging pattern, it was called chaotic. If the expression of genes was considered to be between ordered and chaotic with the formation of identifiable patterns, then it was called complex.

Reil observed that even after manual perturbations in the model, gene expression usually returned to the attractors that emerged previously. It must be emphasized that the artificial genomes endured no evolution. The behaviours observed were the result of the properties of genomes entirely generated at random. Reil hypothesized that robustness in natural genomes might be an inherent property of the template matching system, rather than the result of the natural selection of the most robust nucleotide sequences (Reil, 1999).

An important advancement in the design of an artificial genome model was made by Banzhaf, who designed a genetic representation based on ARNs (Banzhaf, 2003). His genome consists of a randomly generated binary string where special sequences signal the beginning of genes. Each gene has an enhancer and an inhibitor region that regulate the expression of proteins. After a protein has been produced, it is then compared on a bit by bit basis with the enhancer and inhibitor sequences on all genes in the genome affecting their protein expression.

After observing the dynamics of proteins from genomes that had experienced no evolution, Banzhaf used Genetic Programming in an attempt to drive the dynamics of gene expression towards desired behaviours. He started by evolving the genome to obtain a target concentration of a particular protein. He found out that in general the evolutionary process quickly converged towards the target state.

Another author that evolved an ARN in order to perform a specific task was Bongard (2002). He designed virtual modular robots that were evaluated for how fast they could travel over an infinite horizontal plane during a time interval previously specified. The robots are composed of one or more morphological units and zero or more sensors, motors, neurons and synapses. Each morphological unit contains a genome, and at the beginning of the evolution a genome and a motor neuron are inserted into the initial unit. Using his model,

Bongard demonstrated that mobile units could be evolved in a virtual environment. His results suggest that a similar model might be applied in the design of physical robots.

Other authors have performed research on ARNs using a number of approaches. Willadsen & Wiles (2003) designed a genome based on the model proposed by Reil (1999). As in other models, the genome consists of a string of randomly generated integers where a promoter precedes a fixed-length gene. Gene products are generated, which can regulate expression of other genes. While their genome model offered no major improvement over previous models, these authors succeeding in showing that there was a strong relationship between gene network connectivity and the degree of inhibition with respect to generating a chaotic behaviour. Low connectivity gene networks were found to be very stable, while in higher connectivity networks there was a significantly elevated frequency of chaotic behaviour. Flann et al. (2005) used ARNs to construct 2D cellular patterns such as borders, patches and mosaics. They implemented the ARN as a graph, where each node represents a distinct expression level from a protein, and each edge corresponds to interactions between proteins. A protein is influenced when its production or inhibition is altered as the function of other protein concentration levels. A set of differential equations was used to define the rate of production or inhibition. These authors conjectured that complex ARNs in nature might have evolved by combining simpler ARNs. Finally, Nehaniv's research group has worked on ARNs aiming at evolving a biological clock model (Knabe et al., 2006). They studied the evolvability of ARNs as active control systems that responded with appropriate periodic behaviours to periodic environmental stimuli of several types.

2.11 Evolutionary Development Model

Kumar & Bentley (2003) designed a developmental testbed that they called the Evolutionary Development System (EDS). It was intended for the investigation of multicellular processes and mechanisms, and their potential application to computer science. The EDS contains the equivalent of many key elements involved in biological development. It implements concepts such as embryos, cells, cell cytoplasm, cell wall, proteins, receptors, transcription factors, genes and *cis*-regulatory regions.

Cells in the EDS are autonomous agents that have sensors in the form of surface receptors capable of binding to substances in the environment. Depending on their current state, cells can exhibit a number of activities such as division, differentiation shown as an external colour, and apoptosis or programmed cell death. A GA with tournament selection was used to evolve the genomes.

The design of the EDS was probably too ambitious by involving many elements that introduced more variables and interactions in the system than desired. Results obtained with the EDS are not as good as expected, considering the number of concepts involved. The system might prove its true potential with a more complex target cellular structure.

3. The French Flag Problem

The problem of generating a French flag pattern was first introduced by Wolpert in the late 1960s when trying to formulate the problem of cell pattern development and regulation in living organisms (Wolpert, 1968). This formulation has been used since then by some authors to study the problem of artificial pattern development.

Lindenmayer & Rozenberg (1972) used the French flag problem to illustrate how a grammar-based L-System could be used to solve the generation of this particular pattern when enunciated as the production of a string of the type $a^nb^nc^n$ over the alphabet $\{a,b,c\}$ and with $n>0$. On the other hand, Herman & Liu (1973) developed an extension of a simulator called CELIA (Baker & Herman, 1970) and applied it to generate a French flag pattern in order to study synchronization and symmetry breaking in cellular development.

More recently, Miller & Banzhaf (2003) used what they called Cartesian genetic programming to evolve a cell program that would construct a French flag pattern. They tested the robustness of their programs by manually removing parts of the developing pattern. They found that some of their evolved programs could repair to some extent the damaged patterns. Bowers (2005) also used this problem to study the phenotypic robustness of his embryogeny model, which was based on cellular growth with diffusing chemicals as signalling molecules.

Gordon & Bentley (2005) proposed a development model based on a set of rules that described how development should proceed. A set of rules evolved by a GA was used to develop a French flag pattern. The morphogenic model based on a multiagent system developed by Beurier et al. (2006) also used an evolved set of agent rules to grow French and Japanese flag patterns. On the other hand, Devert et al. (2007) proposed a neural network model for multicellular development that grew French flag patterns. Finally, even models for developing evolvable hardware have benefited from the French flag problem as a test case (Tyrrell & Greensted, 2007; Harding et al., 2007).

4. Cell Pattern Generation Model

In the proposed model of artificial development, cellular patterns are generated by means of the selective activation and inhibition of development genes under the constraints of morphogenetic gradients. Cellular growth is achieved through the expression of structural genes, which are in turn controlled by an ARN evolved by a GA. The ARN establishes the time at which cells can reproduce and determines which structural gene to use at each time step. At the same time, morphogenetic gradients constrain the position at which cells can replicate. The combination of the ARN and the structural genes constitutes the artificial cell's genome.

4.1 Cellular Growth Testbed

In order to evaluate the performance of the development program obtained with the model, their evolved genomes were applied to a cellular growth testbed designed to generate simple geometrical shapes (Chavoya & Duthen, 2006b). This growth model is based on the extensively studied CA paradigm.

Cellular automata are simple mathematical models that can be used to study self-organization in a wide variety of complex systems (Wolfram, 1983). CA are characterized by a regular lattice of N identical cells, an interaction neighbourhood template η, a finite set of cell states Σ, and a space- and time-independent transition rule ϕ which is applied to every cell on the lattice at each time step.

In the cellular growth model presented here, a 33×33 regular lattice with non-periodic boundaries was used. The set of cell states was defined as $\Sigma=\{0,1\}$, where 0 can be interpreted as an empty cell and 1 as an occupied or active cell. The interaction template η

used was an outer Moore neighbourhood. The CA's rule ϕ was defined as a lookup table that determined, for each local neighbourhood, the state (empty or occupied) of the objective cell at the next time step. For a 2-state CA, these update states are termed the rule table's "output bits". The lookup table input was defined by the binary state value of cells in the local interaction neighbourhood, where 0 meant an empty cell and 1 meant an occupied cell (Chavoya & Duthen, 2006a).

Figure 1 shows an example of the relationship between a CA neighbourhood template and the corresponding lookup table. For each neighbourhood configuration, the output bit determines whether or not a cell is to be placed at the corresponding objective cell position. In this example, if there is only an active cell at the objective cell's right position, then the objective cell is to be filled with an active cell (second row of the lookup table in Fig. 1). The actual output bit values used have to be determined for each different shape and are found using a GA. For the sake of simplicity, the neighbourhood shown in the figure is an outer Von Neumann template, but as mentioned above the neighbourhood used in the testbed was an outer Moore template with the eight nearest cells surrounding the central objective cell.

Neighborhood template

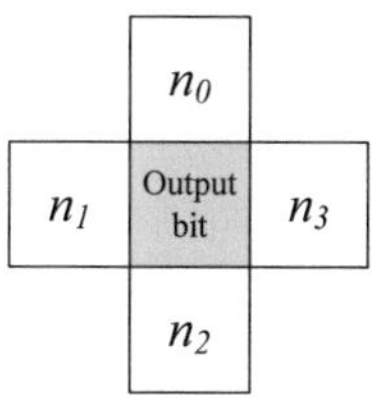

Lookup Table

n_0	n_1	n_2	n_3	Output bit
0	0	0	0	0
0	0	0	1	1
0	0	1	0	1
0	0	1	1	0
0	1	0	0	1
	⋮			⋮
1	1	1	1	0

Figure 1. Relationship between a cellular automaton neighbourhood template and the corresponding lookup table. The output bit values shown are used only as an example

A cell can become active only if there is already an active cell in the interaction neighbourhood. Starting with an active cell in the middle of the lattice, the CA algorithm is applied allowing active cells to reproduce for 100 time steps according to the rule table. During an iteration of the CA algorithm, the order of reproduction of active cells is randomly selected to avoid artifacts caused by a deterministic order of cell reproduction. Finally, cell death is not considered in the present model for the sake of simplicity.

4.2 Morphogenetic Gradients

Since Turing's seminal article on the theoretical influence of diffusing chemical substances on an organism's pattern development (Turing, 1952), the role of these molecules has been confirmed in a number of biological systems. These organizing substances have been termed *morphogens* due to their role in driving morphogenetic processes. In our proposed development model, morphogenetic gradients were generated similar to those found in the eggs of the fruit fly *Drosophila*, where orthogonal gradients offer a sort of Cartesian coordinate system (Carroll et al. 2005). These gradients provide reproducing cells with positional information in order to facilitate the spatial generation of patterns. The artificial morphogenetic gradients were set up as suggested in (Meinhardt, 1982), where morphogens diffuse from a source towards a sink, with uniform morphogen degradation throughout the gradient.

Before cells were allowed to reproduce in the cellular growth model, morphogenetic gradients were generated by diffusing the morphogens from one of the CA boundaries for 1000 time steps. Initial morphogen concentration level was set at 255 arbitrary units, and the source was replenished to the same level at the beginning of each cycle. The sink was set up at the opposite boundary of the lattice, where the morphogen level was always set to zero. At the end of each time step, morphogens were degraded at a rate of 0.005 throughout the CA lattice. We defined two orthogonal gradients on the CA lattice, one generated from left to right and the other from top to bottom (Fig. 2).

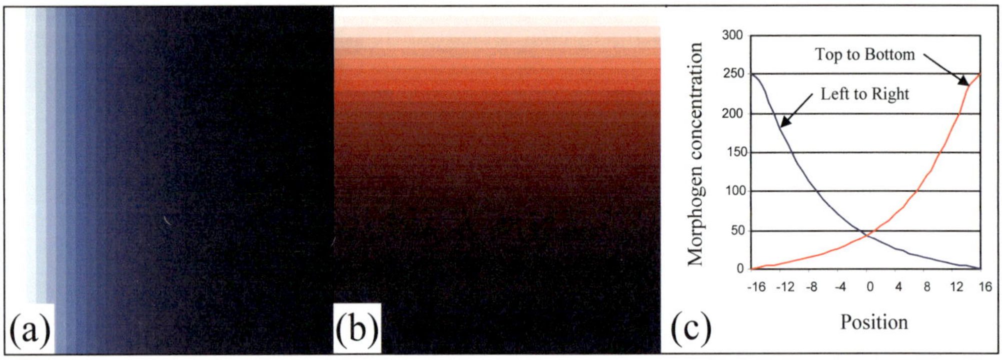

Figure 2. Morphogenetic gradients (a) Left to Right; (b) Top to Bottom; (c) Morphogen concentration graph

4.3 Genome

Genomes are the repository of genetic information in living organisms. They are encoded as one or more chains of DNA, and they regularly interact with other macromolecules, such as RNA and proteins. Artificial genomes are typically coded as strings of discrete data types. The genome used in the proposed model was defined as a binary string starting with a series of regulatory genes, followed by a number of structural genes.

The series of regulatory genes at the beginning of the artificial genome constitutes an ARN. For the sake of simplicity, the term "regulatory gene" is used in this model to comprise both the elements controlling protein expression and the regions coding for the regulatory protein. On the other hand, structural genes code for the particular shape grown by the reproducing cells and they will be described in more detail in Subsection 4.3.2.

4.3.1 Artificial Regulatory Networks

In nature, gene regulatory networks have been found to be a central component of an organism's genome. They actively participate in the regulation of development and in the control of metabolic functions in living organisms (Davidson, 2006). Artificial Regulatory Networks on the other hand are computer models whose objective is to emulate to some extent the gene regulatory networks found in nature. ARNs have previously been used to study differential gene expression either as a computational paradigm or to solve particular problems.

The ARN model presented here (shown as the series of regulatory genes of the genome in Fig. 3) was originally based on the ARN proposed by Banzhaf (Banzhaf, 2003). However, unlike the ARN model developed by this author, the ARN implemented in the present work does not have promoter sequences and there are no unused intergene regions. All regulatory genes are adjacent and have predefined initial and end positions. Furthermore, the number of regulatory genes is fixed and their internal structure has been modified by adding more inhibitor/enhancer sites and by allowing their role to evolve. The number of regulatory sites was extended with respect to the original model, in order to more closely follow what happens in nature, where biological regulatory genes involved in development typically have several regulatory sites associated with them (Davidson, 2006). Another addition was the incorporation of morphogen threshold activation sites in the regulatory gene.

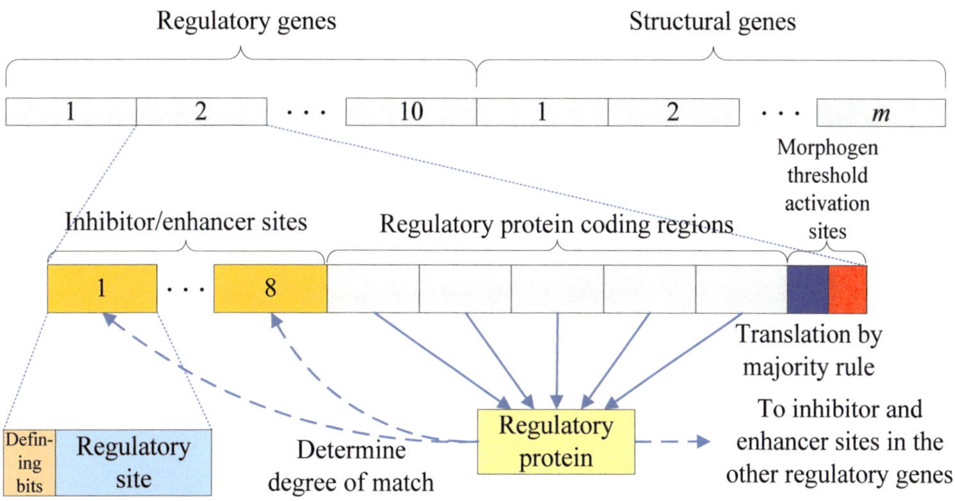

Figure 3. Genome structure and regulatory gene detail

Each regulatory gene consists of a series of eight inhibitor/enhancer sites, a series of five regulatory protein coding regions, and two morphogen threshold activation sites that determine the allowed positions for cell reproduction (Fig. 3). Inhibitor/enhancer sites are composed of a 12-bit function defining region and a regulatory site. The values used for the number of inhibitor/enhancer sites and the number of function defining bits are those that previously gave the best results under the conditions tested (Chavoya & Duthen, 2007c). Regulatory sites can behave either as an enhancer or an inhibitor, depending on the configuration of the function defining bits associated with them. If there are more 1's than 0's in the defining bits region, then the regulatory site functions as an enhancer, but if there are more 0's than 1's, then the site behaves as an inhibitor. Finally, if there is an equal number of 1's and 0's, then the regulatory site is turned off (Chavoya & Duthen, 2007b).

Regulatory protein coding regions "translate" a protein using the majority rule, i.e. for each bit position in these regions, the number of 1's and 0's is counted and the bit that is in majority is translated into the regulatory protein. The regulatory sites and the individual protein coding regions all have the same size of 32 bits. Thus the protein translated from the coding regions can be compared on a bit by bit basis with the regulatory site of the inhibitor and enhancer sites, and the degree of matching can be measured. As in (Banzhaf, 2003), the comparison was implemented by an XOR operation, which results in a "1" if the corresponding bits are complementary. Each translated protein is compared with the inhibitor and enhancer sites of all the regulatory genes in order to determine the degree of interaction in the regulatory network.

The influence of a protein on an enhancer or inhibitor site is exponential with the number of matching bits. The strength of excitation *en* or inhibition *in* for gene *i* with $i=1,...,n$ is defined as

$$en_i = \frac{1}{v}\sum_{j=1}^{v} c_j e^{\beta(u_{ij}^{+} - u_{\max}^{+})} \tag{1}$$

$$in_i = \frac{1}{w}\sum_{j=1}^{w} c_j e^{\beta(u_{ij}^{-} - u_{\max}^{-})}, \tag{2}$$

where n is the total number of regulatory genes, v and w are the total number of active enhancer and inhibitor sites, respectively, c_j is the concentration of protein j, β is a constant that fine-tunes the strength of matching, u_{ij}^{+} and u_{ij}^{-} are the number of matches between protein j and the enhancer and inhibitor sites of gene i, respectively, and $u_{\max}^{+}$ and $u_{\max}^{-}$ are the maximum matches achievable (32 bits) between a protein and an enhancer or inhibitor site, respectively (Banzhaf, 2003).

Once the *en* and *in* values are obtained for all regulatory genes, the corresponding change in concentration c for protein i in one time step is calculated using

$$\frac{dc_i}{dt} = \delta(en_i - in_i)c_i, \tag{3}$$

where δ is a constant that regulates the degree of protein concentration change.

Protein concentrations are updated and if a new protein concentration results in a negative value, the protein concentration is set to zero. Protein concentrations are then normalized so that total protein concentration is always the unity. Parameters β and δ were set to 1.0 and 1.0×10^6, respectively, as previously reported (Chavoya & Duthen, 2007a).

The morphogen threshold activation sites provide reproducing cells with positional information as to where they are allowed to grow on the CA lattice. There is one site for each of the two orthogonal morphogenetic gradients described in Subsection 4.2. These sites are 9 bits in length, where the first bit defines the allowed direction (above or below the threshold) of cellular growth, and the next 8 bits code for the morphogen threshold activation level, which ranges from 0 to 2^8 -1=255. If the site's high order bit is 0, then cells are allowed to replicate below the morphogen threshold level coded in the lower order eight bits; if the value is 1, then cells are allowed to reproduce above the threshold level. Since in a regulatory gene there is one site for each of the two orthogonal morphogenetic gradients, for each pair of morphogen threshold activation levels, the pair of high order bits defines in which of the four relative quadrants cells expressing the associated structural gene can reproduce. Quadrants can have irregular edges because morphogenetic gradients are not perfectly generated due to local morphogen accumulation close to the non-periodic boundaries of the CA lattice.

Genome size in bits is dependent on the number and size of its component genes. For all simulations the following parameter values were used: The number of structural genes took values from 3, 4 or 8, depending on the experiment performed, as explained in Section 5. The number of regulatory genes was chosen as 10 because this figure was within the range of values previously reported for this kind of ARN (Banzhaf, 2003), and it was found that this value gave a desirable behaviour in the protein concentration variations needed to control cell reproduction. Parameter values for the number of regulatory protein coding regions and the region size in bits are 5 and 32, respectively, and are equal to those used in (Banzhaf, 2003). Finally, structural genes are always 256 bits in length, which results from the use of an outer Moore neighbourhood with its eight cells surrounding the central objective cell. Since each cell in the template can take a value of 1 or 0, the lookup table coding for the structural gene has $2^8 = 256$ rows (Chavoya & Duthen, 2006a).

4.3.2 Structural Genes

Structural genes code for the particular shape grown by the reproducing cells (Chavoya & Duthen, 2006a) and they correspond to the CA rule table's output bits from the cellular growth testbed presented in Section 4.1. Previously to being attached to the regulatory genes to constitute the genome, structural genes were evolved by a GA in order to produce predefined simple 2D shapes, such a square or a line.

Structural genes are always associated to the corresponding regulatory genes, that is, structural gene number 1 is associated to regulatory gene number 1 and its related translated protein, and so on. A structural gene was defined as being active if and only if the regulatory protein translated by the associated regulatory gene was above a certain concentration threshold. The value chosen for the threshold was 0.5, since the sum of all protein concentrations is always 1.0, and there can only be a protein at a time with a concentration above 0.5. As a result, only one structural gene can be expressed at a particular time step in a cell. If a structural gene is active, then the CA lookup table coded in it is used to control cell reproduction.

In the series of simulations presented in Section 5, the number of structural genes used in the genome depended on the particular pattern grown and this number was always less than the number of regulatory genes. Thus, some regulatory proteins both regulated concentration for other proteins and directly controlled structural gene expression, while other proteins only had a regulatory role. Structural gene expression is visualized in the cellular growth testbed as a distinct external colour for the cell.

4.4 Genetic Algorithm

A simple GA was chosen in this work for evolving the genomes due to the discrete and fixed-size nature of the artificial genome used. Moreover, it was considered that the GA was the evolutionary computation paradigm that resembled the most the actual evolutionary mechanism seen in nature. GAs are search and optimization methods based on ideas borrowed from natural genetics and evolution (Holland, 1992). A GA starts with a population of chromosomes representing vectors in search space. Each chromosome is evaluated according to a fitness function and the best individuals are selected. A new generation of chromosomes is created by applying genetic operators on selected individuals from the previous generation. The process is repeated until the desired number of generations is reached or until the desired individual is found.

The GA in this work uses tournament selection with single-point crossover and mutation as genetic operators. Single-point crossover consists in randomly selecting two chromosomes with a certain probability called crossover rate, and then randomly selecting a single bit position in the chromosome structure. From this point on, the remaining fragments of the two chromosomes are exchanged. The resulting chromosomes then replace the original ones in the chromosome population. On the other hand, mutation consists in randomly flipping one bit in a chromosome from 0 to 1 or vice versa. The probability of each bit to be flipped is called the mutation rate.

After several calibration experiments, the parameter values described next were considered to be appropriate. The initial population consisted of either 500 binary chromosomes chosen at random for evolving the form generating genes, or 1000 chromosomes for the simulations involving the ARN models. Tournaments were run with sets of 3 individuals randomly selected from the population. Crossover rate was 0.60 in all cases, whereas the mutation was 0.015 for the evolution of structural genes, and 0.15 for the evolution of ARNs. The crossover rate of 0.60 was chosen because it was reported to give the best results when trying to evolve a binary string representing a CA using a GA (Breukelaar & Bäck, 2005). As for the mutation rate, it was decided to use a value one order of magnitude higher in the evolution of the ARN models than the one used in the same report, due to the great influence that single bits can have in the convergence towards optimal solutions (Chavoya & Duthen, 2007a). Finally, the number of generations was set at 50 in all cases, since there was no significant improvement after this number of generations.

When evolving the ARNs with the goal of synchronizing the expression of structural genes, the chromosomes used for the GA runs were simply the ARN chains themselves. Chromosome size in this case depended on the values of the parameters chosen. Under the conditions tested, the ARN binary string has a size of 6560 bits, which represents a search space of $2^{6560} \approx 5.7 \times 10^{1974}$ vectors. Evidently, search space grows exponentially with the number of regulatory genes. But even for the simplest of ARNs, the one consisting of only two regulatory genes, the search space has a size of $2^{1312} \approx 8.9 \times 10^{394}$, which is still too large to be explored deterministically. It should be evident that the search space for the ARN model is far too large for any method of exhaustive assessment. Therefore, the use of an evolutionary search algorithm for finding an appropriate synchronization of gene expression is amply justified.

For evolving the ARNs that synchronized the expression of structural genes, the fitness function used by the GA was defined as

$$Fitness = \frac{1}{c} \sum_{i=1}^{c} \frac{ins_i - \frac{1}{2} outs_i}{des_i} \tag{4}$$

where c is the number of different coloured shapes, each corresponding to an expressed structural gene, ins_i is the number of filled cells inside the desired shape i with the correct colour, $outs_i$ is the number of filled cells outside the desired shape i, but with the correct colour, and des_i is the total number of cells inside the desired shape i. In consequence, a fitness value of 1 represents a perfect match. This fitness function is an extension of the one used in (de Garis, 1992), where the shape produced by only one "gene" was considered. To account for the expression of several structural genes, the combined fitness values of all structural gene products were introduced in the fitness function used.

During a GA run, each chromosome produced in a generation was fed to the corresponding CA model, where the previously evolved structural genes were attached and the cells were allowed to reproduce controlled by the ARN found by the GA. Fitness was evaluated at the end of 100 time steps in the cellular growth testbed, where a coloured pattern could develop. This process continued until the maximum number of generations was reached or when a fitness value of 1 was obtained.

5. Results

For all experiments, the GA previously described was used to evolve the ARN for the desired coloured patterns. The goal was to combine different coloured shapes expressed by structural genes in order to generate a predefined pattern. After an ARN was obtained and the previously evolved structural genes were attached to constitute the artificial genome, an initial active cell in the middle of the CA lattice was allowed to reproduce controlled by the structural gene activation sequence found by the GA. In order to achieve the desired pattern with a predefined colour for each cell, the genes in the ARN had to evolve to be activated in a precise sequence and for a specific number of iterations. It should be mentioned that not all GA experiments rendered an ARN capable of forming the desired pattern. Furthermore, some difficulties were found when trying to evolve appropriate ARNs for developing patterns involving four structural genes.

In order to explore the result of combining different structural genes that are expressed for a different number of time steps, three different genes were used to grow a French flag pattern. One gene drove the creation of the central white square, while the other two genes extended the central square to the left and to the right, expressing the blue and the red colour, respectively. The last two structural genes do not code specifically for a square, instead they extend a vertical line of cells to the left or to the right for as many time steps as they are activated.

For the generation of the French flag pattern, the central square could be extended to the left or to the right in any of the two orders, that is, first extend to the left and then to the right, or vice versa. This endowed the GA with flexibility to find an appropriate ARN. Figure 4 shows a 27x9 French flag pattern grown from the expression of the three structural genes mentioned above. The graph of the corresponding regulatory protein concentration change over time is shown in 4(e). Starting with a single white cell (a), a white central square is formed from the expression of gene number 1 (b), the left blue square is then grown (c), followed by the right red square (d). The evolved morphogenetic fields are shown for each of the three structural genes. Since the pattern obtained was exactly as desired, the fitness value assigned to the corresponding ARN was the unity (Chavoya & Duthen, 2007d).

In order to explore once again the result of combining different structural genes that are expressed for a different number of time steps, four structural genes were used to grow a French flag with a flagpole pattern. Unlike previous reports where only the French flag itself was produced, the flagpole was added in order to increase the complexity of the pattern generated. The same three structural genes used previously for growing the French flag pattern were used. The fourth gene added created the brown flagpole by means of growing a single line of cells downward from the lower left corner of a rectangle.

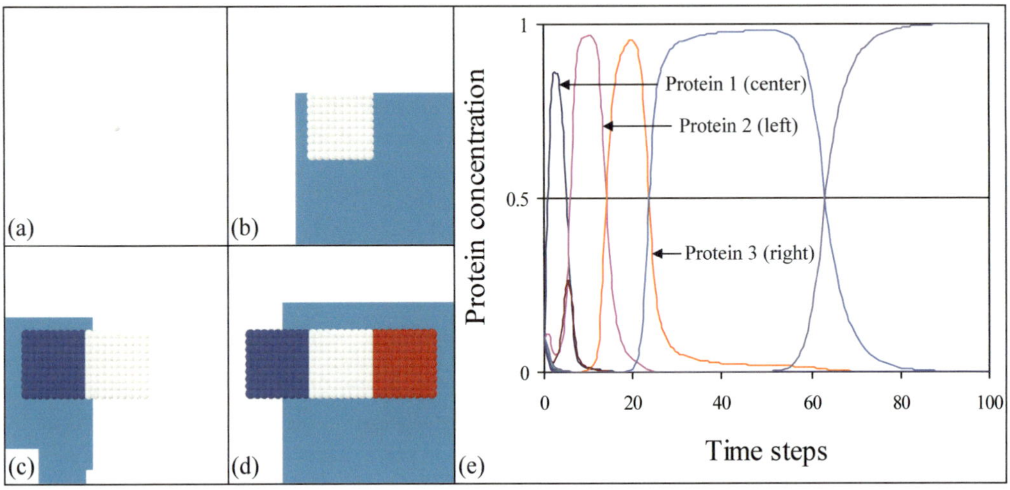

Figure 4. Growth of a French flag pattern. (a) Initial cell; (b) Central white square with morphogenetic field for gene 1 (square); (c) White central square and left blue square with morphogenetic field for gene 2 (extend to left); (d) Final flag pattern with morphogenetic field for gene 3 (extend to right); (e) Graph of protein concentration change from the genome expressing the French flag pattern

When trying to evolve an ARN to produce the French flag with a flagpole pattern, it was found that the GA could not easily evolve an activation sequence that produced the desired pattern. In consequence, it was decided to use the approach of setting a tandem of two identical series of the four structural genes that could produce the desired pattern. In that manner, for creating the white central square, the ARN could express either structural gene number 1 or gene number 5, for the left blue and right red squares it could use genes 2 or 6, or genes 3 or 7, respectively, and finally for the flagpole it could express structural genes 4 or 8. In this way the probability of finding an ARN that could express a French flag with a flagpole pattern was significantly increased.

The 21x7 French flag with a flagpole pattern produced by the expression of this configuration of structural genes is shown in Fig. 5. The graph for the corresponding regulatory protein concentration change is shown in 5(e). After the white central square is formed (a), a right red pattern (b) and the left blue square (c) are sequentially grown, followed by the creation of the flagpole (d). The evolved morphogenetic fields are shown for each of the four structural genes expressed. Note that the white central square is formed from the activation of the first gene from the second series of structural genes, while the other three genes are expressed from the first series of the tandem. It should also be noted that the last column of cells is missing from the red right square, since the morphogenetic field for the gene that extends the red cells to the right precluded growth from that point on (Fig. 5(b)). On the other hand, from the protein concentration graph in 5(e), it is clear that this morphogenetic field prevented the growth of red cells all the way to the right boundary, as gene 3 was active for more time steps than those required to grow the appropriate red square pattern. The fitness value assigned to this pattern was 0.96, which corresponded to the most successful simulation obtained when trying to grow this particular pattern (Chavoya & Duthen, 2007d).

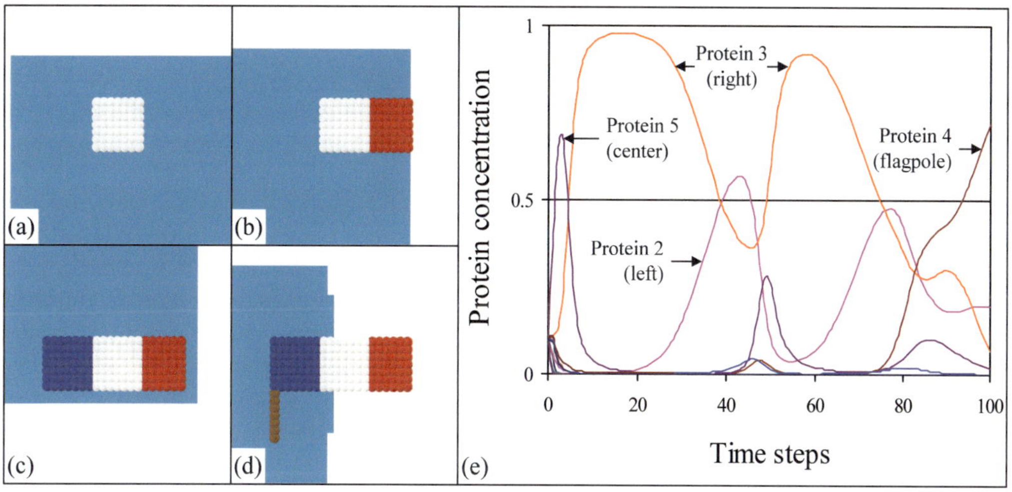

Figure 5. Growth of a French flag with a flagpole pattern. (a) Central white square with morphogenetic field for gene 5 (square); (b) White central square and right red pattern with morphogenetic field for gene 3 (extend to right); (c) White central square, right red pattern and left blue square with morphogenetic field for gene 2 (extend to left); (d) Finished flag with a flagpole pattern with morphogenetic field for gene 4 (flagpole); (e) Graph of protein concentration change from the genome expressing the French flag with a flagpole pattern

Unlike the problem of growing a sequential pattern, where one gene had to finish forming the corresponding shape before the next gene could become activated, there is a certain amount of flexibility in the activation sequence needed to grow a French flag pattern. In particular, after the white central square is fully formed, the genes that extend the central square to either side can be activated in any order, and their corresponding activations can even alternate before either one has finished growing (Chavoya & Duthen, 2007a). However, in the case of the French flag with a flagpole pattern, unless the morphogenetic fields preclude growth of cells at undesired locations, it is essential that the flag is fully formed before the flagpole can begin to grow. It is evident that the left blue square has to be complete in order to start growing the flagpole at the correct position, but consider the case where the right red square is not fully formed after the flagpole, or part of it, was grown. In this case, if the gene that extends a vertical line of cells to the right is activated, it would not only produce the cells required to finish the red right square, but it would equally start to extend the flagpole to the right if allowed by the corresponding morphogenetic field, since the flagpole also consists of a vertical line of cells.

6. Conclusions

As is often the case, by studying how nature works, insight can be gained that aid in proposing approaches for solving a particular problem. In this case, it was decided that the number of enhancer and inhibitor sites in the regulatory network could be increased with respect to the original ARN model, as biological gene regulatory networks usually contain a number of such sites. Likewise, the role as enhancer or inhibitor of the regulatory sites was allowed to be evolved, as is the case in biological genomes, where the role of regulatory sites depends on the particular nucleotide sequence present at the appropriate places.

Simulations involving the artificial development model proposed show that a GA can give reproducible results in evolving a genome to grow predefined simple 2D cell patterns starting with a single cell. In particular, it was found that using this model it was feasible to reliably synchronize up to three structural genes. However, some problems were encountered when trying to synchronize the activation of more than three structural genes in a precise sequence. Despite its limitations, this model demonstrated that the synchronization of structural genes similar to the gene expression regulation found in nature was feasible.

In a previous model, apart from the gene activation sequence coded in the genome, cells only had local information to determine whether or not to reproduce. In particular, cells had no global positional information, since the shape grown was mainly due to a self-organizing mechanism driven by the ARN (Chavoya & Duthen, 2007b). However, in order to achieve more complex shapes, it was considered necessary to allow cells to extract information from their environment through the use of diffusing morphogens.

Morphogenetic fields should in principle assist in the creation of more complex patterns by providing positional constraints to cellular growth. However in the results obtained with the present model, it was apparently harder for the GA to find an activation sequence for the creation of the French flag with a flagpole pattern. One possible explanation is that with the addition of the morphogen threshold activation sites to the ARN, the search space grew even larger than in the previous ARN model, making it more difficult for the GA to find an appropriate activation sequence. However, since individual simulation times usually took several hours to complete, it could be that the number of simulations essayed was not high enough to draw an unambiguous conclusion.

On the other hand, there is evidence that the fitness landscape on which the GA performs the search to evolve the ARNs is very rugged. This has been illustrated previously with the influence of single bits on the fitness values of an evolving model. In one of the simulations, it took the shift of one bit value in the genome string of the basic ARN model to go from a fitness value of 0.50 to 0.93, and one additional single bit shift led the fitness value to a perfect match (Chavoya & Duthen, 2007a). In this particular case, that meant that adjacent vectors in the search space had very dissimilar values in fitness evaluation. It is conjectured that this behaviour is widespread in the search spaces defined in the model developed, given the difficulties encountered in synchronizing what could be considered just a handful of structural genes.

One restriction of the model presented is that all cells synchronously follow the same genetic program, as a sort of biological clock. This has obvious advantages for synchronizing the behaviour of developing cells, but it would also be desirable that cells had an individual program —possibly a separate ARN— for reacting to local unexpected changes in their environment. Morphogenetic fields provide a means to extract information from the environment, but an independent program would lend more flexibility and robustness to a developing organism. After all, living organisms do contain a series of gene regulatory networks for development and metabolism control. One could even envision either a hierarchy of ARNs, where some ARNs could be used to regulate others ARNs, or a network of ARNs, where all ARNs could influence and regulate each other.

Additional work is needed in order to explore pattern formation of more complex forms, both in 2D and 3D. It is also desirable to search for a development model that can reliably synchronize the activation of more than four genes. In order to achieve the activation sequence of five or more structural genes using the approach presented of ARN synchronization, it is probably necessary to change the representation of the model, so that a smoother fitness landscape could be obtained. Furthermore, in order to increase the usefulness of the model, interaction with other artificial entities and extraction of information from a more physically realistic environment may be necessary. Until now this work has been devoted to generating predefined patterns in a kind of directed evolution. However, it would be desirable to let cells evolve into a functional pattern under environmental constraints without any preconceived notion of the final outcome.
The approach used in the model proposed was used to shed light on the problem of determining how the physical arrangement of cells in body structures is achieved. However, it is not difficult to see that the spatial distribution of cells can have a decisive role in determining aspects of biological function. As an example, the distribution of neurons in the developing brain can constrain the creation of synapses and hence have an influence on the patterns of electrical and chemical signals that can travel through the neural paths.
The long-term goal of this work is to study the emergent properties of the artificial development process. It can be envisioned that one day it will be feasible to build highly complex structures arising mainly from the interaction of myriads of simpler entities.

7. References

Baker, R.W. & Herman, G.T. (1970). Celia - a cellular linear iterative array simulator, *Proceedings of the Fourth Annual Conference on Applications of Simulation*, pp. 64-73, Winter Simulation Conference

Banzhaf, W. (2003). Artificial regulatory networks and genetic programming. In: *Genetic Programming Theory and Practice*, Riolo, R.L. & Worzel, B. (Ed.), 43-62, Kluwer

Beurier, G.; Michel, F. & Ferber, J. (2006). A morphogenesis model for multiagent embryogeny, *Proceedings of the Tenth International Conference on the Simulation and Synthesis of Living Systems (ALife X)*, pp. 84-90

Bongard, J. (2002). Evolving modular genetic regulatory networks, *Proceedings of the 2002 Congress on Evolutionary Computation (CEC2002)*, pp. 1872-1877, Honolulu, USA, May 2002, IEEE Press, Piscataway, NJ

Bowers, C.P. (2005). Simulating evolution with a computational model of embryogeny: Obtaining robustness from evolved individuals, *Proceedings of the 8th European Conference on Artificial Life (ECAL 2005)*, pp. 149-158, Canterbury, UK, September 2005, Springer

Breukelaar, R. & Bäck, T. (2005). Using a genetic algorithm to evolve behavior in multi dimensional cellular automata: emergence of behavior, *Proceedings of the 7th Annual Conference on Genetic and Evolutionary Computation (GECCO '05)*, pp. 107-114, Washington, D.C. USA, June 2005, ACM Press

Carroll, S.B.; Grenier, J.K. & Weatherbee, S.D. (2004). *From DNA to Diversity: Molecular Genetics and the Evolution of Animal Design*, Blackwell Science, 2nd edition

Chavoya, A. & Duthen, Y. (2006a). Evolving cellular automata for 2D form generation, *Proceedings of the Ninth International Conference on Computer Graphics and Artificial Intelligence 3IA'2006*, pp. 129-137, Limoges, France, May 2006

Chavoya, A. & Duthen, Y. (2006b). Using a genetic algorithm to evolve cellular automata for 2D/3D computational development, *Proceedings of the 8th Annual Conference on Genetic and Evolutionary Computation (GECCO'06)*, pp. 231-232, Seattle, WA, USA, July 2006, ACM Press, New York, NY, USA

Chavoya, A. & Duthen, Y. (2007a). Evolving an artificial regulatory network for 2D cell patterning, *Proceedings of the 2007 IEEE Symposium on Artificial Life (CI-ALife'07)*, pp. 47-53, Honolulu, USA, April 2007, IEEE Computational Intelligence Society

Chavoya, A. & Duthen, Y. (2007b). Use of a genetic algorithm to evolve an extended artificial regulatory network for cell pattern generation, *Proceedings of the 9th Annual Conference on Genetic and Evolutionary Computation (GECCO'07)*, pp. 1062, London, UK, July 2007, ACM Press, New York, NY, USA

Chavoya, A. & Duthen, Y. (2007c). A cell pattern generation model based on an extended artificial regulatory network, *Proceedings of the 7th International Workshop on Information Processing in Cells and Tissues (IPCAT'07)*, pp. 149-158, Oxford, UK, August 2007

Chavoya, A. & Duthen, Y. (2007d). An artificial development model for cell pattern generation, *Proceedings of the 3rd Australian Conference on Artificial Life (ACAL'07)*, pp. 61-71, Gold Coast, Australia, December 2007

Davidson., E.H. (2006). *The Regulatory Genome: Gene Regulatory Networks in Development and Evolution,* Academic Press

Dawkins., R. (1996). *The Blind Watchmaker: Why the Evidence of Evolution Reveals a Universe without Design,* W. W. Norton

de Garis, H. (1991). Genetic programming: artificial nervous systems artificial embryos and embryological electronics, *Proceedings of the First Workshop on Parallel Problem Solving from Nature*, pp. 117-123, Dortmund, Germany, Springer-Verlag, Berlin, Germany

de Garis, H.; Iba, H. & Furuya, T. (1992). Differentiable chromosomes: The genetic programming of switchable shape-genes, *Proceedings of the Second Conference on Parallel Problem Solving from Nature*, pp. 489-498, Brussels, Belgium, September 1992

Devert, A.; Bredeche, N. & Schoenauer, M. (2007). Robust multi-cellular developmental design, *Proceedings of the 9th Annual Conference on Genetic and Evolutionary Computation (GECCO'07)*, pp. 982-989, ISBN, London, UK, July 2007, ACM Press, New York, NY, USA

Eggenberger, P. (1997a). Creation of neural networks based on developmental and evolutionary principles, *Proceedings of the Seventh International Conference of Artificial Neural Networks (ICANN'97)*, pp. 337-342, Springer

Eggenberger, P. (1997b). Evolving morphologies of simulated 3D organisms based on differential gene expression, *Proceedings of the 4th European Conference on Artificial Life (ECAL)*, pp. 205-213, Springer

Flann, N.; Hu, J. ; Bansal, M.; Patel, V. & Podgorski, G. (2005). Biological development of cell patterns: Characterizing the space of cell chemistry genetic regulatory networks, *Proceedings of the 8th European Conference on Artificial Life (ECAL'05)*, pp. 57-66, Canterbury, UK, September 2005, Springer

Fleischer K. & Barr, A.H. (1992). A simulation testbed for the study of multicellular development: The multiple mechanisms of morphogenesis, *Proceedings of the Workshop on Artificial Life (ALIFE'92)*, pp. 389-416, Addison-Wesley

Gierer, A. (1981). Generation of biological patterns and form: Some physical, mathematical, and logical aspects. *Prog. Biophys. Molec. Biol.,* Vol. 37, pp. 1-47

Gierer, A. & Meinhardt, H. (1972). A theory of biological pattern formation. *Kybernetik,* Vol. 12, pp. 30-39

Gordon, T.G.W. & Bentley, P.J. (2005). Bias and scalability in evolutionary development, *Proceedings of the 7th Annual Conference on Genetic and Evolutionary Computation (GECCO'05),* pp. 83-90, Washington, D.C., USA, June 2005, ACM Press, New York, NY, USA

Harding, S.L.; Miller, J.F. & Banzhaf, W. (2007). Self-modifying Cartesian genetic programming, *Proceedings of 9th Annual Conference on Genetic and Evolutionary Computation (GECCO'07),* pp. 1021-1028, ISBN, ACM Press, New York, NY, USA

Herman, G.T. & Liu, W.H. (1973). The daughter of Celia, the French flag and the firing squad, *Proceedings of the 6th Conference on Winter Simulation,* pp. 870, ACM Press, New York, NY, USA

Holland, J.H. (1992). *Adaptation in Natural and Artificial Systems: An Introductory Analysis with Applications to Biology, Control and Artificial Intelligence,* MIT Press, Cambridge, MA, USA

Kauffman, S.A. (1969). Metabolic stability and epigenesis in randomly constructed genetic nets. *Journal of Theoretical Biology,* Vol. 22, pp. 437-467

Kauffman, S.A. (2004). *Investigations,* Oxford University Press

Kitano, H. (1990). Designing neural networks using genetic algorithms with graph generation system. *Complex Systems,* Vol.4, pp. 461-476

Kitano, H. (1994). A simple model of neurogenesis and cell differentiation based on evolutionary large-scale chaos. *Artificial Life,* Vol. 2, No. 1, pp. 79-99

Knabe, J.F.; Nehaniv, C.L.; Schilstra, M.J. & Quick, T. (2006). Evolving biological clocks using genetic regulatory networks, *Proceedings of the Artificial Life X Conference (ALife 10),* pp. 15-21, MIT Press

Kumar, S. & Bentley, P.J. (2003). An introduction to computational development, In: *On Growth, Form and Computers,* Kumar, S. & Bentley, P.J., (Ed.), 1-44, Academic Press, New York, NY, USA

Lindenmayer, A. (1968). Mathematical models for cellular interaction in development Parts I and II. *Journal of Theoretical Biology,* Vol. 18, pp. 280-315

Lindenmayer, A. & Rozenberg, G. (1972). Developmental systems and languages, *Proceedings of the Fourth Annual ACM Symposium on Theory of Computing,* pp. 214-221, ACM Press, New York, NY, USA

Mech, R. & Prusinkiewicz, P. (1996). Visual models of plants interacting with their environment, *Proceedings of SIGGRAPH 96,* pp. 397-410

Meinhardt, H. (1982). *Models of Biological Pattern Formation,* Academic Press, London

Miller, J.F. & Banzhaf, W. (2003). Evolving the program for a cell: from French flags to Boolean circuits, In: *On Growth, Form and Computers,* Kumar, S. & Bentley, P.J., (Ed.), 278-301, Academic Press, New York, NY, USA

Prusinkiewicz, P. (1993). Modeling and Vizualization of Biological Structures, *Proceedings of Graphics Interface '93,* pp. 128-137, ISBN, May 1993

Prusinkiewicz, P. & Lindenmayer, A. (1990). *The Algorithmic Beauty of Plants,* Springer-Verlag

Reil, T. (1999). Dynamics of gene expression in an artificial genome - implications for biological and artificial ontogeny, *Proceedings of the 5th European Conference on Artificial Life (ECAL'99)*, pp. 457-466, Lausanne, Switzerland, Springer Verlag, New York, NY, USA

Stewart, F.; Taylor, T. & Konidaris, G. (2005). METAMorph: Experimenting with genetic regulatory networks for artificial development, *Proceedings of the 8th European Conference on Artificial Life (ECAL'05)*, pp. 108-117, Canterbury, UK, September 2005, Springer

Turing, A.M. (1952). The chemical basis of morphogenesis. *Philosophical Transactions of the Royal Society of London. Series B, Biological Sciences,* Vol. 237, No. 641, August 1952, pp. 37-72

Tyrrell, A.M. & Greensted, A.J. (2007). Evolving dependability. *J. Emerg. Technol. Comput. Syst.*, Vol. 3, No. 2, pp. 7

Willadsen, K. & Wiles, J. (2003). Dynamics of gene expression in an artificial genome, *Proceedings of the IEEE 2003 Congress on Evolutionary Computation*, pp. 199-206, IEEE Press

Wolfram, S. (1983). Statistical mechanics of cellular automata. *Reviews of Modern Physics,* Vol. 55, pp. 601-644

Wolpert, L. (1968). The French flag problem: a contribution to the discussion on pattern development and regulation, In: *Towards a Theoretical Biology,* Waddington, C. (Ed.), 125-133, Edinburgh University Press, New York, NY, USA

Wolpert, L. (1969). Positional information and the spatial pattern of cellular differentiation. *J. Theor. Biol.,* Vol. 25, pp. 1-47

5

I'm Sorry to Say, But Your Understanding of Image Processing Fundamentals Is Absolutely Wrong

Emanuel Diamant
VIDIA-mant, Kiriat Ono
Israel

1. Introduction

Among the five human senses through which we explore our surrounding, vision takes a unique and a remarkable place. The lion part of information about our near, medium, and distant environment comes to us via the vision channel. It is, therefore, not surprising that almost a half of our cortex is devoted to visual information processing (Milner & Goodale, 1998). In the course of millions of years of evolution, we have even developed a very special attitude to it - we feel an everlasting "hunger" for new visual information. We are "Infovores", as Irving Biederman (Biederman & Vessel, 2006), one of the founders of the contemporary vision theory, wittily defined.

Maybe, this perpetual yearning is the incentive that made us so inclined to various forms of visual information gathering and accumulation. The story about explosive expansion of camera phones may be a good example here: At the end of the year 2007, Nokia manage to sell almost 440 million mobile phones (obviously, each one equipped with a tiny video camera) which accounted for 40% of all global mobile phone sales (Nokia, 2008). That means, more than a billion mobile phones have been soled worldwide only in one last year!

By the late 2009, the total number of camera phones will exceed that of both conventional and digital cameras shipped since the invention of photography (Thevenin et al., 2008). The result is - an unprecedented and previously unknown flood of visual information in our environment. According to a leading market research firm, Internet video consumption has increased by nearly 100% over the past year: from an average of 700 terabytes/day in 2006, to 1200 terabytes/day in 2007. Internet video uploads have reached 500K uploads/day in 2007 and will grow to 4800K in 2011 (Mobile video, 2008).

That places an urgent demand for a new and previously unknown way of visual information flow handling and management. Certainly, it must be human-like and human-compatible, because Human Visual System (HVS) is the sole information processing system we know that is capable to cope with such problems.

However, by saying that we immediately fall into a trap - we don't know how HVS so perfectly performs its duties. What we do know is that video data sampled by 126 millions of photoreceptors at the eye's retina is immediately converted (as long as the visual input propagates from the eyes to the higher brain processing levels) into meaningful disjointed visual objects, of various complexities. It must be stressed again and again - we do not know how this semantic segmentation is accomplished. But we certainly know that the bulk of visual processing accomplished in the human's brain is performed at the semantic information processing level. Artificial visual systems that we have tirelessly attempted to construct over the last half of a century have always lacked such an ability. The bulk of visual processing carried out in artificial visual systems is constrained to visual data processing only: Pure, exhaustive data processing and nothing more than that.

The apparent difference and incompatibility between these two image processing modalities - pure low-level data processing in human-made visual systems and enigmatic high-level semantic information processing in natural human visual systems - is often overlooked and commonly misinterpreted in the computer vision community. This leads to many funny things that are ubiquitous in computer vision design practice, but they seem far less funny when the production scale of such lapses is regarded. Here are some examples:

The perceptual quality of an image is usually strictly tied with image primary resolution. More pixels in a frame - more valued is the image. Undeniably, this philosophy is the driving force behind the race for megapixel-large image sensors for portable phone cameras, or the High Definition Television Standard for stationary devices. In each case, image high resolution is directly associated with an extremely high volume of raw image data.

Communication bandwidth constraints, power-on-hand limits and other design restrictions request effective signal compression techniques to be used in such data abundant cases. Indeed, carefully designed and skillfully adjusted compression/decompression (encoding/decoding) techniques are generally implemented. Their prime and single purpose: to reduce the data-handling burden. But in the end, the compressed/ decompressed image data would be always again presented to a human observer for final treatment and semantic information processing.

A smart design approach would attempt from the very beginning to encode the semantic objects buried in the image data and to deliver only them to the human disposal. That is exactly what the MPEG-4 Standard designers have in mind when they have introduced the standard's innovative features: VO (Visual Object), VOP (Visual Object Plane), VOL (Visual Object Level). That happened in the year 1994 (Puri & Eleftheriadis, 1998), and expectations for the new video code were very high.

However, as the time passed, nothing has come about in the field. And for a very simple and sad reason: visual object is a semantic entity, which cannot be attained by data manipulations. Standard designers were aware of this problem, and for this reason nothing was said about the way the visual objects have to be discovered and delineated. Hence, all further improvements and modifications the standard went through (and there were a lot of them, the last version of the standard is even named differently - H.264 or MPEG-4 Advanced Video Coding (H.264/AVC)) are concerned only with data coding improvements (Sullivan & Wiegand, 2005).

The consequences of this are easily imaginable: for stationary environments where power dissipation, processing speed limitations and cost restrictions are not a concern, extremely powerful DSPs (Digital Signal Processors) like Analog Devices TigerSHARC ADSP-TS201S with 3.6 GFLOPs processing power are put into work. For those who are not satisfied with such a might - BittWare offers a PCI Mezzanine Card featuring four TigerSHARCs on a single board with a general processing power of 57 GFLOPs (Bittware, 2007).

For the mobile applications, where the restrictions are stern and fixed, the only possible solution is to compromise on image resolution (size). While the sensor resolution has steadily grown from 1.5 Megapixels (1280x1024) to 5 (2580x1930), 8 (3264x2444), 12 (4220x2820), and at last 14 Megapixels (4570x3050), the actually operated camera-phone images were of the size 80x60 pixels, or 160x120, or finally 352x288 pixels, which is the CIF (Common Intermediate Format) Standard. That is all what the infovore people can get in the real life circumstances.

Another field where vision technology is extensively used is video surveillance. Spurred by increasing public and private security concerns (especially after 9/11), video surveillance systems market is observing an unprecedented growth and expansion. Global video surveillance camera revenue is forecast to grow from $4.9 billion in 2006 to more than $9 billion by 2011 (Video surveillance, 2007).

The general stance is that the driving force behind this expansion is the networked Internet Protocol (IP) video surveillance cameras and IP video servers. Indeed, the IP technology provides the basis for a great leap in video surveillance systems design. However, it has a serious drawback: in terms of useful image resolution the 352x288 CIF standard is the predominating one. From the standpoint of a surveillance system user, the quality of an image in such a system is very dubious. But not this peculiar feature is now in the focus of our concern - visual surveillance implies that the delivered picture is examined and analyzed for scene changes and suspicious event developments (to be detected) and appropriated countermeasures triggered in response. As it was already explained above, this is a sheer semantic information-processing task that only a human being can perform, and none of the existing video surveillance systems can cope with such a task autonomously. What fallows from this, is that a human observer must be attached to the system's display forever: 24 hours a day/7 days a week/52 weeks a year. Otherwise the system is ineffective and useless. However, for such monotonous and boring work humans are the worst candidates. But who cares? To save on expenses, the observer's display usually contains not a single camera output, but is shared between 4, 8, and even 16 camera outputs. The effectiveness of such surveillance systems is less than illusive. The arrogant indifference to human/machine disparities in visual stuff handling is celebrating again. And the market - keeps on growing continuously, every time more and more.

2. Tears do not solve problems

The urgent need for machine-based visual systems, which are capable of processing visual information in a human-like intelligent manner, is well understood and widely acknowledged today. Impressive research programs that European Commission runs under its auspice are a good example for this understanding. But the scale of the efforts and billions of Euro put into the enterprise (European IST Research, 2006), cannot explain the lack of the progress we witness during all phases of the projects development. We are now in the 7th Framework Programme (FP7), but nothing serious has happen, and the things seemed to be stalled in a dead-end alley.

That is a proper moment to check again the basic principles we adhere to when we are pursuing our routine research goals. Since we are aimed on human-like visual information processing, we first have to scrutinize the available knowledge about the HVS performance and then to analyse how this knowledge is used in modelling various human-like image-processing tasks.

The classical paradigm of human visual information processing has been established few decades ago by the seminal works of David Marr (Marr, 1978; Marr, 1982), Anne Treisman

(Treisman & Gelade, 1980), Irving Biederman (Biederman, 1987), and a large group of their associates and followers. Treisman's "Feature-integration theory" (Treisman & Gelade, 1980) is considered as the most fitting incarnation of the idea. It regards human visual information processing as an interplay of two inversely directed processing streams. One is an unsupervised, bottom-up directed process of initial image information pieces discovery and localization. The other is a supervised, top-down directed process, which conveys the rules and the knowledge that guide the linking and binding of these disjoint information pieces into perceptually meaningful image objects.

Essentially, as an idea, this conception was not entirely new. About two hundred years ago, Kant had depicted the "faculty of (visual) apperception" as a "synthesis" of two constituents: the raw sensory data and the cognitive "faculty of reason" (Hanna, 2004). A century later, Herman Ludwig Ferdinand von Helmholtz (the first who scientifically investigated our senses) had reinforced this view, positing that sensory input and perceptual inferences are different, yet inseparable, faculties of human vision (Gregory, 1979). The novelty of the modern approach was in an introduction of a new concept used for the idea clarification - "visual information" (Marr, 1978). However, a suitable definition of the term was not provided, and the mainstream of relevant biological research has continued (and continues today) to investigate the puzzling duality of the phenomenon by capitalizing on traditional vague definitions of the matters: local and global image content, perceptual and cognitive image processing, low-level computer-derived image features versus high-level human-derived image semantics (Barsalou, 1999; Palmeri & Gauthier, 2004). Putting aside the terminology, the main problem of human visual information processing remains the same: in order to fulfill the intuitively effortless low-level information pieces agglomeration into meaningful semantic objects, the system has to be provided with some high-level knowledge about the rules of this agglomeration. Needless to say, such rules are usually not available. In biological vision research, this dilemma is known as the "binding problem". Its importance was recognized at very early stages of vision research, and massive efforts have been directed into it in order to reach a suitable and an acceptable solution. Despite the continuous efforts, any discernable success has not been achieved yet. (For more details, see Treisman (1996) and the special issue of Neuron (vol. 24, 1999), entirely devoted to this problem).

Unable to reach the required high-level processing (binding) rules, vision research took steps in a forbidden, but possibly an appealing and an enticing direction – to try to derive the needed high-level knowledge from the available low-level information pieces. A rank of theoretical and experimental work has been done in order to support and justify this just-mentioned shift in research aspirations. Two approaches could be distinguished in this regard: chaotic attractor modeling approach (McRae, 2004; Johanson & Lansner, 2006), and saliency attention map modeling approach (Treue, 2003; Itti, 2005). There is no need to review the details of these approaches here. I will only make a note that both of them presume low-level bottom-up processing as the most proper way for high-level information recovery. Both are computationally expensive. Both definitely violate the basic assumption about the leading role of high-level knowledge in the low-level information processing.

In computer vision, the situation is even more bizarre. In fact, computer vision community is so busy with its everyday problems that there is no time to raise basic research ventures. Principal ideas (and their possible solutions) are usually borrowed from biological vision research. Therefore, following the trends in biological vision, the computer vision R&D for decades has been deeply involved in bottom-up pixel-oriented image processing. Low-level image computations have become its prime and persistent goal, while the complicated issues of high-level processing were just neglected and disregarded.

However, it is impossible to ignore them completely. It is generally acknowledged that any kind of image processing is unfeasible without incorporation into it the high-level knowledge ingredients. For this reason, the whole history of computer-based image processing is an endless saga on attempts to seize the needed knowledge in any possible way. The oldest and the most common ploy is to capitalize on the expert domain knowledge and adapt it to each and every application case. It is not surprising, therefore, that the whole realm of image processing has been (and continues to be) fragmented (segmented) according to high-level knowledge competence of the domain experts. That is why we have today: medical imaging, aerospace imaging, infrared, biologic, underwater, geophysics, remote sensing, microscopy, radar, biomedical, X-ray, and so on "imagings".

The advent of the Internet, with huge volumes of visual information scattered over the web, has demolished the long-lasting custom of capitalizing on the expert knowledge. Image information content on the Web is unpredictable and diversified. It is useless to apply specific expert knowledge to a random set of distant images. To meet the challenge, the computer vision community has undertaken an enterprise to develop appropriate (so-called) Content-Based Image Retrieval (CBIR) technologies (Lew et al. 2006). However, deprived of any reasonable sources of the desired high-level information, computer vision designers were forced to proceed in the only one possible direction - trying to derive the high-level knowledge from the available low-level information pieces (Mojsilovic & Rogowitz, 2001; Zhang & Chen, 2003).

It will be a mistake to say that computer vision people are not aware of these discrepancies. On the contrary, they are well informed about what is going on in the field. However, they are trying to justify their attempts by promoting a concept of a "semantic gap", an imaginary gap between low- and high-level image features. They sincerely believe that some day they would be able to bridge over it (Hare et al., 2006).

It is worth to mention that all these developments (feature binding in biological vision and semantic gap bridging in computer vision) are evolving in an atmosphere of total indifference towards preceding claims about high-level information superiority in the general course of visual information processing. Such indifference seems to stem from a very loose understanding about what is the concept of "information", what is the right way to use it properly, and what information treatment options could arise from this understanding.

3. Trying to define "What is information?"

I was very proud of myself when it has become clear to me that the problem image processing is subjected to stems from misunderstanding and confusing the duties that machine vision and human vision systems are destined to perform: machine vision systems are for data processing, human vision systems - for information processing. It was clear to me that data and information are different things, and therefore a careless blending of them is harmful and counterproductive (as it follows from the examples provided above). However, my conjectures have not been readily welcomed. My paper submitted to BMCV 2002 Conference was rejected, and the reviewer was very strict in his comments: "The

distinction between information and data processing is superficial - you have to be more specific (after all, data is information, isn't it?)".
I was hurt by what has seemed to me as reviewer's ignorance. But later I was forced to learn that that is a well-established, widespread and quite common view on the matters. Luciano Floridi's papers (Floridi, 2003; Floridi 2005; Floridi 2007) are busy with refining "the Standard Definition of semantic information as meaningful data" (!!!). Alas, you cannot quarrel with Floridi. Especially, as your own definition is so vague and muddle-headed that it is better for you to take a stance that "information" is an indefinable entity, like "time" or "space" in classical physics. (Later I have found out that a similar stance is taken by Aaron Sloman (Sloman, 2006) when he compares the indefinable notion of "information" with the indefinable notion of "energy").
Following my own intuition, I have finally hit on something I was so desperately looking for - an information definition fitting my image processing requirements. It turns out that this definition can be derived from Solomonoff's theory of Inference (Solomonoff, 1997), Chaitin's Algorithmic Information theory (Chaitin, 1977), and Kolmogorov's Complexity theory (Kolmogorov, 1965). The results of my investigation have been already published on several occasions, (Diamant, 2003; Diamant, 2004; Diamant, 2005; Diamant, 2007), and interested readers can easily get them from a number of freely accessible repositories (e.g., arXiv, CiteSeer (the former Research Index), Eprintweb, etc.). Therefore, I will only repeat here some important points of these early publications, which properly reflect my current understanding of the matters.
The main point is that **information is a description**, a certain alphabet-based or language-based description, which Kolmogorov's theory regards as a program that, being executed, trustworthy reproduces the original object (Vitany, 2006). In an image, such objects are visible data structures from which an image consists of. So, a set of reproducible descriptions of image data structures is the information contained in an image.
The Kolmogorov's theory prescribes the way in which such descriptions must be created: at first, the most simplified and generalized structure must be described. (Recall the Occam's Razor principle). Then, as the level of generalization is gradually decreased, more and more fine-grained image details (structures) become revealed and depicted. This is the second important point, which follows from the theory's pure mathematical considerations: image **information is a hierarchy of recursive decreasing level descriptions** of information details, which unfolds in a coarse-to-fine top-down manner. (Attention, please: any bottom-up processing is not mentioned here. There is no low-level feature gathering and no feature binding!!! The only proper way for image information elicitation is a top-down coarse-to-fine way of image processing.)
The third prominent point, which immediately pops-up from the two just mentioned above, is that the top-down manner of image **information elicitation does not require incorporation of any high-level knowledge** for its successful accomplishment. It is totally free from any high-level guiding rules and inspirations. That is why I call it **Physical Information** - information that is totally independent of any high level interpretation of it.
What immediately follows from this is that high-level image semantics is not an integrated part of image information content (as it is traditionally assumed). It cannot be seen more as a natural property of an image. Image semantics, therefore, must be seen as a property of a human observer that watches and scrutinizes an image. That is why we can definitely say:

semantics is assigned to an image by a human observer. That is strongly at variance with the contemporary views on the concept of semantic information.
Following the new information elicitation rules, it is impossible to continue to pretend that semantics can be **extracted from an image**, (as for example in (Naphade & Huang, 2002)), or should be **derived from low-level information features** (as in (Zhang & Chen, 2003; Mojsilovic & Rogowitz, 2001), and many other analogous publications). That simply does not hold any more.

4. Reification of the proposed idea

The new definition of information has forced us to reconsider the traditional way of doing things in image processing. The inevitable change in design philosophy, the validity of new assumptions, the consequences that acceptance of new assumptions imply, all this has motivated us to test the proposed novelties in a framework of visual robot design enterprise - an enterprise, which is aimed on creating an artificial vision system with some human-like cognitive capabilities.
As follows from the preceding discussion, the proposed arrangement must be comprised of two separate loosely coupled parts: Physical Information processing part and Semantic Information processing part. The proposed block-scheme of this arrangement is depicted in Fig. 1.

4.1 Physical information processing

The purpose of the Physical Information processing part is to extract the physical information buried in the image data. That is, to provide a description of discernable image data structures present in a given image. In simple words, to provide an initial segmentation of the input image. Afterwards the segmented pieces would be submitted to a process of image analysis and interpretation (in terms of our approach - Semantic Information would be assigned to the input image).
As one can see, the proposed Physical Information processing part is comprised of three sub-units: the bottom-up processing path, the top-down processing path and a stack where the discovered information content (the generated descriptions of it) are actually accumulated. (More details about Physical Information processing can be found in (Diamant, 2004; Diamant, 2005; Diamant, 2005a).
As follows from the early-defined information processing principles (which prescribe that the most general and simplified descriptions have to be derived first), the purpose of the bottom-up processing path is to provide a simplified (compressed, squeezed) copy of an input image. The original image is squeezed along this path to a small size of approximately 100 pixels. The rules of this shrinking operation are very simple and fast: four non-overlapping neighbor pixels in an image at level L are averaged and the result is assigned to a pixel in a higher (L+1)-level image, (a so-called 4 to 1 image compression). At the top of the shrinking pyramid, the image is segmented, and each segmented region is labeled. Since the image size at the top is significantly reduced and since in course of the bottom-up image squeezing a severe data averaging is attained, the image segmentation/classification procedure does not demand special computational efforts.
From this point on, the top-down processing path is commenced. At each level, the segmentation maps (intensity and region labels) are expanded to the size of an image at the

nearest lower level, (a 1 to 4 expansion). Since the regions at different hierarchical levels do not exhibit significant changes in their characteristic intensity, the majority of newly assigned pixels are determined in a sufficiently correct manner. Only pixels at region borders and seeds of newly emerging regions may significantly deviate from the assigned values. Taking the corresponding current-level image as a reference (the left-side unsegmented image), these pixels can be easily detected and subjected to a refinement cycle. The region labels map is corrected accordingly. In such a manner, the process is subsequently repeated at all descending levels until the segmentation of the original input image is successfully accomplished.

At each processing level, every segmented image object-region (whether just recovered or an inherited one) is registered in the objects' appearance list (the Stocked Level Descriptions rectangle in Fig. 1), which is the third constituting part of the proposed scheme.

The registered object parameters are the available simplified object's attributes, such as size, center-of-mass position, average object intensity and hierarchical and topological relationship within and between the objects ("sub-part of…", "at the left of…", etc.). They are sparse, general, and yet specific enough to capture the object's characteristic features in a variety of descriptive forms.

This way, a practical algorithm based on the announced above principles has been developed and subjected to some systematic evaluations. The results were published, and can be found in (Diamant, 2004; Diamant, 2005; Diamant, 2005a). There is no need to repeat again and again that excellent, previously unattainable segmentation results have been attained in these tests, undoubtedly corroborating the new information processing principles. Not only an unsupervised segmentation of image content has been achieved, (in a top-down coarse-to-fine processing manner, without any involvement of high-level knowledge), a hierarchy of descriptions for each and every segmented lot (segmented sub-object) has been achieved as well. It contains a set object related parameters, which enable subsequent object reconstruction. That is exactly what we have previously defined as **information**. That is the reason why we specify this information as "physical information", because that is the only information present in an image, and therefore **the only information that can be extracted from an image**.

4.2 Semantic information processing

Semantic information, which (as we understand now) conveys the property of an external observer, is completely dissociated from the physical information contained in an image. Therefore it must be treated (or modeled) in accordance with observer-specific (his/her) cognitive information processing rules.

What are these rules? A consensus view on this topic does not exist as yet in the biological vision theories as well as in the computer vision practice. So, we have to blaze our own trails. We decided, thus, to meet this challenge by suggesting a new approach based on our previously declared information elicitation principles. The preliminary results of our first attempt have been published elsewhere (Diamant, 2006). As in the case of physical information, we will not repeat here all the details of this publication. Possible implementation details of the Semantic Information processing part (solution) are depicted in Fig. 1. Here we will proceed only with a brief explanation of some of them.

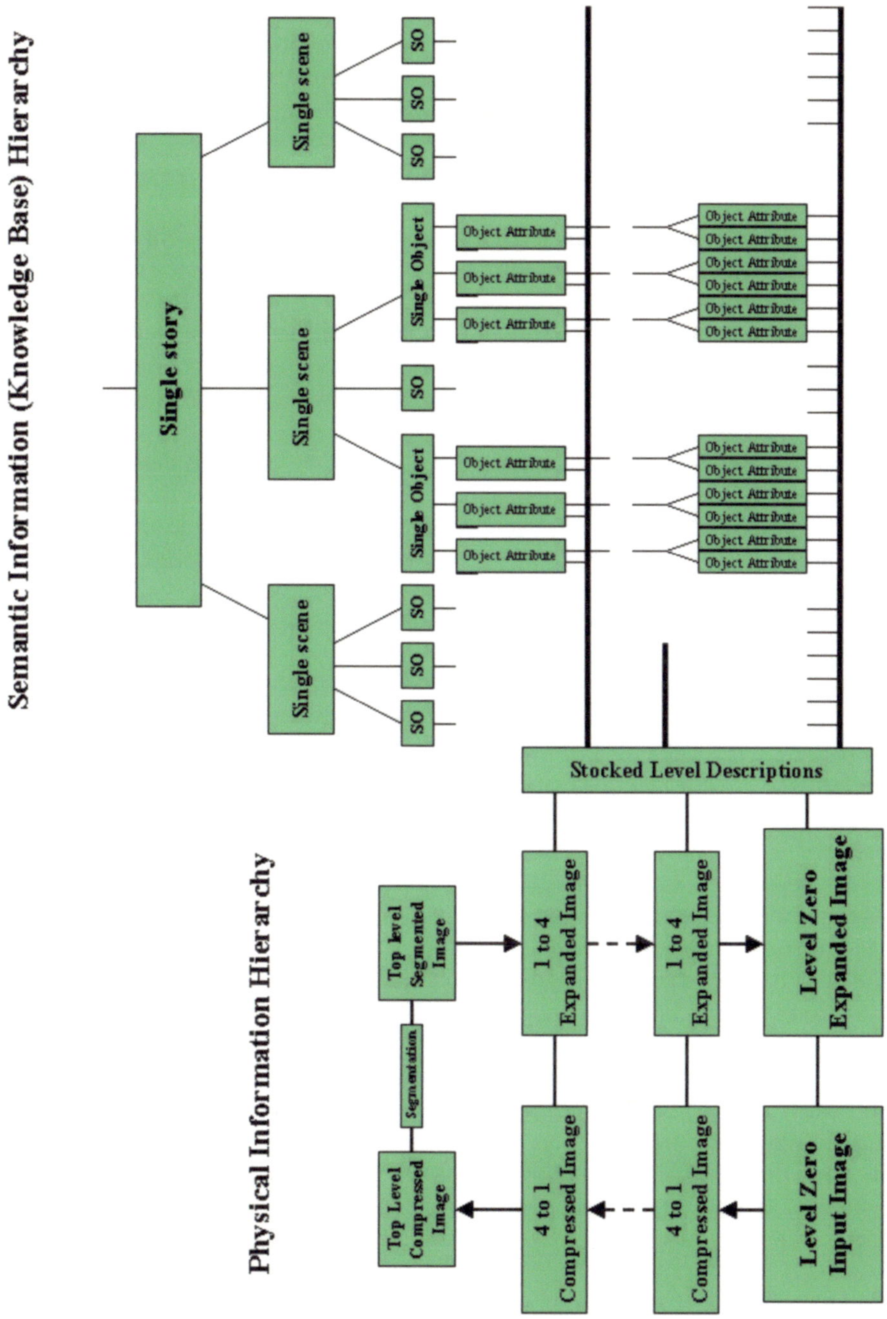

Figure 1. Arrangement of Physical and Semantic Information Hierarchies and their interconnection

Human's cognitive abilities (including the aptness for image interpretation and the capacity to assign semantics to an image) are empowered by the existence of a huge knowledge base about the things in the surrounding world kept in human brain/head.
This knowledge base is permanently upgraded and updated during the human's life span. So, if we intend to endow our visual robot with some cognitive capabilities we have to provide it with something equivalent to this (human) knowledge base.
It goes without saying that this knowledge base will never be as large and developed as its human prototype. But we are not sure that such a requirement is valid in our case. After all, humans are also not equal in their cognitive capacities, and the content of their knowledge bases is very diversified too. (The knowledge base of aerial photographs interpreter is certainly different from the knowledge base of X-ray images interpreter, or IVUS images, or PET images). The knowledge base of our visual robot has to be small enough to be effective and manageable, but sufficiently large to ensure the robot's acceptable performance. Certainly, for our feasibility study we can be satisfied even with a relatively small, specific-task-oriented knowledge base.
The next crucial point is the knowledgebase representation issue. To deal with it, we first of all must arrive at a common agreement about what is the meaning of the term "knowledge". (A question that usually has no commonly accepted answer.) We state that in our case a suitable and a sufficient definition of it would be: "**Kownledge is a memorized information**". Consequently, we can say that knowledge (like information) must be a hierarchy of descriptive items, with the grade of description details growing in a top-down manner at the descending levels of the hierarchy.
What else must be mentioned here, is that these descriptions have to be implemented in some alphabet (as it is in the case of physical information) or in a description language (which better fits the semantic information case). Any farther argument being put aside, we will declare that the most suitable language in our case is the natural human language. After all, the real knowledge bases that we are familiar with are implemented in natural human languages.
The next step, then, is predetermined: if natural language is a suitable description implement, the suitable form of this implementation is a narrative, a story tale (Tuffield et al., 2005). If the description hierarchy can be seen as an inverted tree, then the branches of this tree are the stories that encapsulate human's experience with the surrounding world. And the leaves of these branches are single words (single objects) from which the story parts (single scenes) are composed of.
The descent into description details, however, does not stop here, and each single word (single object) can be farther decomposed into its attributes and rules that describe the relations between the attributes.
At this stage the physical information reappears. Because the words are usually associated with physical objects in the real world, words' attributes must be seen as memorized physical information (descriptions). Once derived (by the HVS) from the observable world and learned to be associated with a particular word, these physical information descriptions are soldered in into the knowledgebase. Object recognition, thus, turns out to be a comparison and similarity test between currently acquired physical information and the one already retained in the memory. If the similarity test is successful, starting from this point in the hierarchy and climbing back up on the knowledgebase ladder we will obtain: first, the linguistic label for a recognized object; second, the position of this label (word) in the context

of the whole story; and third, the ability to verify the validity of an initial guess by testing the appropriateness of the neighboring parts composing the object or the context of a story. In this way, object's meaningful categorization can be reached, and the first stage of image annotation can be successfully accomplished, providing the basis for farther meaningful (semantic) image interpretation.

One question has remained untouched in our discourse: How this artificial knowledgebase has to be initially created and brought into the robot's disposal? The vigilant reader certainly remembers the fierce debates about learning capabilities of neural networks and other machine learning technologies. We are aware of these debates. But in our case we can state certainly: they are irrelevant. For a simple reason: the top-down fashion of the knowledge base development pre-determines that all responsibilities for knowledge base creation have to be placed on the shoulders of the robot designer.

Such an unexpected twist in design philosophy will be less surprising if we recall that human cognitive memory is also often defined as a "declarative memory". And the prime mode of human learning is the declarative learning mode, when the new knowledge is explicitly transferred to a developing human from his external surrounding: From a father to a child, from a teacher to a student, from an instructor to a trainee. So, our proposal that robot's knowledgebase has to be designed and created by the robot supervisor is sufficiently correct and is fitting our general concept of information use and management.

5. More explanation is required

The proposed Semantic Information Processing scheme must be so annoyingly different from other knowledge-management forms that farther explanations in its defence must be provided. The vigilant reader has certainly paid attention to the fact that the term "ontology" does not appear in the text, albeit ontology is a ubiquitously used technique for human knowledgebase creation and representation. I have chose to avoid the use of the term ontology for the following reason.

More than twenty years ago, a famous Soviet mathematician, Israel Gelfand, and his colleagues were trying to devise a knowledge-based system for medical diagnostic problem solving. From the very beginning, the need for an adequate description language has become apparent, and extensive research efforts were spent moving toward this goal. The notion of ontology has not been yet known – the seminal paper of Thomas Gruber would appear only in the year 1993 (Gruber, 1993). However, in the preface to the book that summarizes their experience, which was well ahead of their time, while referring to the language creation difficulties, Israel Gelfand writes: "There are two ways to create a language: to compose literature scripts or to compile a dictionary. We all know how significant for the Russian language were the works of Pushkin and Dhale" (Gelfand et al., 1989). (We would add accordingly – Shakespeare and Dr. Johnson, for the English language).

The problem is that in contemporary knowledge-based systems design, ontology is used in only one of its manifestations – a vocabulary, a thesaurus. That is, certainly, a miss and a fault, which in our design we are trying to avoid. Imagine a Martian guest that is trying to understand our world relying only on the Oxford Concise Dictionary. On the other hand, you can easily recall the picture books with stories that the grandmother has read to you again and again in the childhood.

The story telling approach that we decided to pursue (and are trying to implement) is also very different from those that could be found in today's research papers. Current trend in story telling research and development is focused on automatic narrative creation, very similar to what is going on in the classical ontology design practice. In this regard it would be a proper place to remind that we reject the tradition of autonomous ontology creation. We are inclined to the "grandmother approach", where, as it was already explained earlier, the new knowledge comes to its possessor from the outside, from someone who already possesses it: A grandmother telling the child her stories, dancing bees that convey to the rest of the hive the information about melliferous sites (Zhang et al., 2005), ants that learn in tandem (Franks & Richardson, 2006), and even bacteria developing their antibiotic resistance as a result of a so-called horizontal gene transfer when a single DNA fragment of one bacteria is disseminated among other colony members (Lawrence & Hendrickson, 2003). That is, in our case this is a job for the robot 's designer. In a story telling manner he has to transfer to the robot his view on the surrounding world and his understanding of a proper behavior in different task-inspired situations.

I am aware that by denying the bottom-up machine-learning-inspired knowledge acquisition I am awaking all the bears in my environment. But sorry, that is only an attempt to find out the way to leave the dead-ended alley where image processing is stalled for so many years.

Let us continue: Vigilant readers have certainly also paid attention to the fact that the name of Claude Shannon (the famous inventor of the Information Theory of Communication) is not mentioned in the paper. The reason for this is clear and plain - Shannon says nothing about the notion of information, about "What is information?" He has invented a measure of information, but that says nothing about the notion of information. Like the measure of time, which we ubiquitously use (second, hour, day, etc.) tells nothing about the notion of time, about "What is time?".

Kolmogorov too was busy with very different things. Randomness has been his main concern. According to the Kolmogorov's theory, a message composed as a sequence of random values cannot be depicted (reproduced) by a description program, which is shorter than the original message. That is, the description of a random message is the message itself. What follows from this, is that nonrandom data structures could be described in a concise compressed form, which Chaitin calls "Algorithmic Information" (Chaitin, 1977), Floridi – "Meaningful data" (Floridi, 2005), Vitanyi – "Meaningful Information" (Vitanyi, 2006). That means that each message can be seen as a composition of: a compressible, information-bearing part of it and a non-compressible, information-devoid, random data part. The first part we call Physical Information, and it is obvious that processing only this part of the message will give us a tremendous gain against the data processing case where meaningful and meaning-less data are inseparable.

The March 2008 issue of the IEEE Signal Processing Magazine is entirely devoted to this problem: in different domains of signal processing people have empirically discovered the advantages of what they call "Compressive Sampling". In the preface to the magazine the guest editors write: "At the heart of the new approach are two crucial observations. The first is that the Shannon/Nyquist signal representation exploits only minimal prior knowledge about the signal being sampled, namely its bandwidth. However, most objects we are interested in acquiring are structured and depend upon a small number of degrees of freedom than the bandwidth suggests. In other words, most objects of interest are sparse or

compressible in the sense that they can be encoded with just a few numbers without numerical or perceptual loss". Bravo! There could be no better explanation to the benefits of information processing versus brute force data processing. The tradition is, however, stronger than the reason - the rest of the magazine is devoted to the alchemy of compressive sampling accomplishment via bottom-up raw data processing.
Some words I would like to spend on the latest developments in the HVS research. While the mainstream of human vision research continues to approach visual information processing in a bottom-up feed-forward fashion (Serre et al., 2005; Kveraga et al., 2007) it turns out that the idea of primary top-down processing was never extraneous to biological vision. The first publications addressing this issue are dated by the early eighties of the last century, (Navon, 1977; Chen, 1982). The prominent authors were persistent in their claims, and farther research reports were published regularly until the recent time, (Navon, 2003; Chen, 2005). However, it looks like they have been overlooked, both in biological and in computer vision research. Only in the last years, a tide of new evidence has become visible and is pervasively discussed now. Although the spirit of these discussions is still different from our view on the subject, the trend is certainly in favor of the foremost top-down visual information processing (Ahissar & Hochstein, 2004; Juan et al., 2004). Again, top-down information processing in the physical information processing part only is assumed here. Information processing partition proposed in this paper is not acknowledged by the contemporary vision researchers.

6. Some conclusions

In this paper, I have proposed a few ideas that are entirely new and therefore might look suspicious. All the novelties come as a natural extension of a new definition of information that is sequentially applied to various aspects of image processing. The most important innovation is positing information image processing as the prime mode of image processing (in contrast to traditionally dominant data image processing). The next novelty is the dissociation between physical and semantic information processing within the information-processing domain. The proposed arrangement of information-processing hierarchies is a further extension of the basic idea of the information-processing nature of the HVS, and its imitation in an artificial vision system - our hypothetical visual robot design.
Despite of the skeptical welcome, the efficiency of the unsupervised top-down directed region-based image segmentation is hard to disprove today. Although the story telling approach to knowledgebase hierarchy creation is not yet so rigorously proved, we hope that this development stage will also be successfully surmounted.
I hope that the time of our persuasive success is not far away.

7. References

Ahissar, M. & Hochstein, S. (2004). The reverse hierarchy theory of visual perceptual learning, *Trends in Cognitive Science*, vol. 8, no. 10, pp. 457-464, 2004.

Barsalou, L.W. (1999). Perceptual symbol systems, *Behavioral and Brain Sciences*, vol. 22, pp. 577-660, 1999.

Biederman, I. (1987). Recognition-by-Components: A Theory of Human Image Understanding, *Psychological Review*, vol. 94, no. 2, pp. 115-147, 1987.

Biederman, I. (2006). Perceptual Pleasure and the Brain, *American Scientist*, vol. 94, pp. 249-255, May-June 2006.

BittWare. (2007). Available: http://www.sarsen.net/sarsen-manufacture-bitware-standard-amc-b2.html.

Chaitin, G. J. (1977). Algorithmic Information Theory, *IBM Journal of Research and Development*, vol. 21, pp. 350-359, 1977.

Chen, L. (1982). Topological structure in visual perception, *Science*, 218, pp. 699-700, 1982.

Chen, L. (2005). The topological approach to perceptual organization, *Visual Cognition*, vol. 12, no. 4, pp. 553-637, 2005.

Diamant, E. (2004). Top-Down Unsupervised Image Segmentation (it sounds like an oxymoron, but actually it isn't), *Proceedings of the 3rd Pattern Recognition in Remote Sensing Workshop (PRRS'04)*, Kingston University, UK, August 2004.

Diamant, E. (2005). Searching for image information content, its discovery, extraction, and representation, *Journal of Electronic Imaging*, vol. 14, issue 1, January-March 2005.

Diamant, E. (2005a). Does a plane imitate a bird? Does computer vision have to follow biological paradigms?, In: De Gregorio, M., et al, (Eds.), *Brain, Vision, and Artificial Intelligence*, First International Symposium Proceedings. LNCS, vol. 3704, Springer-Verlag, pp. 108-115, 2005. Available: http://www.vidiamant.info.

Diamant, E. (2006). In Quest of Image Semantics: Are We Looking for It Under the Right Lamppost?, http://arxiv.org/abs/cs.CV/0609003.

Diamant, E. (2007). Modeling human-like intelligent image processing: An information processing perspective and approach, *Signal Processing: Image Communication*, vol. 22, pp.583-590, 2007.

European IST Research (2005-2006): Building on Assets, Seizing Opportunities. Available: http://europa.eu.int/information_society/.

Floridi, L. (2003). From Data to Semantic Information, *Entropy*, vol. 5, pp. 125-145, 2003.

Floridi, L. (2005). Is Semantic Information Meaningful Data? *Philosophy and Phenomenological Research*, vol. LXX, no. 2, pp. 351-370, March 2005.

Floridi, L. (2007). In defence of the veridical nature of semantic information, *European Journal of Analytic Philosophy*, vol. 3, no. 1, pp. 31-41, 2007.

Floridi, L. (2007). Trends in the Philosophy of Information, In: P. Adriaans, J. van Benthem (Eds.), *"Handbook of Philosophy of Information"*, Elsevier, (forthcoming). Available: http://www.philosophyofinformation.net.

Franks, N. & Richardson, T. (2006). Teaching in tandem-running ants, *Nature*, 439, p. 153, January 12, 2006.

Gelfand, I.M.; Rosenfeld, B.I.; Shifrin, M.A. (1989). Essays on Collaboration of Mathematicians and Physicians, Nauka Pablisher, 1989.

Gruber, T.R. (1993). Toward Principles for the Design of Ontologies Used for Knowledge Sharing, In: *Formal Ontology in Conceptual Analysis and Knowledge Representation*, Kluwer Publisher, 1993. Avl.: http://kls-web.stanford.edu/authorindex/Gruber.

Hare, J., Lewis, P., Enser, P., and Sandom, C. (2006). Mind the Gap: Another look at the problem of the semantic gap in image retrieval, *Proceedings of Multimedia Content Analysis, Management and Retrieval Conference*, SPIE vol. 6073, 2006. Available: http://www.ecs.soton.ac.uk/people/.

Itti, L. (2005). Models of Bottom-Up Attention and Saliency, In: *Neurobiology of Attention*, (L. Itti, G. Rees, J. Tsotsos, Eds.), pp. 576-582, San Diego, CA: Elsevier, 2005.

Johansson, C. & Lansner, A. (2006). Attractor Memory with Self-organizing Input, *Workshop on Biologically Inspired Approaches to Advanced Information Technology (BioADIT 2005)*, LNCS, vol. 3853, pp. 265-280, Springer-Verlag, 2006.

Juan, C-H.; Campana, G. & Walsh, V. (2004). Cortical interactions in vision and awareness: hierarchies in reverse, *Progress in Brain Research*, vol. 144, pp. 117-130, 2004.

Kolmogorov, A. (1965). Three approaches to the quantitative definition of information, *Problems of Information and Transmission*, vol. 1, No. 1, pp. 1-7, 1965.

Kveraga, K.; Ghuman, A. & Bar, M. (2007). Top-down predictions in the cognitive brain, *Brain and Cognition*, vol. 65, pp. 145-168, 2007.

Lawrence, J. & Hendrickson, H. (2003). Lateral gene transfer: when will adolescence end?, *Molecular Microbiology*, vol. 50, no. 3, pp. 739-749, 2003.

Lew, M.S., Sebe, N., Djeraba, C. and Jain, R. (2006). Content-based Multimedia Information Retrieval: State of the Art and Challenges, In: *ACM Transactions on Multimedia Computing, Communications, and Applications*, February 2006.

Marques, O. & Furht, B. (2002). Content-Based Visual Information Retrieval, In: (T.K. Shih, Ed.), *Distributed Multimedia Databases: Techniques and Applications*, Idea Group Publishing, Hershey, Pennsylvania, 2002.

Marr, D. (1978). Representing visual information: A computational approach, *Lectures on Mathematics in the Life Science*, vol. 10, pp. 61-80, 1978.

Marr, D. (1982). Vision: A Computational Investigation into the Human Representation and Processing of Visual Information, Freeman, San Francisco, 1982.

McRae, K. (2004). Semantic Memory: Some insights from Feature-based Connectionist Attractor Networks, Ed. B. H. Ross, *The Psychology of Learning and Motivation*, vol. 45, 2004. Available: http://amdrae.ssc.uwo.ca/.

Milner, D. & Goodale, M. (1998). The Visual Brain in Action, *Oxford Psychology Series*, No. 27, Oxford University Press, 1998.

Mobile video. (2008). Available: http://www.dspdesignline.com/howto/207100795.

Mojsilovic, A. & Rogowitz, B. (2001). Capturing image semantics with low-level descriptors, In: *Proceedings of the International Conference on Image Processing (ICIP-01)*, pp. 18-21, Thessaloniki, Greece, October 2001.

Naphade, M. & Huang, T.S. (2002). Extracting Semantics From Audiovisual Content: The Final Frontier in Multimedia Retrieval, *IEEE Transactions on Neural Networks*, vol. 13, No. 4, pp. 793-810, July 2002.

Navon, D. (1977). Forest Before Trees: The Precedence of Global Features in Visual Perception, *Cognitive Psychology*, 9, pp. 353-383, 1977.

Navon, D. (2003). What does a compound letter tell the psychologist's mind?, *Acta Psychologica*, vol. 114, pp. 273-309, 2003.

Nokia. (2008). Available: http://en.wikipedia.org/wiki/Nokia.

Palmeri, T. & Gauthier, I. (2004). Visual Object Understanding, *Nature Reviews: Neuroscience*, vol. 5, pp. 291-304, April 2004.

Puri, A. & Eleftheriadis, A. (1998). MPEG-4: An object-based multimedia coding standard, *Mobile Networks and Applications*, vol. 3, issue 1, pp. 5-32, 1998.

Serre, T.; Kouh, M.; Cadieu, C.; Knoblich, U.; Kreiman, G. & Poggio, T. (2005). A theory of object recognition: computations and circuits in the feedforward path of the ventral stream in primate visual cortex, *CBCL MIT paper*, November 2005. (Available: http://web.mit.edu/serre/...)

Sloman, A. (2006). What is information? Meaning? Semantic content?, Available: http://www.cs.bham.ac.uk/research/projects/cosy/papers/.

Solomonoff, R. J. (1997). The Discovery of Algorithmic Probability, *Journal of Computer and System Science*, vol. 55, No. 1, pp. 73-88, 1997.

Sullivan, G. & Wiegand, T. (2005). Video Compression - From Concepts to the H.264/AVC Standard, *Proceedings of the IEEE*, vol. 93, no. 1, pp. 18-31, January 2005.

Thevenin, M., Paindavoine, M., Letellier, L., Heyrman, B. (2008). Embedded processor extensions for image processing, *Proceedings of SPIE*, vol. 7001, April 2008.

Treisman, A. & Gelade, G. (1980). A feature-integration theory of attention, *Cognitive Psychology*, vol. 12, pp. 97-136, Jan. 1980.

Treisman, A. (1996). The binding problem. *Current Opinion in Neurobiology*, vol. 6, pp.171-178, 1996.

Treue, S. (2003). Visual attention: the where, what, how and why of saliency, *Current Opinion in Neurobiology*, vol. 13, pp. 428-432, 2003.

Tuffield, M.; Shadbolt, N. & Millard, D. (2005). Narratives as a Form of Knowledge Transfer: Narrative Theory and Semantics, *Proceedings of the 1st AKT (Advance Knowledge Technologies) Symposium*, Milton Keynes, UK, June 2005.

Video Surveillance. (2007). Networking/IP to drive video surveillance market growth. Available: http://semiconductors.tekrati.com/research/8608/.

Vitanyi, P. (2006). Meaningful Information, *IEEE Transactions on Information Theory*, vol. 52, No. 10, pp. 4617-4624, October 2006. Availbl: http://www.cwi.nl/~paulv/papers.

Zhang, C. & Chen, T. (2003). From Low Level Features to High Level Semantics, In: *Handbook of Video Databases: Design and Applications*, by Furht, Borko/ Marques, Oge, Publisher: CRC Press, October 2003.

Zhang, S.; Bock, F.; Si, A.; Tautz, J. & Srinivasan, M. (2005). Visual working memory in decision making by honey bees, *Proceedings of The National Academy of Science of the USA (PNAS)*, vol. 102, no. 14, pp. 5250-5255, April 5, 2005.

Zhou, X.S. & Huang, T.S. (2000). CBIR: From low-Level Features to High-Level Semantics, *Proceedings SPIE*, vol. 3974, pp. 426-431, San Jose, CA, January 24-28, 2000. Available: http://www.ifp.uiuc.edu/~xzhou2/.

6

Multiple Image Objects Detection, Tracking, and Classification using Human Articulated Visual Perception Capability

HeungKyu Lee
MarkAny Corporation
Republic of Korea

1. Introduction

This chapter examines the multiple image objects detection, tracking, and classification method using human articulated visual perception capability in consecutive image sequences. The described artificial vision system mimics the characteristics of the human visual perception. It is a well known fact that a human being, first detects and focuses motion energy of a scene, and then analyzes only a detailed color region of that focused region using a storage cell from a human brain.

From this fact, the spatio-temporal mechanism is derived in order to detect and track multiple objects in consecutive image sequences. This mechanism provides an efficient method for more complex analysis using data association in spatially attentive window and predicted temporal location. In addition, occlusion problem between multiple moving objects is considered. When multiple objects are moving or occluded between them in areas of visual field, a simultaneous detection and tracking of multiple objects tend to fail. This is due to the fact that incompletely estimated feature vectors such as location, color, velocity, and acceleration of a target provide ambiguous and missing information. In addition, partial information cannot render the complete information unless temporal consistency is considered when objects are occluded between them or they are hidden in obstacles. To cope with these issues, the spatially and temporally considered mechanism using occlusion activity detection and object association with partial probability model can be considered. Furthermore, the detected moving targets can be tracked simultaneously and reliably using the extended joint probabilistic data association (JPDA) filter. Finally, target classification is performed using the decision fusion method of shape and motion information based on Bayesian framework. For reliable and stable classification of targets, multiple invariant feature vectors to more certainly discriminate between targets are required. To do this, shape and motion information are extracted using Fourier descriptor, gradients, and motion feature variation on spatial and temporal images, and then local decisions are performed respectively. Finally, global decision is done using decision fusion method based on Bayesian framework. The experimental evaluations show the performance and usefulness of introduced algorithms that are applied to real image sequences. Figure 1 shows the system block-diagram of multi-target detection, tracking, and classification.

In section 2, we describe the target detection and feature selection procedure employing occlusion reasoning from detail analysis of spatio-temporal video frame sequences. In section 3, multi-target tracking based on modified joint probabilistic data association filter is described. In section 4, we describe the multi-target classification using local and global decision rules based on Bayesian framework. Finally, concluding remarks are described in section 5.

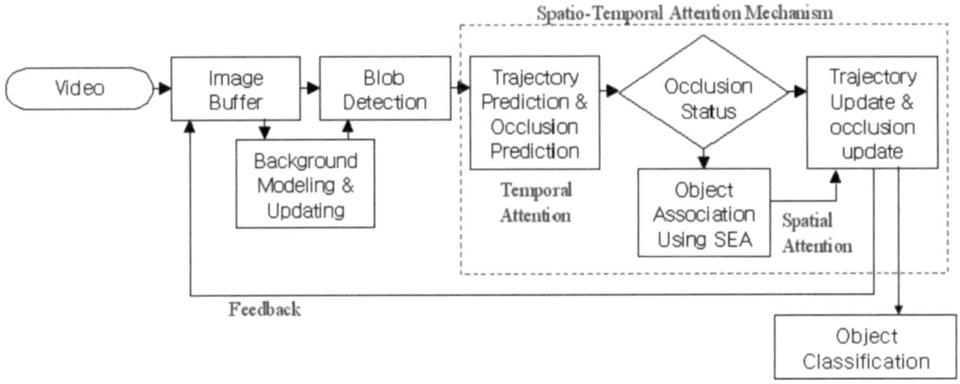

Figure 1. System block-diagram for multi-target detection, tracking, and classification

2. Target Detection and Feature Selection

In video frame sequences, extracting moving blobs is very important task to identify the target. Its performance affects the accuracy of the detection, tracking and classification because the detected moving blobs might include the false alarms. To increase the accuracy of moving blob extraction, adaptive background model generation is required. From this model, accurate estimation of moving blob region can be done just by subtracting accurately estimated adaptive background model from original video frame. For doing this, lots of researches have been done (Y.L.Tian et al. 2005, C.Stauffer et al. 1999, A.Elgammal, et al. 2002, K. Kim, et al. 2004). These researches make the time variant background model using temporal information, and then subtract it from the original video frame sequence. In addition, spatial directional information using motion estimation can be applied.

2.1 Moving Blobs Detection

For moving blobs detection, the spatio-temporal information is very important task to accurately estimate the just moving parts from the complex background. The human eye first stimulates motion information such as time difference image to recognize the moving objects, and then focus on the spatial information such as detail color distribution in detected motion information group.

To mimic the human eye, motion information is first estimated. For doing this, moving blob detection is achieved by adaptively estimating the fixed background model and then by subtracting the background model from the original video frame sequences. For estimating background model in this chapter, the extended adaptive change detection algorithm (Huwer, et al. 2000) that improves change detection accuracy by combining both the temporal difference and the spatial difference using weighted accumulation is applied. The function that accumulates consecutive video frame sequences is given by $\phi(\hat{f}_i, f_i, \tau)$ representing a measure for the number of past values.

$$\begin{aligned} \hat{f}_{i+1}(x,y) &= \phi(\hat{f}_i(x,y), f_i(x,y), \tau) \\ &= f_i(x,y)\left(1 - e^{-1/\tau}\right) + \hat{f}_i(x,y)e^{-1/\tau} \end{aligned} \tag{1}$$

where f_i is the video frame sequences and τ is the length of the video frame accumulation. Using this accumulated video frames, mean background image μ_i is computed. Then, the detection of the background change region, B_i is then done by thresholding the absolute difference between the current video frame f_i and the mean background video frame, μ_i with the background standard deviations, σ_i. Figure 2 shows the moving blob detection example.

$$B_i(x,y) = \{(x,y) \in I / |\mu_i(x,y) - f_i(x,y)| > \sigma_i(x,y)\} \tag{2}$$

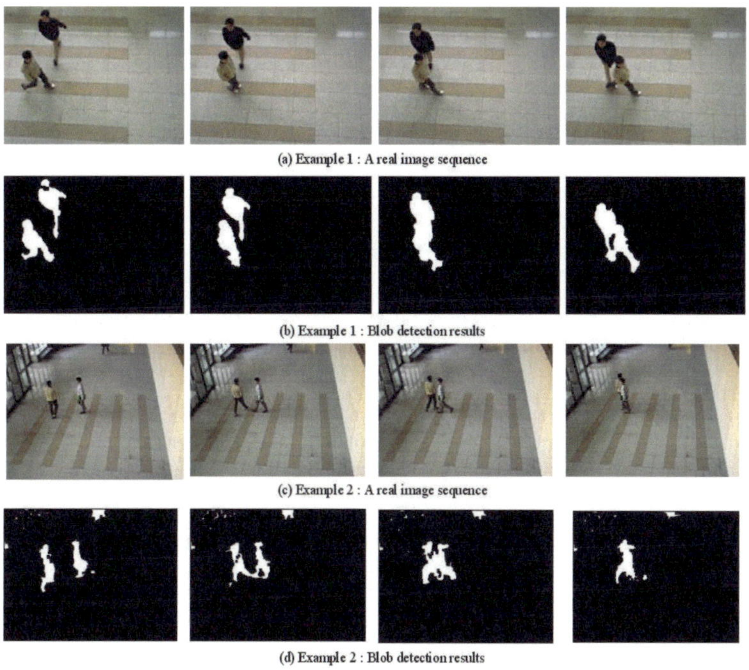

Figure 2. Moving blobs detection using time difference of current video frame and adaptive background model

In addition, the optical flow estimation (S.S. Beauchemin, et al. 1995) is done between the previous video frame sequence and current video frame sequence. The optical flow estimation result, B_{opt} is combined for the detection of the background change region as given

$$B_i(x,y) = \max(B_i(x,y), B_{opt}(x,y)) \tag{3}$$

Background adaptation procedure is recursively performed to deal with changes in illumination. To reliably detect moving blobs as shown in Figure 3, the time difference method using shape and motion information is applied as follows:

$$B_{t,i}(x,y) = \left|B_i(x,y) - f_i(x,y)\right| \tag{4}$$

(a) Object detection using shape information (b) Object detection using shape and motion information

Figure 3. Moving blobs detection example

On the segmented image, $B_{t,i}(x,y)$, a connected components analysis is then applied in order to fill holes in probable regions of interest. It is due to the fact that initial segmentation region is usually noisy. So, the low-pass filter and morphological operations are required. Next time, the segmented foreground region is labeled. At this time, a blob map of current video frame is computed. The blob map, $b_i(t)$ is represented by

$$b_i(t) = \bigcup_x \left|d_x(t) > \Gamma\right| \tag{5}$$

where $d_x(t)$ is a segmented foreground region, and Γ is a threshold to rule out small region. The blob map, $b_i(t)$ is recomputed for obtaining the color distribution (M. J. Swain, et al. 1991) of a blob as follows.

$$MB_{i,j}(x,y) = \begin{cases} f_i(x,y) & \text{if } b_i(x,y) == 1 \\ 0 & else \end{cases} \tag{6}$$

where $MB_{i,j}(x,y)$ is a moving bob having color model, i is a moving blob index, and j is a frame index. This moving blob color model can be used in order to associate a specific blob of occluded region with a real target when the occlusion status is enabled. Thus, this model is saved during short-time period. Meanwhile, it is not stored in queue during the occlusion status is enabled. We then compute the centroids (center points) of labeled blobs as feature vectors by calculating the geometric moment of moving blobs by using

$$M'_{p,q} = \int_{-\infty}^{\infty}\int_{-\infty}^{\infty} x^p y^p f(x,y)\,dx\,,dy \tag{7}$$

where f(x,y) is a moving blob to be analyzed and (p_x, p_y) is a centroid. The center point is stored at the trajectory variable, and it computes the width, $MV_w(i)$ and height, $MV_h(i)$ to represent the bounding region as a minimum bounding rectangle (MBR) (Rasmussen, et al. 1998). The respective centroid points in video frame sequences can give the object's kinematic status information such as walk, running, turn over and so on. Thus, we would be able to utilize them for analyzing objects behavior pattern.

2.2 Occlusion

In feature based multiple target tracking, occlusion issue is challenging one to be considered. Combining feature points derives the tracking failure on the tracking filter. Thus, the separation procedure should be done. To perform the separation procedure, detail analysis should be done in combined (or occluded) region between moving objects. For doing this, temporal information having time difference energy and motion can be utilized. If the modeling of object movement is applied, we can predict the object movement from the LTM(Long Term Memory). Thus, we can utilize the predicted motion information when the multiple objects are occluded between them or hidden back to obstacles even if it is an inaccurate estimation. For doing this, occlusion activity detection algorithm can be applied (H. K. Lee, et al. 2006). This method predicts the occlusion status of next step by employing a kinematics model of moving objects as shown in Figure 4, and notifies it for next complex analysis. Thus, this describes the temporal attention model. Then, the occlusion status is updated in current time of captured image after comparing the MBR of each object in attention window. Proposed occlusion activity detection algorithm has two-stage strategies as follows.

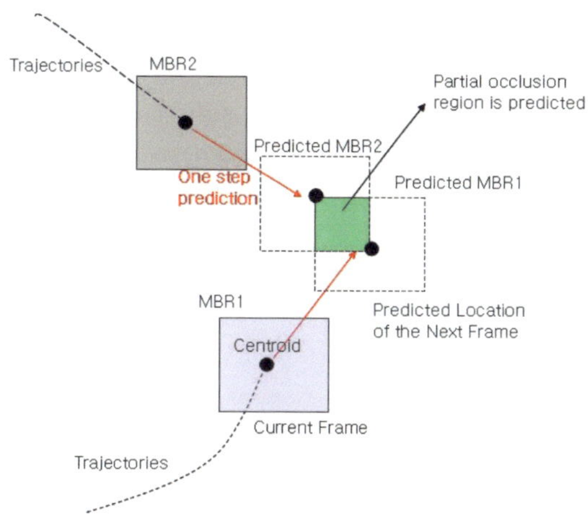

Figure 4. Occlusion reasoning and prediction using Kalman prediction

- STEP 1: Occlusion Prediction Stage

This step predicts the next center points of blobs by employing the Kalman prediction (Y. Bar-Shalom, et al. 1995) as follows:

$$\hat{S}(k+1/k) = F(k)\hat{S}(k/k) + u(k) \tag{8}$$

$$\hat{Z}(k+1/k) = H(k+1)\hat{S}(k+1/k) \tag{9}$$

where S(k+1/k) is the state vector at time k+1 given cumulative measurements to time k, F(k) is a transition matrix, and u(k) is a sequence of zero-mean, white Gaussian process noise. Using the predicted center points, we can determine the redundancy of objects using the intersection measure in attention window. The occlusion activity is computed by comparing if or not there is an overlapping region between MBR_i of each object in the predicted center points as follows.

$$Fg = \begin{cases} 1 & if \ (MBR_i \cap MBR_j) \neq \phi \\ 0 & otherwise \end{cases} \tag{10}$$

where the variable, i, j=1,…,m, the variable, Fg is an occlusion alarm flag, the subscript i and j are the index of the detected target at the previous frame, and m is a number of a target. If a redundant region has occurred at the predicted position, the probability of occlusion occurrence in the next step will be increased. Therefore, the occlusion activity status is notified for next complex analysis.

(a) MBR without occlusion reasoning

(b) MBR using occlusion reasoning

(c) MBR without occlusion reasoning

(d) MBR using occlusion reasoning

Figure 5. Minimum bounding rectangle for representing a validation region using occlusion reasoning

- STEP 2: Update Stage of Occlusion Status

The occlusion activity status can be updated in the current frame. The first, the size of the labeled blobs is verified whether they are contained within the validation region or not. If the shape of labeled blobs is contained within the validation region, the occlusion status flag is disabled. Otherwise, we conclude that the occlusion has occurred at the region, and the occlusion status is enabled. At this time, we apply the predicted center points of the previous step to the system model and the predicted MBR is recomputed as in Figure 5. Then, the Kalman gain is computed and the measurement equation is updated.

2.3 Feature Selection

Each feature sets describing multiple objects is integrated into a set of feature map. This feature map is used for visual search process to associate each blob with a real target. In this paper, color, location, velocity, and acceleration are used to describe object shape and model the kinematics of moving objects (Y. Bar-Shalom, et al. 1995).

Let o = [o_1, o_2, ..., o_M] denote the set of objects to track, φ denotes the movement directions for object o_i and x=[x_i , y_i]^T denote the vector of points of center corresponding to o_i , with v= [$\dot{x}_i, \dot{y}_i$]^T ,where $\dot{x}_i$ and $\dot{y}_i$ denote the derivative of x_i and y_i with respect to t, respectively. First, center points of moving objects are computed, and then movement directions are computed using motion vectors extracted by the optical flow method (Kollnig, et al. 1994). To obtain the movement directions of objects, we compute the direction of motion vector for each pixel. The direction, φ of the vector is defined and computed using the Lucas-Kanade tracking equation (Tomasi, C. et al.) as follows:

$$\begin{aligned} \varphi(rad) &= angle(\frac{v_y}{v_x}) \qquad 0 \le \varphi < 2\pi \\ &= \{\varphi / \sin\varphi = v_y / \|v\|\} \cap \{\varphi / \cos\varphi = v_x / \|v\|\} \cap \{\varphi / \tan\varphi = v_y / v_x\} \end{aligned} \tag{11}$$

where v_x and v_y are motion vectors for x and y direction respectively, and $\|v\| = \sqrt{v_x^2 + v_y^2}$. From Equation (11), we know $\dot{x} = \|v\| \cos\varphi$ and $\dot{y} = \|v\| \sin\varphi$. The equations are differentiated with respect to t as follows.

$$\frac{d}{dt}\varphi = -\frac{1}{\|v\| \sin\varphi}\ddot{x} = \frac{1}{\|v\| \cos\varphi}\ddot{y} = \frac{1}{2\|v\|}\left(\frac{1}{\cos\varphi}\ddot{y} - \frac{1}{\sin\varphi}\ddot{x}\right) \tag{12}$$

Using equation (11) and (12), the proposed system model is given by

$$\dot{s} = \Psi s + \Pi u^e + v \qquad v \sim M(0, Q) \tag{13}$$

$$\Psi = \begin{bmatrix} O_{2\times2} & I_2 & O_{2\times2} & O_{2\times1} \\ O_{2\times2} & -G^{-1}\Sigma & O_{2\times2} & O_{2\times1} \\ O_{2\times2} & O_{2\times2} & O_{2\times2} & O_{2\times1} \\ O_{1\times2} & O_{1\times2} & \frac{1}{2\|v\|}[-\csc\varphi \quad \sec\varphi] & 0 \end{bmatrix} \tag{14}$$

$$\Pi = \begin{bmatrix} O_{2\times2} \\ -G^{-1}I_2 \\ O_{2\times2} \\ O_{1\times2} \end{bmatrix} \tag{15}$$

where $O_{m\times n}$ is an m×n zero matrix, I_m is an m×m identity matrix and s = [x^T , v^T , a^T, φ]^T denote the system state, which is composed of center points, velocity, acceleration and direction of moving object. In the proposed method, the acceleration component in state vector is included to cope with maneuvering of object. The model assumes random acceleration with covariance Q, which accounts for changes in image velocity. As the eigen-values of Q become larger, old measurements are given relatively low weight in the adjustment of state. This allows the system to adapt to changes in the object velocity. Since time interval Δt between one frame and next is very small, it is assumed that F is constant over the (t_k , t_{k+1}) interval of interest. The state transition matrix is simply given by

$$F_k = e^{\Psi \Delta t} = \begin{bmatrix} I_2 & I_2 \Delta t & \frac{\Delta t^2}{2} I_2 & O_{2\times1} \\ O_{2\times2} & I_2 - G^{-1}\Sigma\Delta t & O_{2\times2} & O_{2\times1} \\ O_{2\times2} & O_{2\times2} & I_2 & O_{2\times1} \\ O_{1\times2} & O_{1\times2} & \frac{\Delta t}{2\|v\|}[-\csc\varphi \quad \sec\varphi] & 1 \end{bmatrix} \tag{16}$$

Let z = [z_1, z_2, …, z_M] and z_i denote the measurement vector for object o_i . In the proposed model, center points and movement directions for each object are treated as system measurements. The measurement vector satisfies:

$$z_i = Hs + w \qquad w \sim N(0, R) \tag{17}$$

$$H = \begin{bmatrix} 1 & 0 & 0 & 0 & 0 & 0 & 0 \\ 0 & 1 & 0 & 0 & 0 & 0 & 0 \\ 0 & 0 & 0 & 0 & 0 & 0 & 1 \end{bmatrix} \tag{18}$$

where matrix H connects the relationship between z_i and s. After all, the object kinematics model is determined by setting the appropriate parameters.

3. Multi-Target Tracking using Data Association

For multi-target tracking, the joint probabilistic data association filter (JPDA) (Y. Bar-Shalom, et al. 1995 , Samuel Blackman, et al. 1999, Rasmussen, et al. 1998) is applied. Similarly to the PDA algorithm (Y. Bar-Shalom, et al. 1995 , Samuel Blackman, et al. 1999), the JPDA computes the probabilities of association of only the latest set of measurements Z(k) to the various targets. The key to the JPDA algorithm is the evaluation of the conditional probabilities of the following joint association events pertaining to the current time k. First, it computes the probabilities of association of only the latest set of moving blob Z(k) to the targets to pursue multiple people simultaneously. Next, steps depict the process for calculating the association probability between multiple people.

Step 1: Construction of validation matrix

First, it defines the validation matrix for the evaluation of the conditional probabilities of the following joint association events pertaining to the current image frame, k.

$$\theta = \bigcap_{j=1}^{m_k} \theta_{jt_j} \tag{19}$$

where θ_{jt} is the moving blob, j originated from person, t, j=1,…,m_k, t=0,…,T. A joint association event, θ can be represented by the matrix;

$$\hat{\Omega}(\theta) = \left[\hat{\omega}_{jt}(\theta)\right] \tag{20}$$

consisting of the units in Ω corresponding to the association in θ, ie.,

$$\hat{\omega}_{jt}(\theta) = \begin{cases} 1 & \text{if } \theta_{jt} \subset \theta \\ 0 & otherwise \end{cases} \tag{21}$$

At this point, a moving blob can have only one source, and no more than one moving blob can originate from one person. This is a necessary condition for validation matrix. On the contrary, if an occlusion is occurred, such a condition is not satisfied.

1. Occlusion Case:

Using the recalculated moving blobs, the proposed system satisfies above condition. It employs the state transition model to handle various occlusion scenarios according to the state transition mode (occlusion mode and non-occlusion mode) within the JPDA filter. The transition of the current state that can be altered according to occlusion prediction and detection rules is just conditionally processed. The occlusion process that consists of the procedure of occlusion prediction and detection, and a splitting of coupled objects according to state transition mode, is performed.

Figure 6 shows a state transition diagram with two states. Each state is used to reflect the states of occlusion at each image frames. Under the occlusion state, a recalculating procedure of the occluded people is performed and then the tracking flow is continued. Seven transition modes are applied as follows. (1) A specific target enters into the scene. (2) Multiple targets enter into the scene. (3) A specific target is moving and forms a group with other targets, or just moves beside other targets or obstacles. (4) A specific target within the group leaves a group. (5) A specific target continues to move alone, or stops moving and then starts to move again. (6) Multiple targets in a group continue to move and interact between them, or stop interacting and then start to move again. (7) (8) A specific target or a group leaves a scene. The events of (1), (4), (5), and (7) can be tracked using general Kalman tracking. In addition, the events of (2), (3), (6) and (8) can be tracked reliably using predictive estimation method.

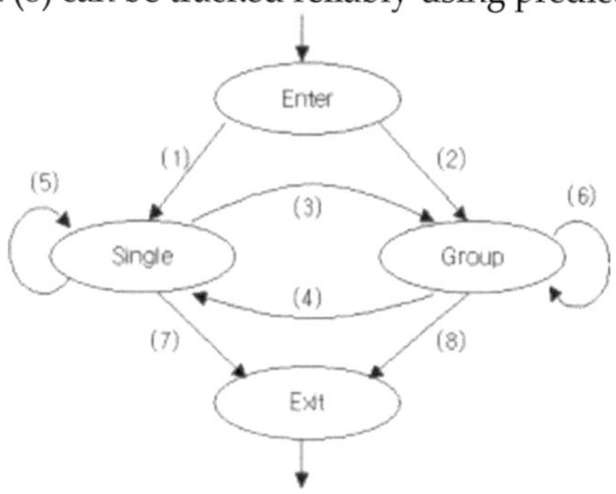

Figure 6. State transition diagram using occlusion reasoning

2. Non-Occlusion Case:

Under the non-occlusion state, a normal JPDA tracking filtering is performed.

Step 2: Compute Joint Association Probability

The purpose at this step is to compute the marginal association probability, β_{jt} that is the probability to be associated between j-th moving blob and person t at current frame k using image sequences. Then, in order to estimate the state and for the purpose of deriving the joint probabilities, it defines the person detection indicator $\delta_t(\theta)$, the moving blob association indicator $\tau_j(\theta)$ and the number of false alarm blobs $\phi(\theta)$ as in Equation (4-22), (4-23), and (4-24).

$$\delta_t(\theta) \equiv \sum_{j=1}^{m_k} \hat{\omega}_{jt}(\theta) \le 1, \qquad t = 1,\ldots,T \tag{22}$$

$$\tau_j(\theta) \equiv \sum_{t=1}^{T} \hat{\omega}_{jt}(\theta), \qquad j = 1,\ldots,m_k \tag{23}$$

$$\phi(\theta) = \sum_{j=1}^{m_k} [1 - \tau_j(\theta)] \tag{24}$$

1. Conditional Probability:

The conditional probability of the joint association event, $\theta(k)$ given the set Z^k of validated moving blobs at current image frame k using Bayes' rule is as follows:

$$\begin{aligned} P\{\theta(k)/Z^k\} &= P\{\theta(k)/Z(k), Z^{k-1}\} \\ &= \frac{1}{c} p[Z(k)/\theta(k), Z^{k-1}] P\{\theta(k)/Z^{k-1}\} \\ &= \frac{1}{c} p[Z(k)/\theta(k), Z^{k-1}] P\{\theta(k)\} \end{aligned} \tag{25}$$

where c is the normalization constant.

2. Likelihood Function

The PDF on the right-hand side in equation (25) is

$$p[Z(k)/\theta(k), Z^{k-1}] = \prod_{j=1}^{m_k} p[z_j(k)/\theta_{jt_j}(k), Z^{k-1}] \tag{26}$$

The conditional PDF of a moving blob given its origin is assumed to be

$$p[z_j(k)/\theta_{jt_j}(k), Z^{k-1}] = \begin{cases} N_{t_j}[z_j(k)] & \text{if } \tau_j[\theta(k)] = 1 \\ V^{-1} & \textit{otherwise} \end{cases} \tag{27}$$

where a moving blob associated with person t_j has Gaussian PDF. Moving blobs not associated with any person are assumed uniformly distributed in the field of view of volume V. Using Equation (27), the PDF (26) can be written as follows:

$$p[Z(k)/\theta(k), Z^{k-1}] = V^{-\phi(\theta)} \prod_{j=1}^{M_e} [N(\hat{x}_j; x_i, \Sigma_i)]^{\tau_j(\theta)} \tag{28}$$

3. Prior Probability:

The prior probability of a joint association event $\theta(k)$ combining equations (30) and (31) in equation (29) yields the equation (32).

$$\begin{aligned} P\{\theta(k)\} &= P\{\theta(k), \delta(\theta), \phi(\theta)\} \\ &= P\{\theta(k)/\delta(\theta), \phi(\theta)\} \cdot P\{\delta(\theta), \phi(\theta)\} \end{aligned} \tag{29}$$

Assuming each event a priori equally likely, first factor in equation (27) has

$$P\{\theta(k)/\delta(\theta), \phi(\theta)\} = \left(P^{m_k}_{m_k-\phi(\theta)}\right)^{-1} = \left(\frac{m_k!}{\phi!}\right)^{-1} = \frac{\phi!}{m_k!} \tag{30}$$

and the last factor is

$$P\{\delta(\theta),\phi(\theta)\} = \prod_{t=1}^{T} \left(P_D^t\right)^{\delta_t} \left(1 - P_D^i\right)^{1-\delta_t} \mu_F(\phi) \tag{31}$$

where P_D^t is the detection probability of person t and $\mu_F(\phi)$ is the prior PMF of the number of false moving blobs.

$$P\{\theta(k)\} = \frac{\phi(\theta)!}{\varepsilon \cdot m_k!} \prod_{t=1}^{T} \left(P_D^t\right)^{\delta_t} \left(1 - P_D^t\right)^{1-\delta_t} \tag{32}$$

The joint association probabilities with Poisson prior are

$$P\{\theta(k)/Z^k\} = \frac{\lambda^{\phi}}{c'} \prod_{j=1}^{m_k} \left[N_{t_j}\left(z_j(k)\right)\right]^{\tau_j} \prod_{t=1}^{T} \left(P_D^t\right)^{\delta_t} \left(1 - P_D^t\right)^{1-\delta_t} \tag{33}$$

where c′ is the new normalization constant and λ is the special density of false moving blobs.

4. Association Probability:

Thus the marginal association probability β_{jt} is calculated as

$$\beta_{jt} \equiv P\{\theta_{jt}/Z^k\} = \sum_{\theta} P\{\theta/Z^k\} \hat{\omega}_{jt}(\theta) \tag{34}$$

where j=1,…,m_k, t=0,…,T because a probabilistic inference can be made on the number of moving blobs in the validation region from the density of false alarms or clutter as well as on their location.

Step 3: State Estimation

Finally, the state estimation equation for each person is computed. The state is assumed to be normally Gaussian distributed according to the latest estimate and covariance matrix. The state update equation is processed as

$$\hat{x}(k/k) = \hat{x}(k/k-1) + W(k)\nu(k) \tag{35}$$

where

$$\nu(k) \equiv \sum_{i=1}^{m_k} \beta_i(k)\nu_i(k) \tag{36}$$

It is highly nonlinear due to the probabilities $\beta_i(k)$ that depend on the innovations. Unlike the standard Kalman filter, the covariance equation is independent of the moving blobs and the estimation accuracy of the error covariance

$$P(k/k) = \beta_0(k)P(k/k-1) + [1-\beta_0]P^c(k/k) + \widetilde{P}(k) \tag{37}$$

Associated with the update state estimate depends upon the data that are actually encountered. Prediction of the state and measurement to image frame k+l is done as in the standard Kalman filter. This JPDA filter extended for resolving occlusion problem in image based tracking is recursively processed. If the step 3 is finished, the step 1 is started again repeatedly in image sequences.

For experimental evaluation, obtained video files were sampled at video rate: example 1 (Figure 7, (b)) (total 640 frames, 15 frames per seconds, and its size is 240×320) and example

2 (Figure 7, (a)) (total 570 frames, 15 frames per seconds, and its size is 240×320) which is processed in a gray level image. In the initial value of the JPDA algorithm to track multi-targets in Figure 7, the process noise variance = 10 and the measurement noise variance = 25 are used. An occlusion state is maintained for 34, 24 frames respectively. We assumed that we know the size of a target to track within field of view. Assumed size of target is set with the following parameters: validation region is (100 pixel, 60~150 pixel) in example 1. In example 2, validation region is (100~120 pixel, 60~170 pixel).

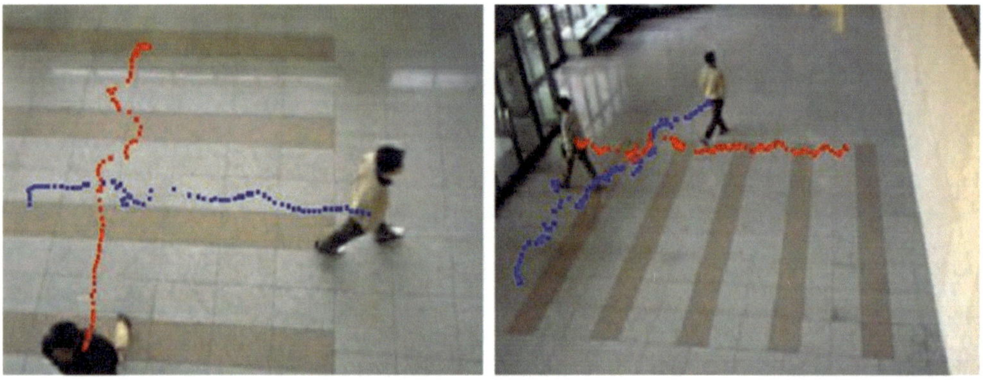

(a) Vertical and horizontal crossing case (b) Diagonal crossing case

Figure 7. Multi-target tracking result and its trajectories

Robustness has been evaluated mainly in terms of location accuracy and error rate of feature extraction and capability to track under occlusion in complex load scenes. The table 1 is an error rate that extracted blobs are not targets within field of view.

Error Rate($\mathcal{E}$)	Error rate of feature extraction		
	Method 1(H. K. Lee, et al. 2005)	Method 2(H. K. Lee, et al. 2005)	Spatio-temporal attention Scheme (H. K. Lee, et al. 2006)
Example 2	0.786	0.796	0.561
Example 1	0.424	0.341	0.336

Table 1. Simulation result of test video sequences

4. Target Classification using Decision Fusion

In this section, the decision problem is considered as binary hypothesis testing to classify the given features into human, vehicle, and animal (H. K. Lee, et al. 2006). From multivariate feature vectors, respective local decisions are made. To extract multivariate feature vectors, shape and motion information are computed using Fourier descriptor, gradients, and motion feature variation (A. J. Lipton, et al. 1998, Y. Kuno, et al. 1996) derived from equation (6) on spatial and temporal images. And then, we apply the global fusion rule based on Bayesian framework to combine local decisions ui, i=1,2,3 based on some optimization criterion for global decision u0. This method provides effective method for the combined decision of respective local feature analysis obtained from shape and motion information.

Once the foreground region is extracted, proposed system consists of three feature extraction procedures: First, Fourier descriptor and gradients representing the shape that is invariant to several change such as translation, rotation, scale, and starting point, is computed, and then classification task for local decision is performed using neural network. Second, classification task for local decision using temporal information is performed using motion information to be obtained from rigidity condition analysis of moving objects. For doing this, skeletonization of the motion region is done, and then motion analysis is done to compute motion feature variation using selected feature points (R. Cutler, et al. 2000, H. Fujiyosi, et al. 2004). Finally, we can classify moving objects through decision fusion method based on Bayesian framework using locally obtained results from shape and motion analysis (M. M. Kokar, et al. 2001, Li. X. R., et al. 2003).

Then, we derive the optimum fusion rules that minimize the average cost in a Bayesian framework (M. M. Kokar, et al. 2001, Li. X. R., et al. 2003). This rule is given by the following likelihood ratio test:

$$\frac{P(u_1,u_2,u_3/H_1)}{P(u_1,u_2,u_3/H_0)} \underset{u_0=0}{\overset{u_0=1}{\gtrless}} \frac{P_0(C_{10}-C_{00})}{P_1(C_{01}-C_{11})} \cong \eta \tag{38}$$

where Cij is the cost of global decision. The left-hand side can be rewritten as given in equation (39) because the local decisions have characteristic of independence.

$$\begin{aligned}\frac{P(u_1,u_2,u_3/H_1)}{P(u_1,u_2,u_3/H_0)} &= \prod_{i=1}^{3}\frac{P(u_i/H_1)}{P(u_i/H_0)} \\ &= \prod_{S_1}\frac{P(u_i=1/H_1)}{P(u_i=1/H_0)}\prod_{S_0}\frac{P(u_i=0/H_1)}{P(u_i=0/H_0)}\end{aligned} \tag{39}$$

where Sj is the set of all those local decisions that are equal to j, j=0,1. In addition, equation (39) can be rewritten in terms of the probabilities of false alarm and miss in detector i. That is why each input to the fusion center is a binary random variable characterized by the associated probabilities of false alarm and miss.

$$\prod_{S_1}\frac{P(u_i=1/H_1)}{P(u_i=1/H_0)}\prod_{S_0}\frac{P(u_i=0/H_1)}{P(u_i=0/H_0)} = \prod_{s_1}\frac{1-P_{M_i}}{P_{F_i}}\prod_{s_0}\frac{P_{M_i}}{1-P_{F_i}} \tag{40}$$

where PFi=P(ui=1/H0) and PMi=P(ui=0/H1). We substitute equation (40) in equation (38) and take the logarithm of both sides as follows:

$$\sum_{s_1}\log\frac{1-P_{M_i}}{P_{F_i}} + \sum_{s_0}\log\frac{P_{M_i}}{1-P_{F_i}} \underset{u_0=0}{\overset{u_0=1}{\gtrless}} \log\left(\frac{P_0(C_{10}-C_{00})}{P_1(C_{01}-C_{11})}\right) \cong \log\eta \tag{41}$$

The equation (41) can be expressed as shown in equations (42) and (43).

$$\sum_{i=1}^{3}\left[u_i\log\frac{1-P_{M_i}}{P_{F_i}} + (1-u_i)\log\frac{P_{M_i}}{1-P_{F_i}}\right] \underset{u_0=0}{\overset{u_0=1}{\gtrless}} \log\eta \tag{42}$$

$$\sum_{i=1}^{3}\left[\log\frac{(1-P_{M_i})(1-P_{F_i})}{P_{M_i}P_{F_i}}\right]u_i \underset{u_0=0}{\overset{u_0=1}{\gtrless}} \log\left[\eta\prod_{i=1}^{3}\left(\frac{1-P_{F_i}}{P_{M_i}}\right)\right] \tag{43}$$

Thus, the optimum fusion rule is applied by forming a weighted sum of the incoming local decisions, and then comparing it with a threshold. At this time, the threshold depends on the prior probabilities and the costs.
For experimental evaluation, training images are obtained in real image sequences. Each class includes three kinds of image view having front, side, and inclined image. Each kinds of image are composed of total 1200 files respectively for training, which is extracted from respective image sequences. Test images were also obtained from image sequences (image size is 480×320) about three targets (human, car, and animal): human (total 400 frames), car (total 400 frames), and animal (total 400 frames) which is a gray level image.

Figure 8. Object detection and classification

Figure 8 shows the detection and classification result of moving objects. To show the robustness of proposed method, we evaluated the proposed method which is compared to other methods such as neural net, and some fusion methods (Y. Bar-Shalom, et al. 1995, Samuel Blackman, et al. 1999, R. R. Brooks, et al. 1998). Majority voting and weighted average score method are fusion methods that are compared to the proposed fusion method. Table 2 shows the experimental results of three methods respectively with respect to the FAR(False Acceptance Rate) and the FRR(False Rejection Rate). Local decision method using neural network showed the lowest classification rate. Each local decision did not show satisfactory results. Thus, some fusion methods are secondly compared using respective local decisions. From the results, majority voting and weight average score methods showed low performance compared to the proposed method considering spatio-temporal information. Thus, we can know that the simple fusion method of final decision does not bring the good performance. In addition, we can know that the fusion method of redundant and complementary information is good choice in feature level and decision level fusion.

Method	FRR(%)	FAR(%)	Recognition Rate(%)
Neural Net	4.0	3.0	96
Majority Voting	2.7	2.5	97.3
Weight Average Score	2.5	2.0	97.5
Decision fusion	1.5	1.3	98.5

Table 2. Experimental evaluations compared to some methods

5. Discussions and Concluding Remarks

The objects are identified consciously within the attentional aperture from human visual system. The particular region of interest rendering motion sensation is focused, and then the complex analysis can be applied. By using this concept, both temporal attention and spatial attention can be considered because temporal attention provides the predictable motion model, and spatial attention provides the detailed local feature analysis. From this fact, the spatio-temporal mechanism is derived in order to detect and track multiple objects in consecutive video frame sequences. This mechanism provided an efficient method for more complex analysis using data association in spatially attentive window and predicted temporal location.

The challenging issue is when multiple objects are moving or occluded between them in areas of visual field. At this time, a simultaneous detection and tracking of multiple objects tend to fail. This is due to the fact that incompletely estimated feature vectors such as location, color, velocity, and acceleration of a target provide ambiguous and missing information. In addition, partial information cannot render the complete information unless temporal consistency is considered when objects are occluded between them or they are hidden in obstacles. Thus, the spatially and temporally considered mechanism using occlusion activity detection and object association with partial probability model should be considered.

Besides, multi-target tracking task has lots of challenging issues under complex situations such as environmental weather conditions; snow, rain, fog, night, and so on. Thus, preprocessing stage is also seriously considered before moving blob detection process. Accurate moving blob detection would derive a high performance of target tracking and recognition. Thus, preprocessing techniques under natural environments would be studied using sensor fusion scheme such as CCDs and IR sensors.

6. References

Y.L.Tian and A.Hampapur, (2005). Robust Salient Motion Detection with Complex Background for Real-time Video Surveillance, in *Proc. Of IEEE Computer Society Workshop on Motion and Video Computing,* January.

C.Stauffer and W.E.L.Grimson, (1999). Adaptive background mixture models for real tracking. *Int. Conf. Computer Vision and Pattern Recognition,* Vol.2, pp.246-252.

A.Elgammal, R.Duraiswami, D.Harwood and L.Davis, (2002). Background and Foreground Modeling Using Nonparametric Kernel Density Estimation for Visual Surveillance, *Proceeding of the IEEE,* Vol.90, No.7, July.

K. Kim, T. H. Chalidabhongse, D. Harwood and L. Davis, (2004). Background Modeling and Subtraction by Codebook Construction, *IEEE International Conference on Image Processing (ICIP).*

Huwer, S.and Niemann, H., (2000). Adaptive change detection for real-time surveillance applications, Visual Surveillance, *IEEE International Workshop* on, pp 37 -46, July.

S.S. Beauchemin and J.L.Barron, (1995). The Computation of Optical flow, *ACM Computing Surveys,* Vol.27, pp.433 - 466.

M. J. Swain and D. H. Ballard, (1991). Colour indexing, *International journal of Computer Vision,* 7(1):11-32.

Rasmussen, C, Hager, G.D, (1998). Joint probabilistic techniques for tracking multi-part objects, Computer Vision and Pattern Recognition, *Proceedings. IEEE Computer Society Conference* on, pp 16 -21, June.

H. K. Lee, June Kim, and Hanseok Ko (2006). Prediction Based Occluded Multi-Target Tracking Using Spatio-Temporal Attention, *International Journal of Pattern Recognition and Artificial Intelligence (IJPRAI) Special Issue on Brain, Vision, and Artificial Intelligence*, Vol.20, No. 6, pp.1-14, World Scientific Press, Sept..

Y. Bar-Shalom and X. R. Li, (1995). Multitarget-multisensor tracking: principles and techniques, YBS Press.

Kollnig, Nagel, Otte, (1994). Association of Motion Verbs with Vehicle Movements Extracted from Dense Optical Flow Fields, *proc. of ECCV94*, pp. 338-350.

Tomasi, C. and Kanade, T., Detection and tracking of point features, *Tech. Rept.* CMUCS-91132, Pittsburgh:Carnegie Mellon University, School of Computer Science.

Samuel Blackman, Robert Popoli, (1999). Design and Analysis of Modern Tracking Systems, *Artech House*.

M. M. Kokar, and J. A. Tomasik, (2001). Data vs. decision fusion in the category theory framework, *Proc. 2nd Int. Conf. on Information Fusion*.

Li. X. R., Zhu, Y., Wang, J., Han, C., (2003). Optimal linear estimation fusion-Part I: Unified fusion rules, *IEEE Trans. Information Theory*. Vol. 49, No. 9, Sep.

A. J. Lipton, H. Fujiyosi, and R. S. Patil, (1998). Moving target classification and tracking from real-time video, *Proc of IEEE Workshop. on Applications of Computer Vision*, pp.8~14, 1998.

Y. Kuno, T. Watanabe, Y. Shimosakoda and S. Nakagawa, (1996). Automated detection of human for visual surveillance system. *Proc. of Int. Conf. on Pattern Recognition*, pp.865~869.

R. Cutler and L. S. Davis, (2000). Robust real-time periodic motion detection, analysis, and applications, *IEEE Trans. Pattern Anal. Machine Intell.*, Vol.22 pp.781~796, Aug.

H. Fujiyosi and J. A. Tomasik, (2004). Real-time human motion analysis by image skeletonization, *IEICE Trans, on Info & Systems*, Vol. E87-D, No. 1, Jan.

M. M. Kokar, and J. A. Tomasik, (2001). Data vs. decision fusion in the category theory framework, *Proc. 2nd Int. Conf. on Information Fusion*.

Li. X. R., Zhu, Y., Wang, J., Han, C., (2003). Optimal linear estimation fusion-Part I: Unified fusion rules, *IEEE Trans. Information Theory*. Vol. 49, No. 9, Sep.

R. R. Brooks and S. S. Iyengar, (1998). Multi-Sensor Fusion: Fundamentals and Applications with software, Prentice Hall.

H. K. Lee, and Hanseok Ko, (2005). Occlusion Activity Detection Algorithm Using Kalman Filter for Detecting Occluded Multiple Objects, *Computational Science*, pp.139-146, LNCS 3514, Springer, May. 2005.

H. K. Lee, and Hanseok Ko, (2005). Spatio-Temporal Attention Mechanism For More Complex Analysis To Track Multiple Objects, *Brain, Vision and Artificial Intelligence*, pp.447-456, LNCS 3704, Springer, October.

H. K. Lee, Jungho Kim, and June Kim, (2006). Decision Fusion of Shape and Motion Information Based on Bayesian Framework for Moving Object Classification in Image Sequences, *Foundations of Intelligent Systems, LNAI 4203*, pp.19-28, Springer, Sept.

7

Consideration of various Noise Types and Illumination Effects for 3D shape recovery

Aamir Saeed Malik and Tae-Sun Choi
Gwangju Institute of Science and Technology
Republic of Korea

1. Introduction

There are a variety of 3D Shape estimation methods. Broadly these methods can be classified into three types, namely, Contact, Transmissive and Reflective methods. The "Contact" method is generally based on some physical contact to acquire data while the "Transmissive" method is based on sending waves (like electromagnetic radiations, sound waves etc) through a body and recording data because of the interaction of wave particles with the object under consideration. The reflective model acquires data based on reflection of wave particles. The reflective method is broadly divided into optical and non-optical techniques.

The optical methods under the reflective model can further be divided into "Passive" and "Active" Techniques. In active techniques, we are projecting light rays while in passive techniques; we simply capture the reflection of light rays without any projections. The passive methods can further be classified as Shape From X (Stereo, Motion, Shading, Focus etc). This chapter deals with Shape From Focus (SFF) which is a passive optical method. The objective of shape from focus is to find out the depth of every point of the object from the camera lens. Hence, we obtain a depth map which contains the depth of all points of the object from the camera lens where they are best focused.

The aim of this chapter is to study the various factors (for example, different types of noise, illumination, window size) that affect SFF. It is shown that the illumination effects can directly result in incorrect estimation of depth map if proper window size is not selected during the computation of focus measure. The large window size results in blurring the image which gives the wrong impression of smoothness of the depth map. So it is important to find the optimum window size for accurate depth map estimation. Further, it is shown that the images need some kind of pre-processing to enhance the dark regions and shadows in the image.

Additionally, a robust focus measure is also discussed in this chapter. This focus measure has shown robustness in the presence of noise as compared to the earlier focus measures. This new focus measure is based on an optical transfer function implemented in the Fourier domain. The focus measure is tested at various levels of noise, i.e., low, medium and high noise levels. The results of this focus measure have shown drastic improvement in estimation of depth map, with respect to the earlier focus measures, in the presence of various types of noise including Gaussian, Shot and Speckle noise.

2. Shape From Focus (SFF)

The basic problem of imaging systems, such as the eye or a video-camera, is that depth information is lost while projecting a 3D scene onto 2D image plane. Therefore, one of the fundamental problem in computer vision is the reconstruction of a geometric object from one or several observations. Various image processing techniques retrieve the lost cue and shape information from the pictorial information. Shape from focus (Krotkov, 1987) is one of such image processing techniques that are used to recover 3D information.
The basic image formation geometry is shown in Figure 1. In the figure, the parameters related to the camera are already known. We need to calculate 'u', i.e., depth of object from the lens. We make a depth map by calculating 'u' for every pixel. We can use the lens formula to calculate 'u'. If the image detector (ID) is placed exactly at a distance v, sharp image P' of the point P is formed. Then the relationship between the object distance u, focal distance of the lens f, and the image distance v is given by the Gaussian lens law:

$$\frac{1}{f} = \frac{1}{u} + \frac{1}{v} \tag{1}$$

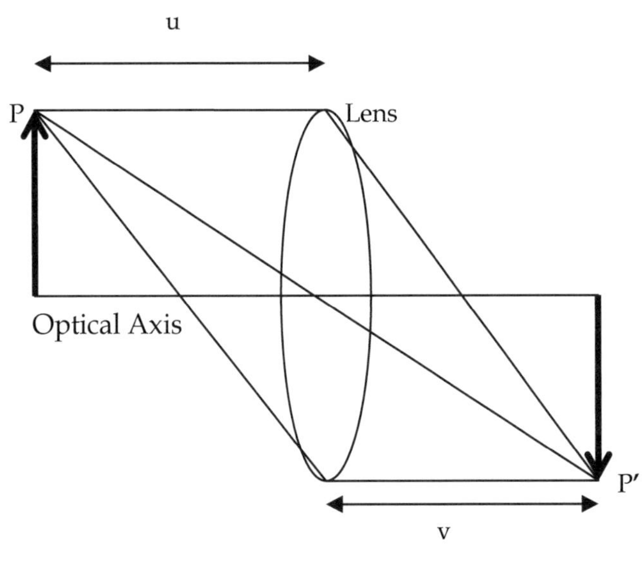

Figure 1. Image Formation of a 3D Object

Therefore, in SFF, a sequence of images that correspond to different levels of object focus is obtained. A sharp image and the relative depth can be retrieved by collecting the best focused points in each image. The absolute depth of object surface patches can be calculated from the focal length and the position of lens that give the sharpest image of the surface patches. The depth or best focus is thus obtained by using some focus measure.
One factor is to be kept in mind that we have finite number of images in the image sequence. The information obtained from them does not represent actual object specification especially in the case of geometrically complex objects. The only way for obtaining accurate results from SFF techniques is estimating object specifications in the gap between images in

the image sequence. Hence, the role of approximation techniques is very important after getting the initial result from focus measure.

The objective of shape from focus is to find out the depth of every point of the object from the camera lens. Hence, finally we get a depth map which contains the depth of all points of the object from the camera lens where they are best focused or in other words, where they show maximum sharpness. Therefore, in SFF, a sequence of images that correspond to different levels of object focus is obtained.

To measure the true focussed point requires large number of images with incremental distance moved towards focus plane. To detect the true focussed point from finite number of images, various focus measures have been proposed by researchers. A focus measure is a quantity which measures the degree of blurring of an image; its value is a maximum when the image is best focused and decreases as blurring increases. Figure 2 shows a focus measure curve for a point in the image.

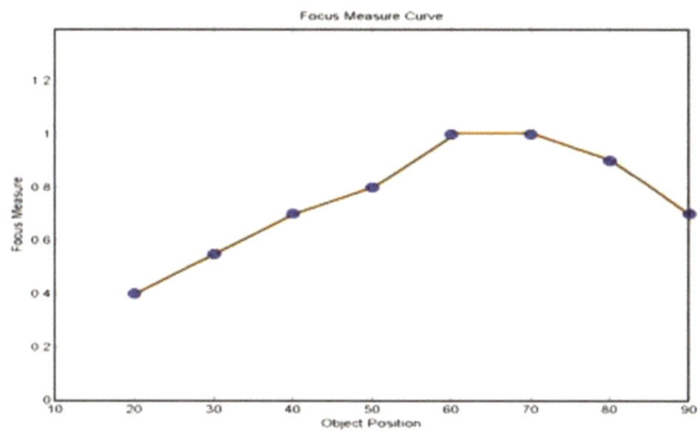

Figure 2. Focus Measure Curve for a point

3. Related Work

3.1 Focus Measure

A Focus Measure operator is one that calculates the best focused point in the image, i.e., focus measure is defined as a quantity to evaluate the sharpness of a pixel locally. The value of the focus measure increases as the image sharpness increases and attains the maximum for the best focused image. (Helmli & Scherer, 2001) summarized the traditional focus measures while introducing new focus measure operators. Existing focus measure operators are given in brief below:

Sum of Modified Laplacian (SML): If the image has rich textures with high variability at each pixel, focus measure can be calculated considering single pixel. In order to improve robustness for weak-texture images, (Nayar & Nakagawa, 1994) presented focus measure at (x,y) as Sum of Modified Laplacian values in a local window (about 5x5) around (x,y).

$$SML(x_0, y_0) = \sum_{p(x,y)\in U(x_0,y_0)} \left(\frac{\partial^2 g(x,y)}{\partial^2 x}\right)^2 + \left(\frac{\partial^2 g(x,y)}{\partial^2 y}\right)^2 \quad (2)$$

Tenenbaum Focus Measure (FM_T): It is gradient magnitude maximization method that measures the sum of squared responses of horizontal and vertical Sobel masks. For robustness, it is also summed in a local window.

$$FM_T(x_0, y_0) = \sum_{p(x,y)\in U(x_0,y_0)} \left(G_x(x,y)^2 + G_y(x,y)^2\right)^2 \tag{3}$$

Gray Level Variance (GLV) Focus Measure: In case of a sharp image, the variance of gray-level is higher than that in a blur image.

$$GLV(x_0, y_0) = \frac{1}{N-1} \sum_{p(x,y)\in U(x_0,y_0)} \left(g(x,y) - \mu_{U(x_0,y_0)}\right)^2 \tag{4}$$

With $\mu_{U(x_0,y_0)}$ the mean of the gray values in the neighborhood $U(x_0,y_0)$

Mean Method Focus Measure (FM_M): The ratio of mean grey value to the center grey value in the neighborhood can also be used as a focus measure. The ratio of one shows a constant grey-level or absence of texture. The ratio is different in case of high variations. It is also summed in a local window. Let FM' is the ratio of mean grey value to the center grey value:

$$FM_M(x_0, y_0) = \sum_{p(x,y)\in U(x_0,y_0)} FM'(x,y) \tag{5}$$

Curvature Focus Measure (FM_C): The curvature in a sharp image is expected to be higher than that in a blur image. First, the surface is approximated using a quadratic equation $f(x,y) = ax + by + cx^2 + dy^2$. The coefficients (a, b, c, d) are calculated using a least squares approximation technique. Then these coefficients are combined to obtain a focus measure.

$$FM_c(x,y) = |a| + |b| + |c| + |d| \tag{6}$$

M_2 Focus Measure: Various focus measures were proposed by (Subbarao et al., 1993). The focus measures proposed were based on image grey level variance (M_1), energy of image gradient (M_2) and energy of image Laplacian (M_3). These focus measures are similar to those described above, i.e., M_1 is similar to Gray Level Variance (GLV) Focus Measure, M_2 is similar to Tenenbaum Focus Measure, and M_3 is similar to Laplacian focus measure. M_2 is computed as:

$$M_2 = \sum_{x=i-N}^{i+N} \sum_{y=j-N}^{j+N} (g_x^2 + g_y^2) \tag{7}$$

where: $g_x(x,y) = g_i(x+1,y) - g_i(x,y)$ & $g_y(x,y) = g_i(x,y+1) - g_i(x,y)$

3.2 Approximation Methods

The discrete number of frames results in some loss of information in between frames. As a result, the optimum value for some pixels may never be calculated. Hence to address this issue among others, approximation techniques can be applied to the results of the focus measures to construct a more accurate depth range image. (Malik & Choi, 2007) summarized

various approximation techniques. They found that in Traditional (TR) SFF, for each image in the sequence the Focus Measure at each pixel can be computed by the Sum Modified Laplacian in the 2D neighborhood around the pixel. Thus, for each pixel, the image frame with the maximum Focus Measure is determined. The camera parameters for this image frame are then used to compute the distance of the object point corresponding to that pixel.
It should be noted that these traditional methods do not consider the fact that an image of 3D object is also three dimensional in image space. Therefore, (Subbarao & Choi, 1995) proposed a new concept they refer to as Focused Image Surface (FIS) applied on SML, which is based on planar surface approximations. The FIS of an object is defined as the surface formed by the set of points at which the object points are focused by a camera lens, after first obtaining an estimate of FIS using a traditional SFF method. This estimate is then refined by searching for a planar surface that maximizes the Focus Measure computed over pixels on FIS. (Choi et al., 1999) proposed the approximation of FIS by a piecewise curved surface rather than through the use of a piecewise planar approximation, where the piecewise curved surface is estimated by interpolation using a second order Lagrange polynomial.
(Asif & Choi, 2001) used Neural Networks on GLV result to learn the shape of FIS by optimizing the Focus Measure over small 3D windows, as due to their nonlinear characteristics, neural networks can be used to approximate any arbitrary function. (Bilal & Choi, 2005) proposed the use of Dynamic Programming (DP) on SML result for handling the computational complexity of FIS. Based on DP definition, a large problem can be split into a series of smaller problems. Thus, unlike the FIS approach, DP can search for the optimal Focus Measure in the whole image volume rather than being limited to a small neighborhood. However, the direct application of DP on 3D data is impractical due to its computational complexity; consequently, they proposed a heuristic model based on DP.

4. Illumination and Window Size

In this section, the main emphasis is on the illumination problems and the corresponding window size affecting the images. The reason for selection of this factor, i.e., illumination, is that almost all the images are affected by illumination. Proper illumination is only possible in well controlled lab conditions. But in real time imaging, it's not possible. Hence, the images have regions with diverse illuminations. However, the regions with low illumination are the ones that require special attention while estimating the depth maps because such regions result in the selection of incorrect focused points for the depth map.
The previous work regarding estimation of depth map using SFF has been discussed in section 3. Here, only the effect of the window sizes are discussed with respect to those methods. In the literature, the trend is to use large window size, e.g., window size of 11x11 has been used commonly to compute various focus measures including Tenenbaum, Gray Level Variance (GLV), Mean Method, Curvature and Point focus measures. (Ahmad & Choi, 2005) mentioned using 15x15 window size for computation of TR SFF. (Subbarao & Choi, 1995) used energy of Laplacian as the focus measure and used window of size 15x15 to compute the focus measure to implement the Focused Image Surface method. For initial estimate, (Choi et al., 1999) used Sum of Modified Laplacian as the focus measure for curved window technique and used window of size 15x15. (Asif & Choi, 2001) used Gray Level Variance (GLV) as the focus measure for their Neural Network based method with window of size 7x7. (Ahmad & Choi, 2005) used Sum of Modified Laplacian as the focus measure for the dynamic programming based method and used window of size 7x7.

Here, we show the results with one of the focus measure, i.e., Gray Level Variance (GLV). We acquired a sequence of 97 real cone images, each at different focus value. Figure 3 shows three fames of the real cone. It is evident from the images that maximum illumination occurs at the upper side of the images hence, the upper part or one side of the cone is quite bright. Then as we move down the image vertically, the illumination decreases but still the sides of the cones are well illuminated. Finally at the bottom of the image, i.e., the region of the image right below the tip of the cone extending till end of the cone is quite dark. Hence three distinct regions of illumination can easily be identified from these images.
Figure 4 shows the images when the GLV focus measure is applied to various frames of the real cone images. The images shown in first column are computed using the window size of 3x3, the ones in second column are computed using window size of 5x5 and window size of 7x7 is used for those in third column. It can be seen from the figure that the parts below the tip of the cone are not well focused because of poor illumination. However, with the increase in the window size, the number of pixels being extracted increase in the low illumination region.
From figure 4, it is clear that the blurring effect is more pronounced in the 3rd column (7x7 window size) as compared to first column (3x3 window size). The number of pixels extracted has increased in the 3rd column because of consideration of more neighborhood pixels with dissimilar values. This clearly indicates that the dependence on sharpness of the pixel value itself has decreased while the dependence on the values of the neighborhood pixels has increased. So, the larger the window size, the more is probability of taking into account higher pixel values of the neighbouring pixels lying far from the pixel in consideration. Hence, the result will be incorrect selection of frame numbers (that may not correspond to the best focus point) during computation of the depth map. We emphasize on this fact because people have used large window size like 7x7, 11x11 and 15x15 etc in the literature as discussed earlier. Although, we can show more results with other focus measures too but the above mentioned two points continue to hold.

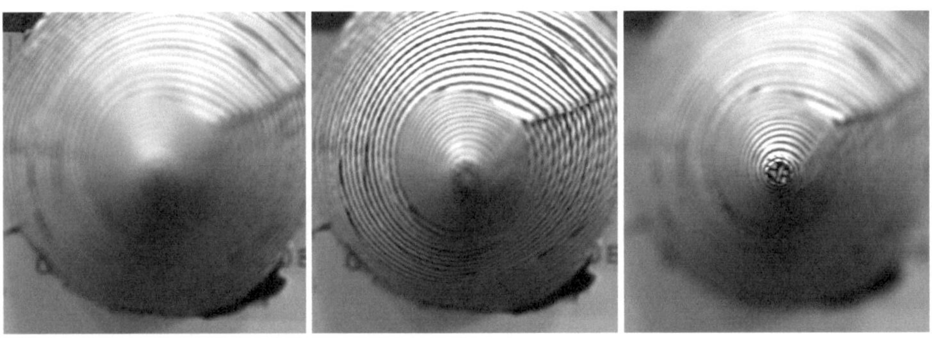

Figure 3. Various frames of real cone at different focus values

Now consider figure 5. We present the results of depth map from Sum of Modified Laplacian using window size of 7x7, 9x9 and 11x11. This figure clearly shows the effects of increasing the size of windows. As the size of the window increase, the result is smoothing and hence we get much smoother depth maps compared to those that are obtained by using smaller window size. This smoothing is because of the blurring effect that is introduced due to large window size. The larger window size takes into account more pixel values which might be quite different from the pixel in consideration. Hence, as the number of neighboring pixels increases, the worth of local intensity variation reduces.

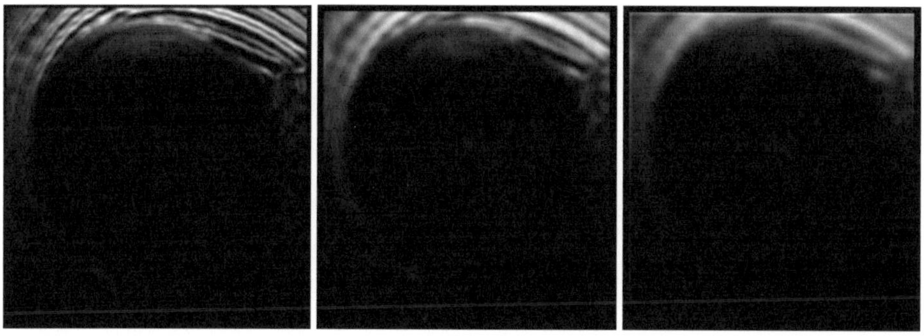

(a) Frame 50

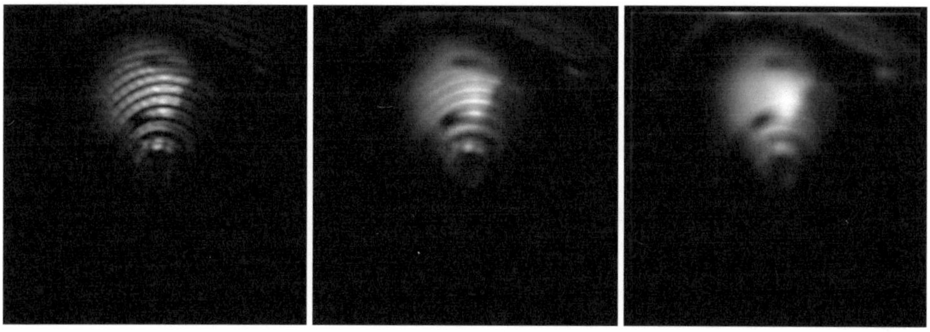

(b) Frame 75

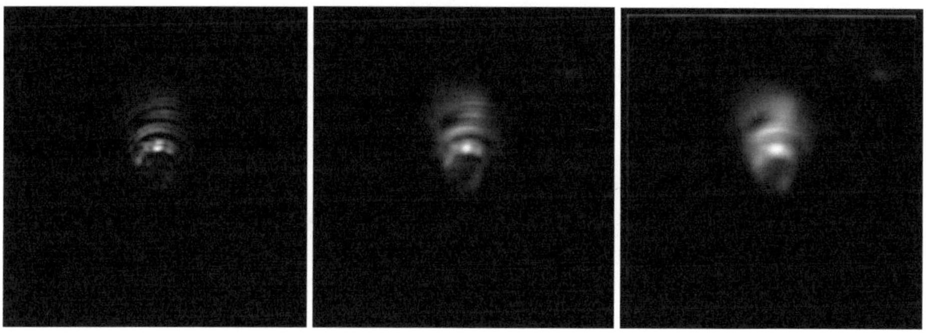

(c) Frame 90

Figure 4. Gray Level Variance operation performed with different window sizes

Also, it can be seen from the images that as the size of the window increases, the number of pixels extracted also increase. Again this is because more neighborhood pixels are taken into account. Those neighborhood pixels might lie in well illuminated region compared to the pixel in consideration that was not extracted earlier. Hence, this results in incorrect estimation of depth map because the dependence is now on the values of the neighbors that lie in or near the high or adequate illuminated region.

So, from all this discussion, we safely conclude that if some parts of the object in an image lie in the region of low illumination then that part of the object cannot be extracted by directly applying the edge extraction methods or techniques that find the sharp points in the images. In such cases, the images need to be pre-processed so that low illumination regions can be enhanced. Further, the larger the window size, the more is probability of taking into account higher pixel values of the neighbouring pixels lying far from the pixel in consideration. Hence, the depth map will contain incorrect frame numbers pointing to the wrong pixel values. So, a smaller window size should be used for computation of focus measures. Window size of 3x3 is adequate for such computations. However, the upper bound or the upper limit on window size should be 5x5. Any selection of window size greater than 5x5 will introduce errors in the depth map estimation (Malik & Choi, 2007).

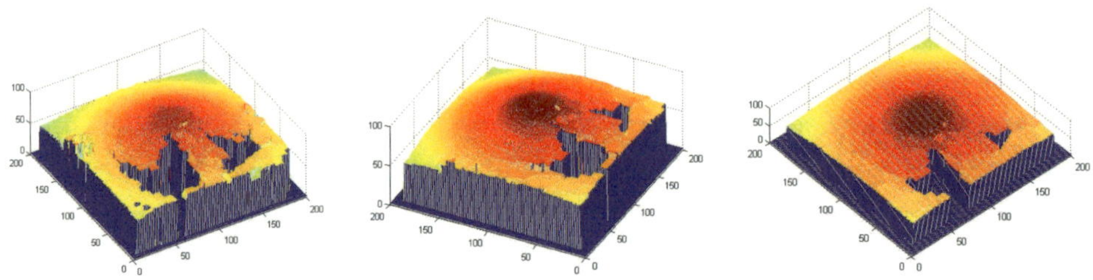

(a) 7x7 (b) 9x9 (c) 11x11

Figure 5. Depth Maps computed from Sum of Modified Laplacian using various window sizes

5. Noise Impact on SFF

As discussed earlier in section 3, there are various focus measures available to estimate the depth map. Three of them are based on second derivative. They are namely Laplacian, Modified Laplacian and Sum of Modified Laplacian. But the problem with second derivative is that it is extremely sensitive to noise. Hence, the result is degraded drastically if there is noise in the image. Another focus measure, Tenenbaum Focus Measure, is based on single derivative technique which again is sensitive to noise although its less sensitive compared to double derivative techniques. Same problem is observed with focus measures incorporating mean and gray level variance values. The pixels, with noise addition, are enhanced and hence taken as sharp focused points when variance values are taken into account. In an extension of variance of gray level method, another method is mean method focus measure. But this technique also suffers from the same problem like gray level variance method.

In this section, three different types of noise are considered, i.e., Gaussian, Speckle and Shot noise. Gaussian noise is used to model the thermal noise which is due to the additional electrons generated within the CCD by physical processes within the CCD itself. Shot noise is found in situations where quick transients, such as faulty switching, take place during imaging. Speckle noise is a physical effect, which occurs when coherent light is reflected from an optically rough surface. Two objects, simulated cone and the real cone, are used and their depth maps are estimated in the presence of these noise types. Now consider figure 6(a). One of the frames of the original cone image is shown without noise. Figure 6(b) shows the same frame when Gaussian noise (mean=0, variance=0.005) is added. Figure 6(c) shows the result of Laplacian operator and it is quite clear that the Laplacian processed result has been degraded significantly.

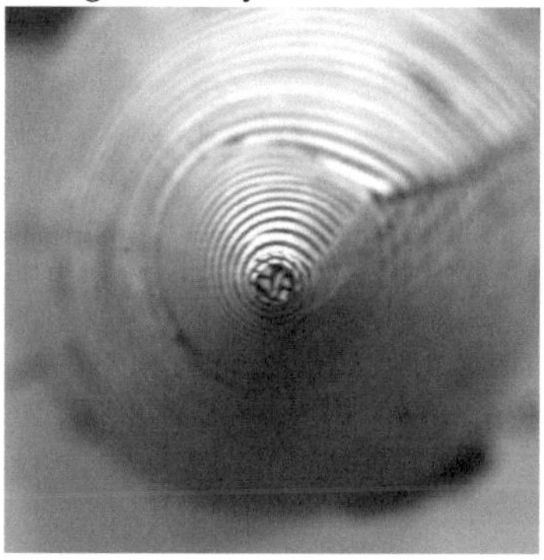

(a) Original

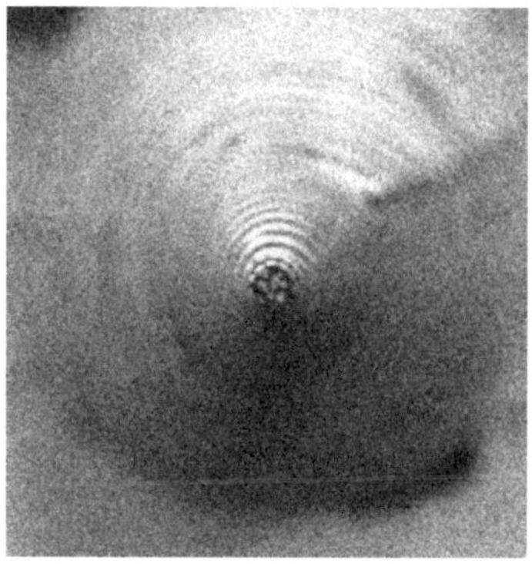

(b) With Gaussian Noise

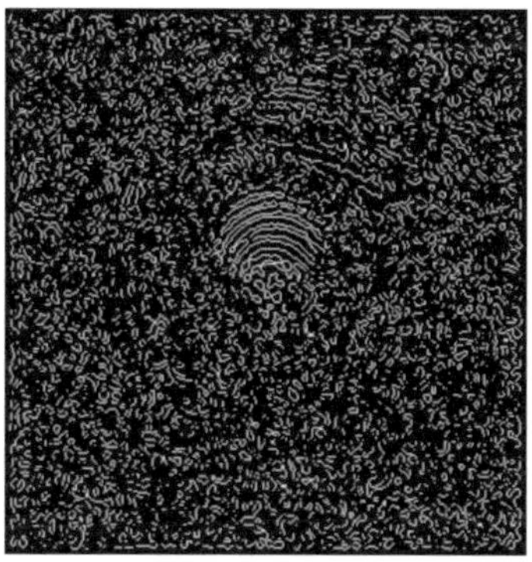

(c) Laplacian

Figure 6. Effect of adding Gaussian noise

Figure 7 shows the depth maps obtained using SML focus measure for simulated cone images. The depth map on the left hand side shows the depth map obtained when no noise is added to the images. The depth map on the right hand side shows the depth map when Gaussian noise (mean=0, variance=0.005) is added to the images. It is evident from these depth maps that the results degrade significantly in the presence of noise.

Figure 8 shows the depth maps obtained using SML focus measure for real cone images. However, this time shot noise is added in figure 8(b) and speckle noise in figure 8(c). It is again evident from these depth maps that the results degrade significantly in the presence of shot and speckle noise. The noise has enhanced the individual pixel values and hence resulted in spikes all over the depth map. With this result, it is not possible to further refine it using some approximation method as discussed in section 3. We have analyzed various focus measures and found that all of the focus measures are effected when noise is present in the images.

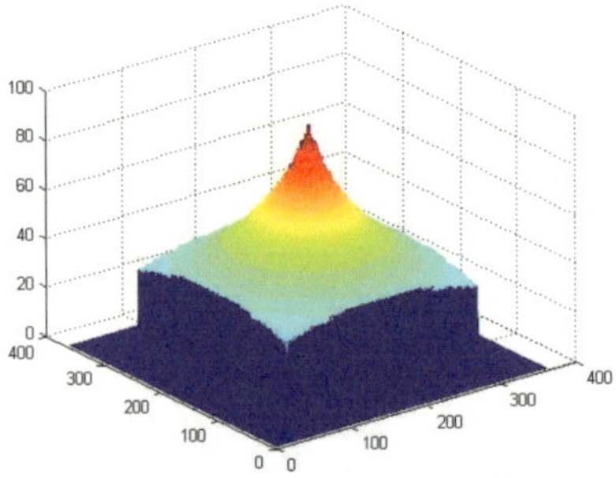

(a) No Noise

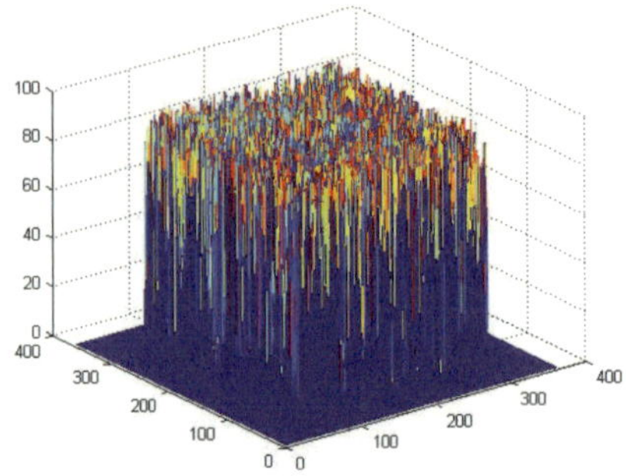

(b) Gaussian Noise

Figure 7. Depth maps using SML for simulated cone images

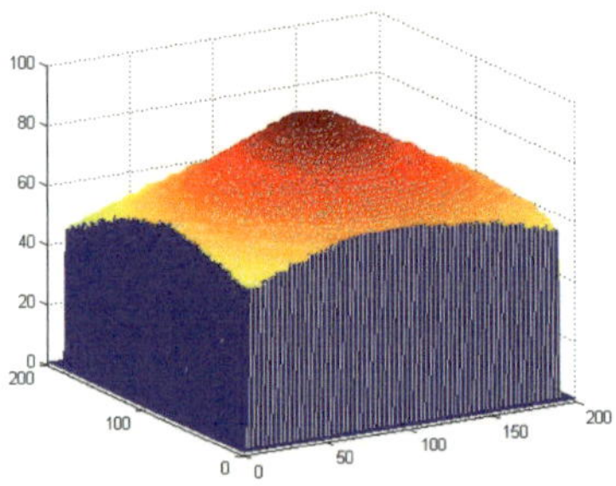

(a) No Noise

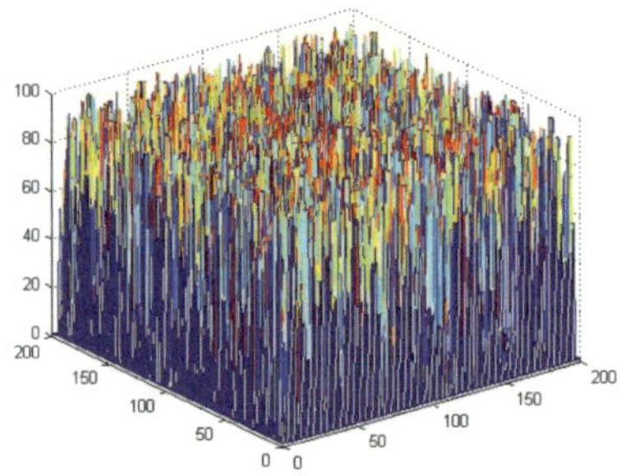

(b) Shot Noise

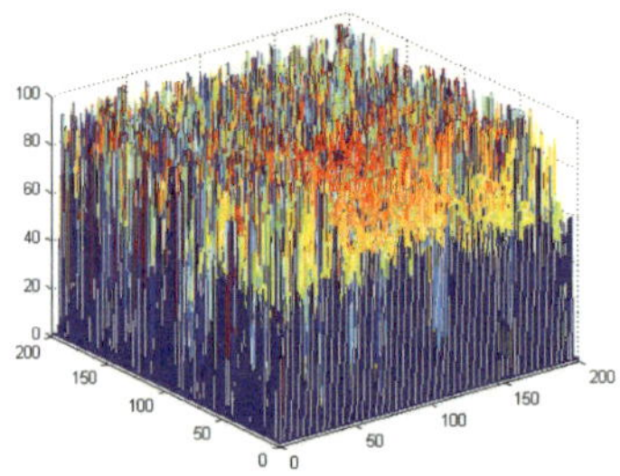

(c) Speckle Noise

Figure 8. Depth maps using SML for real cone images (Shot and Speckle Noise)

6. Robust Focus Measure

Based on the results shown in section 5, a robust focus measure is required that can perform well even in the presence of noise. In this section, a robust focus measure is presented for estimation of depth map. That depth map can further be used in techniques and algorithms leading to recovery of three dimensional structure of the object which is required in many high level vision applications. The focus measure presented here has shown robustness in the presence of noise as compared to the earlier focus measures. This new focus measure is based on an optical transfer function implemented in the Fourier domain. The results of the proposed focus measure have shown drastic improvement in estimation of depth map, with respect to the earlier focus measures, in the presence of various types of noise including Gaussian, Shot and Speckle noise. The focus measure is based on bipolar incoherent image processing and we call it Optical Focus Measure and denote it as FM_O. (Poon and Banerjee, 2001) has discussed bipolar incoherent image processing in detail. Let g(x,y) be input image frames, F & F^{-1} be Fourier and inverse Fourier transform, k_x and k_y be spatial frequencies, σ_1 and σ_2 be filtering parameters, then mathematically, this focus measure is represented as:

$$FM_O\,(i,j) = \sum_{x=i-N}^{i+N} \sum_{y=j-N}^{j+N} \text{Real}\left[F^{-1}\left\{S(k_x,k_y)H(k_x,k_y)\right\}\right] \tag{8}$$

where: $S(k_x,k_y) = F\left|g(x,y)\right|^2$, $H(k_x,k_y) = \exp\{-\sigma_1(k_x^2+k_y^2)\} - \exp\{-\sigma_2(k_x^2+k_y^2)\}$

Hence, this focus measure becomes a filtering operation that provides the sharpness at pixel points in an image. The filtering operation depends upon σ_1 and σ_2. These values are adjusted to provide sharp focus measure even in the presence of noise. The operator responds to the high and medium frequency variations in the image intensity. The high and the medium frequency component of an image area is determined by processing in the Fourier domain and analyzing the frequency distribution. The processing in the frequency domain is particularly useful for noise reduction as the noise frequencies are easily filtered out. Figure 9 shows the filter with σ_1= 0.01 and σ_2= 0.1.

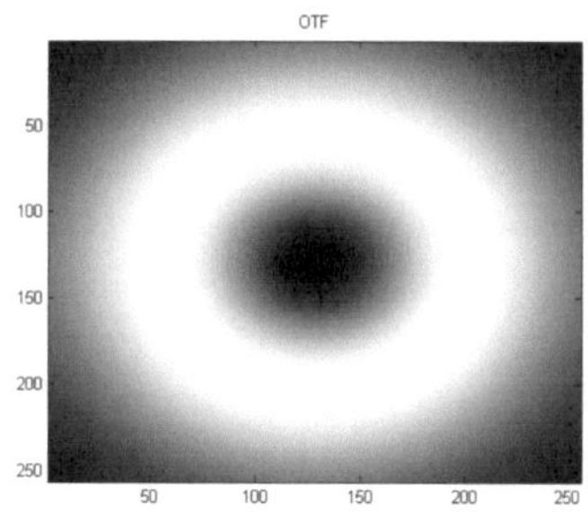

Figure 9. Filter designed with σ_1= 0.01 and σ_2= 0.1

This focus measure is applied on a sequence of 97 simulated cone images, 97 real cone images and 87 slanted planar object images. The resolution of the images is 360x360 pixels for both the simulated and real cone images and it is 200x200 pixels for the planar object. The results are compared with Sum of Modified Laplacian (SML), Gray Level Variance (GLV) method, Tenenbaum and M_2 focus measures.

Consider Figure 10. Noise is added to the sequence of the images of simulated cone. Noise added is Gaussian with zero mean and variance equal to 0.05. Figures 10(a) to 10(e) show the depth maps calculated using Tenenbaum, SML, GLV, M_2 and FM_O. As can be seen from the figures, the 3D depth map obtained using FM_O is clearly recognizable but that of SML and M_2 have degraded significantly. Infact, the noise added to the pixel values is enhanced in the depth map for SML and M_2 and hence it results in spikes originating from pixels all over the image. On the other hand, the result for FM_O has also degraded but that degradation is very minor and various approximation techniques can still use this depth map to refine the result. Further, the results for Tenenbaum and GLV in Figures 10(a) & (c) have also degraded with spikes on one side of the image. However, the central part of the cone is still recognizable.

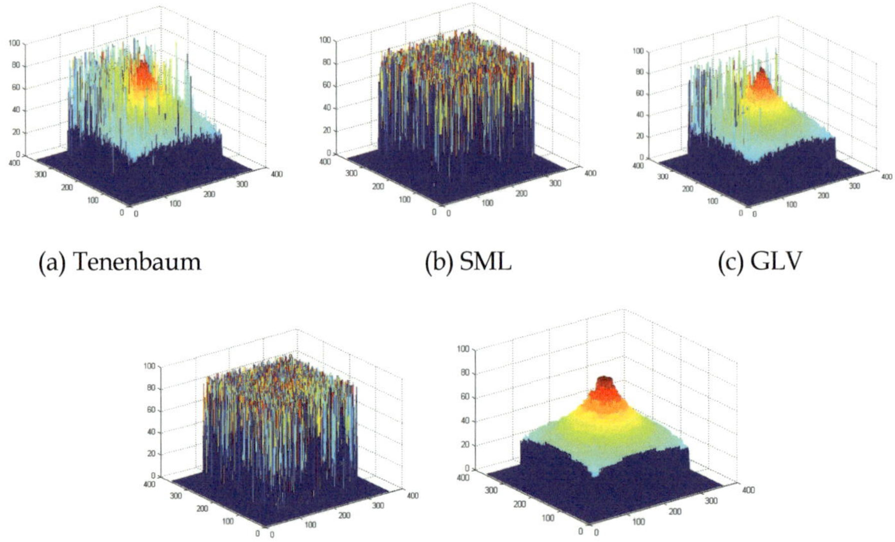

(a) Tenenbaum (b) SML (c) GLV

(d) M_2 (e) FM_O

Figure 10. Depth maps for the simulated cone object when Gaussian noise is added

We used two metrics to compare these focus measures; Root Mean Square Error (RMSE) and Correlation. After comparing the results of RMSE of above mentioned focus measures, we found that the RMSE values are lowest for FM_O in almost all the cases. Also, we found that FM_O is highly correlated with the reference image and the correlation coefficient of FM_O is highest among almost all the five focus measures. The reference image for comparison is the ground truth depth map for the simulated cone.

Consider tables 1 and 2 which show the results of the five focus measures in the presence of Gaussian noise. Table 1 is for RMSE and table 2 is for correlation result. From these tables, it is quite clear that the RMSE values are lowest for FM_O and correlation is highest for FM_O. The result is shown for data with Gaussian noise of zero mean and varying variance values, i.e., variance = 0.5, 0.05, 0.005, 0.0005, 0.00005. The performance of SML and M_2 is the worst in this case till noise variance level of 0.0005. GLV and Tenenbaum performance degrades for upper two noise levels while their performance increases considerably for the lower three noise levels. On the other hand, performance of FM_O is almost constant for all noise levels. Figure 11 depicts this clearly. Similar results were observed for shot and speckle noise too.

Variance	Tenenbaum	SML	GLV	M_2	FMo
0.5	28.5273	29.4557	28.3896	29.2447	15.1542
0.05	20.4283	29.2709	20.0483	27.9341	14.2388
0.005	19.639	20.8646	19.6283	19.6486	14.1992
0.0005	19.6663	19.6249	19.6631	19.6258	14.2148
0.00005	19.6779	19.6329	19.6682	19.6245	14.2117
No Noise	19.7017	19.6557	19.6816	19.6535	14.2114

Table 1. RMSE for Simulated Cone (Gaussian Noise)

Variance	Tenenbaum	SML	GLV	M_2	FMo
0.5	0.6138	0.5897	0.6165	0.5965	0.8707
0.05	0.8699	0.5976	0.8829	0.6347	0.9116
0.005	0.8985	0.8520	0.8982	0.8974	0.9124
0.0005	0.898	0.8982	0.8978	0.8980	0.9120
0.00005	0.8973	0.8979	0.8972	0.8981	0.9120
No Noise	0.8991	0.8999	0.8985	0.9005	0.9119

Table 2. Correlation for Simulated Cone (Gaussian Noise)

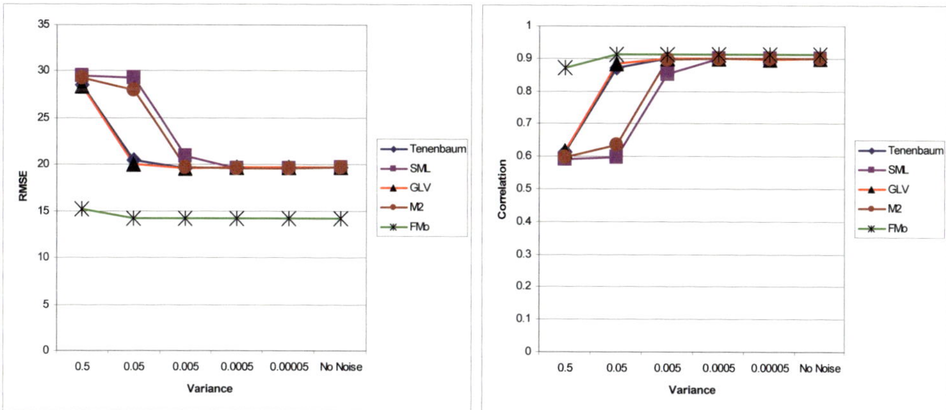

(a) RMSE (b) Correlation

Figure 11. Comparison of Focus Measures (Gaussian Noise)

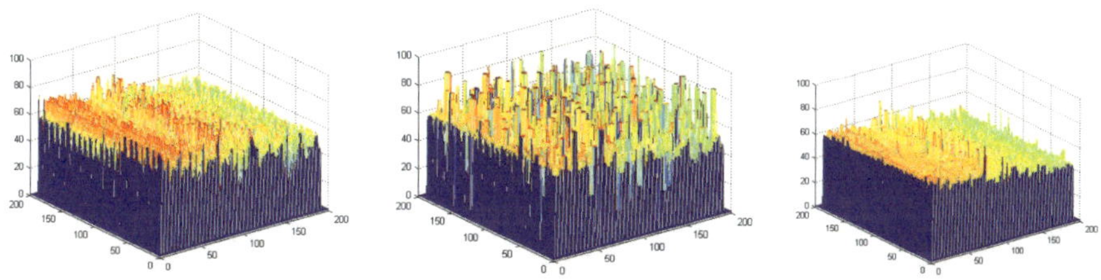

(a) Tenenbaum (b) SML (c) GLV

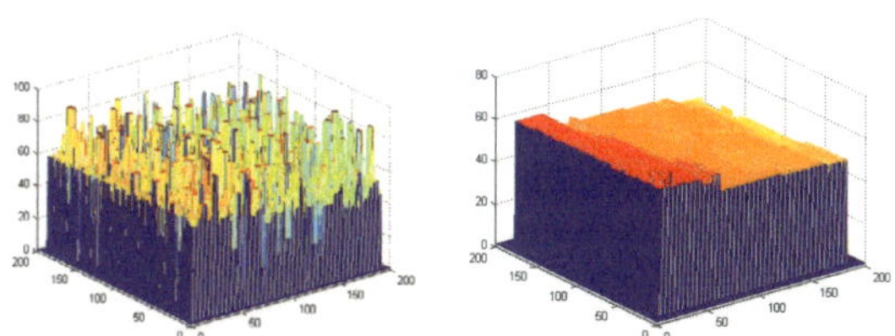

(d) M_2 (e) FM_O

Figure 12. Depth maps for the planar object when shot noise is added to the images

Now we add the shot noise to the sequence of images of the planar object. Consider figure 12 where figures 12 (a) to (e) show the depth maps for Tenenbaum, SML, GLV, M_2 and FM_O, when the bipolar shot noise is added to the planar sequence of images. The noise density used is 0.0005. As can be seen from the images, the depth maps for SML and M_2 are again degraded with spikes originating from the pixels all over the image hence making the shape of the planar object unrecognizable. Further it cannot be used for more processing by any approximation techniques since the initial estimate is not good enough. However, it can also be seen from the depth maps that the result of Tenenbaum and GLV is better than SML and M_2. On the other hand, consider figure 12(e). It shows the depth map calculated using the proposed focus measure FM_O. Although there are few steps in the depth map but still the result is very good. Hence, again FM_O performs better than rest of the focus measures. Similar results were observed for speckle noise too.

Keeping in view the results of all the objects, the following evaluations are made (Malik & Choi, 2008):

- High noise level:
  - Performance of all focus measures is affected in the presence of all noise types.
  - Overall performance: FM_O is the best followed by GLV & Tenenbaum, and then SML & M_2.
- Low noise level:
  - Gaussian noise: It affects the performance of SML and M_2 but rest of the focus measures are not influenced.
  - Shot noise: It affects all the focus measures except FM_O.
  - Speckle noise: Focus measures are not affected by speckle noise.
  - Overall performance: FM_O is the best followed by GLV & Tenenbaum, and then SML and M_2.
- At medium noise levels:
  - Performance of all focus measures is affected in the presence of all noise types.
  - Gaussian noise: Performance of FM_O, GLV and Tenenbaum is comparable followed by SML & M_2.
  - Shot noise: FM_O outperforms other focus measures followed by Tenenbaum & GLV, and then SML and M_2.
  - Speckle noise: FM_O outperforms other focus measures followed by GLV & Tenenbaum, and then SML and M_2.
  - Overall performance: FM_O is the best followed by GLV & Tenenbaum, and then SML and M_2.
- Overall Performance:
  - Gaussian Noise:
    - FM_O outperforms at high and low noise levels and is comparable at medium noise level
    - GLV and Tenenbaum show good performance too
    - SML and M_2 should be avoided except for low noise levels
  - Shot Noise:
    - FM_O outperforms at all noise levels
    - Rest of the focus measures should be avoided in the presence of shot noise
  - Speckle Noise:
    - FM_O outperforms at all noise levels
    - GLV and Tenenbaum exhibits better performance
    - SML and M_2 should be avoided except for low noise levels

7. Conclusion

In this chapter, we considered the effects of illumination and window sizes on the focus measures for accurate calculation of depth map. We showed that the illumination effects can directly result in incorrect estimation of depth map if proper window size is not used for computation. We used two well established focus measures, i.e., Sum of Modified Laplacian and Gray Level Variance. We proved that larger window size results in two major errors. One is the introduction of blurring which results in smoothing of the object hence giving false impression of 3D smoothing in depth map. Second is the wrong extraction of frame numbers for depth map corresponding to the sharpest pixel values in the sequence of the images. Hence, it is suggested that smaller window size should be used with the upper bound of 5x5 on the size of the window. Hence, without pre-processing for image enhancement and without use of proper window size, it is not possible to obtain the accurate depth map for 3D shape recovery. It is worth noting that the problem defined in this chapter is not limited to Shape From Focus only. Rather most of the image processing techniques (especially 3D image recovery algorithms) based on window processing are marred with this problem, i.e., usage of large window size. Hence, this chapter provides guidance for research in this direction too.

In addition, we have presented a focus measure based on robustness in the presence of noise. We tested and compared this focus measure using simulated cone images, real cone images and slanted planar object images. The results show that this focus measure tends to perform better than the traditional focus measures when the noise is present in the images. We have shown the performance of various focus measures with three different types of noise, i.e., Gaussian, Shot and Speckle noise. The various focus measures used for comparison include Sum of Modified Laplacian (SML), Gray Level Variance (GLV), Tenenbaum and M_2 focus measures which clearly indicate that the optical focus measure is equally good for images without noise and at the same time, it shows much enhanced performance in comparison to others in the presence of noise. It can be argued that some noise removal filter can be used before processing with the focus measure. However, as shown, the result of the proposed focus measure (FM_O) is better even in the absence of noise. Further, FM_O does not require noise removal filter because noise removal property is inherent within this technique. Lastly, we know that different types of noise removal filter are employed for different types of noise, e.g., median filter for shot noise, Weiner filter for Gaussian noise etc. Hence, some knowledge of noise is required before hand for the application of such filters. We used RMSE and Correlation metric measures to compare the performance of the earlier focus measures with our optical focus measure. The results clearly indicate that the RMSE values are lowest while the correlation values are the highest for the presented focus measure when compared with the SML, GLV, Tenenbaum and M_2 focus measures at almost all the noise levels for all objects. It is concluded from the results that the best performance is shown by FM_O followed by GLV, Tenenbaum, M_2 and SML.

8. Acknowledgements

This work was supported by the Korea Science and Engineering Foundation (KOSEF) grant funded by the Korean government (MOST) (No. R01-2007-000-20227-0). The authors also acknowledge the support of Dr Asifullah Khan during the review of this chapter.

9. References

Krotkov, E.P. Focusing, *International Journal of Computer Vision*, (1987) pp. 223-237.

Helmli, F.S. & Scherer, S. (2001). Adaptive shape from focus with an error estimation in light microscopy, *2nd International Symposium on Image and Signal Processing and Analysis (ISPA01)*, pp. 188-193, Pula, Croatia

Nayar, S.K. & Nakagawa, Y. Shape from focus, *IEEE Transactions on Pattern Analysis and Machine Intelligence*, Vol. 16, No. 8 (August 1994) pp. 824-831

Subbarao, M., Choi, T.-S. & Nikzad, A. Focusing techniques, *Optical Engineering*, Vol. 32, No. 11 (November 1993) pp. 2824-2836

Malik, A.S. & Choi, T.-S. Application of passive techniques for three dimensional cameras, *IEEE Transactions on Consumer Electronics*, Vol. 53, No. 2 (May 2007) pp. 258-264

Subbarao, M. & Choi, T.-S. Accurate recovery of three dimensional shape from image focus, *IEEE Transactions on Pattern Analysis and Machine Intelligence*, Vol. 17, No. 3, (March 1995) pp. 266-274

Choi, T.-S., Asif, M. & Yun, J. (1999). Three-dimensional shape recovery from focused image surface, *IEEE International Conference on Acoustics, Signal and Speech Processing*, Vol. 6, pp. 3269-3272, Arizona, US

Asif, M. & Choi, T.-S. Shape from focus using multilayer feedforward neural network, *IEEE Transactions on Image Processing*, Vol. 10, No. 11 (November 2001) pp. 1670-1675

Ahmad, M.B. & Choi T.-S. A Heuristic approach for finding best focused shape, *IEEE Transactions on Circuits and Systems for Video Technology*, Vol. 15, No. 4 (April 2005) pp. 566-574

Malik, A.S. & Choi, T.-S. Consideration of illumination effects and optimization of window size for accurate calculation of depth map for 3D shape recovery, *Pattern Recognition*, Vol. 40, No. 1, (January 2007) pp. 154-170

Poon, T.-C. & Banerjee, P. (2001). *Contemporary optical image processing*, 1st ed., Elsevier Science Ltd., New York

Malik, A.S. & Choi, T.-S. A Novel Algorithm for Estimation of Depth Map using Image Focus for 3D Shape Recovery in the Presence of Noise, *Pattern Recognition*, Vol. 41, No. 7, (July 2008) pp. 2200-2225

8

Cooperative intelligent agents for speeding up the Replication of Complement-Based Self-Replicated, Self-Assembled Systems (CBSRSAS)

Mostafa M. H. Ellabaan
Cairo University
Egypt

Abstract

Self-replication of CBSRSAS may occur as a result of completing the complementary parts of the system or self-assembly of the whole system. Self-replication process is a time-consuming process that depends on the dynamics of the system components and environmental factors that describe how system components are distributed across the media and how viscous is the media when the viscosity of the media means how the media supports or burdens the movements of system components. Therefore, we will suggest different models for Multi-agent systems that can speed up the replication process of CBSRSAS systems; we will describe how agents can help in the replication process either at the initiation of replication or through the replication process by bringing system components to their system complementary parts. We will measure how far the degree of cooperation between agents and their intelligence level affect the process of replication.

1. Introduction

CBSRSAS, The complement-based self-replicated and self-assembled system, was introduced as a general model for self-assembled and self-replicated systems inspired from bio-molecular system by (Ellabaan (A), 2007). It differs from cellular automata model that used by Jan Van Neumann to represent his model for self-replication systems (Neumann, 1966). CBSRSAS systems bases on system components that have the capabilities of interaction with each other and dynamical behavior that brings them to interact, while cellular automata model bases on specific number of cells, each cell state can be changed to one state of the states pool defined in advance. CBSRSAS systems are more related to biological systems while cellular automata related in general to chemical and physical systems and in specific to particle systems (Neumann, 1956). CBSRSAS systems give the ability to produce in a very simple manner robust self-assembled and self-replicated systems.

CBSRSAS systems replication may be difficult in some circumstances. This difficulty emerges from the barriers within the environment surrounding CBSRSAS systems. These difficulties can be summarized in how system components are capable to move freely in the environments. In some environments, the viscosity is too high, which burdens the movement of the CBSRSAS system components making their accessibility to CBSRSAS complementary divided parts difficult, and consequently making CBSRSAS self-replication more difficult. So, the need for external agents that have greater dealing with the environment is beneficial.

Aiming at making self-replication process more natural, robust and efficient, it is suggested to utilize the concept of agents. In bimolecular system such as DNA and RNA, their replication processes occur as a process of interaction between DNA systems with some agents or enzymes that initiate the process of replication and bring system components or nucleotides to the appropriate interaction sections. Hence, utilizing agents is a natural case. Moreover, utilizing agents that varies of their capabilities can lead to the specialization which leads to a quick production of the replication process as the agents will be experts in their areas of specialization. Moreover, specialization requires agents to know less and do more work. The process of replication would be more powerful if it is done in a cooperative manner between intelligent agents. Solving the problem by utilizing multi-agents system has many advantages than any other approaches. An agent can represent computer program, human, and robots, so it is a general approach as CBSRSAS systems is. CBSRSAS can be applied for biological systems, nano-scale machines, games and robotics. Moreover, there are a lot of research has been dedicated to Multi-agents system that leads to making the concepts of multi-agents system more obvious and much easier to be understood, and we can utilize this work to build advanced models of multi-agent system that can be utilized in the replication process of CBSRSAS.

In this chapter, we introduce three models for multi-agent systems that can be used to support replication process of CBSRSAS systems. In the first model, we utilize homogeneous stigmergy multi-agent system that can utilize the concept of stigmergy (i.e. to put sign) (Theraulaz, 1999) to communicate between agents. Having homogeneous Multi-agent system requires its agent to have a quite big database of rules to deal with environments. Finding appropriate rules may take times leading to slowing the replication process down little bit. In addition, having such a lot of rules may sometimes lead to choose a wrong one which, consequently, may lead to inappropriate replication or mutation of the replica. Moreover, to learn a lot of rules may also require a lot of time, so at the initial stage of agents life the replication process is noticeably slow.

In the second model, we suggested another multi-agent system, the heterogeneous stigmergy-based multi-agent system, which also utilizes the stigma as an approach for communication among agents in the multi-agent system. This approach has proven its success especially when agents are specialized and distributed in a comparable manner with the distribution of system components in CBSRSAS. Balanced workload among agents is supported by this approach. Moreover, this model has approved that simple rules with clear objectives and a simple cooperation scheme can achieve superiority over very complicated systems with a huge database of rules as the case in the previous model.

In heterogeneous Multi-agent system, we introduced a simple model of diversity between agents with a limited level of cooperation powered by stigma. So in the third model, we introduced another model with a higher level of diversity and communication called *Robosoccer Team-based Multi-agents system*. This model was inspired from soccer robots player (Nebel, 2001) where robots have to work in teams, have to be able to localize both itself and the ball, and planning their path and motion in a cooperative manner. Based on these lessons, we introduce the third model, but this model has a different feature. This feature refers to that the teams are not working against each other, and they also work in cooperative manner to arrange the path planning between agents belonging to different teams.

This chapter consists of four sections, the first one gives an overview about CBSRSAS systems in terms of their basic concepts and their potential applications. The second section provides a detailed introduction about multi-agent systems in terms of what is the agent? What are the main types of agent-based systems and multi-agent systems? In addition, it involves a detailed explanation of two famous models of multi-agent systems: stigmergy-based or Ant colony inspired multi-agent system and Soccer-inspired multi-agent system. In the third section, we provide three models of the multi-agents that can be used to speed up the replication process of CBSRSAS. Two of these models utilize stigmergy-based model, but they differ according the difference between agents. They can be also classified into: homogeneous stigmergy-based multi-agent system where agents have same structure and capabilities, and heterogeneous stigmergy-based multi-agent system where agents vary in their capabilities and structures. The final model is *the Robosoccer team-based multi-agent system* where agents vary in their capabilities and structures but they work in a cooperative manner and compete with other teams. In the fifth section, we give a detailed discussion and future work of the application of multi-agent systems in CBSRSAS.

2. Complement Based Self-Replicated, Self-assembled System (CBSRSAS): An overview

CBSRSAS, the complement-based self-replicated and self-assembled system, bases on the generalization of the concepts of assembly and replication of bio-molecular systems such as DNA and RNA. CBSRSAS systems base on two rule sets: the assembling rule set and the complementary based replication rule set. These rule sets control the interaction between self-assembling sections of the CBSRSAS and self-replication sections of CBSRSAS. The CBSRSAS consists of a group of items called system components. Each system component consists of two types of sections controlling its interactions with other system components such as self-assembling section types and complement-interaction section types. Thus, system components can interact with each other once they are close enough. For autonomous interaction, system components should be given a behavioral model that controls how these components move or behave. This model is represented by a dynamical or kinematical model that will be explained later in this section. These concepts are the main concepts required for building systems of the CBSRSAS type. So how can CBSRSAS self-replicate into more other systems? For the replication phase of the CBSRSAS systems, as biologically inspired CBSRSAS systems, to replicate, the replication process should be initiated. This case is modeled in CBSRSAS systems as the replication initiation rule set which determines in which condition the CBSRSAS system will start to self-replicate. The replication process itself can be done by two ways: the first refers to the autonomous version of self-replication where system components dynamical behavior and interactions through complementary-interaction sections build the new CBSRSAS sibling systems guided by the complementary parts of the parent CBSRSAS; the second approach bases on supporting of agents spread over the nearby environment; this approach called the agent-based replication machinery which will be explained in details throughout the chapter. CBSRSAS may be considered as a blue print for systems that can exhibit the living organisms' features of self-assembly and self-replication. In this section, we will give an overview of the basic concepts of CBSRSAS systems and their potential application

2.1 Basic Concepts of CBSRSAS

In this section, we will explain the main components and rules suggested for generating complement-based self-replicated and self-assembled systems. We will explain what the basic system components and what the characteristics of these main components are, and how these characteristics may lead to autonomous replication and assembling of the systems (Ellabaan (A), 2007).

Firstly, defining *System component* is one of the most important steps in defining CBSRSAS systems. It is considered as the basic building blocks of the CBSRSAS. Defining system components should be driven from the application area. In CBSRSAS systems, system components are composed of two types of sections: self-assembly section type, and complement interaction section.

The first section type or self-assembly section type defines the section that its interactions are controlled by self-assembly rule set that will be described later in this section. A system component may have more than one interaction section. In bio-molecular systems such as DNA or RNA, system components or nucleotides in case of DNA or RNA have two self-assembly sections (See Figure 1)

The second section type, the complement interaction section type, defines sections at which interaction between complementary system components occurs. This part plays an important role in self-replication process and in generating replicates. A system component may have more than one complement interaction section. The more the complement interaction sections a system component has, the more replicas can be generated by CBSRSAS system through the self-replication process.

Secondly, all types of system components are represented by *system component set*. If CBSRSAS systems composed of N system component X, then X should be included in *system Component set*

$$Y \text{ is CBSRSAS system and } Y = (x_1 \quad x_2 \quad .. \quad x_i \quad .. \quad x_n) \text{ where } x_i \text{ is a system component}$$
$$\textit{and } x_i \in \rho \text{ and } \rho \text{ is system component set}$$

CBSRSAS system is considered as spatial order of basic system components chosen from the system components set. CBSRSAS length may be larger than system component set.

Thirdly, each item in ρ (*the system component set*) may have one or more complements. Each pair of items (item and its complement) is called a *complement-based replication rule*. *Complement-based replication rule set*, which is donated by ξ, includes all system complement-based replication rules. There are three types of complement-based replication rule set:

1. Complement-based replication rule set for many to many relationships between system components. This kind of system has a very high mutation level during self-replication process due to the many complementary relationships that a system component has. So it is recommended for high variability or evolvable systems.

$$\xi = \{(A, A), (A, B), (A, C), (B, D), (C, C), (D, F)\}$$

2. Complement-based replication rule set bases on one-to-one relationships between system components. Each system component has one and only one relationship with

either itself or with another system component. The mutation level is expected to be very small if existed.

$$\xi = \{(A, B), (C, C), (D, F)\}$$

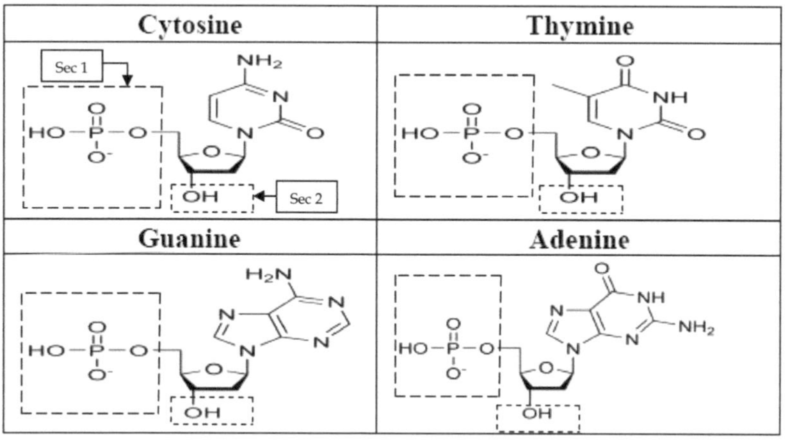

Figure 1. Show that DNA has two self-assembly parts surrounding by dashed rectangles

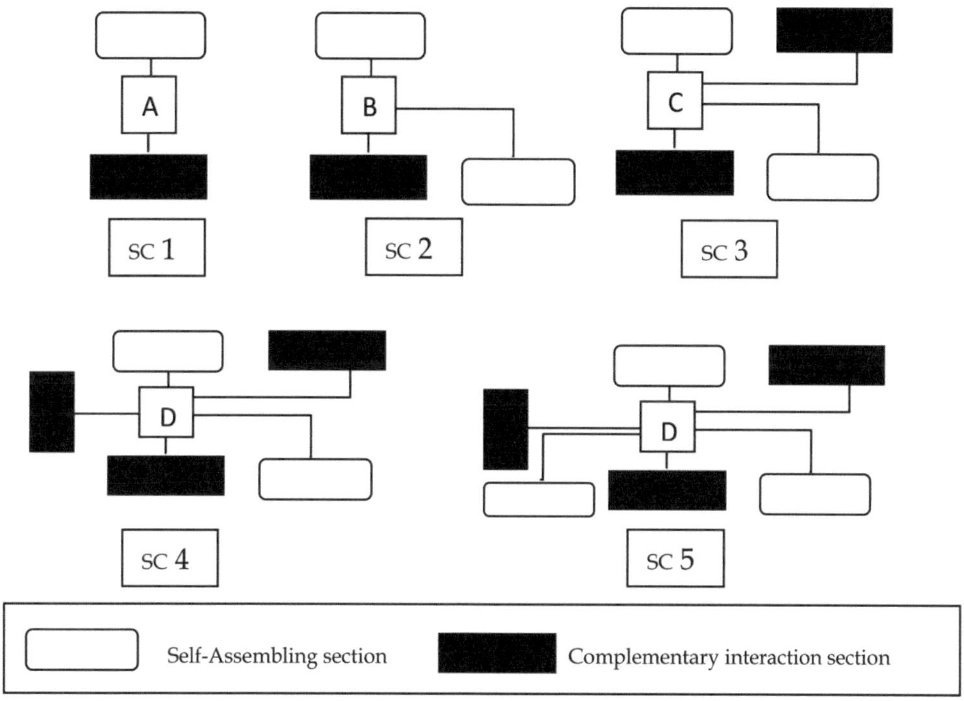

Figure 2. Shows different examples of system components where SC1 is a system component composed of a complement interaction and a self-assembly interaction section, SC2 is composed of two self-assembly sections and one complement interaction section, and SC5 is composed of three self-assembly interaction sections and three complement interaction sections (Ellabaan (A), 2007)

3. Incomplete complement-based replication rule set refers to the complement-based replication rule set that has one or more system components that do not involved in a complementary relationship with either itself or other system components. So the mutation at this point will be very high either at self-replication process or at normal life of CBSRSAS systems.

$$\xi = \{(A, B), (D, F)\}$$

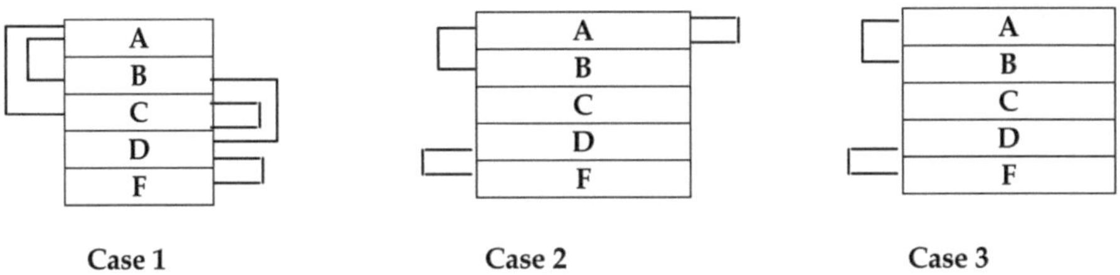

Figure 3. (Case 1) Replication rule set with a many to many relationship; (Case 2) Replication rule set with a one to one relationship; (Case 3) refers to incomplete replication rule set where one or more items have no complementary replication rule with itself or with its

Fourthly, *the assembling rule set* determines how system components interact with each other in case of collision between self-assembling sections of system components. This idea is driven from Wang tile or Wang dominoes proposed by (Wang, 1961). His main purpose was to use a given finite set of geometrical tiles to determine whether they could be arranged using each tile as many times as necessary to cover the entire plan without gap (Ellabaan and Brailsford, 2006). In the assembling rule set, the interactions between colors (distinctive options for self-assembly section) are stored in a symmetric matrix called the interaction matrix (Ellabaan (B), 2007). To illustrate, assume we have two system components. Each one has one self-assembling section with color A for the first system component and color B for the second one. If the interaction between color A and B in the case of collision satisfies a specific rule, they either stay together if they satisfy the stability condition defined in the rule or continue moving according their previous states.

Fifthly, *kinematics model* represents the basic behavior of the basic system component. Each system component should have capabilities to move freely and autonomously. This movement should not burden the capabilities of objects to interact with each other from the side of either self-assembly or self replication section. The kinematics model is not only dedicated to the kinematics model of the system components, but it may also include a kinematics model of the complement interaction sections and self-assembly interaction sections.

Sixthly, *replication-initiation rule sets* are the main signals that may be required to initiate the replication process. By these signals, the complementary relations of the system are broken leading to break the system into its complementary parts. The number of complementary parts depends on the number of the complement interaction sections in the system components. If the system component has N complement interaction sections, then the process of breaking system component will lead to N complementary parts. Each complementary part can generate the system again. Although the advantages of having more than one complement interaction sections, generating many replicates requires a difficult procedure for setting replication-initiation rule sets.

Seventhly, *replication Machinery* refers to the approach utilized for *CBSRSAS'* replication. To illustrate, let us drive an example. To replicate *CBSRSAS* systems, it is required to break the system into its complementary parts and bring the system components for each of these parts. There are two machinery types for handling this type of replication. The first type of machinery depends totally on system components and its kinematics model which is called the *autonomous replication machinery*. The second machinery depends on the interaction between the system and other systems or *agents*. This machinery is called the *agent-based replication machinery*. The agent-based replication machinery is the most famous in biological or natural systems, and will be extensively studied in this chapter.
In this section, we have described the seven basic principles that outline the CBSRSAS systems by which it is easy to generate robust self-replicated and self-assembling machines. In the following subsection we will discuss some of the potential application areas for CBSRSAS systems.

2.2 Applications

CBSRSAS systems has a good potential as a general framework for self-replicated and self-assembled system inspired from the most robust self-assembled and self-replicated bio-molecular systems. This generality and robustness inherited from the most robust biological system makes CBSRSAS system a good model to be applied for wide areas of research that have recently attracted a lot of scientists' interests such as artificial life, robotics, multi-agents systems and systems biology.
Firstly, building artificial system that can behave like biological system is one of the main objectives of artificial life. CBSRSAS system can generate itself (i.e. to self-replicate) and can aggregate from simple subsystems or system components (i.e. self-assemble), so artificial life can be seen as one of the application area of the CBSRSAS systems. Secondly, applying CBSRSAS to robotics may be an interesting future investigation. CBSRSAS can help building self-assembled and self-replicated robots. If robots are built with CBSRSAS characteristics, defining self-assembly interaction sections and complement interaction sections and defining self-assembling rule set as well as self replication rule set, It may generate a powerful robots with interesting behavior and capabilities of generating themselves either through self assembly or self-replication. Thirdly, Investigating the possibility of generating CBSRSAS at atomic or molecular details in Chemistry may lead to discovering other systems with higher assembling and replication rate than the existed ones such as DNA and RNA and, consequently, creating a new type of living systems (Ellabaan (A), 2007).

3. Multi-Agent system: an Introduction

Multi-agent systems refer to the systems composed of multiple interacting intelligent agents, which can be utilized to solve the problem with high complexity that makes it too difficult to be solved by a single agent system or monolithic systems. The main characteristics that distinguish the multi-agent systems form the other kinds of systems can be summarized in the following three properties: The first is the *autonomy* which refers to the agent should be at least partially autonomous. The second is *local view* which means that agent can only recognize the local area where it lies. In other words, it cannot have a global view of the system and environments as the system may be too complex to be understood even if the global view is available to the agent. The third feature is the *decentralization* which means that there is no agent having a full control over the system (Wooldridge, 2002). By these features, the multi-agent systems are not only able to provide distributed parallelism, but they also gives the flexibility to add new agents to the system as the complexity of the problem, which the multi-agent system tries to solve, increases. There are many examples for problems solved utilizing the concept of multi-agent system such as online trading (Rogers, 2007), disaster response (Schurr, 2005), and modeling social structure(Sun, 2004).

Multi-agent systems have been applied to lots of applications in real word. For example, they have been used in computer games, film production and in analyzing massive scientific data. Relative to military wise, scientists are trying to build multi-agent system for coordinated defense system (Gagne, 1993) (Beautement, 2005). They have been also applied to transportation, logistic and graphics. Moreover, they have been utilized in network and mobile technology to achieve automatic and dynamic load balance, high scalability, and self-healing networks. Nowadays, scientists try to utilize Multi-agent system as a frame work for studying complex systems as explained in (Boccara, 2004).

In this section, we will explain the basic concepts of multi-gent systems. What is the agent? And what are the basic components of the agents? These questions will be explained in agent definition subsection. In addition, the different categorization of the agent-based systems will be explained as well as the Multi-agent classification. By the end of this section, we will explain in details some important multi-gent system models widely used as multi-agent system models for solving problems.

3.1 Agent Definition

The main concept that should be clarified in the multi-agent system is the concept of the agent. An agent is an entity with the power to act (Flores-Mendez, 1999). The agent may be represented as an animated character in animation or computer graphics, a robot, or a software component. In this chapter, we consider agents nature as same as the nature of CBSRSAS systems. In other words, if CBSRSAS systems are modeled or represented as animated systems on computer graphics then the agents will be represented as animated characters. If CBSRSAS systems are modeled in a robotic-wise, then the agents will be also modeled in a robotic-wise.

Agent designing is an important process in designing multi-agent systems. The gent designer should consider four important aspects of agents. The first aspect relates to where the agent will be; the second aspect how the agent will sense or perceive the surrounding environment; in response to either internal or external stimulus, how the agent will behave in response to these stimulus, and finally, how the agent will move in its surrounding environment (see figure 4). All these questions are considered in the following four models that the designer should consider in agent design process as proposed by (Millar et al, 1999):

1. ***Environmental model***: refers to the environment where the agent lies. This model determines the basic characteristics of the environment such as viscosity and obstacles.
2. ***Perception model*** refers to how an agent perceives its environment. There are many approaches that can enable an agent perceiving its environments: the first approach is the zonal approach by which the agent is equipped with ability to sense specific regions or perception regions. The agent will be able to perceive any object if it lies in these regions. The smaller the zonal region, the weaker collision avoidance and path planning capabilities will be. The larger the zonal region, the more computationally expensive it will be. The second approach refers to *the sensory approach* which involves placing

synthetic sensors on the character such as sensors for smelling, hearing, and seeing. Agent designer should be careful about the orientation and location of each sensor to enable alertness and high quality perception. *Synthetic vision approach* is the third method that can be used by an agent as a perception model. This approach can utilize the advancement in human vision to give the agent a vision of its surrounding world. This approach is only useful for vision; no other stimuli will be detected.

3. ***Behavioral model*** refers to how the agent responds to internal or external stimulus perceived by perception model. There are many approaches for handling behavioral aspect of the agent. For example, the rule-based approach can be utilized to handle the behavioral aspect of the agent by giving the agent a set of rules defining his behavioral aspects relative to different situations. In addition, designers also can utilize network approaches, cognitive approaches, and mathematical approaches for deal with behavioral aspect of the agents. Cognitive or AI approaches are preferred because it can utilize the advanced models for intelligent behavior suggest in AI.
4. ***Motor model*** handles the movement of the agents only, while path planning is handled by the behavioral model or components. This model is responsible only for achieving a movements request from its behavioral components and execute the request by using specific motor movement approach.

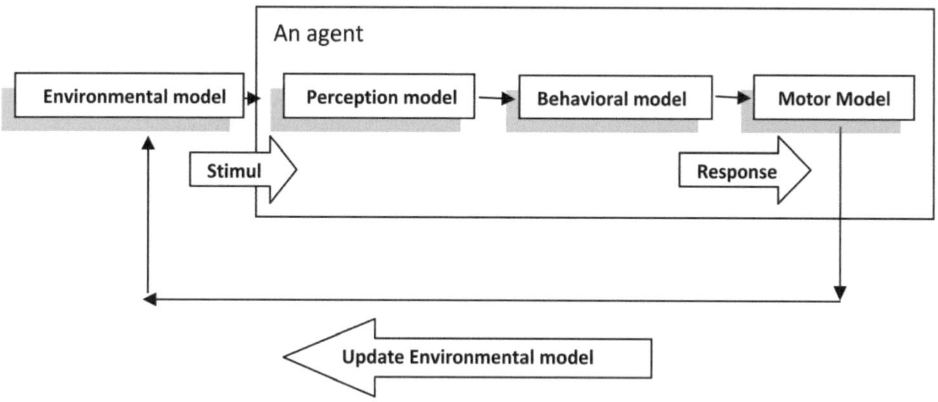

Figure 4. Shows the interaction between the agent and the surrounding environment

3.2 Types of Agent-based systems:

Here, we will explain two important types: Centralized agent system and General multi-agent system.

- Centralized agent System - Single Agent system

Single agent systems refer to agent systems that have a single agent making all the decision, while the others act as remote slaves. Single agent system might have multiple entities for example several actuators or even several robots provided that each entity sends its perceptions to and receives its action from a single and central process. In other word, all agents work as a single agent (Stone & Veloso, 2000).

- Distributed or General Multi-agent systems

Unlike the centralized agent system, Distributed or general multi-agent system is composed of multiple autonomous, interacting and intelligent agents. Each agent in such model concerns about its own interest, does its work in autonomous manner, and shares its sensory information if the sharing will not be against its own interest. Moreover, the global view is not available. Decision making process is done in distributed manner. In other words, each agent takes decision by itself and according to the profit that will be gained which can be described by the local view of the system. To conclude, these features of the agents determine the essential three properties -(autonomy, local view, and decentralization)- of multi-agent system.

3.3 Multi-agent system Classification

There are many approaches for classifying multi-agent systems. Multi-agent systems can be classified, for example, according to the management prospective into centralized and decentralized multi-agent systems, and according to the similarity of the agents into homogenous multi-agent system and heterogeneous multi-agent system. In this section, we will explain in details of the similarity-based multi-agent classification. This classification divides multi-agent system into two groups according to the similarity between agents in the multi-agent system. The first type is the homogeneous multi-agent systems in which agent are very similar in, for example, their capabilities and domain knowledge. The second type refers to the heterogeneous multi-agent system in which agents varies in their capabilities, goals and/or domain knowledge.

3.3.1 Multi-agent system classification based on the similarity among agents:

We will study here how we can classify multi-agent system based on the similarities and/ or differences between the agents involved in the multi-agent system.

3.3.1.1 Homogenous Multi-agent systems

A Homogenous Multi-agent system refers to the Multi-agent system with several agents having identical structure (domain knowledge, decision functions, and sensors and effectors). These agents situated differently in the environments as they have different sensor inputs and effectors outputs. They make their own decision regarding which action to take. Multi-agent system requires different effectors output, otherwise it will not be considered as multi-agent systems. Consequently, homogeneous multi-agent system must have different sensor input, otherwise they will act identically leading to violating the necessity conditions of multi-agent systems previously mentioned. This scenario of systems assumes that the agents cannot communicate directly (see figure 5).

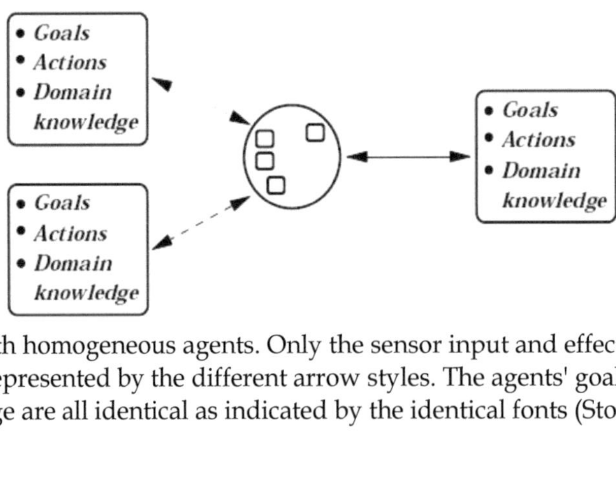

Figure 5. MAS with homogeneous agents. Only the sensor input and effectors output of agents differ, as represented by the different arrow styles. The agents' goals, actions, and/or domain knowledge are all identical as indicated by the identical fonts (Stone & Veloso, 2000)

3.3.2 Heterogeneous Multi-agent Systems

Heterogeneous multi-agent systems refer to multi-agent systems with significantly different agents having different domain knowledge, goals and/ or actions which refer to heterogeneity conditions. In this scenario, agents are situated in the environment differently, causing them to have different sensory inputs and necessitating different actions. This kind of scenario provides system designers a great deal of power over system. There are two different scenarios for these types of system: *Heterogeneous non-communicating multi-agent systems* and *Heterogeneous communicating multi-agent systems*.

Heterogeneous non-communicating multi-agent systems refer to multi-agent systems having different agents that do not sharing their knowledge, goals and their sensory inputs. They just interact together indirectly See figure 6.

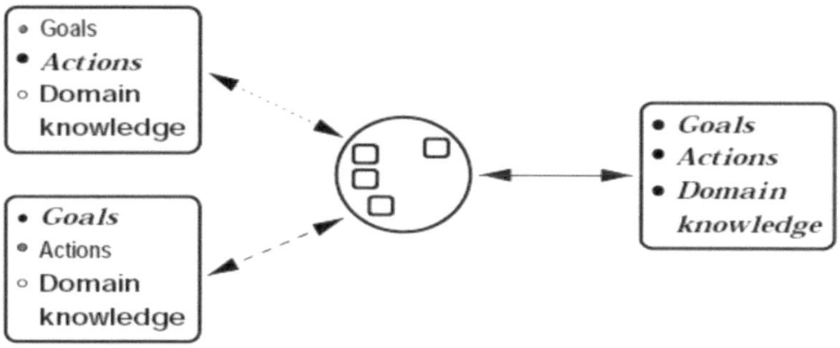

Figure 6. The general heterogeneous MAS scenario. Now agents' goals, actions, and/or domain knowledge may differ as indicated by the different fonts. The assumption of no direct interaction remains (Stone and Veloso, 2000)

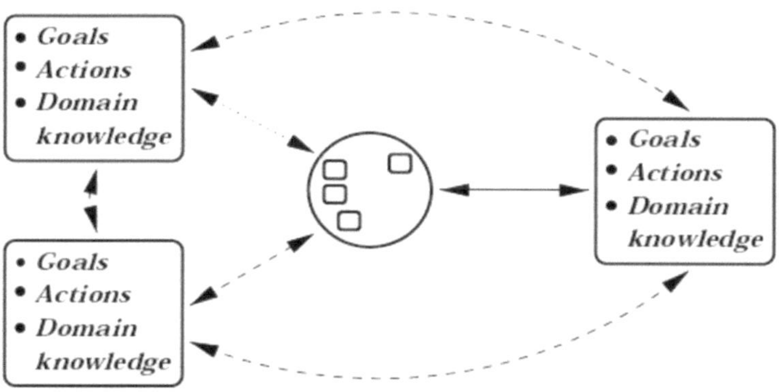

Figure 7. The general communicating MAS scenario. Agents can be heterogeneous to any degree. Information can be transmitted directly among agents as indicated by the arrows between agents. Communication can either be broadcast or transmitted point-to-point (Stone and Veloso, 2000)

In heterogeneous communicating multi-agent systems (see figure 7), agents have capabilities to communicate with each others. Having agents with different sensory data, goal, actions and domain knowledge and empowered with communication capabilities can provide a very complex and powerful multi-agent systems. Adding the concept of communication can turn multi-agent systems into single-agent system or centralized agents systems if there is an agent capable to send its sensory inputs and commands to other agents who in turn just achieve the commands. Therefore, the heterogeneous multi-agent system scenario can span the full range of the complexity in agent systems.

3.4 Important Multi-agent System Models:

Here, we will explain two famous examples of multi-agent system models that are widely used as models for different multi-agent systems such as (Valckenaers, et al, 2001), (Nebel, 2001), and (Theraulaz, 1999). These models either inspired from biological system as the stigmergy-based multi-agent systems or inspired from the soccer game as the robosoccer multi-agent system model (Theraulaz, 1999). Literature has a lot of work that have been done to investigate the possibility enabling robots to play games like human beings (Nebel, 2001), and (Gutmann, 2000). Soccer game is a very famous game, representing the complex cooperative behavior of team players. It is a good area to investigate the cooperative team-work where agents cooperatively work together to achieve their teams' goal as it will be explained in robosoccer multi-agent systems model.

3.4.1 Stigmergy-based Multi-agents systems

This model is inspired from ant-colony where ants put signs or stigmas (i.e. pheromone) to influence other ants' behavior. Like ants in ant-colony, agents in stigmergy multi-agent system model utilizes stigma or signs to communicate or affect the performance of each others. With stigmergy, agents observed sign in their environments and act upon them without the need to synchronize with other agents. Stigmergy can be classified as indirect interactions between agents (Valckenaers, et al, 2001). This model enables agents to utilize locally available signs to learn about the global properties of the system. In this model, agents work in the same manner as the ant foraging for food or search for food where food foraging ants execute a simple procedure in which their behavior is guided by permanently changing environment. Ants forage for food works as explained in Figure 8. As ants start their work by random search, the agents will start searching for their targets or CBSRSAS systems, put signs at the CBSRSAS system components. When other agents find it, they start searching for the complementary system components to the one at which they find the stigma. In section four, we will explain in details different stigmergy-based multi-agent system models and how each one of these models work.

Ant Foraging for food

1. *In absence of any signs in the environment (consisting of by scents from chemical substance called a pheromone), ants perform a randomized search for food.*
2. *When an ant discovers a food source, it drops a chemical smelling substance – i.e. pheromone – on its way back to the nest while carrying some of the food. Thus it creates a pheromone trail between nest and food source.*
3. *When an ant sense sings in form of a pheromone trail it will b e urged by its instinct to follow this trail to the food source.*

Figure 8. Pseudo code for Ants Food foraging (Valckenaers, et al, 2001)

The main advantages of stigmergy-based multi-agent system model can be summarized as follow: firstly, utilizing a simple model of communication reduces the complexity in agent

design; secondly, this model considers the environment as a part of the solution; thirdly, global information is locally made available. On its way through the system this information is transformed in appropriate manners, to enable the agents to make local decisions based on locally available information while being aimed at global goals.
But this model also suffers from many drawbacks. For example, stigmergy-based multi-agent system model utilizes a simple communication approach which based on stigmas which fails to support high level of cooperation between agents. Thus, it is difficult to find team-working in such model. In addition, Task achievement in this model is randomly done due to the absence of cooperative planning. Conflict is unavoidable in such models, and its possibility is higher due to the limited communication, and consequently limited cooperation. To sum up, the simplicity of communication inherited from stigmergy method is behind the limited or absence of cooperation, and, consequently, behind high level of conflict expected from stigmergy-based multi-agent system.

3.4.2 Robosoccer Multi-agent system model

Unlike the stigmergy-based multi-agent system model, Robosoccer multi-agent system model have a higher level of cooperation between agents belonging to the same team as this model is built based on the existence of high level of communication between agents. This system works in similar way as robot players. As the agents start their work searching for the ball, once finding it, they pass it to each other, until achieving their goal. There are many lessons to be learned from robosoccer team such as cooperative sensing and cooperative path and motion planning. We will discuss three main lessons of the robosoccer team in the following subsections.

3.4.2.1 Cooperative-Sensing:

Cooperative-sensing refers to observations sharing process among a group of agents. The main advantage of this approach is the compensation of sensor limitation that may restrict the region in which an object can be sensed. Moreover, it is providing agent with combined estimates that the agent can utilize to narrow down their hypotheses to correct their estimates. In Soccer Robot wise, it can be beneficial in two aspects. Firstly, in *cooperative self-localization*, an agent is able to utilize the sharing of observations with other agents to determine its current position. Secondly, in *cooperative object localization*, agents utilize sharing of observation to localize the object or ball in case of soccer robot. Cooperative sensing has proven its powerful as more accurate and reliable tool for localization (Nebel, 2001).

3.4.2.2 Cooperative Path and motion planning:

Basic motion planning problem (Latombe, 1991) is the problem of moving single object in an Euclidian space which called work space from an initial position (and orientation) to a target position. Robots are responsible for planning their own trajectory from the initial state to the goal state avoiding obstacles in non-cooperative motion planning. In cooperative path and motion planning, a group of robots is sharing their views to plan the motion trajectories for them. Cooperative sensing leads to more accurate and reliable tools for localization (Nebel, 2001). Therefore, the initial and goal are reliably and accurately determined. This approach facilities the process of path and motion planning. Although cooperative sensing is computationally reasonable, the computation cost of cooperative path planning is much more difficult and expensive.

There are two types of cooperative path and motion planning:

- Cooperative path planning with global communication:

This schema of cooperative path planning assumes that all agents can communicate with each other. There are two approaches utilizing this schema. The first one in which the multi-robot path planning problem can be solved centrally which so-called *centralized approach*. This approach does not guarantee optimality and completeness. Moreover it is not efficient enough for even only a moderate number of robots (Nebel, 2001).

In *decoupling approach*, the second one, (Latombe, 1991) one robot or agent plans independent path trajectories for all robots and then combine them, resolving conflicts when they happen. It is a good method in reducing complexity, but it does not also assure completeness and optimality. In literature, there are two methods basis in decoupling approach. The first one is path coordination methods in which robots planning their paths independently and afterword coordinate their movements without leaving their plans. Coordination methods usually utilize a collision-free schedule and coordination diagram to solve the problem of path planning. The second one is the prioritized planning approach. In this approach, multi-robot path planning problem solved as a sequence of path planning problems (Erdmann & Lozano-Perez, 1987). This approach may lead to *deadlock* (Nebel, 2001).

- Cooperative path planning with only local communication:

In cooperative path planning with local communication, agents or robots planning their path independently, and utilize local coordination to solve conflicts (Nebel, 2001).

3.4.2.3 Role Assignment in dynamic environment

How to assign roles for a member of groups is one of the main issues to be considered in teamwork-based multi-agent system design. The problem of role assignment in dynamic environment can be solved by associating a set of behavioral pattern with agents in order to support coordination between the agents (Nebel, 2001).There are two methods suggested to handle this problem. The first one is CS Freibrug team done in 1998 (Gutmann et al, 2000). This approach based on using fixed assignments. The second approach is CMUnited's SPAR method (stone et al, 1999) which is more advanced than the previous one. This approach is able to handle the problem of role assignments in dynamic environments to account for the current positioning and to support team reconfiguration after break down or removal of individual team members, and having flexibly positioning that takes into account the entire situation on the field (Nebel, 2001).

4. Multi-agent Systems for speeding up the Replication of Complement-Based Self-Replicated, Self-Assembled Systems (CBSRSAS)

In this section, we will explain three multi-agent systems. Two of these systems are inspired form biological system or ants' colony. In these systems, agents act as ants search for food, once finding it, they leave pheromones or stigmas as signs for other ants to be able to discover food as soon as they become near to it. Relative to the other multi-agent system, it was inspired from the robosoccer teams where agents work as they search for the ball and pass it to each other until achieving the goal. This system bases on high level of cooperation among the agents. To achieve this high cooperation level, Agents utilize a higher level of communication than level of communication of the previously mentioned stigmergy-based multi-agent systems. The details will be explained in the following subsections.

4.1 Stigmergy-based Multi-agent system for speeding up the replication process of CBSRSAS systems:

Stigmergy refers to the process by which agents put signs or stigmas as in Greek to influence each other's behavior. Stigmergy which was introduced in (Grasse, 1959) is a good approach for small-grained interactions compared to coordination methods that require an explicit rendezvous among agents. When agents observe signs in their environments, they act upon them without need to synchronize with other agents. The stigmergy-based multi-agent systems are the multi-agent systems that utilize the concept of stigmergy or putting signs or stigma as a communication approach between agents. This system works in the same manner as the ants foraging for food as explained in figure 8 (Valchenaers et al, 2001).

Here, we suggested two models based on stigmergy: the first one is the *heterogeneous stigmergy-based multi-agent system*. In this model, agents specialized in specific task. Some of the agents are specialized in discovering and putting signs at CBSRSAS's system components, called discoverer agents and others which are specialized in searching and carrying system components to their complementary system components in CBSRSAS systems, called carrier agents. For carrier agents, we classified them into two kinds of carriers: specialized carriers referring to the agents that able to discovery and carry only specific type of system components (see figure 9) and general carrier referring to the agents with abilities to discover and carry any system components. The same classification also works for the discoverers agents. The second model is *homologous stigmergy-based multi-agent* in which all agents are of the same type and with same capabilities. These models will be explained in details in following subsections.

4.1.1The heterogeneous stigmergy-based multi-agent system

This system consists of at least two types of agents. Each type is specialized in a specific task. These types are categorized into: discoverer agents, and carrier agents. Discoverer agents are responsible for discovering the existence of CBSRSAS system and put sign, stigma, at the system components. There are two options for implementing discoverer agents. The first option is to generate a general discoverer agent that can discover any system components belongs to the CBSRSAS systems, and generate different kinds of stigma that differ according to system components. The second option is to generate a specialized discoverer agent that can deal with a specific type of system components. A discoverer agents start its mission by random search for CBSRSAS as Ants search for its food, once recognizing the nearest system component, it assign a specific sign (stigma) to the system component. After that it continues another search for another specific system component in case of specialized discoverer agent or the next system component in the case of the general discoverers.

Relative to carrier agents, it should be able to have the capabilities for recognizing free system components in the media, to be able to carry them, and to be able to recognize stigma of the carried system components. Carrier agents start random search for a specific free system components if it is *a specialized carrier agent* or any free system component if it is *a general carrier agent*, once carried it, the carrier agent starts searching for the nearest stigma to target its movement toward the stigma and searching for the shortest path.

The intelligent behavior of the suggest system depends on rule-based modeling of intelligent behavior. Agents having many rules makes decision little bit slower; as the agents require traversing their database of rules to determine the appropriate decision to take. Moreover, having a lot of rules may lead to contradictions which may lead to the failure of the replication process, so specialized agents make their decision faster and more reliable than general or multi-tasking agents. Therefore, it is recommended to utilize specialized agents with larger systems. Sometimes, it is recommended to utilize some of the generalized agents to assure the load balance among agents especially if the specialized agents are not equally distributed compared to the distribution of CBSRSAS's system components types.

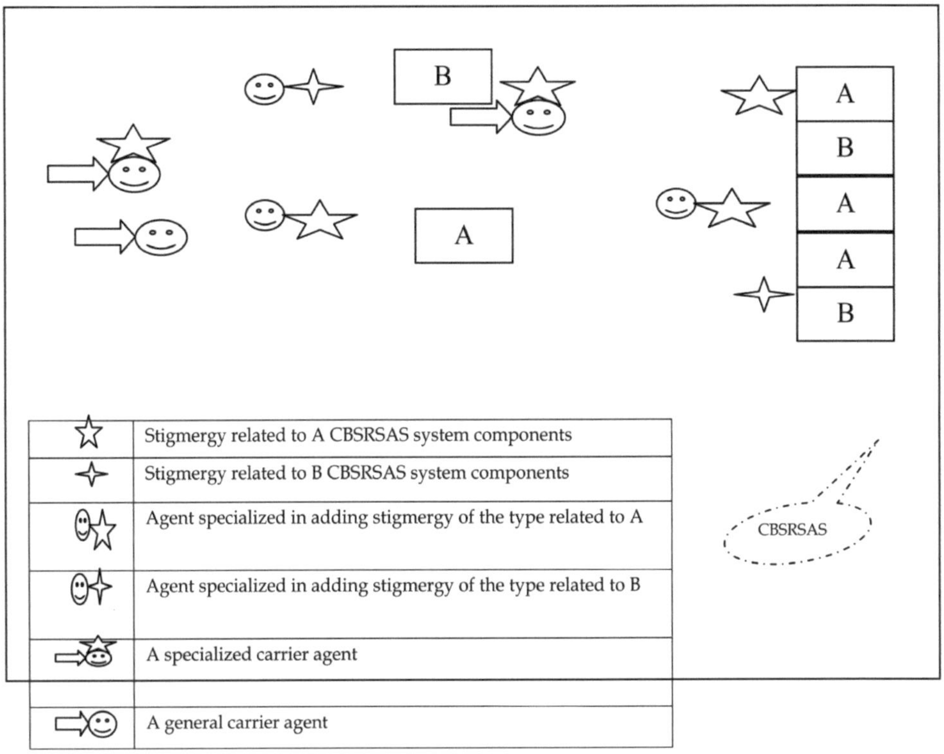

Figure 9. show a simple representation of heterogeneous Multi-agent System and how it can support the replication process of CBSRSAS systems

The behaviour of the heterogeneous multi-agent system can be represented:

$$F_{Total} = \sum_{i}^{M} \sum_{k}^{n} x_{i,j}^{\to CBSRSAS} + x_{i,j}^{\to SC} \tag{1}$$

M refers to the number of agents. N refers to the number of system components in the CBSRSAS system that their complementary parts have been carried by carrier agent i. $x_{i,j}^{\to CBSRSAS}$ refers to the effort that the carrier agent i exerts to bring system components to their complementary ones in CBSRSAS. $x_{i,j}^{\to SC}$ refers to effort that the carrier agent i exerts to find the appropriate system components. The main goal is to minimize this function considering balanced work load among the agents. This function can also represent the total required time to achieve replication process of CBSRSAS systems.

$x_{i,j}^{\to SC} = (\xi_{i,j}^{\to SC} + d_{i,j}^{\to SC})$ ξ is utilized to describe time required by the carrier agent to recognize required system component SC. $x_{i,j}^{\to CBSRSAS} = (\rho_{i,j}^{\to CBSRSAS} + d_{i,j}^{\to CBSRSAS})$ ρ is utilized to describe time required by the agent to recognize the stigma associated with the system component j.

$$F_{Total} = \sum_{i}^{M}\sum_{k}^{n}(\rho_{i,j}^{\rightarrow CBSRSAS} + d_{i,j}^{\rightarrow CBSRSAS}) + (\xi_{i,j}^{\rightarrow SC} + d_{i,j}^{\rightarrow SC}) \quad (2)$$

This new model (Equation[2]) consider how the level of agent intelligence affect the agent-based replication process of CBSRSAS system represented in recognition factor that vary from agent to another and from interaction to another.

For heterogeneous systems, ξ , the intelligent factor, for specialized carrier agent is slightly lower than ξ for general carrier agents, as specialized agent has small size of rules, it can arrive a decision quicker than the general one. Moreover the experience the agents in a specific field can improve his recognition level. Consequently, it is recommended to design this kind of multi-agent system with specialized carrier agents and to make the distribution among these agents comparable to the distribution of different system components in CBSRSAS systems.

Added to the recognition factor, there is another factors which is $\rho_{i,j}^{\rightarrow CBSRSAS}$ that measures the recognition level of carrier agent *i* to the stigma at j[th] system component in CBSRSAS systems. Consequently, $\rho_{i,j}^{\rightarrow CBSRSAS}$ value depends on the recognition of the agent which associates to his level of intelligence and the ability of discoverer agents to put signs or stigma. To illustrate, if the carrier agent *i* was successful detecting the system component *k* and discoverer agent was not able at that time to recognize the complement system, this action will result in delaying the delivery of system component *k* to its complementary system component in CBSRSAS system. Consequently, the general behavior of the system will be affected by the behaviour of less intelligent agents.

Task sharing for the heterogeneous stigmergy-based multi-agent system is at least assured even if there are only general carriers and general discovers. Task sharing here is achieved autonomously without pre-intention. As one of the general agent will be required to assign stigma, while the other will be required to search for free system components to bring.

Relative to conflict, as inherited form the stigmergy approach, agents can not directly communicate with each other. This prevents agents with same goal - for example two agents targeting the same stigma- from discovering that they are targeting the same goal. Therefore, the possibility of conflict is high in such model.

Relative Speed Up of Replication process

Relative speed up of the replication process can be measured as the ratio between a single agent system and a multi-agent system of M agents. This model includes the intelligent factor as factor the speeding up the replication process equation [3].

$$\text{Relative Speed up} = \frac{M\left(\sum_{j}^{L}(\rho_{1,j}^{\rightarrow CBSRSAS} + d_{1,j}^{\rightarrow CBSRSAS}) + (\xi_{1,j}^{\rightarrow SC} + d_{1,j}^{\rightarrow SC})\right)}{\left(\sum_{i}^{M}\sum_{j}^{N}(\rho_{i,j}^{\rightarrow CBSRSAS} + d_{i,j}^{\rightarrow CBSRSAS}) + (\xi_{i,j}^{\rightarrow SC} + d_{i,j}^{\rightarrow SC})\right)} \quad (3)$$

4.1.2 The homogenous stigmergy-based multi-agent system

In this system, all agents have similar capabilities (perception model, behavioral model and motor model). An agent can discover CBSRSAS systems, assign stigma to system components and carry system components to their complementary parts in CBSRSAS system. Designers of the homogenous stigmergy-based multi-agent system should consider a complex behavioral model as the agent should be trained for different functions.

In the homogenous stigmergy-based multi-agent system model, an agent starts working by doing a random search for either CBSRSAS systems or system components. In case of finding CBSRSAS systems, the agent puts a sign or stigma at the nearest system component of the CBSRSAS system, afterword agents start searching for the complementary system component of the discovered CBSRSAS system components. If the agent finds a system component earlier than CBSRSAS systems, the agent carries it and determines the position of the nearest stigma and start path and motion planning toward it.

Conflicts may occur in this model with a higher probability than the previous one because of the lack of specialization and the limitation of communication inherited from the stigmergy-based communication model. For instance, path and motion planning is done by each individual. There is no sharing of path planning details which may lead to conflict between agents when they collide together. Moreover agents also conflict when they are targeting the same stigma. Targeting the same stigma is frequent case in this model. To resolve this type of conflicts, the agents have to re-planning their path to the target for the first type conflict, and to retarget another stigma for the second type of conflict.

Task sharing is difficult to be arranged in this model as limited specialization and communication, so the conflict and unbalanced work load is expect with high probability in the homogeneous stigmergy-based multi-agent systems.

The behavior of this the homogenous multi-agent system can be represent as in Equation (4):

F_{Total} = cost of assigning stigma to CBSRSAS + cost of bringing system components to their complementary parts at CBSRSAS systems

$$F_{Total} = \sum_{i}^{M} x_{i,j} + \sum_{i}^{M+K} \Upsilon_{i,j} \tag{4}$$

M refers to the number of system components belonging to CBSRSAS systems, K refers to the number trails that agents tried to bring system components to the stigma and find that it is already achieved by another agent. $x_{i,j}$ represents the effort that the agent j has done to assign stigma at the ith system component of system components in CBSRSAS systems. $\Upsilon_{i,j}$ refers to the effort that the jth agent does to bring the system component to its complementary system component in CBSRSAS systems. $\sum_{i}^{M+K} \Upsilon_{i,j}$ can be divided into $\sum_{i}^{M+K} \Upsilon_{i,j} + \sum_{i}^{K} \Upsilon_{i,j}$. $\sum_{i}^{K} \Upsilon_{i,j}$ represents the effort wasted as result of conflict between agents. To illustrate, two agents bring two system components to the same complementary system component in CBSRSAS systems. The complementary part might accept only one. So the effort done by one of the agents is wasted. The main goal of this behavioral model is to minimize the energy or efforts.

Relative Speed Up of this model:

Assume we have a system of only one agent, then the time required to brings all system components to their complementary components in CBSRSAS system can be expressed

$$F_{Total}(t) = \sum_{i}^{M} x_i(t) + \sum_{i}^{M} \Upsilon_i(t) \tag{5}$$

Where $x_i(t)$ refers to the time required by the agent to put stigma at the ith system components in CBSRSAS systems. $\Upsilon_i(t)$ is the time that the agent requires to bring the complementary system components to the ith system components in CBSRSAS systems. $F_{Total}(t)$ refers to the total time required to achieve the replication process by single agent.

$$F_{Total,N}(t) = \frac{\sum_{i}^{M} x_{i,j}(t) + \sum_{i}^{M} \Upsilon_{i,j}(t)}{N} \quad \text{where } 1 \le j \le N \tag{6}$$

This model refers that the total time required by N agents to achieve replication of CBSRSAS systems. This model assumes that there is no any conflict between multi-agents systems, so the maximum speed up for the replication process that can be achieved by the homogenous multi-agent system can be computed as:

$$SpeedUp(N) = \frac{N\left(\sum_{i}^{M} x_i(t) + \sum_{i}^{M} \Upsilon_i(t)\right)}{\left(\sum_{i}^{M} x_{i,j}(t) + \sum_{i}^{M} \Upsilon_{i,j}(t)\right)} \tag{6}$$

But this representation of speed up does not include the intelligent behavior, so the following model considers the time required by decision making processes which differ from an agent to another, from a system component to another and from function to another. Many factors are involved, but we summarized the measure of intelligent behavior into factor $\xi_{i,j}(t)$ which describe the time required by the jth agent to take a decision about the ith system component and make the appropriate stigma that fit with the ith system component and factor $\gamma_{i,j}(t)$ which describes the time required to take decision about whether the agent found the system component or not which system components to carry the following equation explain the speed up.

$$SpeedUp(N) = \frac{N\left(\sum_{i}^{M} \left(x_i(t) + \xi_{i,1}(t)\right) + \sum_{i}^{M} \left(\Upsilon_i(t) + \gamma_{i,1}(t)\right)\right)}{\left(\sum_{i}^{M} \left(x_{i,j}(t) + +\xi_{i,j}(t)\right) + \sum_{i}^{M} \left(\Upsilon_{i,j}(t) + \gamma_{i,j}(t)\right)\right)} \tag{7}$$

4.2 A Robosoccer Team-Based Multi-agent System for speeding up the replication process of CBSRSAS systems:

In this system, agents have different capabilities (perception model, behavioral model and motor model), but they have the same capabilities to communicate. A group of agents agrees to work together forming a team work. Working as a team provides agents with cooperative sensing which means the limited sensing capabilities of an agent can be overcome by support from other agents (Nebel, 2001) this gives the group capabilities to localize the objects which, in our case, are system components in CBSRSAS systems and their complementary system components. Moreover, cooperative sensing provides agents with capabilities to localize themselves by either indentifying their position using (Rekleitis et al, 1997) schema which depends on well known immobile agents or identify their relative position using multiple-hypothesis approach (Fox et al, 2000). The first approach for localization is best for avoiding odometry error and the second is good for dealing with well know environments (Rekleitis et al, 1997).

In this model, agents start their work by building teams or coalitions. They negotiate together till forming the teams (Dignum et al, 1999). Once formed, each agent in the team start searching for a goal to the team. The goal can be determined by either finding free system components in the environments or finding the CBSRSAS systems. For the first case, the goal is to find CBSRSAS systems that can utilize these system components in the replication process. For the second case, the goal is to find system components that help in CBSRSAS system replication. Once, the goal is determined, the team agents start cooperatively planning their motion and path using local communication between team agents to avoid conflict among team agents and global communication among teams to avoid conflict between teams' agents. Moreover, agents communicate together to help each other in dynamic environments. Once an agent find system component, the agent broadcast its findings to other team agents that, in turn, plan faster achievement of the task by defining sequence of passing system components to each other till providing system components to their complementary system components in CBSRSAS systems.

The advantages of this model of multi-agent systems are enormous. Firstly, this model follows the main theme of nature which is the *diversity* (Loreau et al, 2006), as the model provides different agents with different capabilities. Secondly, since agents vary according their capabilities, *delegation of responsibilities* of this model is an important issue handled by this model as it is team-based multi-agent system (Norman and Reed, 2000). To illustrate, if an agent x in team y has higher capabilities to deal very well with current situation, and an agent z carries a system component, the agent z will broadcast its findings and environmental conditions, and the best free agent will handle it. Thirdly, *cooperation between agents* in this model of multi-agent system is much better than the previously mentioned stigmergy-based multi-agent systems. Fifthly, *load balance among agents* is assured. For example, if agent x did a lot of work and feel tired, it will not respond to the broadcast from the agents holding system components. Sixthly, *passing of objects* is the main powerful characteristic inherited from soccer playing model, as the agent will pass the system components to another agents, afterwards it will be free to participate in another job, saving extra time. Seventhly, this model provides different way for optimizing the behavior of all system. For example, number of teams and average number of agents a team can be used to optimize behavior. Moreover, policies utilized through agent-to-agent and team-to-team interactions can be optimized. Consequently, there are many parameters used to improve the total behavior of entire multi-agent system. To conclude, soccer inspired team-based multi-agent system is a powerful multi-agent system with enormous advantages.

Total cost & relative speed up

To measure the total effort or cost exerted by this type of multi-agent system, we propose the following function. The main goal we seek is to minimize this objective function as much as we can. This function consists of three terms. The first, $\gamma_{i,j}(t)$, refers to the effort i^{th} team exerts to find out the system component j. The second, $\psi_{i,j}(t)$, expresses the effort team i exerts to find the CBSRSAS's system component that its complementary is the one that the team has. $\Im_{i,j}(t)$, the third, is utilized to express the total effort done by the team agents to bring the system component *j* to its complementary at CBSRSAS systems.

$$F_{Total} = \sum_{i}^{Tms}\sum_{j}^{I_{Sc}}\left(\gamma_{i,j}(t) + \psi_{i,j}(t) + \Im_{i,j}(t)\right) \tag{9}$$

Tms refers to the number of teams participate in replication process of the CBSRSAS systems, and I_{Sc} refers to the number of system components that the ith team brings to their complementary system components in CBSRSAS system.

Relative to speed up, to compute the relative speed up that N teams of agents can achieve, we propose the following equation [10]. The relative speed up of a multi-agent system is the ratio between the period of time required by a team of one agent to get all the system components to their complementary system components in CBSRSAS systems to the period of time required by the n teams to achieve the same objective.

$$SpeedUp(N) \le \frac{N\left(\sum_{j}^{M}\left(\gamma_{1,j}(t) + \psi_{1,j}(t) + \Im_{1,j}(t)\right)\right)}{\left(\sum_{i}^{N}\sum_{j}^{I_{Sc}}\left(\gamma_{i,j}(t) + \psi_{i,j}(t) + \Im_{i,j}(t)\right)\right)} \tag{10}$$

5. Discussion and future work

Replication is not only an important process of CBSRSAS, but It is also important process for all living creatures by which they maintain their existence. Industrially, it has a lot of advantages, but the main advantage of this process is the massive production of the product. The Autonomous replication of CBSRSAS system is a time consuming process as it depends not only on the kinematic capabilities of the system components, but also on the viscosity environments.

So, in this chapter, we have proposed three multi-agent system models to be used in speeding up this process. These models vary in their way of organizations, communication, and cooperation. In the first and second models: the heterogeneous stigmergy-based multi-agent systems, and the homogeneous stigmergy-based multi-agent systems, we have utilized the concept of stigmergy or putting signs which is inspired from ant-colony as an approach for communication between agents. By stigmergy, on one hand, we succeeded to make the global goal which is to bring free system components to their complementary in CBSRSAS systems locally available to the agents.

But, on the other hand, we expect that the conflict between agents in stigmergy-based approaches is high because of the limited cooperation and communication capabilities of agents. These limitations prevent agents from collective behavior where many agents are involved. To illustrate, carrier agents may collide or conflict together, which may lead to system components carried by these agents either to self-assemble into bigger complex which may be difficult to be carried by one of them or to be lost leading them to restart searching for free system components. Moreover, conflict may happen when two agents target the system stigma, leading to lose efforts that have done by one of them and subsequently to *ineffectiveness* in achieving tasks.

The third model, the robosoccer team-based multi-agent system, utilizes high level of communication and cooperation between agents. Agents belonging to one team have many advantages. For example, they utilize the cooperative sensing where the limitation of the agent sensing capabilities has been overcommed. In addition, they can arrange their work in a cooperative manner through utilizing the cooperative path and motion planning and dynamic role assignments to deal with different conditions and circumstances. To explain, agents with higher capabilities to deal with complicated environment where a lot of burdens exist arrange themselves to help other agents through such kind of environments.

Relative to the task sharing among agents, the stigmergy-based multi-agent system does not assure sharing of tasks among agents in general. The heterogeneous type is better than homogenous one from the tasking sharing wise, but this task sharing is evolved not as matter of cooperation but as the result of heterogeneity among agents that lead subsequently specialization among agents. This specialization assures that the agents do only a specific piece of the task. In the robosoccer team-based multi-agent systems, the task sharing among agents is a dynamic process and varies according the environmental conditions. Thus, task sharing is an added advantage of the robosoccer multi-agent systems.

In this chapter, we theoretically derive some mathematical models that represent how these models can relatively speed up the replication process of the CBSRSAS systems. These mathematical models take in consideration how the cooperation among agents and their intelligence level affect the replication process of CBSRSAS systems. The models can be considered by multi-agent systems designers to balance between the cost of the multi-agent system and the objectives.

$$\text{Absolute speed up} = \frac{F_{total}^{\text{Autonomous Replication CBSRSAS}}}{F_{total}^{\text{Multi-agent -based replication of CBSRSAS}}} \quad (11)$$

To measure the absolute speed up of the multi-agent system, we have to compare the replication of CBSRSAS utilizing the multi-agent system against the autonomous replication of CBSRSAS system (see Equation [11].). The absolute measure of the speed up is not only a good evidence of how the multi-agent system is supportive to the replication of CBSRSAS systems compared to the autonomous replication of CBSRSAS systems, but it is also a good measure of which multi-agent system performs better relative to common criteria or the execution time required by the autonomous replication of CBSRSAS systems. Unlike the absolute speed up, the relative speed up measures how the number of agents affects the speed up of the replication process. Thus, the relative speed up is a good approach for determining the best number of agents to be utilized, while the absolute speed up is a good approach for determining which multi-agent system model is better for the current situation or circumstances for replication of CBSRSAS.

Relative to future investigation, we are looking for integrating these multi-agent system models with multi-agent modeling tools such as MASON (Luke et al, 2004), and JADE. In addition, we are looking for utilizing advanced cooperation methodologies that clearly explained in literature such as the market model (Smith, 1988), and scientific community metaphors such as (Kornfieldeld, 1979), and (Lenat, 1975) to fully utilize the agents' capabilities.

The multi-agent system models suggested in this chapter assume that the CBSRSAS system replication rule set is of the 2nd category (see section 1) where each system components have one and only complementary system components and one and only complement interaction section, leading to a very simple model of CBSRSAS systems. Thus, one of the major directions for future investigation is to build a general multi-agent system capable of handling the potential complexity of CBSRSAS systems. To handle such complexity in the future, the agents should be integrated with a powerful learning strategy and an AI induction or reasoning approach as well as a good cooperation approach.

6. References

Beautement P., Allsopp D., Greaves M. , Goldsmith S., Spires S, Thompson S. G. and Janicke H. Autonomous Agents and Multi -agent Systems (AAMAS) for the Military - Issues and Challenges, *International Workshop on Defence Applications of Multi-Agent Systems, DAMAS 2005* pp. 1-13, Utrecht, The Netherlands, July 25, 2005

Boccara N. 2004, *Modeling complex systems*, ISBN0-387-40462-7, P:1-36, Springer Berlin/ Heidelberg 2004

Dignum F., Dunin-Ke B. ¸plicz, and Verbrugge R.. Dialogue in team formation: a formal approach. In: F. Dignum and B. Chaib-draa (eds.), *IJCAI Workshop on Agent Communication Languages*, Stockholm, 1999, pp. 39–50

Doran J., Agent-based modeling of ecosystems for sustainable resource management , *proceeding of ACAI 2001*, , ISBN: 3-540-42312-5, LNAI 2086, PP. 383-403, 2001 Pargue, Czech Republic, July, 2001.

Ellabaan M. (A) (2007): Complement-Based Self-Replicated, Self-assembled Systems (CBSRSAS), *Progress in artificial life, proceeding of third Australian conference*, ISBN: 978-3-540-76930-9, LANI 4828. pp. 168-178, 2007, ACAL 2007, Gold Coast, Australia, December 2007.

Ellabaan M. (B) (2007): Activation energy-based simulation for self-assembly of multi-shape tiles, *GECCO'07*, July 7–11, 2007, London, England, United Kingdom. July, 2007.

Ellabaan M, Brailsford T. (2006) Wang Cube Simulation of Self-assembly, *Proceeding of Information & Communications Technology*, 2006. ICICT '06, ISBN: 0-7803-9770-3, Cairo, Egypt, 2006.

Erdmann M. and Lozano-Perez, T. On Multiple Moving Objects. *Algorithmica*, 2(4):477-521, 1987.

Flores-Mendez R., A Towards a standardization of multi-agent system framework, *Cross rood*, 5 (4), p:18-24, 1999, ACM, New york, USA, 1999.

Fox D., Burgard W.,. Kruppa H, and Thrun S. Collaberative mutli-robot localization, autonomous Robots, 8(3), 2000.

Gagne, D., Nault, G, Garant, A, & Desibiens, J. Aurora: A multi-agent proto type Modelling Crew Interpersonal communication Network., in *Proceeding of the 1993 DND workshop on knowledge based systems robotics*. Ottawa, Ontario, 1993

Grasse, P. La theorie de la stigmergy: essai d'interpretation du comportement des termites constructerus, insects sociaux 6 (1959)

Gutmann J., Herrmann W., Nebel F., Rittinger f., Toppor A., and Weigel T., The CS Freibrug team: Playing robotic soccer based on an explicit world model. *The AI Magazine*, 21 (1): 37-46, 2000.

Kornfieldeld A. ETHER: A Parallel Problem Solving System. In *Proceedings of the 1979 Joint Conference on Artificial Intelligence* (IJCAI), 1979,490-492.

James E. Rauch & Diana Weinhold, 1999. Openness, Specialization, and Productivity Growth in Less Developed Countries, *Canadian Journal of Economics, Canadian Economics Association*, vol. 32(4), pages 1009-1027, August. [Specialization]

Lenat D. B. BEINGS: Knowledge as Interacting Experts. In *Proceedings of the Fourth Joint Conference on Artificial Intelligence* (IJCAI). 1975,126-133.

Latombe, J. Robot Motion Planning. Kluwer, dordrech, Holland 1991

Loreau M., Oteng-Yeboah A., Arroyo M., Babin D., Barbault R., Donoghue M., Gadgil M., Häuser C., C. Heip, A. Larigauderie, K. Ma, G. Mace, H. A. Mooney, C. Perrings, P. Raven, J. Sarukhan, P. Schei, R. J. Scholes & R. T. Watson. Diversity without representation, *Nature* 442, 245-246 (20 July 2006

Luke S., Cioffi-Revilla C., Panait L, and Sullivan K. MASON: A New Multi-Agent Simulation Toolkit. 2004. *Proceedings of the 2004 SwarmFest Workshop.*

Millar R., Hanna J., and Kealy S. A review of behavioral animation, *Computers and Graphics,* 23(1):127-143, 1999.

Nebel B., Cooperative physical robotis: A lesson in playing robotic soccer , *proceeding of ACAI 2001,* , ISBN: 3-540-42312-5, LNAI 2086, PP. 404-414, 2001 Pargue, Czech Republic, July, 2001.

Rekleitis I.M., Dudek G ., and Milios E.E. Multi-robot exploration of an unkown environment, efficiently reducing the odometry error. In *proceeding of the 15th international joint conference on artificial Intelegence* (IJCAI-97), pages 1340-1345, Nagoya, Japan, August, 1997.

Neumann J. von (1951) The General and Logical Theory of Automata, in *Cerebral Mechanisms in Behavior—The Hixon Symposium,* 1—41, John Wiley, New York, NY. Originally presented in 1948.

Neumann J. V. (1966) Theory of Self-Reproducing Automata, University of Illinois Press, Urbana, IL. Edited and completed by A. W. Burks 1966.

Rogers A., David E., Schiff J., and N.R. Jennings. The Effects of Proxy Bidding and Minimum Bid Increments within eBay Auctions, *ACM Transactions on the Web,* 2007,

Norman T. and Reed C. Delegation and responsibility. In C. Castelfranchi and Y. Lesp´erance, editors, *Intelligent Agents* VII. Agent Theories, Architectures and Languages 7th. International Workshop, ATAL-2000, Boston, MA, USA, July 7-9, 2000.

Theraulaz, G. A brief History of stigmergy, *artificial life* 5 (1999) pp.97-116

Schurr N, Marecki J., M Tambe and Paul Scerri et.al. The Future of Disaster Response: Humans Working with Multiagent Teams using DEFACTO, 2005

Smith R. The Contract Net Protocol: High-Level Communication and Control in a Distributed Problem Solver. In A. Bond, (Ed), *Readings in Distributed Artificial Intelligence.* Morgan Kaufmann,1988, 357-366.

Stone P., Veloso M., and Riley, P.: The CMUnited-98 champion simulator team. In M. Asada and H. Kitano, editors, *RoboCup-98: Robot Soccer World Cup* 11, pp. 61-76, Springer-Verlag, Berlin, Heidelber, New York, 1999

Stone P., and Veloso M., Multiagent Systems: A Survey from a Machine Learning Perspective *In Autonomous Robotics* volume 8, number 3. July, 2000.

Sun R., Naveh I. Simulating Organizational Decision-Making Using a Cognitively Realistic Agent Model, *Journal of Artificial Societies and Social Simulation,* 2004.

Valckenaers P., Brussel H., Kollingbaum M., and Bochmann, O. J., Multi-agent coordination and control using strigmergy applied to manufacturing control , *proceeding of ACAI 2001,* , ISBN: 3-540-42312-5, LNAI 2086, PP. 317-334, 2001 Pargue, Czech Republic, July, 2001.

Wang, H. (1961), Bell System Tech. *Journal* 40(1961), pp. 1-42.

Wooldridge M., an Introduction to Multi Agent Systems, John Wiley & Sons Ltd, 2002, ISBN 0-471-49691-X.

9

Investigating the Performance of Rule-based Models with Increasing Complexity on the Prediction of Trip Generation and Distribution

Elke Moons[1], Geert Wets and Marc Aerts
Hasselt University
Belgium

1. Introduction

Modelling travel behaviour has always been a major research area in transportation analysis. After the second World War, due to the rapid increase in car ownership and car use in Western Europe and the United States, several models have been developed by transportation planners. In the fifties and sixties, travel was assumed to be the result of four subsequent decisions that were modelled: trip generation, trip distribution, mode choice and the assignment of trips to the road network (Ruiter & Ben-Akiva, 1978). These original trip-based models have been extended to ensuing tour-based models (Daly et al., 1983) and activity-based models (Pendyala et al., 1995; Ben-Akiva & Bowman, 1998; Kitamura & Fujii, 1998; Arentze & Timmermans, 2000; Bhat et al., 2004). In tour-based models, trips are explicitly connected in tours, i.e. chains that start and end at the same home or work base. This is carried out by introducing spatial constraints, hereby dealing with the lack of spatial interrelationship which was so apparent in the traditional four-step trip-based model. In activity-based models, travel demand is derived from the activities that individuals and households need or wish to perform. Decisions with respect to travel are driven by a collection of activities that form an activity diary. Travel should therefore be modelled within the context of the entire agenda, or as a component of the activity scheduling decision. In this way, the relationship between travel and non-travel aspects is taken into account. The reason why people undertake trips is one of the key aspects to be modelled in an activity-based model.

However, every working transportation model still exists of at least these original four components of trip generation, distribution, mode choice and assignment. In order to fully understand the structure of a traditional transportation model, we need to elaborate on it some more. As shown in Figure 1, trip generation encompasses both the modelling of production (P) and attraction (A) of trips for a certain region (zone). Production is mainly being modelled at the level of the household, incorporating household characteristics (income, car ownership, household composition, …), features of the zone (land price, degree of urbanization) and accessibility of the zone, whereas attraction is modelled at zone level,

[1] Corresponding author (E-mail: elke.moons@uhasselt.be)

taking into account employment, land use (for industry, education, services, shopping, etc.) and accessibility (Ortúzar & Willumsen, 2001).

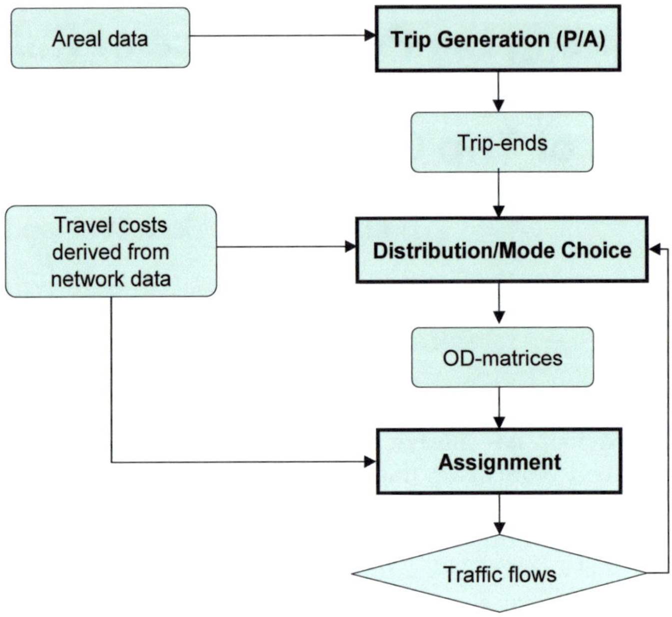

Figure 1. Structure of the traditional trip-based model

In the trip distribution step, the produced and attracted trips, that either depart or arrive at a certain zone will be combined, so after the first two steps (generation and distribution), the result is an origin-destination (OD) matrix, where each cell denotes the number of trips going from and to a particular zone. In step three (modal split), these OD-matrices will be split up per mode of transport, and these trips will be assigned to the network in the fourth step, taking into account some generalised network costs.

After a short history of transportation models and a description of the structure of the traditional model to understand the notions of trip generation and distribution, this introduction will focus on the different types of activity-based (AB) models, since they have become the standard today and the need of AI techniques within the fastest rising type of AB models (i.e. rule-based models) will be shown.

Activity-based models aim at predicting which activities will be conducted where, when, with whom, for how long and the transport mode that was used to arrive at the location of the activity. This sequence of choices immediately shows the usefulness of applying AI techniques, since one of the most important application areas of artificial intelligence is decision making, which clearly happens multiple times a day when a trip is planned. In general, AI can be split up into two broad categories: the symbolic AI that focuses on the development of knowledge-based systems, and the computational AI, which includes neural networks, fuzzy systems and genetic algorithms. In this chapter, we will focus on the latter category of methods, more in specific on the use of induction techniques for prediction. But first, it needs to be shown how induction techniques are applied within AB models.

Actually, several types of models can be distinguished to build an activity-based travel demand model. They range from constraints-based simulation models to utility-maximising and rule-based (computational process) models. Constraints-based simulation models have their roots in time geography, but they are limited in use, because they lack the necessary mechanisms to predict adjustment behaviour of individuals. Currently, the utility-maximising models based on the logit model (multinomial, nested, mixed, paired combinatory, spatially correlated (Ben-Akiva & Lerman, 1985; Hensher & Greene, 2003; Koppelman & Wen, 2000; Bhat & Guo, 2003 a.o.)) are still the most popular choice, however, because of their flexibility, rule-based systems based on AI algorithms are gaining more and more interest. Examples of utility-maximising models are Starchild (Recker et al., 1986), PCATS (Kitamura & Fujii, 1998) and CEMDAP (Bhat et al., 2004), while AMOS (Pendyala et al., 1995, 1998), FAMOS (Pendyala, 2004) and Albatross (Arentze & Timmermans, 2000, 2005) are examples of rule-based models. Utility-maximising models consider different facets of travel patterns simultaneously, however, the process by which individuals arrive at their choices is not modelled at all. Rule-based models represent an attempt of modelling this scheduling process, hereby disregarding the utility-maximising framework. After all, a lot of researchers have argued that people do not always necessarily arrive at 'optimal' choices, but rather use heuristics that may be context dependent. In its most simple form, a rule-based model uses a set of simple IF-THEN rules, that take on the following form: IF (condition = X), THEN (perform action Y). This process of rule induction is similar to the process of parameter estimation in algebraic, econometric models. Although these rule-based models perform very well when induction techniques are used (Wets et al., 2000), they also show some limitations. Most of them are based on a quite complex set of rules. However, already in the Middle Ages, William of Occam's razor (Tornay, 1938) stated that 'Nunquam ponenda est pluralitas sin necesitate' meaning that 'Entities should not be multiplied beyond necessity'. Now it has come to be seen as one of the fundamental tenets of modern science and it is often invoked by learning theorists as a justification for preferring simpler models over more complex ones. However, Domingos (1998) teaches us that it is tricky to interpret Occam's razor in the right way. The interpretation 'Simplicity is a goal in itself' is essentially correct, while 'Simplicity leads to greater accuracy' is not. Moreover, research in the field of psychology (Gigerenzer et al., 1999; Zellner et al., 2001) shows that there is empirical evidence that simple models, based on fast and frugal heuristics that employ a minimum of time, knowledge and computation, often predict human behaviour very well.

Moons et al. (2001) examined the performance of simple classifiers for the transport mode dimension of the Albatross model system. It was discovered that the predictive performance of these simple heuristics was only slightly less than that of a more complex induction algorithm. Moons et al. (2002a, 2002b, 2005) investigated the influence of irrelevant attributes on the performance of the decision tree for the transport mode, the travel party, the activity duration and the location agent of the Albatross model system and it was found that a trimmed decision tree, involving considerable less decision rules, did not result in a significant drop in predictive performance compared to the original larger set of rules that was derived from the activity-travel diaries. Similar techniques have been applied in completely different research domains: marketing (Buckinx et al., 2004), artificial intelligence (Koller & Sahami, 1996; Kohavi et al., 1994), bioinformatics (Zheng et al., 2003), etc. In this chapter, the question `To what extent can this result be generalised in a sequential execution of the full set of nine decision trees that make up the complete Albatross model system?' is inspected.

For reasons outlined above, it was opted to use several induction techniques with an increasing complexity within a rule-based model. Very simple and more complex decision tree induction algorithms are measured against each other, and the resulting predicted OD matrices are compared to the original matrix to investigate the performance of a sequential execution of these (simple) models. The next Section will discuss the methods that are used to arrive at these simple and complex decision trees, whereas in Section 3 a short introduction to the data is given, together with a discussion on the comparison of the performance of the different methods. In Section 4, the results are presented, while the final Section provides the conclusions and some avenues for future research.

2. Methods

First of all, the modelling framework is explained, so that one understands which are the different responses that need to be modelled sequentially. Next, the different methods to determine simple and complex decision are presented.

2.1 Modelling framework

Albatross, the most complex fully-operational rule-based model to date, was developed for the Dutch Ministry of Transportation (Arentze and Timmermans, 2000, 2005). This chapter uses the activity-diary data that were collected to determine the rules of the original Albatross system. The activity scheduling process happens sequentially at micro level. Figure 2 provides a schematic representation of the Albatross scheduling model.

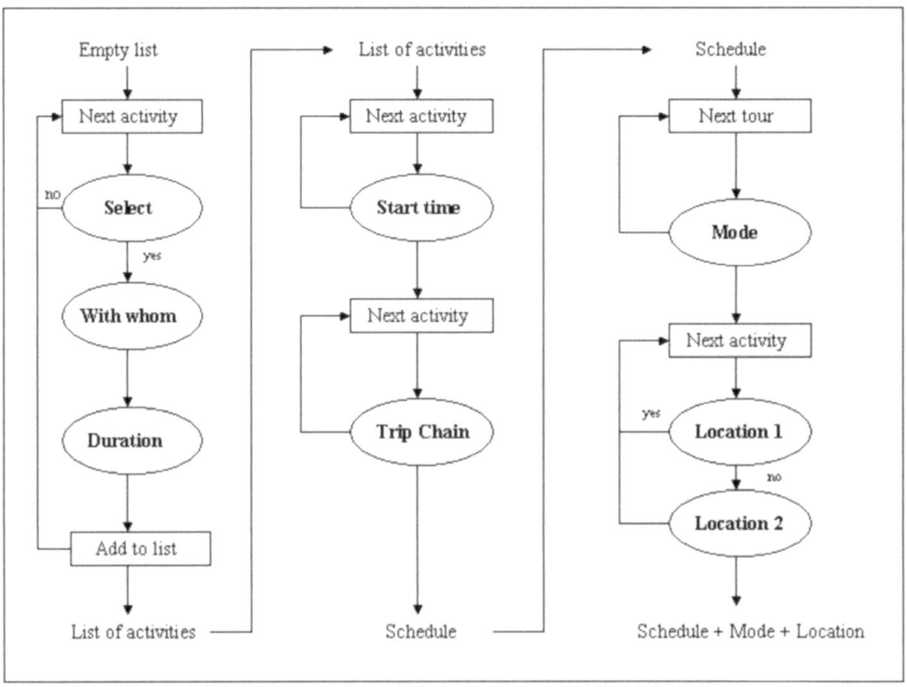

Figure 2. Sequential decisions making up the Albatross model

The activity scheduling agent of Albatross is based on an assumed sequential execution of nine decision trees to predict activity-travel patterns. The model first executes a set of decision rules to predict whether or not a particular activity will be inserted in the schedule. At the same time, the transport mode for the primary work activity is chosen, further referred to as 'mode for work'. If the activity is added, the travel party and the duration of the activity are determined, based on other sets of rules, before a next activity is considered. The order in which activities are evaluated is pre-defined as: daily shopping, services, non-daily shopping, social and leisure activities. Time constraints are used in this step to determine the feasibility of the chosen activities. Subsequently, in order of priority, a general notion of time of the day (e.g. early morning, around noon, ...) is determined for each activity. Based on this, for each activity, a preliminary position is determined in the schedule. Hereafter, trip links (i.e. trip chaining decisions) between activities are considered, which means that when tours are included in the schedule, they are identifiable as sequences of one or more out-of-home activities that start at home and end at home. These trip chaining decisions are not only important for timing activities but also for organising trips into tours. For each tour, a transport mode is then determined. Note that if the activity is the primary work activity, then the transport mode was already chosen, if not, the choice of transport mode is made here in the scheduling process. Finally, the location of each activity is set. Possible interactions between mode and location choices are taken into account by using location information as conditions of mode selection rules. Institutional, spatial and time constraints are adopted in this step to determine which locations are feasible.

The predictions for each model are based on a simulation procedure. This involves building an activity pattern for each person-day by successively making a decision on each of the nine choice dimensions. A decision involves selecting a choice alternative based on the predicted probability distribution across alternatives on the choice facet concerned.

2.2 The methods

A brief literature review indicates that very simple rules may achieve a surprisingly high accuracy on many data sets. For example, Rendell and Seshu (1990) occasionally remark that many real world data sets have 'few peaks (often just one)' and are therefore 'easy to learn'. Further evidence is provided by studies of pruning methods (e.g. Buntine & Niblett, 1992; Clark & Niblett, 1989; Mingers, 1989), where the accuracy is rarely seen to decrease as pruning becomes more severe. This is even so when the rules are pruned to the extreme, using only one or two variables. The most compelling initial indication that very simple rules often perform well, occurs in Weiss et al. (1990). In four of the five data sets studied, classification rules involving two or fewer attributes outperformed the more complex rules.

Therefore, in the next subsections, three induction techniques with an increasing complexity are presented. At first, a very simple classifier, called One R, will be used in order to set up the set of rules for each of the dimensions in the Albatross system. Next, we will discuss a feature selection technique that will applied first to determine the relevant variables before a decision tree is determined. And finally, the C4.5 algorithm to determine a decision tree will shortly be introduced.

2.2.1 One R

Holte developed a very simple classifier that provides a rule based on the value of a single attribute. This algorithm, which he called One R, may compete with state-of-the-art techniques used in the field (Holte, 1993).

Like other algorithms, One R takes as input a set of several attributes and a class variable. Its goal is to infer a rule that predicts the class given the values of the attributes. The One R algorithm chooses the most informative single attribute and bases the rule solely on this attribute. Full details can be found in Holte's paper, but the basic idea is given below. The accuracy is measured by the percentage of correctly classified instances.

```
For each attribute a, form a rule as follows:
        For each value v from the domain of a,
                Let c be the most frequent class in the set of
                        instances where a has value v.
                Add the following clause to the rule for a:
                        If a has value v then the class is c
        Calculate the classification accuracy of this rule.
Use the rule with the highest accuracy.
```

The algorithm assumes that the attributes are discrete. If not, they must be discretised. Any method for turning a range of values into disjoint intervals must take care to avoid creating large numbers of rules with many small intervals. This is known as the problem of 'overfitting', because such rules are overly specific to the data set and do not generalise well. Holte achieves this by requiring all intervals (except the rightmost) to contain more than a predefined number of examples in the same class of the outcome variable. Empirical evidence (Holte et al., 1989) led to a value of six for data sets with large number of instances and three for smaller data sets (with less than 50 instances).

2.2.2 Relief-F: a feature selection technique

Feature selection strategies are often applied to explore the effect of irrelevant attributes on the performance of classifier systems. A feature selection method ranks all the attributes or conditions (features) in descending order of relevance. This relevance can be measured in several ways, leading to two large subclasses in feature selection methods: the filter and the wrapper approach. The fundamental difference between these approaches is the evaluation criterion used to select or rank attributes. For wrappers, the selection or ranking results from the estimation of the performance on the associated induction algorithm, while the filter approach only makes use of the characteristics of the data itself. Both methods have been compared extensively (Hall, 1999a, 1999b; Koller & Sahami, 1996). In this analysis, the filter approach, more specifically the Relief-F feature selection method is chosen because it can handle multiple classes of the dependent variable (the nine different choice facets that we are predicting range from two to seven classes) and because it can easily be combined with the C4.5 induction algorithm (Quinlan, 1993).

Feature selection strategies can be regarded as one way of coping with correlation between attributes. This is relevant because the structure of trees is sensitive to possible multicollinearity, which implies that some variables would be simply redundant (given the presence of other variables). Redundant variables do not affect the impact of the remaining variables in the tree model, but it would simply be better if they were not used for splitting. Therefore, a good feature selection method would search for a subset of relevant features that are highly correlated with the class or action variable that the tree-induction algorithm is trying to predict, while mutually having the lowest possible correlations.

Relief (Kira & Rendall, 1992), the predecessor of Relief-F, is a distance-based feature weighting algorithm. It orders attributes according to their importance. To each attribute it assigns the initial value of zero that will be adapted with each run through the instances of the dataset. The features with the highest values are considered to be the most relevant, while those with values close to zero or with negative values are judged irrelevant. Thus Relief imposes a ranking on features by assigning each a weight. The weight for a particular feature reflects its relevance in distinguishing the classes.

In determining the weights, the concepts of *near-hit* and *near-miss* are central. A *near-hit* of instance i is defined as the instance that is closest to i (based on Euclidean distance) and which is of the same class (concerning the output or action variable), while a *near-miss* of i is defined as the instance that is closest to i (based on Euclidean distance) and which is of a different class (concerning the output variable). The algorithm attempts to approximate the following difference of probabilities for the weight of a feature X:

$$W_X = P(\text{different value of X} \mid \text{nearest instance of different class}) - P(\text{different value of X} \mid \text{nearest instance of same class})$$

Thus, Relief works by random sampling an instance and locating its nearest neighbour from the same and opposite class. The nearest neighbour is defined in terms of the Euclidean distance. That is, in an n-dimensional space, the following distance measure: $d(x,y)=\left(\sum_{i=1}^{n}(x_i-y_i)^2\right)^{1/2}$, where x and y are two n-dimensional vectors.

By removing the context sensitivity provided by the 'nearest instance' condition, attributes are treated as mutually independent, and the previous equation becomes:

$$Relief_X = P(\text{different value of X} \mid \text{different class}) - P(\text{different value of X} \mid \text{same class}).$$

Relief-F (Kononenko, 1994) is an extension of Relief that can handle multiple classes and noise caused by missing values, outliers, etc. To increase the reliability of Relief's weight estimation, Relief-F finds the k nearest hits and misses for a given instance, where k is a parameter that can be specified by the user. For multiple class problems, Relief-F searches for nearest misses from each different class (with respect to the given instance) and averages their contribution. The average is weighted by the prior probability of each class.

2.2.3 C4.5: a decision tree algorithm

Decision tree induction is similar to parameter estimation methods in econometric models. The goal of tree induction is to find the set of Boolean rules that best represents the empirical data. The original Albatross system was derived using a Chi-square based approach. In this study, however, the decision trees were re-induced using the C4.5 method (Quinlan, 1993) because this method is a benchmarking method in the data mining community. Wets et al. (2000) found approximately equal performance of these two tree induction algorithms in terms of goodness of fit in a representative case study.

The C4.5 algorithm works as follows. Let there be given a set of choice observations *i* taken from activity-travel diary data. Consider the *n* different attributes or conditions $X_{i1}, X_{i2}, ..., X_{in}$ and the choice or action variable $Y_i \in \{1,2,...,p\}$ for $i = 1, \ldots I$. In general, a decision tree consists of different layers of nodes. It starts from the root node in the first layer or first parent node. This parent node will split into daughter nodes on the second layer. In turn, each of these daughter nodes can become a new parent node in the next split, and this process may continue with further splits. A leaf node is a node, which has no offspring nodes. Nodes in deeper layers become increasingly more homogeneous. An internal node is split by considering all allowable splits for all variables and the best split is the one with the most homogeneous daughter nodes. The C4.5 algorithm recursively splits the sample space on *X* into increasingly homogeneous partitions in terms of *Y*, until the leaf nodes contain only cases from a single class. Increase in homogeneity achieved by a candidate split is measured in terms of an information gain ratio. To understand this concept, the following definitions are relevant:

Definition 1: Information of a message

The information conveyed by a message depends on its probability and can be measured in bits as minus the logarithm to base 2 of that probability. ■

For example, if there are four equally probable messages, the information conveyed by any of them is - $\log_2 (1/4) = 2$ bits.

Definition 2: Information of a message that a random case belongs to a certain class

$$-\log_2\left(\frac{freq(C_i,T)}{|T|}\right) bits$$

with *T* a training set of cases, C_i a class *i* and freq(C_i, *T*) the number of cases in *T* that belongs to class C_i. ■

Based on these definitions, the average amount of information needed to identify the class of a case in a training set (also called entropy) can be deduced as follows:

Definition 3: Entropy of a training set

$$\text{info}(T) = -\sum_{i=1}^{k} \frac{freq(C_i,T)}{|T|} \times \log_2\left(\frac{freq(C_i,T)}{|T|}\right) bits$$

with *T* a training set of cases, C_i a class *i* and freq(C_i, *T*) the number of cases in *T* that belongs to class C_i. ■

Entropy can also be measured after that *T* has been partitioned in *n* sets using the outcome of a test carried out on attribute X. This yields:

Definition 4: Entropy after the training set has been partitioned on a test X

$$\text{info}_X(T) = \sum_{i=1}^{n} \frac{|T_i|}{|T|} \times \text{info}(T_i) \quad ■$$

Using these two measurements, the *gain criterion* can be defined as follows:

Definition 5: Gain criterion

$$\text{gain}(X) = \text{info}(T) - \text{info}_X(T) \quad ■$$

The gain criterion measures the information gained by partitioning the training set using the test *X*. In ID3, the ancestor of C4.5, the test selected is the one which maximizes this information gain because one may expect the remaining subsets in the branches will be the most easy to partition. Note, however, that by no means this is certain because we have looked ahead only one level deep in the tree. The gain criterion has only proved to be a good heuristic. Although the gain criterion performed quite well in practice, the criterion has one serious deficiency, i.e. it tends to favour conditions or attributes with many outcomes. Therefore, in C4.5, a somewhat adapted form of the gain criterion is used. This criterion is called the *gain ratio criterion*. According to this criterion, the gain attributable to conditions with many outcomes is adjusted using some kind of normalisation. In particular, the split info(*X*) measure is defined as:

Definition 6: Split info of a test X

$$\text{split info}(X) = -\sum_{i=1}^{n} \frac{|T_i|}{|T|} \times \log_2\left(\frac{|T_i|}{|T|}\right) \blacksquare$$

This indicates the information generated by partitioning T into n subsets. Using this measure, the gain ratio is defined as:

Definition 7: Gain ratio

$$\text{gain ratio}(X) = \text{gain}(X) \;/\; \text{split info}(X) \blacksquare$$

This ratio represents how much of the gained information is useful for classification. In case of very small values of split info(*X*) (in case of trivial splits), the ratio will tend to infinity. Therefore, C4.5 will select the condition which maximises the gain ratio, subject to the constraint that the information gain must be at least as large as the average information gain over all possible tests.

After building the tree, pruning strategies are adopted. This means that the decision tree is simplified by discarding one or more sub-branches and replacing them with leaves.

3. Model comparison

3.1 The data

The analyses are based on the activity diary data used to derive the original Albatross system. The data are collected in February 1997 for a random sample of 1649 respondents in the municipalities of Hendrik-Ido-Ambacht and Zwijndrecht (South Rotterdam region) in the Netherlands. The data consist of full activity-diaries, implying that both inhome and out-of-home activities were reported. Respondents are asked, for each successive activity, to provide information about the nature of the activity, the day, start and end time, the location where the activity took place, the transport mode (chain), the travel time per mode and, if relevant, accompanying individuals. A pre-coded scheme is used for activity reporting. More details can be found in Arentze and Timmermans (2000).

A 75-25% split was made on the data set as a whole, where the first 75% are used to build the nine different models, whereas the remaining 25% was left to validate them.

3.2 Model performance

Model performance tests are conducted at two levels: the choice facet level, i.e. the level of the separate decision trees and the trip matrix level. Recall that the Albatross system consists

of nine different choice facets or dimensions and that each of them determines a different response variable. For every dimension, a separate model needs to be built. The strategy for building the C4.5 trees and the trees after feature selection was as follows. The C4.5 trees were induced based on one simple restriction: the final number of cases in a leaf node must meet a minimum of 15, except for the very large data set of the 'select'-dimension, where this number was set to 30. In the feature selection analysis, all the irrelevant attributes were first removed from the data by means of Relief-F feature selection method with the *k* parameter set equal to 10. Next, the C4.5 trees were built based on the same restrictions as before, though only the remaining relevant attributes were used. To determine the variable selection, several decision trees were built, each time removing one more irrelevant attribute. For each of these decision trees, the accuracy was calculated and compared to the accuracy of the decision tree of the C4.5 approach. The smallest decision tree, which resulted in a maximum decrease of 2% in accuracy compared to the decision tree including all features, was chosen as the final model for a single choice facet in the feature selection approach. This strategy was applied to all nine dimensions of the Albatross model.
At choice facet level, we will compare the number of attributes used to build the decision trees and the obtained accuracy. To have an idea about the complexity of the modelling process, the general statistics for the decision tables for each of the nine dimensions can be found in Table 1. This table describes the statistics on the training set.

Dimension	**Nr. of cases**	**Nr. of independent variables**
Mode for work (MW)	858	32
Selection (S)	14190	40
With-whom (WW)	2970	39
Duration (D)	2970	41
Start time (ST)	2970	63
Trip chain (TC)	2651	53
Mode other (MO)	2602	35
Location 1 (L1)	2112	28
Location 2 (L2)	1027	28

Table 1. General statistics per dimension

At the trip matrix level, the observed and predicted Origin-Destination (OD) matrices are compared. The basic unit for generating an OD-matrix is a trip. It contains the frequency of trips for each combination of origins (rows) and destinations (columns). The Albatross system consists of 20 zones (i.e. origins and destinations) that are used as basis for each OD-matrix. A general OD-matrix is generated, and next to this, it can also be broken down according to a variable like e.g. the transport mode (car driver, slow mode, car passenger, public transport, unknown transport mode), such that different OD-matrices for each mode of transport are obtained (see also Figure 1). Note that the number of cells and hence, the degree of disaggregation, differs between the matrices. For example, the basic OD-matrix has 20x20=400 cells, while the OD-matrix by transport mode has 5x20x20 = 2000 cells. The measure that will be used for determining the degree of correspondence between the observed and predicted matrices is the correlation coefficient. It will be calculated between observed and predicted matrix entries in general and for the trip matrices that are disaggregated on transport mode. How can one determine the correlation coefficient between matrices? In both cases, the cells of the OD-matrices are rearranged into a single vector across categories and the correlation coefficient will be calculated by comparing the corresponding elements in the observed and the predicted vector. Thus, for the OD-matrices disaggregated on the transport mode, the cells of the matrices on car driver, slow transport, car passenger, public transport and unknown mode are rearranged into five separate vectors, and these five vectors are combined into one single vector. This occurs for the observed and the predicted matrices, and the correlation coefficient between this observed and predicted vector is the performance measure at trip matrix level. An advantage of the use of the correlation coefficient is that it is insensitive to the difference in scale between column frequencies (i.e. the difference in the total number of trips).

4. Results

Note that for reasons of comparison, the results of the Zero R classifier have also been added in this results Section. This Zero R classifier automatically classifies new instances to the majority class.

Firstly, we will take a closer look at the average length of the observed and predicted sequences of activities. In the observed patterns, the average number of activities equals 5.160 for the training set and 5.155 for the test set. This average length offers room for 1-3 flexible activities complemented with 2-4 in-home activities. Considerable variation occurs, however, as indicated by the standard deviation of approximately 3 activities. The average length of the predicted patterns for the four modelling approaches is shown in Table 2.

Method	Training set	Test set
Zero R	5.217 (3.241)	5.199 (3.333)
One R	5.198 (3.182)	5.178 (3.128)
Feature Selection	5.014 (3.033)	4.907 (2.921)
C4.5	5.286 (2.953)	5.286 (2.937)

Table 2. Average number of predicted activities in the sequences (standard deviation)

On average, when comparing the simple classifiers, Zero R and One R overestimate the number of activities, however, this overestimation is somewhat less pronounced on the test set. All models seem to overestimate the variance a little, both on the training set and on the test set. We observe that in general the C4.5 approach predicts activity sequences that are somewhat too long, while those of the feature selection approach are rather a little bit too short. The results of these different methods will now be compared at two other levels, the choice facet level and the trip matrix level.

Secondly, the results at the level of each decision tree separately are compared to each other. The models have an increasing complexity in the number of variables that they take into account, but we will also look at the total complexity of the decision tree (i.e. the number of final leaves). Furthermore, the accuracy of the four modelling approaches will also be compared. Table 3 summarises the results.

Method	Measure	MW	S	WW	D	ST	TC	MO	L1	L2
Zero R	Variables	0	0	0	0	0	0	0	0	0
	Leaves	1	1	1	1	1	1	1	1	1
	Accuracy	52.5	66.9	35.5	33.4	17.2	53.3	38.8	37.5	20.0
One R	Variables	1	1	1	1	1	1	1	1	1
	Leaves	6	5	5	3	4	2	4	3	3
	Accuracy	59.5	67.7	40.8	34.8	22.7	69.9	41.3	43.5	23.4
Feature	Variables	2	0	4	4	8	10	11	6	8
Selection	Leaves	6	1	51	38	1	13	60	15	14
	Accuracy	59.5	66.9	46.7	36.8	17.2	81.1	50.8	51.3	31.2
C4.5	Variables	3	15	19	28	28	4	15	8	15
	Leaves	8	35	72	148	121	8	63	30	47
	Accuracy	59.8	68.6	49.9	43.1	40.8	80.2	52.4	54.0	37.2

Table 3. Performance at the level of the decision trees

The results show that One R clearly improves on the results of Zero R. Furthermore, the feature selection approach generally generates considerably less complex decision trees than the C4.5 approach. One exception is the 'trip chaining' dimension, which has more final leaves in the decision trees with feature selection, when compared to the tree without.

Although it is interesting to investigate the results at the level of the decision tree itself, the results are as expected. More complex trees lead to a higher accuracy, although the gain in accuracy is not that high, while much more complexity is required. Therefore, it seems more interesting to look at the result after the whole scheduling process has been carried out and the trips that are predicted are distributed over origins and destinations.

Thirdly, the results are compared at trip matrix level, where the observed number of trips from a certain origin to a certain destination is compared to the predicted number of trips, and this for each OD-pair. Correlations are calculated between the final observed and predicted OD-matrices, and also between the OD-matrices that were disaggregated on travel mode, so after step two and step three in the traditional four-step trip-based transportation model.

Method	**Training data**		**Test data**	
	ρ(o,p)	ρ(o,p) mode	ρ(o,p)	ρ(o,p) mode
Zero R	0.938	0.841	0.925	0.787
One R	0.936	0.880	0.928	0.862
Feature Selection	0.957	0.887	0.947	0.849
C4.5	0.962	0.885	0.942	0.856

Table 4. Model performance at trip matrix level

Table 4 shows that all correlation coefficients are quite similar. The test set is the most relevant dataset for comparison of the models, so therefore we will focus on this latter one. After the trip distribution step, the feature selection approach shows the highest correlation on the test set. While after the disaggregation of trips according to the different transport modes, the One R approach even shows the highest correlation. This clearly indicates the non-inferior performance of simpler models when compared to the most complex model (C4.5). Table 5 shows the results on the test set more in detail.

Mode	Observed	Zero R	One R	Feature sel.	C4.5
Car	1609	1580	1609	1466	1573
Slow	814	1020	1013	920	1038
Public	79	83	81	107	113
Car passenger	294	356	321	333	375

Table 5. Number of trips at trip matrix level: Test set in detail

It can be seen that the number of trips undertaken as a car driver is correctly predicted by the One R approach and underestimated by the remaining approaches, while the use of any other transport mode appears to be overestimated.

The stability of the different models has also been tested, and the extent to which over-fitting may have occurred is approximately the same and at an acceptable level for all models.

5. Conclusions and future research

Rule-based models that predict travel behaviour based on activity diary data have been suggested in the literature over the past two decades. These models usually perform very well, though, very often, they are based on a very complex set of rules.

Moreover, research in the field of psychology has learned us that simple models often predict human behaviour very well. In fact, the call for simplicity is a question of all ages. Occam's razor, that has to be situated already in the Middle Ages, being an important example.

In addition, one has to be careful in interpreting these previous studies, they only support the proposition 'Simplicity is a goal in itself', not that simplicity would lead to greater accuracy or better models. It is in this light that this chapter should be regarded. We regarded two ways of simplifying the complex set of rules used to determine the Albatross system. On the one hand, we used two simple classifiers to predict the nine dimensions, while on the other hand we performed two similar analyses: one with and one without irrelevant variables. The results of the tree-induction algorithms can namely be heavily influenced by the inclusion of irrelevant attributes. On the one hand, this may lead to over-fitting, while one the other hand, it is not evident whether the inclusion of irrelevant attributes would lead to a substantial loss in accuracy and/or predictive performance. The aim of the study reported in this chapter therefore was to further explore this issue in the context of the Albatross model system, currently the most comprehensive operational computational, rule-based process model of travel demand.

The results of the simple classifiers do indicate that the 'simpler' models do not perform better, but, on the other hand, it is also not the case that they are inferior to the complex C4.5

approach. It is rather logical that the model that always takes the majority class (Zero R) does not perform that well, conversely, the models that make up their decisions based on one or a few variables are not in any case second to the complex analysis. This comes as a welcome bonus.

The results of the analyses conducted at the two different levels of performance, indicate that, also in the second way of simplification, the simpler models do not necessary perform worse. In fact, more or less the same results were obtained at trip generation level, with or without disaggregating on transport mode. At the choice facet level, one can observe that a strong reduction in the size of the trees as well as in the number of predictors is possible without adversely affecting predictive performance too much. Thus, at least in this study, there is no evidence of substantial loss in predictive power in the sequential use of decision trees to predict activity-travel patterns.

The results indicate that using feature selection in a step prior to tree induction can improve the performance of the resulting sequential model. It should be noted, however, that predictive performance and simplicity are not the only criteria. The most important criterion is that the model needs to be responsive to policy sensitive attributes and it needs to be able to model the behavioural mechanisms. For that reason, policy sensitive attributes, such as for example service level of the transport system, or particular behavioural attributes should have a high priority in the selection of attributes if the model is to be used for predicting the impact of policies. The feature selection method allows one to identify and next eliminate correlated factors that prevent the selection of the attributes of interest during the construction of the tree, so that the resulting model will be more robust to policy measures.

By these findings, the primary belief that people rely for their choices on some simple heuristics is endorsed. In real life, every person is limited in both knowledge and time and it is infeasible to consider all the different possibilities, before trying to make an optimal choice. Since, in the Albatross system, we are trying to predict nine different choices on travel behaviour made by human beings, this might give an idea on why these simple models do not necessarily perform worse than the complex models. In fact, this is not totally true. If simple models are able to predict the choices of a human being, this can mean two things: either the environment itself is perceived as simple, or the complex choice process can be described by simple models. Since activity-based transport modellers keep developing systems with an increasing complexity in order to try to understand the travel behaviour undertaken by humans, we acknowledge that the environment is not simple. However, whether it is perceived as simple by human beings, remains an open question.

6. References

Arentze, T.A. & Timmermans, H.J.P. (2000) *Albatross: A Learning-Based Transportation Oriented Simulation System*, Eindhoven University of Technology, EIRASS.

Arentze, T.A. and H.J.P. Timmermans (2005). *Albatross 2: A Learning-Based Transportation Oriented Simulation System*, European Institute of Retailing and Services Studies. Eindhoven, The Netherlands.

Ben-Akiva, M. & Lerman, S. (1985) *Discrete Choice Analysis*, M.I.T. Press, Cambridge, MA.

Ben-Akiva, M.E. & Bowman, J.L. (1998) Integration of an activity-based model system and a residential location model. *Urban Studies*, 35(7), pp. 1231-1253.

Bhat, C.R. & Guo, J. (2003) A mixed spatially correlated Logit model: formulation and application to residential choice modeling. *Paper presented at the 82nd Annual Meeting of the Transportation Research Board*, Washington, D.C.

Bhat, C.R.; Guo, J.; Srinivasan, S. & Sivakumar, A. (2004) Comprehensive econometric microsimulator for daily activity-travel patterns, *Electronic proceedings of the 83rd Annual Meeting of the Transportation Research Board*, Washington, D.C., USA.

Buckinx W.; Moons, E.; Van den Poel, D. & Wets, G. (2004) Customer-adapted coupon targeting using feature selection. *Expert Systems with Applications*, 26(4), pp. 509-518.

Buntine, W. & Niblett, T. (1992) A further comparison of splitting rules for decision-tree induction. *Machine Learning*, 8, pp. 75--86.

Clark, P. & Niblett, T. (1989) The CN2 induction algorithm. *Machine Learning*, 3, pp. 261-283.

Daly, A.J.; van Zwam, H.H. & van der Valk, J. (1983) Application of disaggregate models for a regional transport study in The Netherlands. *Paper presented at the 3rd World Conference on Transport Research*, Hamburg, Germany.

Domingos, P. (1998) Occam's two razors: The sharp and the blunt. *Proceedings of the Fourth International Conference on Knowledge Discovery and Data Mining*, pp. 37-43.

Gigerenzer, G.; Todd, P.M. & the ABC Research Group. (1999) *Simple Heuristics That Make Us Smart*, Oxford University Press, New York.

Hall, M.A. (1999a) Correlation-*based Feature Selection for Machine Learning*. Ph.D. dissertation, Department of Computer Science, University of Waikato, Hamilton.

Hall, M.A. (1999b) Feature selection for machine learning: Comparing a correlation-based filter approach to the wrapper. *Proceedings of the Florida Artificial Intelligence Symposium (FLAIRS)*, Orlando, Florida, USA.

Hensher, D. & Greene, W.H. (2003) The mixed logit model: The state of practice, *Transportation*, 30(2), pp. 133–176.

Holte, R.C.; Acker, L. & Porter, B.W. (1989) Concept learning and the problem of small disjuncts. *Proceedings of the eleventh international joint conference on artificial intelligence*, pp. 813-818, Morgan Kaufmann.

Holte, R.C. (1993) Very simple classification rules perform well on most commonly used datasets. *Machine Learning*, 11, pp. 63-90.

Kira, K. and Rendall, L.A. (1992) A practical approach to feature selection. *Proceedings of the 9th International Conference on Machine Learning, Aberdeen, Scotland, UK*, Sleeman, D.H. & Edwards, P. (eds.), pp. 249-256, Morgan Kaufmann Publishers, San Mateo.

Kitamura, R. & Fujii, S. (1998) Two computational process models of activity-travel choice. In: *Theoretical Foundations of Travel Choice Modeling*, Gärling, T.; Laitila, T. & Westin, K. (eds.), pp. 251 – 279, Elsevier, Oxford.

Kohavi, R., Becker, B. & Sommerfield, D. (1997) Improving simple bayes. *Poster papers of the 9th European conference on machine learning*, pp. 78-87.

Koller, D. & Sahami, M. (1996) Toward optimal feature selection. In: *Proceedings of the 13th International Conference on Machine Learning*, Saitta, L. (ed.), pp. 284-292, Bari, Italy.

Kononenko, I. (1994) Estimating attributes: analysis and extensions of relief. *Proceedings of the 7th European Conference on Machine Learning, Catania, Italy*, Bergadano, F. & De Raedt, L. (eds.), pp. 171-182, Springer Verlag.

Koppelman, F. & Wen, C-H. (2000) The Paired Combinatorial Logit model: Properties, estimation and application. *Transportation Research B*, 34(2), pp. 75-89.

Mingers, J. (1989) An empirical comparison of pruning methods for decision tree induction. *Machine Learning*, 4(2), pp. 227-243.

Moons, E.; Wets, G.; Vanhoof, K.; Aerts, M. & Timmermans, H. (2001) How well perform simple rules on activity diary data. *Proceedings of the 7th International Computers in Urban Planning and Urban Management Conference*, Honolulu, USA.

Moons, E.; Wets, G.; Aerts, M. & Vanhoof, K. (2002a) The role of Occam's razor in activity based modeling. In: *Computational Intelligent Systems for Applied Research - Proceedings of the 5th International FLINS Conference*, Ruan, D., D'hondt, P. and Kerre, E.E. (Eds.), pp. 153-162, Gent, Belgium.

Moons, E.; Wets, G.; Vanhoof, K.; Aerts, M.; Arentze, T. & Timmermans, H. (2002b) The impact of irrelevant attributes on the performance of classifier systems in generating activity schedules. Proceedings *of the 81st Annual Meeting of the Transportation Research Board*, Washington D.C., USA.

Moons, E.A.L.M.G.; Wets, G.P.M.; Aerts, M.; Arentze, T.A. & Timmermans, H.J.P. (2005) The impact of simplification in a sequential rule-based model of activity scheduling behavior. *Environment and Planning A*, 37(3), pp. 551-568.

Ortúzar, J. de D. & Willumsen, L.G. (2001). *Modelling Transport* (3rd ed.), Wiley.

Pendyala, R.M.; Kitamura, R. & Reddy, D.V.G.P. (1995) A rule-based activity-travel scheduling algorithm integrating neural networks of behavioral adaptation. *Paper presented at the EIRASS Conference on Activity-Based Approaches*, Eindhoven, The Netherlands.

Pendyala, R.M.; Kitamura, R. & Reddy, D.V.G.P. (1998) Application of an activity-based travel demand model incorporating a rule-based algorithm. *Environment and Planning B*, 25, pp. 753-772.

Pendyala, R.M. (2004) FAMOS: Application in Florida. *Paper presented at the 83rd Annual Meeting of the Transportation Research Board*, Washington, D.C., USA.

Quinlan, J.R. (1993) *C4.5 Programs for Machine Learning*, Morgan Kaufmann Publishers, San Mateo.

Recker, W.W.; McNally, M.G. & Root, G.S. (1986) A model of complex travel behavior: Part 2: an operational model. *Transportation Research A*, 20, pp. 319-330.

Rendell, L. & Seshu, R. (1990) Learning hard concepts through constructive induction. *Computational Intelligence*, 6, pp. 247-270.

Ruiter, E.R. & Ben-Akiva, M. (1978) Disaggregate travel demand models for the San Francisco bay area. *Transportation Research Record*, 673, pp. 121-128.

Tornay S. (1938) *Ockham: Studies and Selections*, La Salle, IL: Open Court.

Weiss, S.M.; Galen, R.S. & Tadepalli, P.V. (1990) Maximizing the predictive value of production rules. *Artificial Intelligence*, 45, pp. 47-71.

Wets, G., Vanhoof, K., Arentze, T. and Timmermans, H. (2000) Identifying decision structures underlying activity patterns: an exploration of data mining algorithms. *Transportation Research Record*, 1718, pp. 1-9.

Zheng, C.L.; de Sa, V.R.; Gribskov, M. & Murlidharan Nair, T. (2003) On selecting features from splice junctions: an analysis using information theoretic and machine learning approaches, *Genome Informatics*, 14, pp. 73--83.

Zellner, A.; Keuzenkamp, H.A. & McAleer, M. (2001). *Simplicity, Inference and Modelling: Keeping It Sophisticatedly Simple*, Cambridge University Press, Cambridge, United Kingdom.

10

Laban Movement Analysis using a Bayesian model and perspective projections

Joerg Rett[1], Jorge Dias[1] and Juan-Manuel Ahuactzin[2]
[1]*Institute of Systems and Robotics - University of Coimbra,* [2]*Probayes SAS, Montbonnot*
[1]*Portugal,* [2]*France*

1. Introduction

Human movement is essentially the process of moving one or more body parts to a specific location along a certain trajectory. A person observing the movement might be able to recognize it through the spatial pathway alone. Kendon (Kendon, 2004) holds the view that willingly or not, humans, when in co-presence, continuously inform one another about their intentions, interests, feelings and ideas by means of visible bodily action. Analysis of face-to-face interaction has shown that bodily action can play a crucial role in the process of interaction and communication. Kendon states that expressive actions like greeting, threat and submission often play a central role in social interaction.

In order to access the expressive content of movements theoretically, a notational system is needed. Rudolf Laban, (1879-1958) was a notable central European dance artist and theorist, whose work laid the foundations for Laban Movement Analysis (LMA). Used as a tool by dancers, athletes, physical and occupational therapists, it is one of the most widely used systems of human movement analysis.

Robotics has already acknowledged the evidence that human movements could be an important cue for Human-Robot Interaction. Sato et al. (Sato et al., 1996), while defining the requirements for 'human symbiosis robotics' state that those robots should be able to use non-verbal media to communicate with humans and exchange information. As input modalities on a higher abstraction level they define channels on language, gesture and unconscious behavior. This skill could enable the robot to actively perceive human behavior, whether conscious and unconscious. Human intention could be understood, simply by observation, allowing the system to achieve a certain level of friendliness, hospitality and reliance. Fong, Nourbakhsh and Dautenhahn (Fong et al., 2003) state in their survey on 'socially interactive robots' that the design of sociable robots needs input from research concerning social learning and imitation, gesture and natural language communication, emotion and recognition of interaction patterns. Otero et al. suggest (Otero et al., 2006) that the interpretation of a person's motion within its environment can enhance Human-Robot Interaction in several ways. They point out, that a recognized action can help the robot to plan its future tasks and goals, that the information flow during interaction can be extended and additional cues, like speech recognition, can be supported. Otero et al. state that body motion and context provide in many situations enough information to derive the person's current activity.

1.1 Related works on computational Human Movement Analysis

There has been an interesting work which also used movement descriptors and a probabilistic framework. Bregler (Bregler, 1997) introduced mid-level descriptors embedded in a thorough probabilistic framework that produced a robust classification for human movements. The concept of multiple hypothesizes is kept from low-level motion clusters to high-level gait categories producing good classification results even for noisy and uncertain evidences in natural environments. Model parameters are learned from training data using the EM-algorithm. The work points towards the concept of atomic phonemes and words used in speech recognition. Bregler defines his 'movemes' as simple dynamical categories, i.e. a set of second order linear dynamical systems. A Hidden Markov Model (HMM) is used to classify three different gait categories: running, walking, and skipping. The critical point on this approach were the 'movemes' themselves. The 'movemes' appear limited in their expressiveness. This might have been caused by their simplicity and that no relations are drawn to models and data of physiological studies of human movements. To overcome this weakness we have tied our descriptors to a well established notational framework: Laban Movement Analysis.

That probabilistic methods can produce very good classification results was also demonstrated for the application of sign language recognition. Starner & Pentland (Starner & Pentland, 1995) based their system on real-time tracking of the hands using color gloves and a monocular camera with 5 frames per second. The learning and classification of the 40 words (signs) was embedded in 400 sentences (sequence of signs) for learning and 100 sentences for classification. The results compared the accuracy when using grammar rules (99.2%) or when not using them (91.3%). The results showed that when constraints can be applied like colored marker, a spatially well defined trajectory and rules that help to deal with a sequence of symbols, high accuracies can be reached. In this approach no mid-level descriptors were needed as the sign language has very well defined spatial pathways and grammars. The application of this approach as a general interface for Human-Robot Interaction is difficult, as it requires the person to learn the sign language.

1.2 Related works on computational Laban Movement Analysis

A long tradition in research on computational solutions for Laban Movement Analysis (LMA) has the group around Norman Badler, who already started in 1993 to re-formulate Labanotation in computational models (Badler et al., 1993). The work of Zhao & Badler (Zhao & Badler, 2005) is entirely embedded in the framework of Laban Movement Analysis. Their computational model of gesture acquisition and synthesis can be used to learn motion qualities from live performance. Many inspirations concerning the transformation of LMA components into physically measurable entities were taken from this work. As the final application was the back-projection of the LMA parameters to an animated character, Zhao (Zhao, 2002) made no attempt to address the problem of gesture recognition. For the same reason video capture was presented for a controlled environment (human wearing black cloth in front of black curtain). The application of LMA to the classification of movements, especially in unconstrained environments is the main goal of our contribution.

In (Nakata et al., 2002) Nakata et al. reproduced expressive movements in a robot that could be interpreted as emotions by a human observer. The first part described how some parameters of Laban Movement Analysis (LMA) can be calculated from a set of low-level features. They concluded further that the control of robot movements oriented on LMA parameters allows the production of expressive movements and that those movements leave the impression of emotional content to a human observer. The critical points on the mapping of low-level features to LMA parameters was, that the computational model was closely tied to the embodiment of the robot which had only a low number of degrees of freedom. For our solution we have chosen low-level features that can be used for an arbitrary object (human full body, body parts, etc.).

1.3 The contribution of this work

This work poses the automatic movement classification task as a problem to recognize a sequence of symbols taken from an alphabet consisting of motion-entities. The alphabet and its underlying model is well defined though Laban Movement Analysis. The LMA parameters serve as mid-level descriptors that can be produced and understood by the system. Our *Tracking* process is two-fold, the technique use for learning based on the active markers of our positioning device produces a robust representation of each object as points. For the visual tracking we use the central point of a boundary box containing the pixels or regions found in the figure–ground segmentation process. The relationship between the two approaches is established through a geometric model (Rett & Dias, 2007-B). This work emphasizes probabilistic methods, i.e. Bayesian approaches, as a tool to model the concept of Laban Movement Analysis (LMA), learn its parameters and classify the movements. The process of segmentation and tracking of image data is also based on a probabilistic method, i.e. the CAMshift algorithm (Bradski, 1998). This work provides a new skill for machines that analyze human movements, i.e. computational Laban Movement Analysis. The system has been implemented in our social robot, 'Nicole' to test several human-robot interaction scenarios (Rett & Dias, 2007-A).

2. Laban Movement Analysis

Laban Movement Analysis (LMA) is a method for observing, describing, notating, and interpreting human movement. It was developed by a German named Rudolf Laban (1879 to 1958), who is widely regarded as a pioneer of European modern dance and theorist of movement education (Zhao, 2002). The general framework was described in 1980 by Irmgard Bartenieff a scholar of Rudolf Laban in (Bartenieff & Lewis, 1980). While being widely applied to studies of dance and application to physical and mental therapy (Bartenieff & Lewis, 1980), it has found little application in the engineering domain. Most notably the group of Norman Badler, who already started in 1993 to re-formulate Labannotation in computational models (Badler et al., 1993). More recently a computational model of gesture acquisition and synthesis to learn motion qualities from live performance has been proposed in (Zhao & Badler, 2005). Also recently but independently, researchers from neuroscience started to investigate the usefulness of LMA to describe certain effects on the movements of animals and humans. Foround and Whishaw adapted LMA to capture the kinematic and non-kinematic aspects of movement in a reach-for-food task by human patients whose movements had been affected by stroke (Foroud & Whishaw, 2006). It was stated that LMA places emphasis on underlying motor patterns by notating how the body segments are moving, how they are supported or affected by other body parts, as well as whole body movement.

The theory of LMA consists of several major components, though the available literature is not in unison about their total number. The works of Norman Badler's group (Chi et al., 2000); (Zhao, 2002) mention five major components shown in Figure 1.

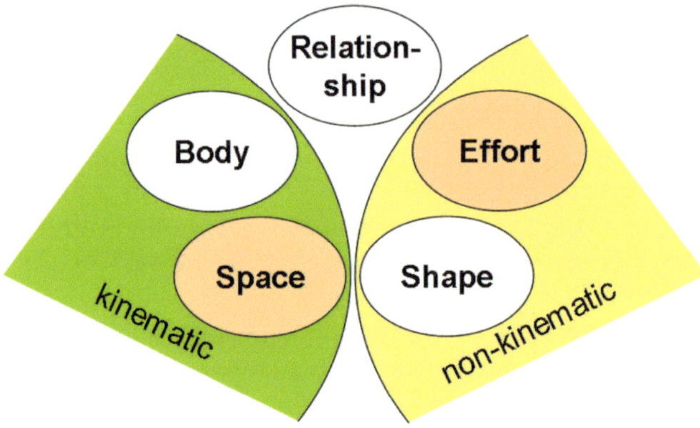

Figure 1. The major components of LMA are Body, Space, Effort, Shape and Relationship

Relationship describes modes of interaction with oneself, others, and the environment (e.g. facings, contact, and group forms). As *Relationship* appears to be one of the lesser explored components, some literature (Foroud & Whishaw, 2006) only considers the remaining four major components. *Body* specifies which body parts are moving, their relation to the body center, the kinematics involved and the emerging locomotion. *Space* treats the spatial extent of the mover's *Kinesphere* (often interpreted as reach-space) and what form is being revealed by the spatial pathways of the movement. *Effort* deals with the dynamic qualities of the movement and the inner attitude towards using energy. *Shape* is emerging from the *Body* and *Space* components and focused on the body itself or directed towards a goal in space. The interpretation of *Shape* as a property of *Body* and *Space* might have been the reason for Irmgard Bartenieff to mention only three major components of LMA. Like suggested in (Foroud & Whishaw, 2006) we have grouped *Body* and *Space* as kinematic features describing changes in the spatial-temporal body relations, while *Shape* and *Effort* are part of the non-kinematic features contributing to the qualitative aspects of the movement as shown in Figure 1. This article concentrates on the *Space* component in order to establish a basis for comparison with subsequent works that include also other components.

2.1 Space

The *Space* component presents the different concepts to describe the pathways of human movements inside a frame of reference, when "carving shapes in space" (Bartenieff & Lewis, 1980). *Space* specifies different entities to express movements in a frame of reference determined by the body of the actor. Thus, all of the presented measures are relative to the anthropometry of the actor. The concepts differ in the complexity of expressiveness and dimensionality but are all of them reproducible in the 3-D Cartesian system. The following definitions were taken from Choreutics (Laban, 1966) and differ in some aspects from those given in Labanotation (Hutchinson, 1970). The most important ones shown in Figure 2 are: I) The *Levels of Space* - referring to the height of a position, II) The *Basic Directions* - 26 target points where the movement is aiming at, III) The *Three Axes* - Vertical, horizontal and sagittal axis, IV) The *Three Planes* - *Door Plane* (vertical) π_v, *Table plane* (horizontal) π_h, and the

Wheel Plane (sagittal) π_s each one lying in two of the axes, and V) The *Icosahedron* - used as *Kinespheric Scaffolding*.

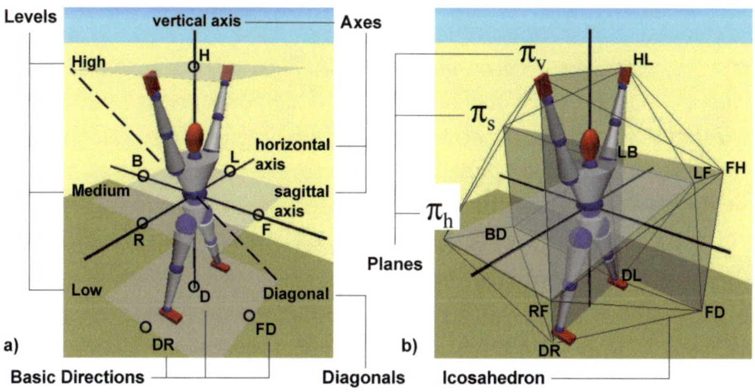

Figure 2. The *Space* component defines several concepts: a) Levels of Space, Basic Directions, Three Axes, and b) Three Planes and Icosahedron

The *Kinesphere* describes the space of farthest reaches in which the movements take place. Levels and Directions can also be found as symbols in modern-day Labanotation (Bartenieff & Lewis, 1980)

Labanotation direction symbols encode a position-based concept of space. Recently, Longstaff (Longstaff, 2001) has translated an earlier concept of Laban which is based on lines of motion rather than points in space into modern-day Labanotation. Longstaff coined the expression *Vector Symbols* to emphasize that they are not attached to a certain point in space. The different concepts are shown in Figure 3.

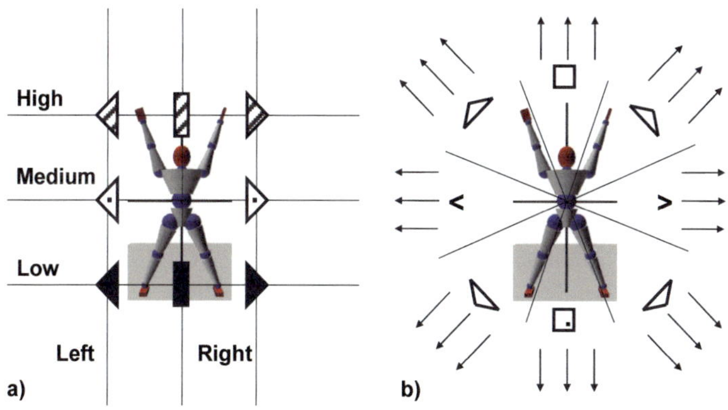

Figure 3. Two different sets of symbols to describe the *Space* component presented through the *Door Plane*. a) Position based symbols of Labanotation represent the 'height' through shading and the horizontal position through shape. b) Direction based vector symbols of Choreographie use different shapes for each direction

The symbols of Labanotation correspond to positions in space like *Left-High* while the *Vector Symbols* describe directions. Figure 3 represents a 2-D view of the vertical (door) plane π_v and thus shows only a fraction of the set of symbols (8) which describes movements in 3-D space. It was suggested that the collection of *Vector Symbols* provides a heuristic for the perception and memory of spatial orientation of body movements. The thirty eight *Vector Symbols* are organized according to *Prototypes* and *Deflections*. The fourteen *Prototypes* divide the Cartesian coordinate system into movements along only one dimension (*Pure Dimensional Movements*) and movements along lines that are equally stressed in all three dimensions (*Pure Diagonal Movements*) as shown in Figure 2 a). Longstaff suggests that the *Prototypes* give idealized concepts for labeling and remembering spatial orientations. The twenty four *Deflections* are mentally conceived according to their relation to the prototype concepts. The infinite number of possible deflecting orientations is conceptualized in a system based on eight *Diagonal Directions*, each deflecting along three possible *Dimensions*.

2.2 Labanotation and Effort Notation

The need to develop some means of recording for the perceptions of movements led to a notation system known as *Labanotation*. It is built of symbols which describe the structure and progression of the movement (shown in Figure 4.). The spatial definitions (Hutchinson, 1970) vary from those stated in Choreutics (Laban, 1966). In Labanotation the three *Levels of Space* are circular causing the distances e.g. *centre-L* and *centre-LD* to be equal. Moreover, distinct frames of reference are defined for the different groups of body parts. e.g. placing the origin of the arm-hand group at the shoulder joint. The symbols reflect which body part does what in space and time and with what kind of dynamic stress. In particular it contains when the movement starts and its duration. The so called *Staff* organizes the body parts in columns where the time proceeds from the bottom up along the length. The placement of a symbol shows that the body part is active, its shape indicates the direction of the movement, its shading shows the level and its length, the duration of the movement. From a properly notated movement sequence, the skilled reader can see at one glance what is happening at any moment in every part of the body.

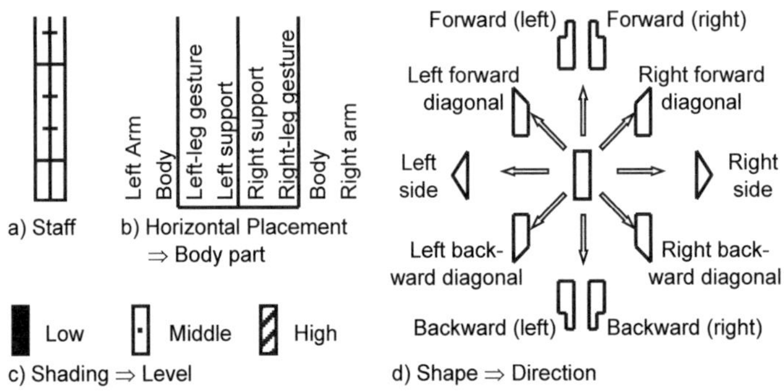

Figure 4. Labanotation: a) The staff is used to place the symbols. b) The horizontal placement of the symbol indicates the body part. c) Shading of the symbol is used to indicate the *Level* (height) of the 3-D position. d) Different shapes of the symbols are used to indicate the position in the *Table Plane*

The example in Figure 5 shows the ballet figure, *Port de Bras*. For the sake of readability we rotated the staff by 90 degrees. Reading from the right (usually bottom), one sees the basic position of neutral standing, arms hanging down. Then move your arms forward middle (shoulder level), followed by an open side movement (for two counts), followed by lowering the arms.

Figure 5. Example of a ballet "Port de Bras" figure. The staff in the center holds the symbols to represent the sequence of positions performed by the actor. Verify with the previous figure: Mainly the left and the right arm symbols are written, the sequence starts and concludes with *Level=low*

2.3 Database of Expressive Movements

We have created a database of 'expressive movements'. Some of the movements are based on suggestions mentioned in (Bartenieff & Lewis, 1980) and (Zhao, 2002) others are commonly used gestures with anticipated *Effort* qualities. In this work we will concentrate only on movements with distinct *Space* component. Table 1 shows such movements.

Movement	**Description**	π_{prin}
Lunging	Lunging for a ball	XY
Maestro	Conducting an orchestra	YZ
Stretch	Stretch to yawn	YZ
Ok	OK-sign gesture	YZ
Point:	Pointing gesture	XY
Byebye	Waving bye-bye	YZ
Shake	Reach for someone's hand	XZ
Nthrow	Waving sagittally (approach sign)	XZ

Table 1. Expressive movements from our database (HID) with principal plane π_{prin} i.e. the plane where the movement can be observed best

Their distinctive *Space* component can be verified by observing the trajectories (see Figure 6).

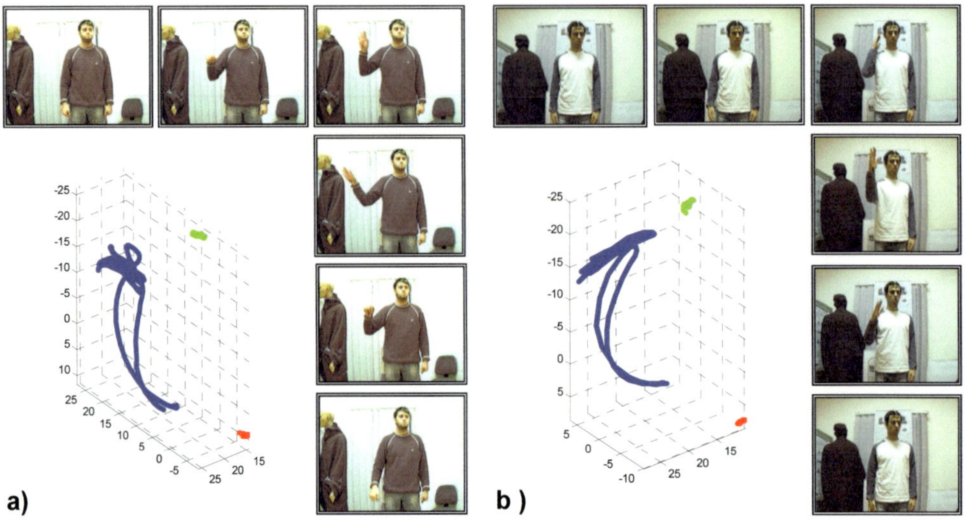

Figure 6. Two movements with distinct *Space* component. a) Horizontal waving (*byebye*) and b) Sagittal waving (*nthrow*)

The *byebye* gesture represents a horizontal waving, while *nthrow* represents a sagittal waving. Both movements are oscillatory and in the case of *byebye* the primary signal can be described by a sequence of left to right *R* and right to left *L Vector Symbols*. In the case of *nthrow* the primary signal would be described by a sequence of forward (*F*) and backward (*B*) *Vector Symbols*.
The case of non-oscillatory movements like the *ok* sign and reaching for someone's hand (*shake*) can be seen in Figure 7.

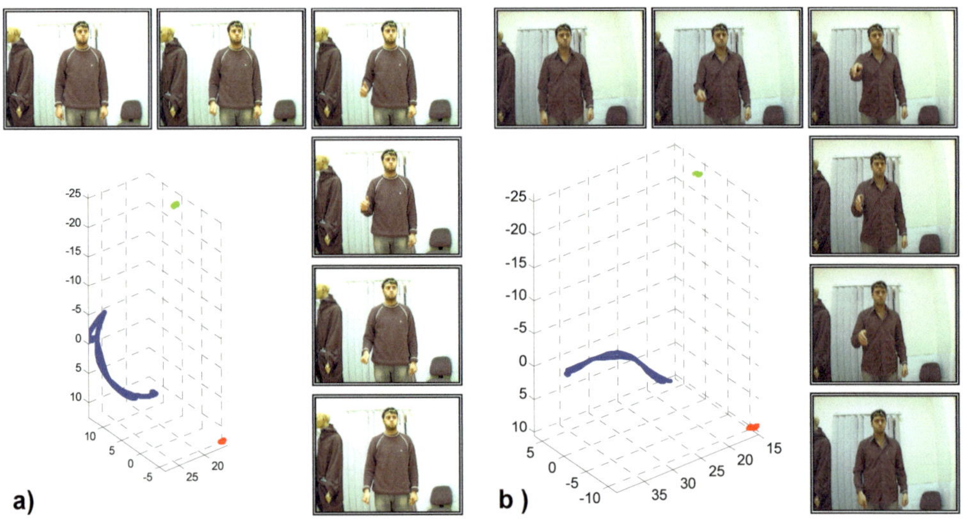

Figure 7. Two movements with distinct *Space* component. a) Showing the *ok* sign and b) Reaching for someone's hand (*shake*)

These two cases can be distinguished by a greater influence of forward (*F*) and backward (*B*) vector symbols in the case of *shake*. The shown trajectories present one trial of one person. The whole set of trials can be seen in (Rett, 2008).
In the case of lunging for a ball (*lunging*) the *Space* component consists mainly of forward (*F*) and backward (*B*) *Vector Symbols* for both hands as shown in Figure 8.

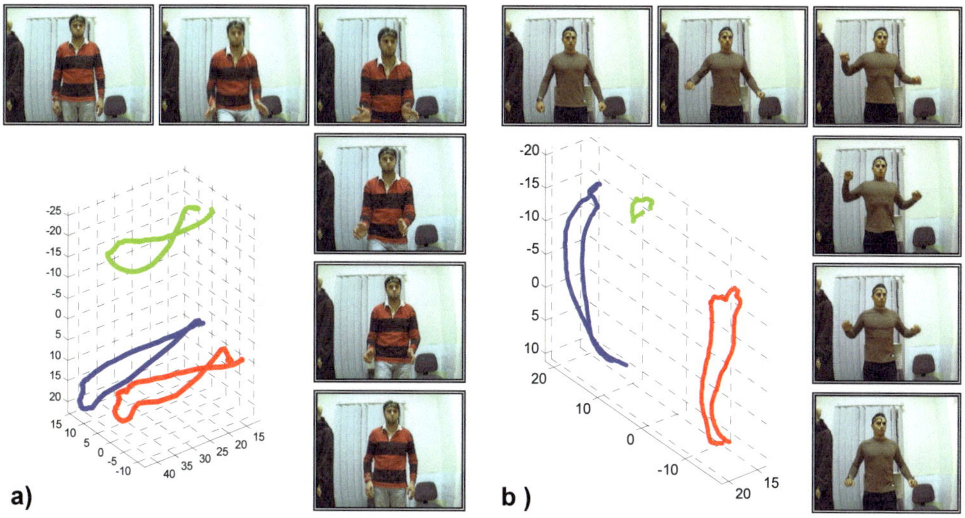

Figure 8. Two movements with distinct *Space* component. a) Forward dab (Lunging for a ball) and b) Upward wring (Stretching to yawn)

The mainly appearing *Vector Symbols* for the 'stretch to yawn' (stretch) movement are upward (*U*) and downward (*D*).

3. Human Movement Tracking

Laban Movement Analysis is essentially defined in a 3-D space related whether with a world frame of reference {W} or an egocentric frame of reference {H} of the human under observation. With a magnetic tracker precise movement data from body parts related to both {W} and {H} can be collected. This kind of sensor system is useful for a stationary Human-Computer-Interface, as it requires a certain preparation-effort from the user (e.g. attaching the sensors). For a mobile robot a visual-based system is more useful as it does not require any preparation, though on the cost of precision, as depicted in Figure 9. Our solution is based on a system which uses both, 3-D magnetic tracker data and 2-D visual data. The relationship between LMA parameters, Low-Level features and the types of movement will be learned by a synchronous acquisition of 3-D tracking and 2-D image data. Additionally, a probabilistic model for the geometry of the frames of reference will be established. The mobile robot will be equipped with a monocular camera only, but additionally with the knowledge from the previous learning.

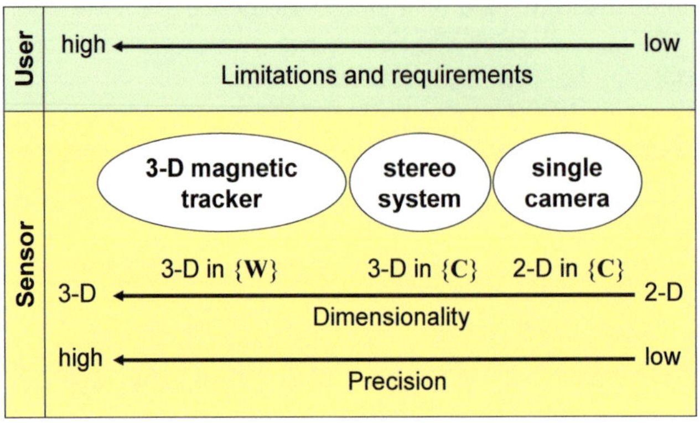

Figure 9. Different sensor modalities and their characteristics

Some sets of movement data have already been introduced in section 2.3. The corresponding database is called Human Interaction Database (HID) and is accessible through *WWW* (Rett, et al. 2007). The database consists of image sequences, high precision 3-D position data and results from our visual tracker and classifier.

Our geometric model needs to address the appearance of sensors and objects in the interaction scenery, i.e. define their frames of reference. Figure 9 shows the frames of reference: the camera referential {C} in which the image is defined and some world coordinate system {W}.

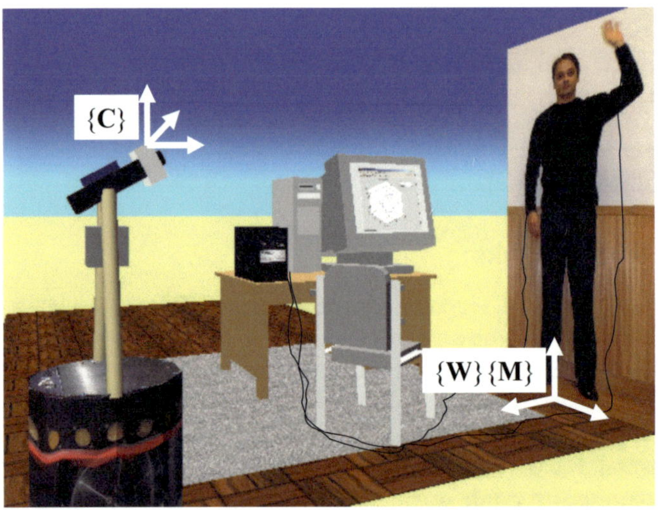

Figure 10. Frames of reference of the scene

In the experimental setup for collecting movement data we have the world frame of reference {W} coinciding with the one of the magnetic tracker {M}.

Using a 6-DoF magnetic tracker provides 3-D position data with a sufficiently high accuracy and speed (50Hz). We use a Polhemus Liberty™ system with sensors attached to several body parts and objects. From the tracker data a set of features is calculated and related to the Laban Movement Parameters (LMP). The 3-D position data is projected in the following step to 2-D planes from which the low-level features are computed.

3.1 Geometric model of the camera

As the learning of human movements is based on a synchronous acquisition of 3-D tracking and 2-D image data we need to establish the geometric relationship in a model. The presented model considers the frame of reference of the world {W} and of the camera referential {C}. As shown in Figure 11 we placed the origin of {W} on the ground level aligned with the gravitational vertical and the sagittal axis of the person.

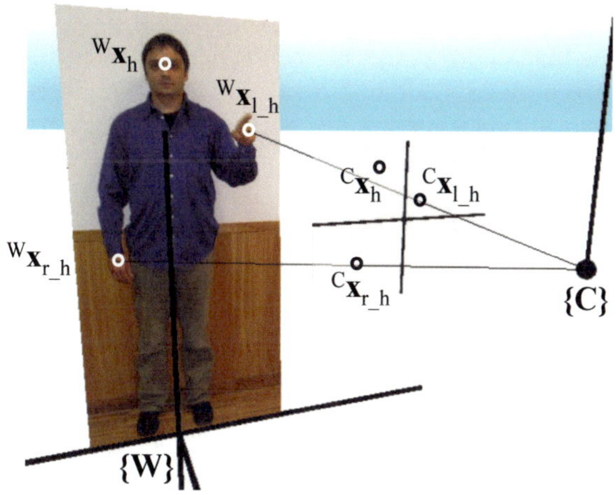

Figure 11. Projection of head and hands position in the camera plane

Any generic 3-D point ${}^{W}\mathbf{X} = [X \;\; Y \;\; Z]^T$ and its corresponding projection ${}^{img}\mathbf{X} = [u \;\; v]^T$ on an image-plane can be mathematically related using projective geometry and the concept of homogeneous coordinates through the following equation, the projective camera relation, where s represents an arbitrary scale factor (Hartley & Zisserman, 2000):

$$\begin{bmatrix} sv \\ su \\ s \end{bmatrix} = \begin{bmatrix} a_{1,1} & a_{1,2} & a_{1,3} & a_{1,4} \\ a_{2,1} & a_{2,2} & a_{2,3} & a_{2,4} \\ a_{3,1} & a_{3,2} & a_{3,3} & a_{3,4} \\ a_{4,1} & a_{4,2} & a_{4,3} & a_{4,4} \end{bmatrix} \begin{bmatrix} X \\ Y \\ Z \\ 1 \end{bmatrix} \quad (1)$$

Matrix **A** is called the projection matrix, and through its estimation it is possible to make the correspondence between any 3-D point and its projection in a camera's image-plane. We can likewise express the matrix **A** by using the parameters of the projective finite camera model, as stated in (Hartley & Zisserman, 2000).

$$\mathbf{A} = \mathbf{C}\left[{}^{\{C\}}\mathbf{R}_{\{W\}} \quad {}^{\{C\}}\vec{\mathbf{t}}_{\{W\}}\right] \quad (2)$$

Where {**C**} is the camera's calibration matrix, more frequently known as the intrinsic parameters matrix, while the camera's extrinsic parameters are represented by the rotation orthogonal matrix **R** and the translation vector **t** that relates the chosen {W} to the camera {C}.

The projective camera presents us, in fact, with the solution for the intersection of planes π_{cam1} and π_{cam2} which, assuming $\mathbf{X}^* = [X \; Y \; Z \; 1]^T$ (i.e. homogeneous coordinates), can be proven from its projection expression to be given by (3) (Dias, 1994).

$$\begin{cases} (\mathbf{a}_1 - u\mathbf{a}_3)^{\mathrm{T}}\ {}^{\mathrm{W}}\mathbf{X} + a_{1,4} - u = 0 \\ (\mathbf{a}_2 - v\mathbf{a}_3)^{\mathrm{T}}\ {}^{\mathrm{W}}\mathbf{X} + a_{2,4} - v = 0 \end{cases} \Leftrightarrow \begin{cases} \mathbf{\Pi}_{cam1}\ \mathbf{X}^* = 0 \\ \mathbf{\Pi}_{cam2}\ \mathbf{X}^* = 0 \end{cases} \tag{3}$$

This solution is called the projection or projecting line, which can be alternatively represented by equation (4) (Dias, 1994).

$$\vec{\mathbf{n}} = (\mathbf{a}_1 - u\mathbf{a}_3) \times (\mathbf{a}_2 - v\mathbf{a}_3) \tag{4}$$

These relations indicate that all 3-D points on the projecting line correspond to the same projection point on the image-plane. A unique correspondence between ${}^{W}\mathbf{X}$ and ${}^{C}\mathbf{X}$ could only be established through additional constraints, such as the intersection with the surface of a sphere, a plane, etc.

3.2 Low-level features

The selection of 'good' features is a general and long known problem in pattern recognition. For the description of the *Space* component we have chosen a feature based on the *displacement angle*. This physical measurable entity represents the *Space* component of LMA very well and the process of computation is simple. When using a low cardinality we can expect a good performance of the Bayesian method for learning and classification. Displacement angles, which also have been used by (Zhao, 2002) can be calculated easily from two subsequent positions. They describe the trace of a curve quite well and are independent from the absolute positions. As the position data is projected to planes, each plane produces a sequence of displacement angles with a certain sampling rate and discretization.

All computations are based on the raw tracking data inside our Human Interaction Database (HID). The tracking data consists of: I) the 2-D or 3-D position $\mathbf{X}_{bp}$ of a point belonging to a body part *bp* and II) the timestamp t_i given by some timer function of the system. The position is defined in a frame of reference ϕ indicated by ${}^{\phi}\mathbf{X}$. This usually indicates the sensor used for input like the camera {C} or the commercial motion capture device {W}. With the sampling (frame) index *i* the sampling interval Δt_{i+1} can be calculated between two conescutive frames *i* and *i*+1. In order to treat 2-D and 3-D data equally the first step is to project the 3-D data to some suitable planes. Usually the three principal planes *Door Plane* (vertical) π_v, *Table plane* (horizontal) π_h, and the *Wheel Plane* (sagittal) π_s are used. To allow for a fast computation we are discretizing the low-level features to a low cardinality. The continuous *displacement angles* are discretized into *directions D* with a cardinality of eight.

$$\mathrm{D} \in \{180°,\ 135°,\ 90°,\ 45°,\ 0°,\ -45°,\ -90°,\ -135°\} < 8 > \tag{5}$$

With this we get one discrete variable *D* per body part and plane. Considering the two most important body parts 'left hand' *lh* and 'right hand' *rh* and the three principal planes we get six *directions*:

$$D_{xy}^{rh}, D_{yz,}^{rh} D_{xz}^{rh},\ D_{xy}^{lh}, D_{yz,}^{lh} D_{xz}^{lh} \tag{6}$$

The angular values of *D* are then translated into the *Vector Symbols* A_{bp}, B_{bp} and C_{bp}. Figure 12 shows this transformation for the *Door Plane* (vertical) π_v and the right hand *rh* using a 'byebye' movement as an example.

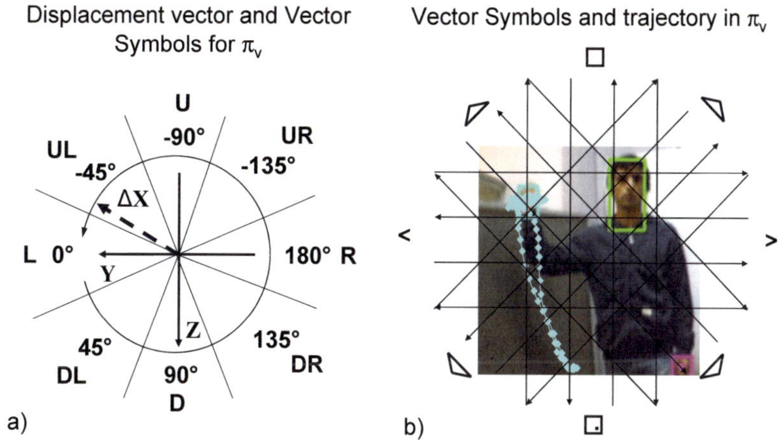

Sequence of Directions and Vector Symbols

Frame i	1	2	3	4	5	6	7	8	.....
Direction D_{yz}^{rh}	-45°	-45°	-90°	-90°	-90°	180°	-45°	0°	.....
Vector Symbols B_{rh}	◸	◸	□	□	□	>	◸	<	.....
	UL	UL	U	U	U	R	UL	L	.....

c)

Figure 12. Vector Symbols for the *Door Plane* and the right hand by means of a 'byebye' movement. a) The *displacement* is converted into the *Vector Symbol* B_{rh}. b) Grid of *Vector Symbols* superimposed on the movement trajectory. c) The continuous computation results in a stream of *Vector Symbols*

In Figure 12 a) the scheme for the conversion from the *displacement* to the *displacement angles* to the *direction* D_{yz}^{rh} and finally to the *Vector Symbol* B_{rh} is shown. In Figure 12 b) the grid of *Vector Symbols* is superimposed on the movement trajectory. As a result of the continuous computation we get a stream of *Vector Symbols* as shown in Figure 12 c). Figure 12 shows both representtations for the Vector Symbols, the signs taken from (Longstaff, 2001) and the letters used by our algorithm.

4. Bayesian Models for Movement Perception

The concepts of Laban Movement Analysis (LMA) and the characteristics of our system to track human movements can be mathematically and computationally modeled using a common framework. The Bayesian theory gives us the possibility to deal with incompleteness and uncertainty, make predictions on future events and, most important, provides an embedded scheme for learning.

Included in the Bayesian framework are specialized models which have a long tradition in many areas and are known under the names, Hidden Markov Models (HMMs), Kalman Filters and Particle Filters. Bayesian models have already been used in a broad range of technical applications (e.g. navigation, speech recognition, etc.). Recent findings indicate that Bayesian models can also be useful in the modeling of cognitive processes. Research on the human brain (and in its computations for perception and action) report, that Bayesian

methods have proven successful in building computational theories for perception and sensorimotor control (Knill & Pouget, 2004).
In the course of our investigation and development we found, that the process of prediction and update during classification represents an intrinsic implementation of the mental concept of anticipation. Using the property of conditional independence the dimensionality of the parameter space that describes the human movements can be reduced. Bayesian nets offer the possibility to represent dependencies, parameters and their values intuitively understandable, which is a frequently expressed request from non-engineers (Loeb, 2001). Furthermore these methods have already proven their usability in the related field of gesture recognition (Starner, 1995); (Pavlovic, 1999).
Probabilistic reasoning needs only two basic rules. The first is the *conjunction rule*, which gives the probability of a conjunction of *propositions*.

$$\begin{aligned} P(a\, b) &= P(a) \times P(b \mid a) \\ &= P(b) \times P(a \mid b) \end{aligned} \tag{7}$$

The second one is the *normalization rule*, which states that the sum of the probabilities of a and $\neg a$ is one.

$$P(a) \wedge P(\neg a) = 1 \tag{8}$$

The two rules are sufficient for any computation in discrete probabilities. All the other necessary inference rules concerning variables can be derived such as the *conjunction rule*, the *normalization rule* and the *marginalization rule for variables* (Rett, 2008).

4.1 Global Model

The global model to describe the phenomenon of computational Laban Movement Analysis (LMA) is shown in Figure 13.

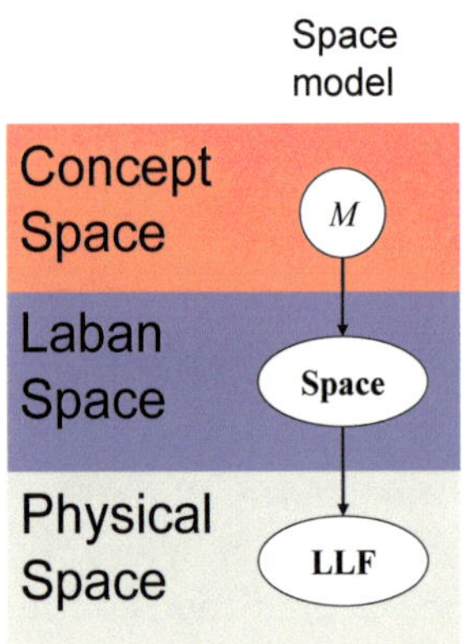

Figure 13. Bayes-Net of the global model with three levels of abstraction (i.e. Concept Level, Laban Space and Physical Space)

Having the concept of a movement represented by the variable M certain characteristics will be exhibited through the sets of variables of LMA (**Space**). The sets of LMA can be observed through the set of low-level features **LLF**. This concept is accompanied by different levels of abstraction by introducing the 'Concept space', the 'Laban space' and the 'Physical space'.

The nodes represent variables (e.g. movement M) and sets of variables (e.g. low-level features **LLF**). The arcs describe the dependencies between the nodes. The movement M represents the parent node which effects the child nodes in the 'Laban space'. The node on the 'Laban space' is a parent for the set of low-level features **LLF**. The dependencies can also be expressed as a joint distribution and its decomposition while omitting the conjunction symbol $\wedge$ as:

$$P(M\,\mathbf{Space}\,\mathbf{LLF}) = P(M)\,P(\mathbf{Space} \mid M)\,P(\mathbf{LLF} \mid \mathbf{Space}) \tag{9}$$

In the following section the *Space* model will be discussed in detail. Additionally a temporal model will be discussed which tackles issues concerning the duration of a movement and the frames of inflection (phase).

4.2 Space Model

The *Space* component of LMA is modeled using the concept of *Vector Symbols*. As defined in the 'global model' (see section 4.1) two sets of variables are used in the model:

$$\mathbf{LLF} = \mathbf{Space} \in \{A, B, C\} \tag{10}$$

It can be seen that **LLF** and **Space** are equal which is due to the fact that the variables {A, B, C} are both, LMA descriptors and low-level features.

The *Vector Symbols* receive one additional value from the velocity variable, i.e. the indication of no movement $v = 0$. As we describe the spatial pathway of a movement by 'atomic' displacements, we refer to the *Vectors Symbols* sometimes as *atoms*. Movements which are parallel to one of the axes are expressed as up, down, left, right, back and forward movement resulting in the values U, D, L, R, B and F respectively. This represents the concept of *Pure Dimensional Movements* within LMA, while the concepts of *Pure Diagonal Movements* and *Deflections* are described as combinations of *Pure Dimensional Movements*.

Of particular interest are the *atoms B*, occurring in the frontal *Door Plane* (YZ-plane) as they convey most of the information found in gestures. The variables and their sample space are shown in

$$\begin{aligned} &M \in \{byebye, \ldots, lunging\}\langle 8\rangle \\ &I \in \{1, \ldots, I_{\max}\}\langle I_{\max}\rangle \\ &A_{bp} \in \{O, F, FR, R, BR, B, BL, L, LF\}\langle 9\rangle \\ &B_{bp} \in \{O, U, UR, R, DR, D, DL, L, UL\}\langle 9\rangle \\ &C_{bp} \in \{O, U, UF, F, DF, D, DB, B, UB\}\langle 9\rangle \end{aligned} \tag{11}$$

The model of LMA-Space assumes that each movement $M = m$ produces certain *atoms* $A_{bp} = a$, $B_{bp} = b$ and $C_{bp} = c$ at a certain point in time, i.e. frame $I = i$ and for a certain *body part bp*. In this model a certain movement m is 'causing' the atoms a, b and c at the frame i. The *evidences* that can be measured are the atoms a, b, c and the frame i. The model might be applied to any number of body parts bp which are treated as independent evidences a thus expressed through a product as shown in the joint distribution as

$$P(M\ I\ A\ B\ C) = P(M)\ \ P(I)\prod_{bp}\{P(A_{bp} \mid M\ I)\ \ P(B_{bp} \mid M\ I)\ \ P(C_{bp} \mid M\ I)\} \tag{12}$$

Figure 14 shows the corresponding representation in a Bayes-net.

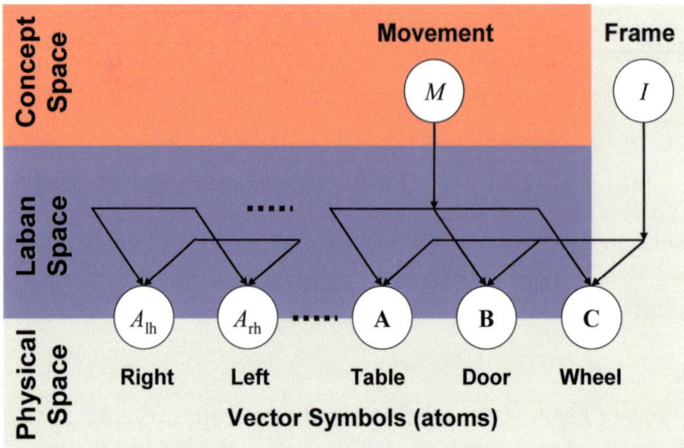

Figure 14. Bayes-Net for the *Space* component of LMA. The movement *M* belongs to the *concept space* while the *Vector Symbols* are part of both, the *Laban space* and the *physical space*. Their instances are in the principal planes *Table*, *Door* and *Wheel* and the left and right hand. The frame *I* is associated with the *physical space* only

Table 2 summarizes the variables used in this model.

Variable	Symbol	Description
Movement	M	Set of movements
Frame	I	Frame index
Body part	bp	e.g. *rh* (right hand)
Vector symbol	A_{bp}	*Vector Symbols* (*Atoms*) in π_h
	B_{bp}	*Vector Symbols* (*Atoms*) in π_v
	C_{bp}	*Vector Symbols (Atoms)* in π_s

Table 2. Space variables

4.3 Temporal Model

The *Space* model is based on the temporal sequence of *atoms*. Different paces and number of repetitions while performing the movement influence the classification result. One solution to deal with this problem is to introduce an additional uncertainty model. For each trial of movements the total length in frames i_{max} can be determined. For all trials the mean and variance can be calculated. The uncertainty about the length i_{max} of a performance can be expressed as a an uncertainty concerning the frame i itself. One may think of this as stretching and shrinking the length of the frames i so they may fit in a static length i_{max}.
Technically one can map an observed frame i_obs to a normal frame i, probabilistically we define a conditional probability

$$P(i\_obs \mid i) \;=\; N(i\_obs;\sigma_i) \tag{13}$$

where for a certain frame i get probability values for all possible values of *i_obs*. It makes sense to assign the highest probability to the case *i_obs* = i and model the relationship as a

Gaussian distribution. The mean of the Gaussian will be the observed frame *i_obs* = *i* itself and the standard deviation may have a value $0 < \sigma_i \leq \sigma_{i\_max}$.
For each newly observed frame *i_obs* the mean of the distribution slides one step further as shown in Figure 15.

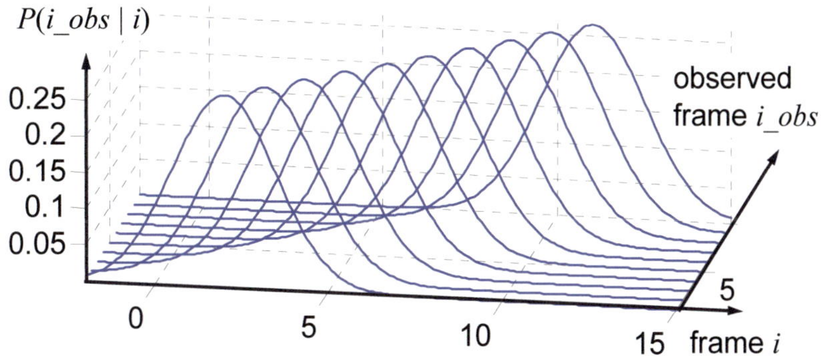

Figure 15. P(*i_obs* | *i*=*i_obs*) as a Gaussian distribution with 'sliding' mean

One might notice that the standard deviation does not change, producing the relation of probabilities e.g. between P(*i_obs* | *i*=*i_obs*) and P(*i_obs* | *i*=*i_obs*+1) for any observed frame in the interval.
The variables and their sample space are shown in (14).

$$I \in \{1,\ldots,I_{\max}\}\langle I_{\max}\rangle$$
$$I\_obs \in \{1,\ldots,I\_obs_{\max}\}\langle I\_obs_{\max}\rangle \tag{14}$$

For the *temporal* model we assume that each frame *I* can show up as an observed frame *I_obs* with a certain probability. Thus, we have a conditional dependency of *I* and *I_obs* as can be seen in Bayes-net of Figure 16.

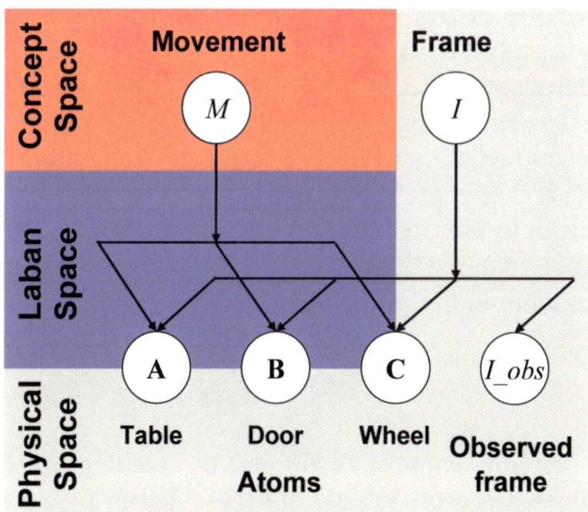

Figure 16. Bayes-Net of the *temporal* model which connects to the *Space* model

The *I_obs* variable is measured directly as hard evidence, the frame *I* can be interpreted as a soft evidence for the *Space* model. The joint distribution embedded *Space* model while omitting the body part index can be expressed as

$$P(M\, I\_obs\; I\, A\, B\, C) \\ = P(M)\quad P(I)\quad P(I\_obs \mid I)\quad P(A \mid M\; I)\quad P(B \mid M\; I)\quad P(C\; \mid M\; I) \tag{15}$$

Table 2 summarizes the variables used in this model.

Variable	Symbol	Description
Frame	*I*	Computed (soft) evidence
Observed Frame	*I_obs*	Measured (hard) evidence

Table 3. Variables used in the *temporal* model.

4.4 Learning of probability tables

The previous sections presented models through Bayesian nets and joint distributions. The latter appeared as a product of several conditional distributions which links the hypothesizes to the data. Thus, the distributions need to represent the data given a certain condition. The question is 'How can we find this distribution?' and the answer is 'Learning'. Many different techniques and forms of representations exist.

The probability distribution can be learned by counting the observations a variable has a certain value (Histogram Learning). For a finite number of discrete values the process can be described as building a histogram. By dividing the counts for each value *i* of the variable *V* (*V*=*i*) by the total number of samples *n* a probability distribution can be computed as

$$P^*([V = i]) = \frac{n_i}{n} \tag{16}$$

The assumptions that apply are: i) All samples *n* come from the same phenomenon. ii) All samples are from a single variable *V*. iii) The order of the samples is not important.

When learning a probability distribution through the histogram some values of *V* might have zero probability, simply because they have never been observed. Whenever these values occur in the later classification stage the corresponding hypothesis(es) will receive also a zero probability. In continuous classifiers, that are based on multiplicative update of beliefs, this leads to an immediate and definite out-rule of the hypothesis(es). Most of the time this is not desirable and appears 'unnatural'.

One way of solving this is to use an equation which produces a minimum probability for non-observed evidences. Equation (17) is based on the Laplace Succession Law and it can be seen that it will produce a minimum probability of $1/(n+\lfloor V \rfloor)$.

$$P^*([V = i]) = \frac{n_i + 1}{n + \lfloor V \rfloor} \tag{17}$$

The atom variable A_{rh} has nine values $\lfloor V \rfloor = 9$ and by learning from six samples *n*=6 each non-observed value will receive a probability of $P^*(V) = 0.0667$ for all values *i* where $n_i = 0$. The learned table *P* (*Atom* | *M I*) holds the probability distribution of the Variables *Atom* e.g. *Table Plane* right hand atom A_{rh}. The variable has two conditions, the movement *M* and the frame *I*. Figure 17 represents this multidimensional table.

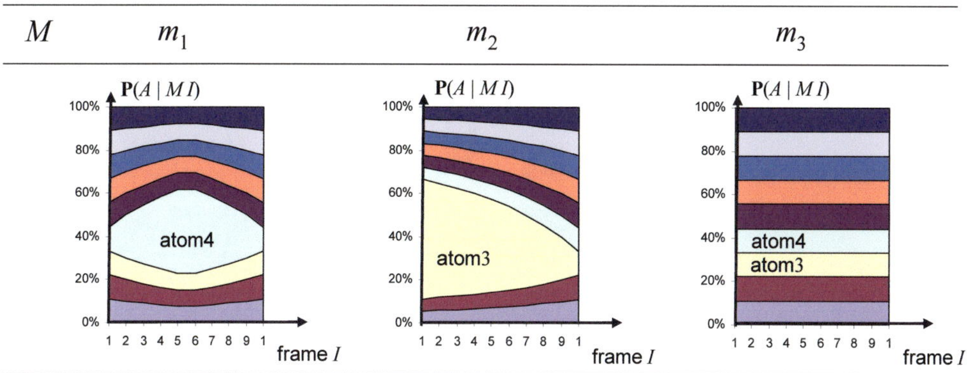

Figure 17. Learned table for generic movements of the type *P(Atom | M I)*. The movements m_1 and m_2 have a dominating *atom* (4 and 3) during certain phases (middle and beginning) while movement m_3 shows no spatial pattern at all

When stacking the probabilities for each value one over each other, patterns can be observed along the time given by the frame *I* and between the movements *M*. From the hypothetical example one can conclude, that in movement $M = m_1$ at frame $I = 5$ most probably *atom* 4 will show up. This shows that after learning the data can be presented in a way that allows an evaluation of both, the hypothesis and the data. The generic movement m_2 has its dominating *atom* 3 at the beginning. Movement m_3 can be seen as a 'white noise' movement where no spatial pattern can be observed along the time. The size of the table is given by the cardinality of *Atom* i.e. nine, the maximum number of frames, e.g. forty and the number of movements, e.g. four. In this example the table will have 1440 entries.

4.5 Continuous classification of movements

Classification is the final step after the model has been established and the tables have been learned. Given our joint distribution (17) we need to formulate a question, i.e. what we want to classify and what we can observe. In our case we are interested to classify an unknown movement from the evidences observed in the *Physical Space*. In the following we continue with a simplified question, i.e. classifying a movement *M* taking into account only the *Vector Symbols* (atoms) *A* and the frame *I*.

The previous step of learning provided us with the possibility to determine the probability that the *atom A* has value *a* given a frame *i* from all possible frames *I* and a given a movement *m* from all possible movements *M*, i.e. $P(a \mid m, i)$. The table $\mathbf{P}(A \mid M, I)$ holds the probability distribution for all possible values of atom *A* given all possible movements *M* and frames *I*.

Knowing the conditional probability $\mathbf{P}(A \mid M, I)$ together with the prior probabilities for the movements $\mathbf{P}(M)$ we are able to apply Bayes' rule and compute the probability distribution for the movements *M* given the frame *I* and the *atom A* with

$$\mathbf{P}(M \mid I\ A) \propto \mathbf{P}(M)\ \ \mathbf{P}(A \mid M\ I) \tag{18}$$

It is possible to compute how likely it is that an observed sequence of *n atoms* was caused by a certain movement *m*. To compute the *likelihood* we assume that the observed *atoms* are independently and identically distributed (i.i.d.). In (19) the sequence of *n* observed values for *atom a* is represented by $a_{1:n}$. For each movement m the joint probability will be the product of the probabilities from frame $i = 1$ to $i = n$, where the j-th frame of the sequence is indicated by i_j.

$$P(a_{1:n} \mid m\, i_{1:n}) = \prod_{j=1}^{n} P(a_j \mid m\, i_j) \tag{19}$$

We can formulate (19) in a recursive way and for all movements M and get

$$P(a_{n+1} \mid M\, i_{1:n+1}) = P(a_n \mid M\, i_{1:n}) \;\; P(a_{n+1} \mid M\, i_{n+1}) \tag{20}$$

The *likelihood computation* (20) can be plugged in our question (18). Assuming that each frame i a new observed direction symbol arrives we can continuously (online) update our classification result.

$$P(M_{n+1} \mid i_{1:n+1}\, a_{1:n+1}) \propto P(M_n) \;\; P(a_{n+1} \mid M\, i_{n+1}) \tag{21}$$

We can see that the prior of step n+1 is the result of the classification of step n. Given a sufficient number of evidences (*atoms*) and assuming that the learned tables represent the phenomenon sufficiently good, the classification will converge to the correct hypothesis. This will happen, regardless of the probability distribution of the 'true' prior for n=0, if there are no zero probabilities assigned to any of the hypothesizes.

The final classification result is given by the maximum a posteriori (MAP) method. Several questions can be formed and compared against each other. The following Table 4 presents some questions and their decompositions.

Movement using 2-D (horizontal) Space model	
Question	$P(M \mid i\, a)$
Decomposition	$P(M)\;\; P(a \mid M\, i)$
Movement using 2-D (vertical) Space with temporal model	
Question	$P(M \mid i\_obs\; b)$
Decomposition	$P(M)\;\; P(i\_obs \mid i)\;\; P(b \mid M\, i)$
Movement using 3-D Space model	
Question	$P(M \mid i\, a\, b\, c)$
Decomposition	$P(M)\;\; P(a \mid M\, i)\;\; P(b \mid M\, i)\;\; P(c \mid M\, i)$

Table 4. Questions for classification and their decompositions

In this example the query variable (usually M) is held in a capital letter, while the observed evidences have small letters.

5. Online Movement Recognition System

The previous sections of this article reflect the steps of designing a probabilistic model. The implementation of the processes and its results can also be organized in steps. The first step is the extraction and computation of the low-level features. In the second step probabilistic variables and conditional kernel tables need to be defined. The third step of learning fills the tables with data from a number of trials. In the fourth step several joint distributions and questions can be defined to investigate different types of models. The fifth and final step is to run the continuous classification and discuss the evolution of the probabilities and the confusion table for several trials. To emphasize the important characteristic of the system it is called *Online Movement Anticipation and Recognition (OMAR)* system. As this section emphasizes the technological aspects of the solution some technical terms will be used such as conditional kernel maps and -tables to represent a probability distribution.

5.1 Learning conditional kernel maps

The second step of implementation is the definition of the probabilistic variables and conditional kernel tables. As this has been done already in section 4 we can proceed to the third step of learning those tables. Figure 18 shows the flow chart of the learning process.

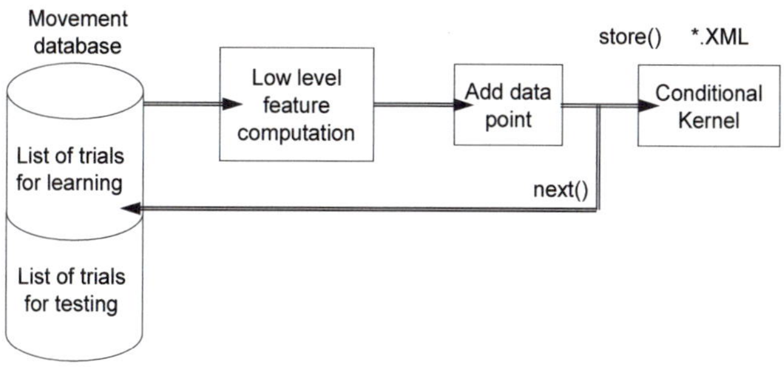

Figure 18. Learning process: Low level features are extracted each frame and 'adds' points to the histogram. After all trials are processed the conditional kernel maps are stored, e.g. in XML-format

From the movement database (HID) a set of trials for learning is chosen and fed into the system for low-level feature extraction. The database consists of five trials per person and movement. Three trials are usually chosen for learning. Each trial produces one data point per feature and frame. Learning based on an histogram approach creates probabilistic tables simply by adding those points until all trials are processed.

5.2 Results: Probability tables for Space

Some of the movements from our database can be described as 'gestures'. Figure 19 shows tables for two 'gestures', i.e. *byebye* and *pointing* with the nine *atoms* of the right hand.

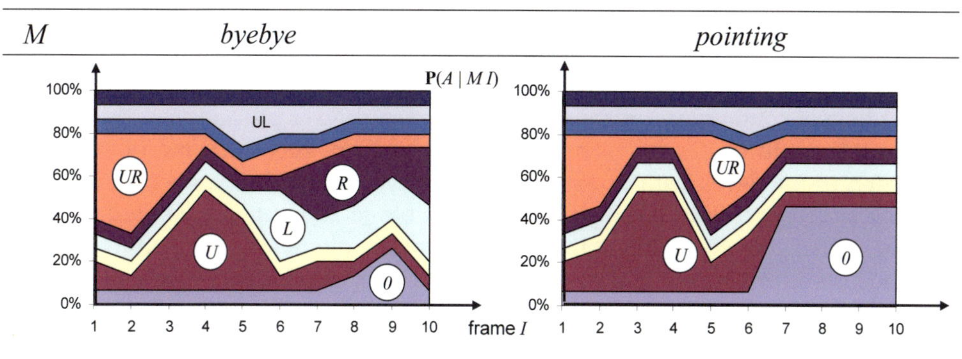

Figure 19. Learned Table $\mathbf{P}(B \mid M\, I)$ for gesture *byebye* and *pointing*

It represents the 'fingerprint' of the gesture prototype for waving *byebye*. The table preserves the possibility to evaluate what has been learned. Figure 19 uses a stacked representation of the probabilities to show which atoms are dominant during certain phases. Two gestures are to be compared: *byebye* on the left and *pointing* on the right. During the first frames the most likely *atoms* to be expected are the ones that go upward and to the right, i.e *UR* and *U*. This is coincides with our intuition, that while we are starting to perform a gesture with the left hand we tend to move up and to the left to gain space to perform the gesture. This is similar for both gestures. From the fifth or sixth frame on, the gestures become distinct. The gesture *byebey* has mainly movements to the left and right (*L* and *R*) with some zero *atoms* 0 at the points of inflection. The gesture *pointing* has mainly non-movement *atoms* (0) leaving the other probabilities at their minimum given by the Laplace assumption. It can be concluded that the movement set 'gestures' has a high spatial distinctiveness and can be used for simple but robust command interaction with a robot.

5.3 The process of recognition

The fourth step of implementation has been presented in section 4. The joint distributions of interest are:

- Movement classification using 2-D Space.
- Movement classification using 3-D Space.

The fifth and final step is the investigation of the evolution of probabilities and the confusion table that can be obtained for all trials of the test set.
Figure 20 shows the flow chart of the classification process.

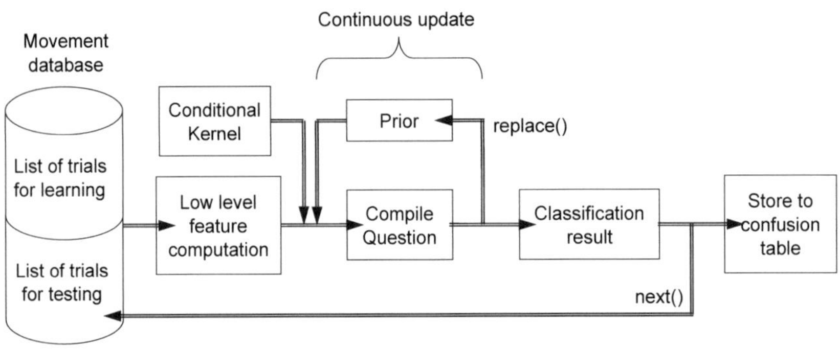

Figure 20. Classification process: The inner loop of continuous update produces the evolution of probabilities, the outer loop of next trial produces the confusion table

The inner loop of continuous update produces the evolution of probabilities, the outer loop of 'next trial' produces the confusion table. Classification uses the same process for the computation of low level features as learning before. With the low level features and the previously stored conditional kernel maps it possible to compute the desired probability distribution. This goes according to the defined joint distribution and the desired question. Inside the probabilistic library the step is known as 'compiling the question'. Through feeding in (replacing) the result of the compiled question as the new prior a continuous update of the classification results for all frames can be obtained. The result of the 'last' frame gives the final result and while looping through all trials for testing a confusion table can be built.

We can conclude that the two processes of learning and classification are based on the same type of observations as shown in Figure 21.

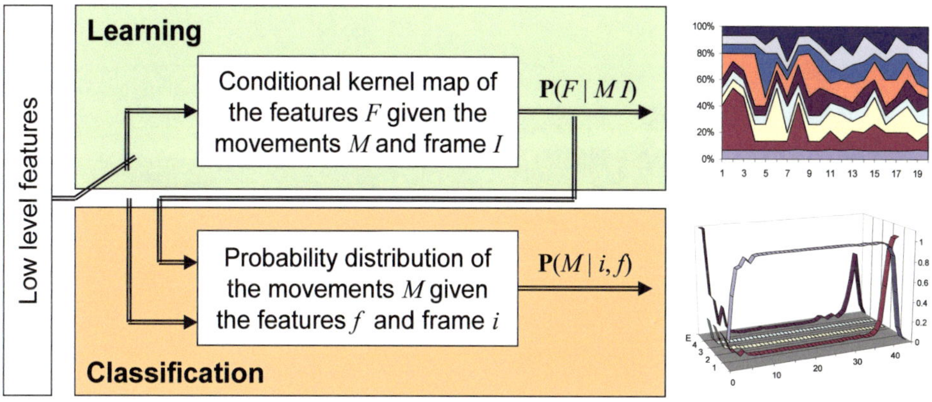

Figure 21. Switching between Bayesian learning and classification

The previously presented scheme starts by learning and, after the conditional kernel maps have been build, continues with classification. An important feature of Bayesian histogram learning is that we can 'switch back' at any time to learn new and more data. This opens the possibility to create artificial agents that are able to continuously learn new data during their daily operation.

5.4 Results: 3-D versus 2-D Recognition

By representing movements using only one plane, some of the spatial information gets lost. This section investigates the loss by comparing the results of classification when using the *Vector Symbols* (*atoms*) of all the tree planes *A*, *B*, *C* to the results gained when only the *atom B* of the *Door Plane* (vertical) plane π_v is used. The results are compared through a confusion table for eight movements, as already presented in Table 1. Table 5 shows the results for using the *B* atoms of the vertical plane π_v.

Movement	**1**	**2**	**3**	**4**	**5**	**6**	**7**	**8**	Σ_e
1 lunging	7			5				1	6
2 maestro		5				8			8
3 stretch			12				1		1
4 ok				8	1		4		5
5 pointing				1	10		1		2
6 byebye						13			0
7 shake				4			9		4
8 nthrow				4			1		5
									31

Table 5. Confusion table using only the 2-D (vertical) *atoms*

The sum of all numbers in each row usually adds up to thirteen, though some movements have fewer trials. In the 2-D case 31 of 95 trials are classified wrongly leaving a recognition rate of 67%. The highest false-rate has the *maestro* sequence which is confused with the *byebye* sequence shown in the second row. By comparing the traces of the two movements (see Figure 22) we can see that they are quite similar, though the vertical plane π_v appears as the most distinctive one.

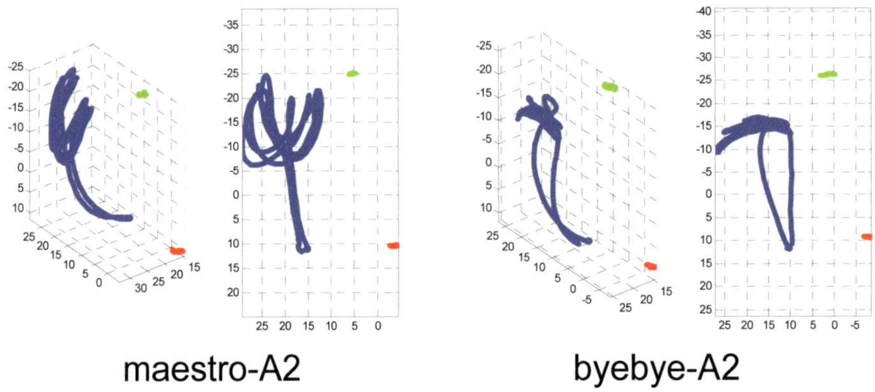

Figure 22. Comparing the traces of the movements *byebye* and *maestro* in 2-D and 3-D

The confusion between the two-hand movement *lunging* and the one-hand gesture *ok* indicated in the first row of the table is partly due to the traces but also due to the model. From Figure 23 it can be seen that for 2-D the right hand traces (blue) are similar leading partly to the confusion.

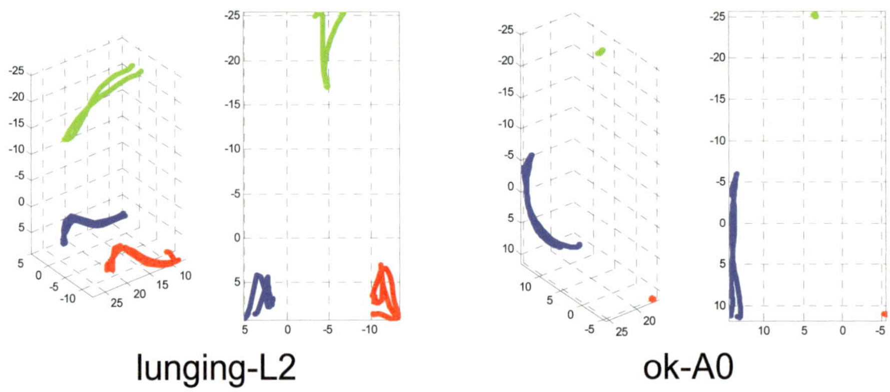

Figure 23. Comparing the traces of the movements *lunging* and *ok* in 2-D and 3-D

The model for the left hand is based on the assumption that we get mostly non-movement *atoms* which is true for both cases. The model can be easily improved by adding an evidence for not having moved at all.

The confusion between the gesture *ok* and the movement *shake* indicated in the fourth row of the table is due to the traces for some trials. From Figure 24 it can be seen that trials where the hand does not reach towards the middle (sagittal plane), but goes straight forward, the 2-D projection can be confused easily.

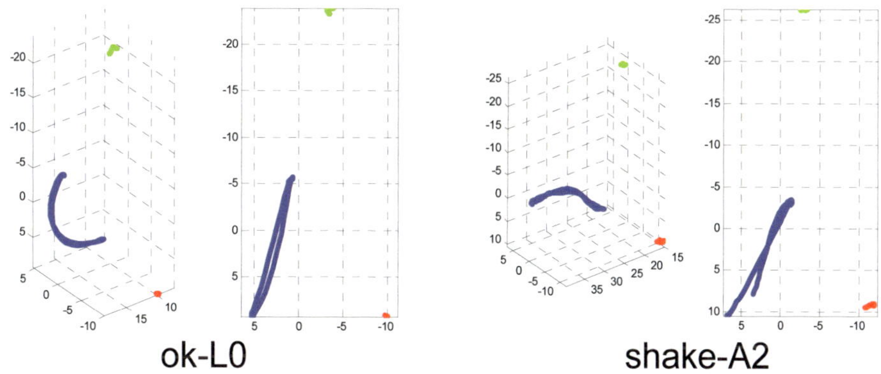

Figure 24. Comparing the traces of the movements *lunging* and *ok* in 2-D and 3-D

In this case the confusion goes in both directions as can be seen in the seventh row.
The final confusion occurs in the eight row. From Figure 25 it can be seen that the 2-D projecttion does not convey the information on the sagittal oszillation the right hand is performing.

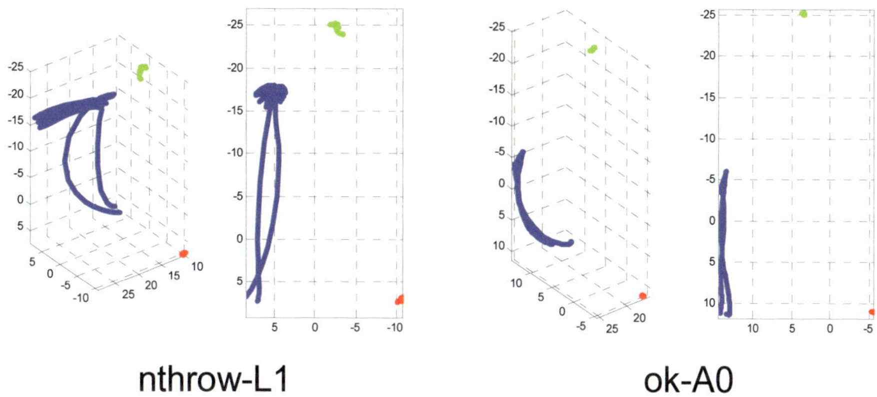

Figure 25. Comparing the traces of the movements *nthrow* and *ok* in 2-D and 3-D

Table 6 shows the results for using the *A*, *B* and *C atoms* of the all planes.

Movement	**1**	**2**	**3**	**4**	**5**	**6**	**7**	**8**	Σ_e
1 lunging	11			1			1		2
2 maestro		2				11			11
3 stretch			12	1					1
4 ok				9			4		4
5 pointing					10		2		2
6 byebye						13			0
7 shake				1			12		1
8 nthrow								5	0
									21

Table 6. Confusion table using 3D (all planes) *atoms*

In the first row it can be seen, that the recognition rate has improved due to the additional evidences indicating the movement in the x-dimension. Similar is true for the seventh row where the hands are usually reaching further in the x-dimension when performing the *shake* movement as compared to the *ok* gesture. The *nthrow* movement is now recognized in all trials as the evidences of the sagittal waving are now processed. In the 3-D case 21 of 95 trials are classified wrongly leaving a recognition rate of 78%. The *maestro* movement of the second row is significantly worse in 3-D which may be due to the fact that the x-dimension does not add additional information for distinction.

We can conclude that the recognition rate improves in general when using evidences from all three planes (from 67% to 78%). Some movements can not be seen in certain planes, e.g. *nthrow* in the vertical plane π_v. It appears that apart from the 'pure' spatial pattern also evidences from the temporal model effect the classification result. A further tuning of the temporal model (sliding mean was used) should improve the results. Further improvements are expected from a variable that indicates if a hand has not moved at all.

6. Conclusions and future works

The work presented in this article started with the premise that the field of computational Human Movement Analysis is in need of an annotated database for human movements. The second section of this article showed that Laban Movement Analysis (LMA) is a good choice for this descriptor. After a brief overview the *Space* component was discussed in detail and the descriptive language Labanotation was presented. This section concluded with examples from our Human Interaction Database (HID) to outline the applicability of LMA for an annotated database.

To allow applications which involve autonomous mobile robots (e.g. 'social robots') a technical solution needed to be found to bring together monocular cameras and high precision data from a 3-D tracking device. The third section showed that we are able to base the computation of our low level features on two very different sensor types, i.e. monocular camera and commercial motion tracking device. This allows to work with a database of rich 3-D position data and sensory input from (a) 2-D projection(s). The section presented the extraction and computation of low level features based on displacement angles.

A suitable framework needed to be chosen which provides a scheme for learning as well as for classification and takes into account that LMA is based on human observations where incompleteness and uncertainty are issues. By suggesting a Bayesian approach in the fourth section the former issues have been taken into account. A probabilistic scheme for learning and classification using models that can be represented as Bayesian nets was shown.

The fifth section presented the implementation as flow charts with some links to functions of the probabilistic library used. It was shown that the probabilistic approach provides the learned data in a way that allows its visual inspection and evaluation. The chosen histogram-based approach for learning provides a simple way of adding data points. The Human Interaction Database (HID) provides several sets of 'expressive movements'. It was shown that 'gestures' has a high spatial distinctiveness and can be used for simple but robust command interaction with a robot. As a benefit of the modularity of the system results for movement classification could be presented and compared using 3-D *Space* and 2-D *Space*. The recognition rate improved in general when using evidences from all three planes (from 67% to 78%). Some movements could not be seen in certain planes, e.g. *nthrow* in the *Door Plane* π_v.

For the future the database of movements with annotated Laban Movement Analysis (LMA) descriptors will be extended by certain classes. The Bayesian models will be extended by additional components taken from LMA. A socially assistive robot will be designed to be used in rehabilitation that records human movements annotated with LMA descriptors. An interface for the smart infrastructure and the socially assistive robot will be designed to show the results of the recorded movement and the evolution of the rehabilitation process. The main goals of the future research will be to establish Laban Movement Analysis (LMA) as a general tool for the evaluation of human movements and provide those communities that collect large amounts of experimental data with technical solutions for labeled data sets. The research will be justified by showing that rehabilitation processes do benefit from evaluations based on LMA. That comparison of experimental data with very distinct experimental set-ups is possible by using the descriptors of LMA. Data from computational LMA opens the possibility to cluster motor deficits and neurological disorders that are similar with regards to LMA.

7. Acknowledgements

The authors would like to thank Luis Santos from the Institute of Systems and Robotics, Coimbra for his work on the implementation. This work is partially supported by FCT-Fundação para a Ciência e a Tecnologia Grant #12956/2003 to J. Rett and by the BACS-project-6th Framework Programme of the European Commission contract number: FP6-IST-027140, Action line: Cognitive Systems to J. Rett and L. Santos.

8. References

Badler, N.I.; Phillips, C.B. & Webber, B.L. (1993). *Simulating Humans: Computer Graphics, Animation, and Control*, Oxford Univ. Press

Bartenieff, I. & Lewis, D. (1980). *Body Movement: Coping with the Environment*, Gordon and Breach Science, New York

Bradski, G.R. (1998). Computer Vision Face Tracking For Use in a Perceptual User Interface, *Intel Technology Journal*, Q2, 15

Bregler, C. (1997). Learning and recognizing human dynamics in video sequences, *Conference on Computer Vision and Pattern Recognition*, San Juan, Puerto Rico,

Chi, D.; Costa, M.; Zhao, L. & Badler, N. (2000). The EMOTE model for Effort and Shape, SIGGRAPH 00, *Computer Graphics Proceedings, Annual Conference Series*, 173-182 ACM Press

Dias, J. (1994). *Reconstrução Tridimensional Utilizando Visão Dinâmica*, University of Coimbra, Portugal,

Fong, T.; Nourbakhsh, I. & Dautenhahn, K. (2003). A survey of socially interactive robots, *Robotics and Autonomous Systems*, 42, 143–166

Foroud, A. & Whishaw, I.Q. (2006). Changes in the kinematic structure and non-kinematic features of movements during skilled reaching after stroke: A Laban Movement Analysis in two case studies, *Journal of Neuroscience Methods* 158, 137-149

Hartley, R. & Zisserman, A. (2000). *Multiple View Geometry in Computer Vision*, Cambridge University Press,

Hutchinson, A. (1970). *Labanotation or Kinetography Laban*, Theatre Arts, New York

Kendon, A. (2004). *Gesture: Visible Action as Utterance*, Cambridge University Press,

Knill, D.C. & Pouget, A. (2004). The Bayesian brain: the role of uncertainty in neural coding and computation, *TRENDS in Neurosciences*, 27, 712-719

Laban, R. (1966). *Choreutics*, MacDonald & Evans., London

Loeb, G.E. (2001). Learning from the spinal cord, *Journal of Physiology*, 533.1, 111-117

Longstaff, J.S. (2001). Translating vector symbols from Laban's (1926) Choreographie, 26. *Biennial Conference of the International Council of Kinetography Laban*, ICKL, Ohio, USA, 70-86

Nakata, T.; Mori, T. & Sato, T. (2002). Analysis of Impression of Robot Bodily Expression, *Journal of Robotics and Mechatronics*, 14, 27-36

Nakata, T. (2007). Temporal segmentation and recognition of body motion data based on inter-limb correlation analysis, *IEEE/RSJ International Conference on Intelligent Robots and Systems*, IROS,

Otero, N.; Knoop, S.; Nehaniv, C.; Syrda, D.; Dautenhahn, K. & Dillmann, R. (2006). Distribution and Recognition of Gestures in Human-Robot Interaction, *The 15th IEEE International Symposium on Robot and Human Interactive Communication*, 2006. ROMAN 2006., 103-110

Pavlovic, V.I. (1999). *Dynamic Bayesian Networks for Information Fusion with Applications to Human-Computer Interfaces*, Graduate College of the University of Illinois,

Rett, J. & Dias, J. (2007-A). Human-robot interface with anticipatory characteristics based on Laban Movement Analysis and Bayesian models, *Proceedings of the 2007 IEEE 10th International Conference on Rehabilitation Robotics*,

Rett, J. & Dias, J. (2007-B). Human Robot Interaction Based on Bayesian Analysis of Human Movements, *EPIA 07*, Neves, J.; Santos, M. & Machado, J. (ed.) 4874, 530-541 Springer, Berlin,

Rett, J. (2008). *Robot-Human Interface using Laban Movement Analysis inside a Bayesian framework*, University of Coimbra,

Rett, J.; Neves, A. & Dias, J. (2007). *Hid-human interaction database*: http://paloma.isr.uc.pt/hid/,

Sato, T.; Nishida, Y. & Mizoguchi, H. (1996). Robotic room: Symbiosis with human through behavior media, *Robotics and Autonomous Systems*, 18, 185-194

Starner, T. (1995). *Visual recognition of american sign language using Hidden Markov Models*, MIT,

Starner, T. & Pentland, A. (1995). Visual recognition of american sign language using hidden markov models, In *International Workshop on Automatic Face and Gesture Recognition*, Zurich, Switzerland, 189-194

Zhao, L. (2002). *Synthesis and Acquisition of Laban Movement Analysis Qualitative Parameters for Communicative Gestures*, University of Pennsylvania,

Zhao, L. & Badler, N.I. (2005). Acquiring and validating motion qualities from live limb gestures, *Graphical Models* 67, 1, 1-16

11

Video System in Robotic Applications

Vincenzo Niola, Cesare Rossi, Sergio Savino and Salvatore Strano
University of Naples "Federico II"
Italy

1. Introduction

The "Artificial Vision" permits industrial automation and system vision able to act in the production activities without humane presence. So we suppose that the acquisition and interpretation of the imagines for automation purposes is an interesting topic.
Industrial applications are referred to technological fields (assembly or dismounting, cut or stock removal; electrochemical processes; abrasive trials; cold or warm moulding; design with CAD techniques; metrology), or about several processes (control of the row material; workmanship of the component; assemblage; packing or storages; controls of quality; maintenance).
The main advantages of these techniques are:

1. elimination of the human errors, particularly in the case of repetitive or monotonous operations;
2. possibility to vary the production acting on the power of the automatic system (the automatic machines can operate to high rhythms day and night every day of the year);
3. greater informative control through the acquisition of historical data; these data can be used for successive elaborations, for the analysis of the failures and to have statistics in real time;
4. quality control founded on objective parameters in order to avoid dispute, and loss of image.

The use of a vision system in a robot application, it concurs to increase the robots ability to interact with their work space, to make more efficient their management.
In this chapter some "Artificial Vision" applications to robotics are described:

- robot cinematic calibration;
- trajectories recording;
- path planning by means of vision system;
- solid reconstruction with a video system on a robot arm.

2. Vision usefullness

The man perceives the characteristics of the external world by means of sense organs. They allow that a sure flow of information, regarding for example the shape, the color, the temperature, the smell of an object, reaches the brain; in this way each man possesses a complete description of that is around him. More in a generalized manner, the man can itself be seen as a system that, for survival reasons, must interact with the external world, and, to be able to make it, he has need of a sensory apparatus able to supply him continuously information. This affirmation can be extended also to not biological systems, like, for example, the automatic machines or the robots. These equipment, carrying out a determined task, interact with the external world and they must be fortified with devices that are able to perceive the world characteristics , this devices are called sensors. A robot or one whichever automatic machine, that is equipped with sensors, is be able to perceive the "stimula " of the external world, in which it works.

What is the difference between sensors and organs of sense, at the operating level?

When we perceive a any sound, for example the voice of a known person, we are able to distinguish the stamp, to establish if it is acute or serious, to feel the intensity and volume. If instead, the same voice is acquired through a microphone, converting its signal in digital and processing it by means of an electronic calculator, the information that we can deduce, increase and they make more detailed: we will be able, for example, to determine the main frequency components, to measure the amplitude in decibel, to visualize the wave shape. In other words, sensors, beyond to having the representative function of the truth, concur also to extrapolate information at quantitative level and they allow us to lead a technical analysis on the acquired data.

Main aim of this chapter is to show how it is possible to equip robot of sight

The main problem of the reliable and precise robot realization, has been to implement the hardware e software structures, that constitute a sturdy and efficient control system.

How does motion control work in the man? The human body has a much elevating number of degrees of freedom and this renders very arduous the nervous system task. For this reason a highly centralized control structure is necessary. It is possible to describe the job of such structure through a simple example: let's image a man, that wants to take an object that is disposed on a table distant some meters. The man observes the table and the object position, while the brain elaborates the trajectory and the nervous impulses to transmit to muscles, characterizing reference points that are acquired from image observed by eyes. Subsequently the man begins to move and after some step, he reaches the table and takes the object. From this example, it can be asserted that, excluding the memory contribution and an elevated development of the other senses, it is not possible to carry out a task without to see.

Therefore the sense of the sight it has a twofold function in the human body motion:

1. to characterize the targets in the space.
2. to control the position and the guidelines of the several parts of the body that move.

In the robots, the motion control is, usually implemented only with joints position transducers. It is clear that, if joints translation and rotations are known, its spatial configuration is known completely; therefore, the second function that has been attributed to human sight is realized. A blind control is less suitable to catch up a target in the work space. In fact, to guide the robot end effector to a point, it is necessary to know, with precision, its cartesian coordinates and "translate" them in the joints space by means of inverse cinematic. For this reason, it is useful to increase robots sensory abilities, equipping them "off sight", by means of vision systems with opportune sensors. In this chapter it will be described in how it is possible to characterize the targets in the work space and to determine the values of the Denavit-Hartenberg cinematic parameters, by means of opportune techniques, and with two television cameras, so as to make simpler, more accurate and efficient both the robot management and the motion planning.

3. Vision process

About the term "vision" applications to industrial robots, the meaning of this word must be enriched and cleared with technical slight knowledge.
In literature, use of the vision like instrument for technical applications, is called "machine vision" or "computer vision".
It is important to explain, in the first place, which is the aim of the computer vision: to recognize the characteristics of objects that are present in the acquired images of work space and to associate them theirs real meant.
The vision process can be divided in following operations:

- Perception
- Pre-elaboration
- Segmentation
- Description
- Recognition
- Interpretation

Perception is the process that supplies the visual image. With this operation, we mean the mechanism of photogram formation by means of a vision system and a support, like a computer.
Pre-elaboration is the whole ~~of~~ noise reduction techniques and images improvement techniques.
Segmentation is the process by means of which the image is subdivided in characteristics of interest.
Description carries out the calculation of the characteristics that segmentation has evidenced, it represents the phase in which it is possible to quantify that only qualitatively has been characterized: lengths, areas ,volumes, ecc.
Recognition consists in assembling all the characteristics that belong to the object, in order to characterize the object. By means of the last phase, called interpretation, it is established the effective correspondence between a characterized shape and the object that is present in the real scene.
To say that a robot "sees", does not mean simply that it has a reality representation, but that it is able to recognize quantitatively the surrounding space, that is to recognize distances, angles, areas and volumes of the objects that are in the observed scene.

4. The perspective transform

In this paragraph, an expression of perspective transformation is proposed, in order to introduce the perspective concepts for the application in robotic field.
The proposed algorithm uses the fourth row of the Denavit and Hartemberg transformation matrix that, for kinematics' purposes, usually contains three zeros and a scale factor, so it is useful to start from the perspective transform matrix.

4.1 The matrix for the perspective transformation [1,5]

It is useful to remember that by means of a perspective transform it is possible to associate a point in the geometric space to a point in a plane, that will be called "image plane"; this will be made by using a scale factor that depends on the distance between the point itself and the image plane.

Let's consider fig.1: the position of point P in the frame O,x,y,z is given by the vector w, while the same position in the frame Ω,ξ,η,ζ is given by vector w_r and the image plane is indicated with R; this last, for the sake of simplicity is supposed to be coincident with the plane ξ,η.

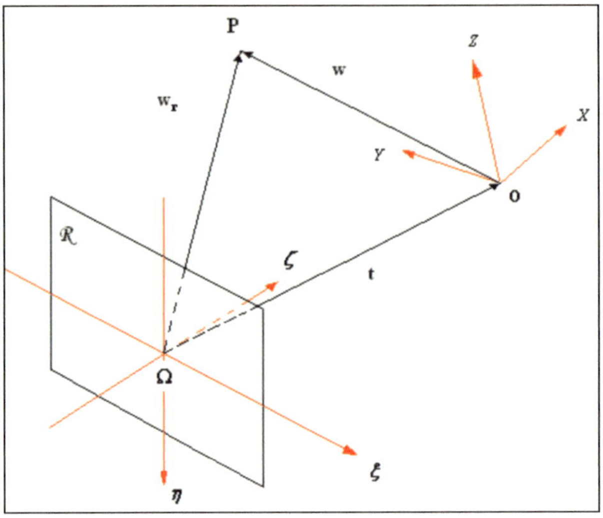

Figure 1. Frames for the perspective transformation

The vectors above are joined by the equation:

$$\begin{Bmatrix} w_{r,x} \\ w_{r,y} \\ w_{r,z} \\ sf \end{Bmatrix} = \begin{bmatrix} R_{11} & R_{12} & R_{13} & t_\xi \\ R_{21} & R_{22} & R_{23} & t_\eta \\ R_{31} & R_{32} & R_{33} & t_\zeta \\ 0 & 0 & 0 & sf \end{bmatrix} = \begin{Bmatrix} w_x \\ w_y \\ w_z \\ sf \end{Bmatrix} \tag{1}$$

where sf is the scale factor; more concisely equation (1) can be written as follows:

$$\tilde{w}_r = T \cdot \tilde{w} \tag{2}$$

where the tilde indicates that the vectors are expressed in homogeneous coordinates.
The matrix T is a generic transformation matrix that is structured according to the following template:

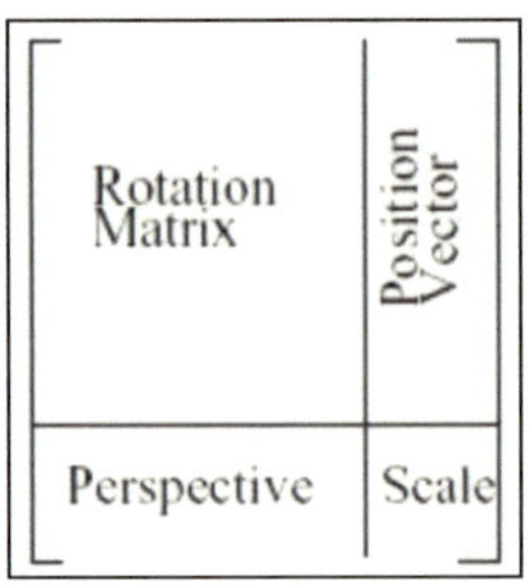

The scale factor will almost always be 1 and the perspective part will be all zeros except when modelling cameras.
The fourth row of matrix [T] contains three zeros; as for these last by means of the prospectic transform three values, generally different by zero, will be determined.
Lets consider, now, fig.2: the vector w*, that represents the projection of vector w_r on the plane ξ,η.

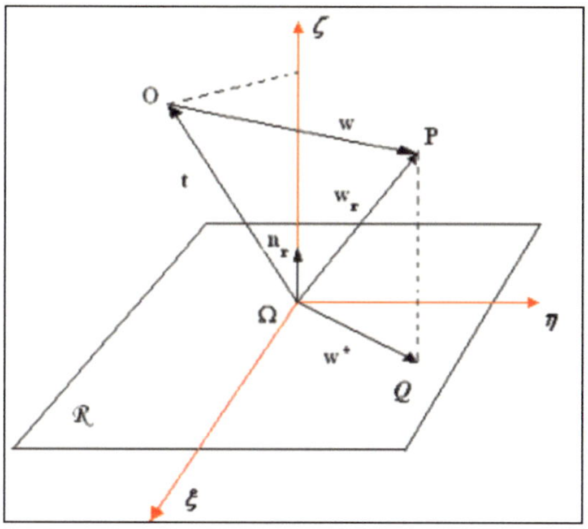

Figure 2. Vectors for the perspective transformation

The coordinates of point P in the image plane can be obtained from the vector w_r, in fact, these coordinates are the coordinates of w*, that can be obtained as follows:
Let's consider the matrix R:

$$R = \begin{bmatrix} \hat{\xi}^T \\ \hat{\eta}^T \\ \hat{\zeta}^T \end{bmatrix} \tag{3}$$

where $\hat{\xi}$ $\hat{\eta}$ $\hat{\zeta}$ are the versor of the frame $\{\Omega,\xi,\eta,\zeta\}$ axes in the frame $\{O,x,y,z\}$.
In fig.2 the vector t indicates the origin of frame O,x,y,z in the frame Ω,ξ,η,ζ and the projection of P on the plane ξ,η is represented by point Q, which position vector is w*. This last, in homogeneous coordinates is given by:

$$\tilde{w}^* = \begin{pmatrix} w_{r,\xi} \\ w_{r,\eta} \\ 0 \\ 1 \end{pmatrix} = \begin{pmatrix} \hat{\xi}^T w + t_\xi \\ \hat{\eta}^T w + t_\eta \\ 0 \\ 1 \end{pmatrix} \tag{4}$$

In the same figure, n_r is the versor normal to the image plane R , and n will be the same versor in the frame $\{O,x,y,z\}$. The perspective image of vector w* can be obtained by assessing a suitable scale factor. This last depends on the distance d between point P and the image plane. The distance d is given from the following scalar product:

$$d = n_r^{T} w_r \tag{5}$$

Let's indicate with $w_{\{\Omega,\xi,\eta,\zeta\}}$ the vector w in the frame $\{\Omega,\xi,\eta,\zeta\}$:

$$\tilde{w}_{\{\Omega,\xi,\eta,\zeta\}} = \begin{pmatrix} w_\xi \\ w_\eta \\ w_\zeta \\ 1 \end{pmatrix} \tag{6}$$

Because $\hat{\xi}$ $\hat{\eta}$ $\hat{\zeta}$ are the versor of the frame $\{\Omega,\xi,\eta,\zeta\}$ axes in the frame $\{O,x,y,z\}$, it is possible to write the coordinates of the vector $w_{\{\Omega,\xi,\eta,\zeta\}}$ in the frame $\{\Omega,\xi,\eta,\zeta\}$:

$$\begin{aligned} w_\xi &= \hat{\xi}^T \cdot w = \xi_x w_x + \xi_y w_y + \xi_z w_z; \\ w_\eta &= \hat{\eta}^T \cdot w = \eta_x w_x + \eta_y w_y + \eta_z w_z; \\ w_\xi &= \hat{\zeta}^T \cdot w = \zeta_x w_x + \zeta_y w_y + \zeta_z w_z; \end{aligned} \tag{7}$$

In the frame $\{\Omega,\xi,\eta,\zeta\}$, it is possible to write w_r as sum of $w_{\{\Omega,\xi,\eta,\zeta\}}$ and t:

$$\tilde{w}_r = \tilde{w}_{\{\Omega,\xi,\eta,\zeta\}} + \tilde{t} = \begin{pmatrix} w_\xi + t_\xi \\ w_\eta + t_\eta \\ w_\zeta + t_\zeta \\ 1 \end{pmatrix} \tag{8}$$

Let's introduce the expressions:

$$\begin{aligned} D_x &= \frac{\left(\xi_x w_x + \xi_y w_y + \xi_z w_z + t_\xi\right) \cdot n_{r,\xi}}{w_x}; \\ D_y &= \frac{\left(\eta_x w_x + \eta_y w_y + \eta_z w_z + t_\eta\right) \cdot n_{r,\eta}}{w_y}; \\ D_z &= \frac{\left(\zeta_x w_x + \zeta_y w_y + \zeta_z w_z + t_\zeta\right) \cdot n_{r,\zeta}}{w_z}; \end{aligned} \tag{9}$$

it is possible to write:

$$d = n_r^T w_r = \begin{pmatrix} D_x \\ D_y \\ D_z \\ 0 \end{pmatrix}^T \cdot \begin{pmatrix} w_x \\ w_y \\ w_z \\ 1 \end{pmatrix} = D^T \cdot w \tag{10}$$

In the equation (10) the vector D is:

$$D = \begin{pmatrix} D_x \\ D_y \\ D_z \\ 0 \end{pmatrix} \tag{11}$$

As vector w* is given by:

$$\tilde{w}^*_p = \begin{pmatrix} \hat{\xi}^T w + t_\xi \\ \hat{\eta}^T w + t_\eta \\ 0 \\ n_r^T w_r \end{pmatrix} \tag{12}$$

The perspective matrix $[T_p]$ can be obtained:

$$\tilde{w}^*_p = T_p \cdot \tilde{w} \Rightarrow T_p = \begin{bmatrix} \xi_x & \xi_y & \xi_z & t_\xi \\ \eta_x & \eta_y & \eta_z & t_\eta \\ 0 & 0 & 0 & 0 \\ D_x & D_y & D_z & 0 \end{bmatrix} \tag{13}$$

The terms Dx, Dy, Dz assume infinity values if the vector w has one of his coordinates null, but this does not influence on generality of the relation $\tilde{w}^*_p = T_p \cdot \tilde{w}$, in fact in this case, the term that assume infinity value, is multiplied for zero.

4.2 The perspective concept

From equation (13) some useful properties can be obtained in order to define how a geometric locus changes its representation when a perspective transform occurs.

As for an example of what above said, let us consider the representation of the displacement of a point in the space: suppose that the displacement occurs, initially, in the positive direction of x axis. Say this displacement Δw, the point moves from the position P to the position P′, that are given by the vectors:

$$w = \begin{pmatrix} w_x \\ w_y \\ w_z \end{pmatrix} \quad \text{and} \quad w' = \begin{pmatrix} w'_x \\ w_y \\ w_z \end{pmatrix} \tag{14}$$

If the perspective transforms are applied we have :

$$p = Tp \cdot w \quad \text{and} \quad p' = Tp \cdot w' \tag{15}$$

the displacement in the image plane is given by:

$$\Delta p = p' - p \tag{16}$$

that is to say:

$$\Delta p = \begin{Bmatrix} \dfrac{\xi_x \cdot [w_x'(D^T w) - w_x(D'^T w')]}{(D^T w)(D'^T w')} \\ \dfrac{\eta_x \cdot [w_x'(D^T w) - w_x(D'^T w')]}{(D^T w)(D'^T w')} \\ 0 \end{Bmatrix} \tag{17}$$

In this way, a displacement Δw along the x axis corresponds to a displacement Δp in the image plane along a straight line which pitch is . So the x axis equation in the image plane is:

$$\eta = (\eta_x / \xi_x) \cdot \xi + \frac{\xi_x t_\eta - \eta_x t_\xi}{\xi_x} \tag{18}$$

The interception was calculated by imposing that the point which coordinates are belongs to the x axis. In the same way it is possible to obtain the y axis and the z axis equations:

$$\text{y axis}: \quad \eta = (\eta_y / \xi_y) \cdot \xi + \frac{\xi_y t_\eta - \eta_y t_\xi}{\xi_y} \tag{19}$$

$$\text{z axis}: \quad \eta = (\eta_z / \xi_z) \cdot \xi + \frac{\xi_z t_\eta - \eta_z t_\xi}{\xi_z} \tag{20}$$

By means of equations (18), (19) and (20) it is possible to obtain a perspective representation of a frame belonging to the Cartesian space in the image plane; that is to say: for a given body it is possible to define it's orientation (e.g. roll, pitch and yaw) in the image plane.

4.3 Perspective transformation in D-H robotic matrix [5]

For kinematics purposes in robotic applications, it is possible to use the Denavit and Hartemberg transformation matrix in homogeneous coordinates in order to characterize the end-effector position in the robot base frame by means of joints variable, this matrix usually contains three zeros and a scale factor in the fourth row. The general expression of the homogenous transformation matrix that allows to transform the coordinates from the frame i to frame i-1, is:

$$A_1^{i-1} = \begin{bmatrix} C\vartheta_i & -C\alpha_i \cdot S\vartheta_i & S\alpha_i \cdot S\vartheta_i & a_i \cdot C\vartheta_i \\ S\vartheta_i & C\alpha_i \cdot C\vartheta_i & -S\alpha_i \cdot C\vartheta_i & a_i \cdot S\vartheta_i \\ 0 & S\alpha_i & C\alpha_i & d_i \\ 0 & 0 & 0 & 1 \end{bmatrix} \tag{21}$$

For a generic robot with n d.o.f., the transformation matrix from end-effector frame to base frame, has the following expression:

$$T_n^0 = A_1^0 \cdot A_2^1 \cdot A_3^2 \cdot \ldots\ldots \cdot A_n^{n-1} \tag{22}$$

With this matrix it is possible to solve the expression:

$$\{P\}_0 = T_n^0 \cdot \{P\}_n \tag{23}$$

where and are the vectors that represent a generic point P in frame 0 and frame n.
It is useful to include the perspective concepts in this transformation matrix; in this way it is possible to obtain a perspective representation of the robot base frame, belonging to the Cartesian space, in an image plane, like following expression shows:

$$\{P\}_p = T_p \cdot \{P\}_0 = T_p \cdot T_n^0 \cdot \{P\}_n = \left[T_p\right]_n^0 \cdot \{P\}_n \tag{24}$$

where is the perspective image of generic point P and is the perspective transformation matrix from end-effector frame to an image plane.
With this representation the fourth row of the Denavit and Hartemberg matrix will contain non-zero elements. A vision system demands an application like this.

5. The camera model

When vision systems are used for robotic applications, it is important to have a suitable model of the cameras.
A vision system essentially associates a point in the Cartesian space with a point on the image plane. A very common vision system is the television camera that is essentially composed by an optic system (one or more lenses), an image processing and managing system and an image plane; this last is composed by vision sensors. The light from a point in the space is conveyed by the lenses on the image plane and recorded by the vision sensor.
Let us confine ourselves to consider a simple vision system made up by a thin lens and an image plane composed by CCD (Charged Coupled Device) sensors. This kind of sensor is a

device that is able to record the electric charge that is generated by a photoelectric effect when a photon impacts on the sensor's surface.
It is useful to remember some aspects of the optics in a vision system.

5.1 The thin lenses model [2,4,13,14]

A lens is made up by two parts of a spherical surfaces (dioptric surfaces) joined on a same plane. The axis, normal to this plane, is the optical axis. As shown in fig.3, a convergent lens conveys the parallel light rays in a focus F at distance f (focal distance) from the lens plane.

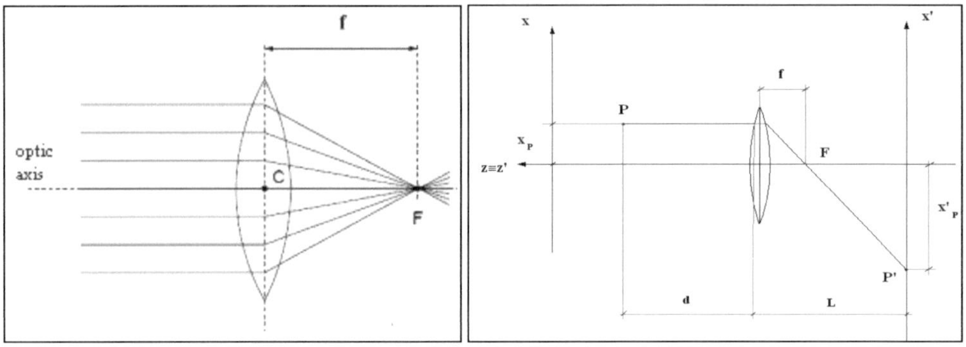

Figure 3. Convergent lens (left), Thin lens (rigth)

The focal distance f, in air, is given by:

$$f = (n-1) \cdot \left(\frac{1}{R_1} - \frac{1}{R_2} \right) \tag{25}$$

where n is the refractive index of the lens and R_1 ed R_2 are the bending radius of the dioptric surfaces.
Now consider a thin lens, a point P and a plane on which the light-rays refracted from the lens are projected as shown in fig.3 the equation for the thin lenses gives:

$$\frac{1}{d} + \frac{1}{L} = \frac{1}{f} \tag{26}$$

It is possible to determinate the connection between the position of point P in the space and it's correspondent P' in the projection's plane (fig.3).
If two frames (xyx for the Cartesian space and x'y'z' for the image plane), having their axes parallel, are assigned and if the thickness of the lens is neglected, from the similitude of the triangles in fig.5 it comes:

$$\frac{x_P}{f} = -\frac{x'_P}{L-f} \tag{27}$$

with the equation of the thin lenses we can write:

$$x'_P = -\frac{f}{d-f} \cdot x_P \tag{28}$$

If we consider that generally the distance of a point from the camera's objective is one meter or more while the focal distance is about some millimetres (d>>f), the following approximation can be accepted:

$$x'_P \cong -\frac{f}{d} \cdot x_P \tag{29}$$

So the coordinates of the point in the image plane can be obtained by scaling the coordinates in the Cartesian space by a factor . The minus sign is due to the upsetting of the image.

5.2 The model of the camera [4]

As already observed a camera can be modelled as a thin lens and an image plane with CCD sensors. The objects located in the Cartesian space emit rays of light that are refracted from the lens on the image plane. Each CCD sensor emit an electric signal that is proportional to the intensity of the ray of light on it; the image is made up by a number of pixels, each one of them records the information coming from the sensor that corresponds to that pixel.
In order to indicate the position of a point on an image it is possible to define a frame u,v (fig.4) which axes are contained in the image plane. To a given point in the space (which position is given by its Cartesian coordinates) it is possible to associate a point in the image plane (two coordinates) by means of the camera. So, the expression "model of the camera" means the transform that associates a point in the Cartesian space to a point in the image space.
It has to be said that in the Cartesian space a point position is given by three coordinates expressed in length unit while in the image plane the two coordinates are expressed in pixel; this last is the smaller length unit that ca be revealed by the camera and isn't a normalized length unit. The model of the camera must take onto account this aspect also.
In order to obtain the model of the camera the scheme reported in fig.4 can be considered.

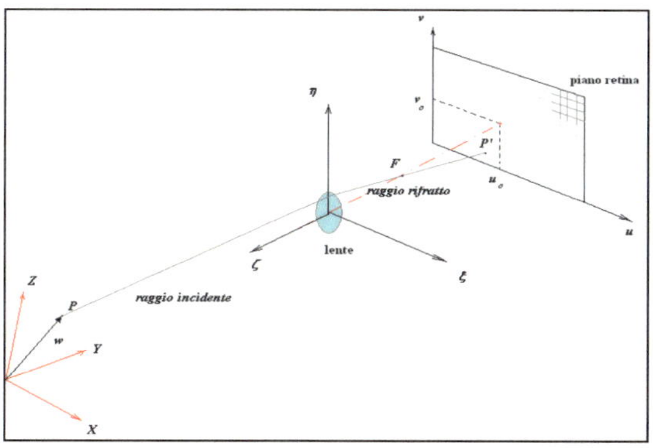

Figure 4. Camera model

Consider a frame xyz in the Cartesian space, the position of a generic point P in the space is given by the vector w. Then consider a frame ξ,η,ζ having the origin in the lens centre and the plane ξ,η coincident with the plane of the lens; hence, the plane ξ,η is parallel to the

image plane and ζ axis is coincident with the optical axis. Finally consider a frame u,v on the image plane so that u_0 and v_0 are the coordinates of the origin of frame ξ,η,ζ expressed in pixel.
As it was already told, the lens makes a perspective transform in which the constant of proportionality is –f . If this transform is applied to vector w, a w_l vector is obtained:

$$\tilde{w}_l = T_l \cdot \tilde{w} \tag{30}$$

Were the matrix T_l is obtained dividing by –f the last row of the perspective transformation matrix T_p.

$$T_l = \begin{bmatrix} \xi_x & \xi_y & \xi_z & t_\xi \\ \eta_x & \eta_y & \eta_z & t_\eta \\ 0 & 0 & 0 & 0 \\ -\frac{D_x}{f} & -\frac{D_y}{f} & -\frac{D_z}{f} & 0 \end{bmatrix} \tag{31}$$

Substantially, the above essentially consists in a changing of the reference frames and a scaling based on the rules of geometric optics previously reported.
Assumed x_l e y_l as the first two components of the vector w_l, the coordinates u and v (expressed in pixel) of P' (image of P) are :

$$\begin{cases} u = \dfrac{x_l}{\delta_u} + u_o \\ v = \dfrac{x_l}{\delta_v} + v_o \end{cases} \tag{32}$$

Where δ_u e δ_v are respectively the horizontal and vertical dimensions of the pixel.
So, by substituting equation (30) in equation (32) it comes:

$$\begin{cases} u = -\dfrac{f}{D^T w}\left[\left(\dfrac{1}{\delta_u}\cdot\hat{\xi} - \dfrac{u_o}{f}\cdot D\right)^T w + \dfrac{1}{\delta_u}\cdot t_\xi\right] \\ v = -\dfrac{f}{D^T w}\left[\left(\dfrac{1}{\delta_v}\cdot\hat{\eta} - \dfrac{v_o}{f}\cdot D\right)^T w + \dfrac{1}{\delta_v}\cdot t_\eta\right] \end{cases} \tag{33}$$

Finally, if we define the vector $m = [u \quad v]^T$, the representation in homogeneous coordinates $\tilde{m} = \left[m_1 \quad m_2 \quad -D^T w/f\right]^T = \left[u \quad v \quad -D^T w/f\right]^T$ of the previous vector can be written :

$$\tilde{m} = M \cdot \tilde{w} \tag{34}$$

Where M is the matrix :

$$M = \begin{bmatrix} \left(\frac{\xi_x}{\delta_u} - \frac{u_o D_x}{f}\right) & \left(\frac{\xi_y}{\delta_u} - \frac{u_o D_y}{f}\right) & \left(\frac{\xi_z}{\delta_u} - \frac{u_o D_z}{f}\right) & t_\xi / \delta_u \\ \left(\frac{\eta_x}{\delta_v} - \frac{v_o D_x}{f}\right) & \left(\frac{\eta_y}{\delta_v} - \frac{v_o D_y}{f}\right) & \left(\frac{\eta_z}{\delta_v} - \frac{v_o D_z}{f}\right) & t_\eta / \delta_v \\ -D_x / f & -D_y / f & -D_z / f & 0 \end{bmatrix} \tag{35}$$

that represents the requested model of the camera.

6. The stereoscopic vision

What above reported concurs to determine the coordinates in image plane (u,v) of a generic point of tridimensional space $w=[w_x\ w_y\ w_z\ 1]^T$, but the situation is more complex if it is necessary to recognise the position (w) of a point starting to its camera image (u, v). In this case the equations (33) becomes a system of 2 equation with 3 unknowns, so it has no solutions.
This obstacle can be overcome by means of a vision system with at least two cameras.
In this way, what above reported can be applied to the recording of a robot trajectory in the three dimensional space by using two cameras. This will emulate the human vision.
Let us consider two cameras and say M and M′ their transform matrixes. We want to recognise the position of a point P, that in the Cartesian space is given by a vector w in a generic frame xyz. From equation (34) we have:

$$\begin{cases} \tilde{m} = M \cdot w \\ \tilde{m}' = M' \cdot w \end{cases} \tag{36}$$

The first equation of the system (36), in Cartesian coordinates (non-homogenous), can be written as:

$$\begin{cases} (u \cdot D + f \cdot \mu_1)^T w = \mu_{14} \\ (v \cdot D + f \cdot \mu_2)^T w = \mu_{24} \end{cases} \tag{37}$$

Where:

$$\begin{aligned} \mu_1 &= \left\{ \left(\frac{\xi_x}{\delta_u} - \frac{u_o D_x}{f}\right) \left(\frac{\xi_y}{\delta_u} - \frac{u_o D_y}{f}\right) \left(\frac{\xi_z}{\delta_u} - \frac{u_o D_z}{f}\right) \right\}; \\ \mu_2 &= \left\{ \left(\frac{\eta_x}{\delta_v} - \frac{v_o D_x}{f}\right) \left(\frac{\eta_y}{\delta_v} - \frac{v_o D_y}{f}\right) \left(\frac{\eta_z}{\delta_v} - \frac{v_o D_z}{f}\right) \right\}; \\ \mu_{14} &= t_\xi / \delta_u \\ \mu_{24} &= t_\eta / \delta_v \end{aligned} \tag{38}$$

In the same way for the camera, whose transform matrix is M′, it can be written:

$$\begin{cases} (u' \cdot D' + f' \cdot \mu'_1)^T w = \mu'_{14} \\ (v' \cdot D' + f' \cdot \mu'_2)^T w = \mu'_{24} \end{cases} \tag{39}$$

By arranging eq.(26) and eq.(27) we obtain:

$$\begin{bmatrix} (u \cdot D + f \cdot \mu_1)^T \\ (v \cdot D + f \cdot \mu_2)^T \\ (u' \cdot D' + f' \cdot \mu'_1)^T \\ (v' \cdot D' + f' \cdot \mu'_2)^T \end{bmatrix} \cdot w = \begin{bmatrix} \mu_{14} \\ \mu_{24} \\ \mu'_{14} \\ \mu'_{24} \end{bmatrix} \tag{40}$$

This last equation represents the stereoscopic problem and consist in a system of 4 equation in 3 unknown (w_x,w_y,w_z). As the equations are more than the unknowns can be solved by a least square algorithm. In this way it is possible to invert the problem that is described by equations (33) and to recognise the position of a generic point starting to its camera image.

6.1 The stereoscopic problem [2]

Relation (40) represents the stereoscopic problem, it consists in a system of 4 equations in 3 unknown, in the form:

$$A(u, u, u', v', w) \cdot w = B \tag{41}$$

where A is a matrix that depends by two couple of camera coordinates (u,v) and (u′,v′), and by vector w, and B is a vector with parameters of cameras configuration.
It is possible to find an explicit form of this problem.
Starting to first equation of (33), it is possible to write:

$$u = -\frac{f}{D^T w}\left[\left(\frac{1}{\delta_u} \cdot \hat{\xi} - \frac{u_o}{f} \cdot D\right)^T w + \frac{1}{\delta_u} \cdot t_\xi\right] \Rightarrow$$

$$\frac{1}{\delta_u}\left(\xi_x \cdot w_x + \eta_x \cdot w_y + \zeta_x \cdot w_z\right) - \tag{42}$$

$$\frac{u_0}{f}\left(D_x \cdot w_x + D_x \cdot w_y + D_x \cdot w_z\right) + \frac{u}{f}\left(D_x \cdot w_x + D_x \cdot w_y + D_x \cdot w_z\right) = -\frac{t_\xi}{\delta_u}$$

By means of equation (9), it is possible to write:

$$
\begin{gathered}
D_x \cdot w_x + D_x \cdot w_y + D_x \cdot w_z = \\
w_x\left(\xi_x \cdot n_{r,\xi} + \xi_y \cdot n_{r,\eta} + \xi_z \cdot n_{r,\zeta}\right) + w_y\left(\eta_x \cdot n_{r,\xi} + \eta_y \cdot n_{r,\eta} + \eta_z \cdot n_{r,\zeta}\right) + \\
w_z\left(\zeta_x \cdot n_{r,\xi} + \zeta_y \cdot n_{r,\eta} + \zeta_z \cdot n_{r,\zeta}\right) + \\
\left(t_\xi \cdot n_{r,\xi} + t_\eta \cdot n_{r,\eta} + t_\zeta \cdot n_{r,\zeta}\right)
\end{gathered} \tag{43}
$$

If we define the elements:

$$
\begin{aligned}
N_\xi &= \left(\xi_x \cdot n_{r,\xi} + \xi_y \cdot n_{r,\eta} + \xi_z \cdot n_{r,\zeta}\right); \\
N_\eta &= \left(\eta_x \cdot n_{r,\xi} + \eta_y \cdot n_{r,\eta} + \eta_z \cdot n_{r,\zeta}\right); \\
N_\zeta &= \left(\zeta_x \cdot n_{r,\xi} + \zeta_y \cdot n_{r,\eta} + \zeta_z \cdot n_{r,\zeta}\right); \\
k &= \left(t_\xi \cdot n_{r,\xi} + t_\eta \cdot n_{r,\eta} + t_\zeta \cdot n_{r,\zeta}\right),
\end{aligned} \tag{44}
$$

equation (33) becomes:

$$
\begin{gathered}
\left(\frac{\xi_x}{\delta_u} - \frac{(u-u_0)\cdot N_\xi}{f}\right)\cdot w_x + \left(\frac{\eta_x}{\delta_u} - \frac{(u-u_0)\cdot N_\eta}{f}\right)\cdot w_y + \left(\frac{\zeta_x}{\delta_u} - \frac{(u-u_0)\cdot N_\xi}{f}\right)\cdot w_z + \\
\frac{u-u_0}{f}\cdot k = -\frac{t_\xi}{\delta_u}
\end{gathered} \tag{45}
$$

An analogous relation can be written for second equation of (33):

$$
\begin{gathered}
\left(\frac{\xi_y}{\delta_v} - \frac{(v-v_0)\cdot N_\xi}{f}\right)\cdot w_x + \left(\frac{\eta_y}{\delta_v} - \frac{(v-v_0)\cdot N_\eta}{f}\right)\cdot w_y + \left(\frac{\zeta_y}{\delta_v} - \frac{(v-v_0)\cdot N_\xi}{f}\right)\cdot w_z + \\
\frac{v-v_0}{f}\cdot k = -\frac{t_\eta}{\delta_v}
\end{gathered} \tag{46}
$$

By arranging equation (45) and (46), it is possible to redefine the stereoscopic problem, expressed by equation (40):

$$
P(u, u, u', v')\cdot w = S \tag{47}
$$

In equation (47) P is a matrix 4x3, whose elements depend only by (u,v) and (u',v'), and B is a vector 4x1, whose elements contain parameters of cameras configuration.
The expression of matrix P is:

$$P = \begin{bmatrix} \frac{\xi_x}{\delta_u} - \frac{(u-u_0)\cdot N_\xi}{f} & \frac{\eta_x}{\delta_u} - \frac{(u-u_0)\cdot N_\eta}{f} & \frac{\zeta_x}{\delta_u} - \frac{(u-u_0)\cdot N_\xi}{f} \\ \frac{\xi_y}{\delta_v} - \frac{(v-v_0)\cdot N_\xi}{f} & \frac{\eta_y}{\delta_v} - \frac{(v-v_0)\cdot N_\eta}{f} & \frac{\zeta_y}{\delta_v} - \frac{(v-v_0)\cdot N_\xi}{f} \\ \frac{\xi'_x}{\delta_{u'}} - \frac{(u'-u'_0)\cdot N_{\xi'}}{f'} & \frac{\eta'_x}{\delta_{u'}} - \frac{(u'-u'_0)\cdot N_{\eta'}}{f'} & \frac{\zeta'_x}{\delta_{u'}} - \frac{(u'-u'_0)\cdot N_{\xi'}}{f'} \\ \frac{\xi'_y}{\delta_{v'}} - \frac{(v'-v'_0)\cdot N_{\xi'}}{f'} & \frac{\eta'_y}{\delta_{v'}} - \frac{(v'-v'_0)\cdot N_{\eta'}}{f'} & \frac{\zeta'_y}{\delta_{v'}} - \frac{(v'-v'_0)\cdot N_{\xi'}}{f'} \end{bmatrix} \tag{48}$$

The expression of vector S is:

$$S = \begin{Bmatrix} -\frac{t_\xi}{\delta_u} - \frac{u-u_0}{f}\cdot k \\ -\frac{t_\eta}{\delta_v} - \frac{v-v_0}{f}\cdot k \\ -\frac{t_{\xi'}}{\delta_{u'}} - \frac{u'-u'_0}{f'}\cdot k' \\ -\frac{t_{\eta'}}{\delta_{v'}} - \frac{v'-v'_0}{f'}\cdot k' \end{Bmatrix} \tag{49}$$

By equation (47) it is possible to invert the problem that is described by eqs. (33) and to recognise the position of a generic point starting to its camera image, by means of pseudoinverse matrix P+ of matrix P.

$$P\cdot w = S \Rightarrow P^T\cdot P\cdot w = P^T\cdot S \Rightarrow w = \left(P^T\cdot P\right)^{-1}\cdot P^T\cdot S \Rightarrow w = P^+\cdot S \tag{50}$$

By means of equation (50), it is possible to solve the stereoscopic problem in all configurations in which is verified the condition:

7. The camera calibration [2, 18]

In order to determine the coordinate transformation between the camera reference system and robot reference system, it is necessary to know the parameters that regulate such transformation. The direct measure of these parameters is a difficult operation; it is better to identify them through a procedure that utilize the camera itself.

Camera calibration in the context of three-dimensional machine vision is the process of determining the internal camera geometric and optical characteristics (intrinsic parameters) and/or the 3-D position and orientation of the camera frame relative to a certain world coordinate system (extrinsic parameters). In many cases, the overall performance of the machine vision system strongly depends on the accuracy of the camera calibration.

In order to calibrate the cameras a toolbox, developed by Christopher Mei, INRIA Sophia-Antipolis, was used. By means of this toolbox it is possible to find the intrinsic and extrinsic parameters of two cameras that are necessary to solve the stereoscopic problem. In order to carry out the calibration of a camera, it is necessary to acquire any number of images of observed space in which a checkerboard pattern is placed with different positions and orientations.

In each acquired image, after clicking on the four extreme corners of a checkerboard pattern rectangular area, a corner extraction engine includes an automatic mechanism for counting the number of squares in the grid. This points are used like calibration points, fig. 5.

The dimensions dX, dY of each of squares are always kept to their original values in millimeters, and represent the parameters that put in relation the pixel dimensions with observed space dimensions (mm).

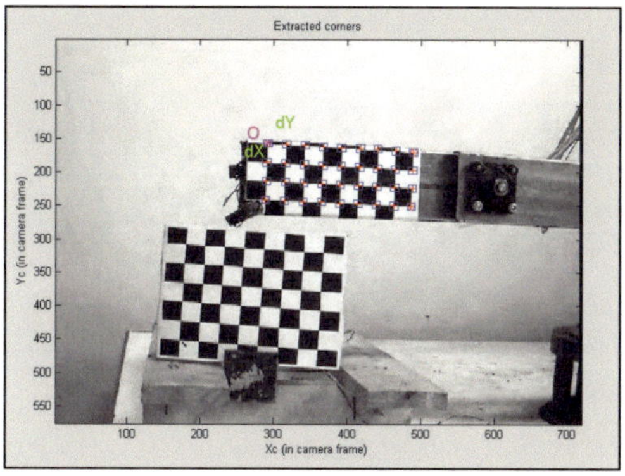

Figure 5. Calibration image

After corner extraction, calibration is done in two steps: first initialization, and then nonlinear optimization.

The initialization step computes a closed-form solution for the calibration parameters based not including any lens distortion.

The non-linear optimization step minimizes the total reprojection error (in the least squares sense) over all the calibration parameters (9 DOF for intrinsic: focal (2), principal point (2), distortion coefficients (5), and 6*n DOF extrinsic, with n = images number).

The calibration procedure allows to find the 3-D position of the grids with respect to the camera, like shown in fig. 6.

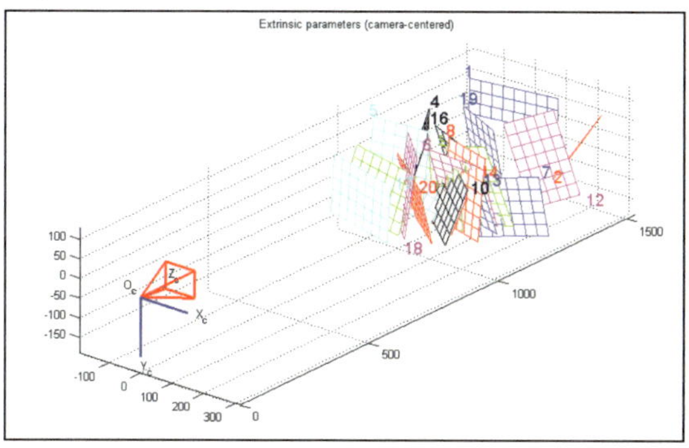

Figure 6. Position of the grids for the calibration procedure

With two camera calibration, it is possible to carry out a stereo optimization, by means of a toolbox option, that allows to do a stereo calibration for stereoscopic problem.
The global stereo optimization is performed over a minimal set of unknown parameters, in particular, only one pose unknown (6 DOF) is considered for the location of the calibration grid for each stereo pair. This insures global rigidity of the structure going from left view to right view. In this way the uncertainties on the intrinsic parameters (especially that of the focal values) for both cameras it becomes smaller.
After this operation, the spatial configuration of the two cameras and the calibration planes may be displayed in a form of a 3D plot, like shown in fig. 7.

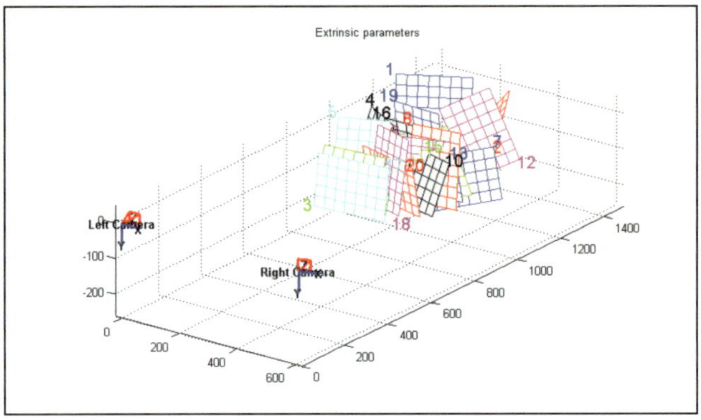

Figure 7. Calibration planes

8. Robot cinematic calibration

Among the characteristics that define the performances of a robot the most important can be considered the repeatability and the accuracy. Generally, both these characteristics depend on factors like backlashes, load variability, positioning and zero putting errors, limits of the transducers, dimensional errors, and so on. The last sources of error essentially depend on the correct evaluation of the Denavit and Hartemberg parameters. Hence, some of the sources of error can be limited by means of the cinematic calibration.
Basically, by the cinematic calibration it is assumed that if the error in the positioning of the robot's end-effector is evaluated in some points of the working space, by means of these errors evaluation it is possible to predict the error in any other position thus offset it.
In few words, the main aim of the technique showed in this paper is to obtain precise evaluations of those Denavit-Hartenberg parameters that represent, for each of the links, the length, the torsion and the offset.

8.1The calibration technique [3, 7]

This calibration technique essentially consists in the following steps:

i. The end-effector is located in an even position in the work space;
ii. A vision system acquires and records the robot's image and gives the coordinates of an assigned point of the end-effector, expressed in pixels in the image plane.
iii. By means of a suitable camera model, it is possible to find a relation between these coordinates expressed in pixels, and the coordinates of the assigned point of the end-effector in the world (Cartesian) frame.

iv. By means of the servomotor position transducers, the values of the joint position parameters are recorded for that end-effector position in the work space.

In this way, for each of the camera images, the following arrays are obtained:

$$\begin{pmatrix} X_i \\ Y_i \\ Z_i \end{pmatrix}, \quad \begin{pmatrix} \theta_{1,i} \\ \theta_{2,i} \\ \theta_{3,i} \end{pmatrix} \tag{51}$$

where: i = 1,…,N, and N is the number of acquired camera images (frames).

If the coordinates in the working space and the joint parameters are known, it's possible to write the direct kinematics equations in which the unknown are those Denavit-Hartenberg parameters that differ from the joint parameters; thus these Denavit-Hartenberg parameters represent the unknown of the kinematic calibration problem.

The expression of these equations is obtained starting from the transform matrix (homogeneous coordinates) that allows to transform the coordinates in the frame i to the coordinates in the frame i-1:

$$^{i-1}A_i = \begin{bmatrix} C\vartheta_i & -C\alpha_i \cdot S\vartheta_i & S\alpha_i \cdot S\vartheta_i & a_i \cdot C\vartheta_i \\ S\vartheta_i & C\alpha_i \cdot C\vartheta_i & -S\alpha_i \cdot C\vartheta_i & a_i \cdot S\vartheta_i \\ 0 & S\alpha_i & C\alpha_i & d_i \\ 0 & 0 & 0 & 1 \end{bmatrix} \tag{52}$$

By means of such matrixes it is possible to obtain the transform matrix that allows to obtain the coordinates in the frame 0 (the fixed one) from those in frame n (the one of the last link) :

$$^{0}T_n = {}^{0}A_1 \cdot {}^{1}A_2 \cdot \ldots \cdot {}^{n-1}A_n \tag{53}$$

As for an example, if we consider a generic 3 axes revolute (anthropomorphic) robot arm, we'll obtain an equation that contains 9 constant kinematic parameters and 3 variable parameters ($\theta_1, \theta_2, \theta_3$).

So, the vector:

$$\pi_{DH} = \begin{pmatrix} a_1 \\ a_2 \\ a_3 \\ d_1 \\ d_2 \\ d_3 \\ \alpha_1 \\ \alpha_2 \\ \alpha_3 \end{pmatrix} \tag{54}$$

represents the unknown of the kinematic calibration problem.

Said:

$$\Theta = \begin{pmatrix} \theta_1 \\ \theta_2 \\ \theta_3 \end{pmatrix} \tag{55}$$

the direct kinematics equation for this manipulator can be written as :

$$w = t_4(\Pi_{DH}, \Theta) \tag{56}$$

where w is the position vector in the first frame and is the fourth row of the Denavit-Hartenberg transform matrix. In equation (56) it clearly appears that the position depends on the joint parameters and on the others Denavit-Hartenberg parameters. Equation (39) can be also seen as a system of 3 equations (in Cartesian coordinates) with 9 unknowns: the elements of vector .
Obviously, it's impossible to solve this system of equations, but it's possible to use more camera images taken for different end-effector positions:

$$\begin{cases} t_4(\Pi_{DH}, \Theta^1) = w_1 \\ t_4(\Pi_{DH}, \Theta^2) = w_2 \\ \dots\dots\dots\dots\dots\dots \\ t_4(\Pi_{DH}, \Theta^N) = w_N \end{cases} \tag{57}$$

with $N \geq 9$.
As, for each of the camera images the unknown Denavit-Hartemberg parameters are the same, equations (57) represent a system of N non linear equations in 9 unknowns. This system can be numerically solved by means of a minimum square technique.
It's known at a minimum square problem can be formulated as follows:
given the equation (56), find the solutions that minimize the expression:

$$\int_{D_\Theta} \left| t_4(\Pi_{DH}, \Theta) - w \right|^2 \cdot d\Theta \tag{58}$$

This method can be simplified by substituting the integrals with summations, thus it must be computed the vector that minimize the expression:

$$\sum_{i=1}^{N} \left| t_4(\Pi_{DH}, \Theta^i) - w_i \right|^2 \tag{59}$$

If we formulate the problem in this way, the higher is the number of images that have been taken (hence the more are the known parameters), the more accurate will be the solution, so it's necessary to take a number of pictures.

8.2 Camera model and D-H robotic matrix [7, 8]

Can be useful to include D-H transformation matrix of equation (24), in camera model (33), in this way it is possible to obtain a perspective representation of the robot in an image plane by means joint coordinates.
In homogeneous coordinates, using matrix notation, it is possible to write equation (33):

$$\begin{Bmatrix} u \\ v \\ 0 \\ 1 \end{Bmatrix} = \frac{1}{w_{r,\zeta}} [K] \cdot \begin{Bmatrix} w_{r,\xi} \\ w_{r,\eta} \\ w_{r,\zeta} \\ 1 \end{Bmatrix} \tag{60}$$

where matrix K is:

$$[K] = \begin{bmatrix} -\frac{f}{\delta_u} & 0 & u_0 & 0 \\ 0 & -\frac{f}{\delta_v} & v_0 & 0 \\ 0 & 0 & 0 & 0 \\ 0 & 0 & 1 & 0 \end{bmatrix} \tag{61}$$

Considering equation (2), it is possible to write (60) in the frame O,x,y,z, external to images :

$$\begin{Bmatrix} u \\ v \\ 0 \\ 1 \end{Bmatrix} = \frac{1}{D_z \cdot w_z} [K] \cdot [T] \begin{Bmatrix} w_x \\ w_y \\ w_z \\ 1 \end{Bmatrix} \tag{62}$$

Considering equation (9), If we define the vector N:

$$\{N\} = \left\{ \varsigma_x, \varsigma_y, \varsigma_z, t_\varsigma \right\}^T \tag{63}$$

(62) becomes:

$$\begin{Bmatrix} u \\ v \\ 0 \\ 1 \end{Bmatrix} = \frac{1}{\{N\}^T \cdot \{w\}} [K] \cdot [T] \begin{Bmatrix} w_x \\ w_y \\ w_z \\ 1 \end{Bmatrix} \tag{64}$$

Equation (64) represents the relation between coordinates (u,v) of an assigned point, (e.g. a robot end-effector point expressed in pixels in the image plane) and the coordinates of the same point in the world (Cartesian) frame. In this equation, it is possible to include D-H transformation matrix, to obtain a model that describes the relation between coordinates (u,v) of robot end-effector expressed in pixels, in image plane, and end-effector coordinates in the robot joints space. The relation that synthetizes the model is following:

$$\{u,v\} = \frac{1}{\{N\}^T \cdot \left[T_n^0 \right] \{\tilde{w}\}_n} [K] \cdot [T] \left[T_n^0 \right] \{\tilde{w}\}_n \tag{65}$$

where:

- $\{u,v\}$: vector with end-effector coordinates expressed in pixel in image plane;

- $\{\tilde{w}\}_n$: end-effector homogeneous coordinates in robot frame n, for a generic robot with n d.o.f;
- $[T_n^0]$: Denavit-Hartenberg robot transformation matrix from base frame to end-effector frame;
- [T]: transformation matrix from camera frame to robot base frame;
- [K]:matrix with geometric and optical camera parameters;
- {N}:vector with expression of optic axis in robot base frame.

8.3 Experimental results

Experimental tests have been executed on a revolute robot prototype with 3 d.o.f., in order to verify the effectiveness of the algorithm.

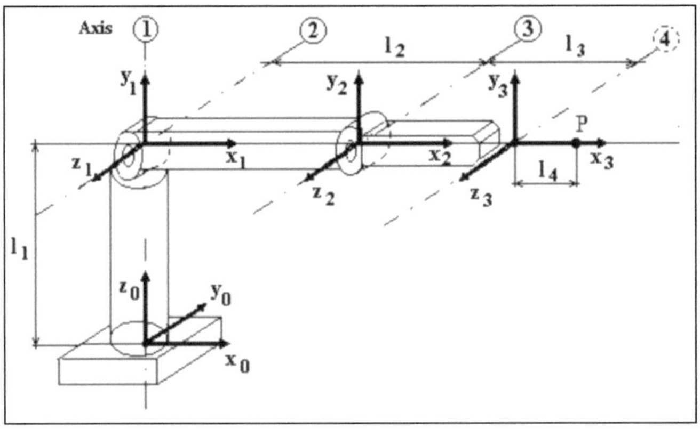

Figure 8. Revolute robot scheme

Twenty images of the robot in twenty different positions of its workspace, with two cameras, have been acquired. After a vision system calibration, by means of an optimization algorithm that uses minimum square technique, it is possible to solve the system of equations (65) and to obtain a numerical solution. Using two cameras we have 2*20=40 equations (65), to find nine D-H parameters that characterize the kinematics structure of a three axis revolute robot.

In the tables 1, real parameters (real) and calculated parameters (comp.) are shown.

Joint	a_i (mm)		α_i (deg)		Θ_i (deg)		d_i (mm)	
	Real	Comp.	Real	Comp.	Real	Comp.	Real	Comp.
1	0	7.04mm	90°	86.28°	-180°÷ 180°	-180°÷ 180°	l_1 = 449mm	l_1 = 447.15mm
2	l_2 = 400mm	l_2 = 396.16mm	0°	0.94°	-90°÷ 45°	-90°÷ 45°	0	10.85mm
3	l_3 = 400mm	l_3 = 413.65mm	0°	0°	-90°÷ 90°	-90°÷ 90°	0	13.75mm

Table 1. Real and calculated prototype D-H parameters

9. Trajectories recording

The trajectory recording, that is essential to study robot arm dynamical behaviour has been obtained by means of two digital television camera linked to a PC.
The rig, that has been developed, is based on a couple of telecameras; it allows us to obtain the velocity vector of each point of the manipulator. By means of this rig it is possible:

- to control the motion giving the instantaneous joint positions and velocities;
- to measure the motions between link and servomotor in presence of non-rigid transmissions;
- to identify the robot arm dynamical parameters.

An example of these video application for robot arm is the video acquisition of a robot arm trajectories in the work space by means of the techniques above reported.
In the figure 9 are reported a couple of frames, respectively, from the right telecamera and the left one. In fig. 10 is reported the 3-D trajectory, obtained from the frames before mentioned; in this last figure, for comparison, the trajectory obtained from the encoders signals is also reported.

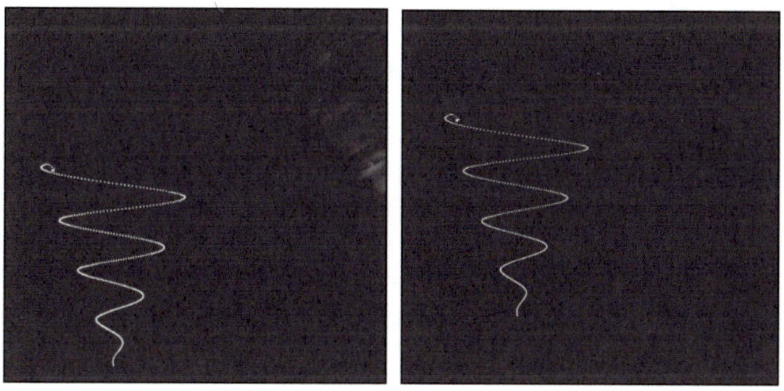

Figure 9. Trajectories in image space: camera position 1(left), camera position 2 (rigth)

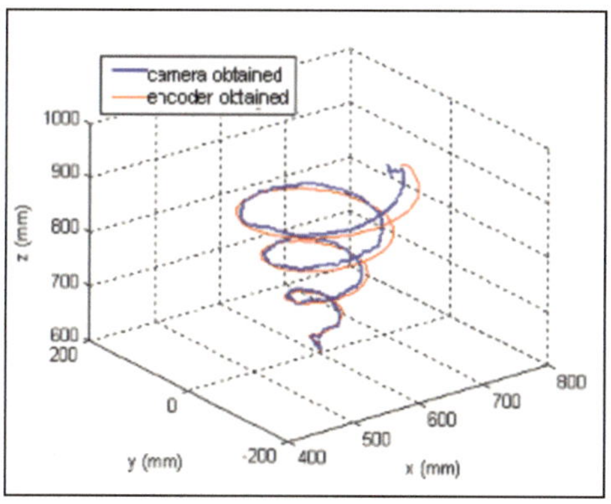

Figure 10. Comparison between trajectory recordings

10. Path planning by means a video system [9]

Was developed a software that allows to choose the end-effector trajectory points. By means of this software, it is possible to select "objective" points, for which the robot must journey, e "obstacle" points, that must be avoided.

The software recognizes the positions of such points in the work space, using a developed camera model.
The procedure starts from a couple of images (taken from two different cameras, fig. 11); the operator selects (with the cursor) a point on the first image of the couple and this will fix a point in a plane. Subsequently, on the second image appears a green line, that represents the straight line that links the focus of the first camera to that point. Now the operator can fix the real position (in the work space) of that point by clicking on this green line.

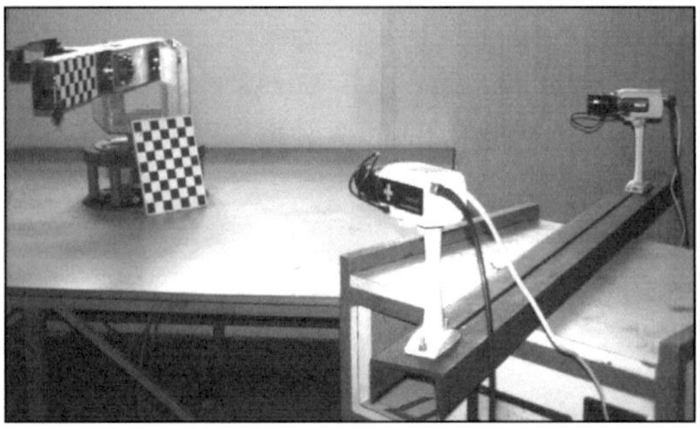

Figure 11. The stereoscopic vision system

In figure 12 the couple of images is reported; on the left is reported the first image and on the right the second one; on the second image is also reported a white solid thick line that is the line that links the focus of the first camera to the point selected on the image on the left.

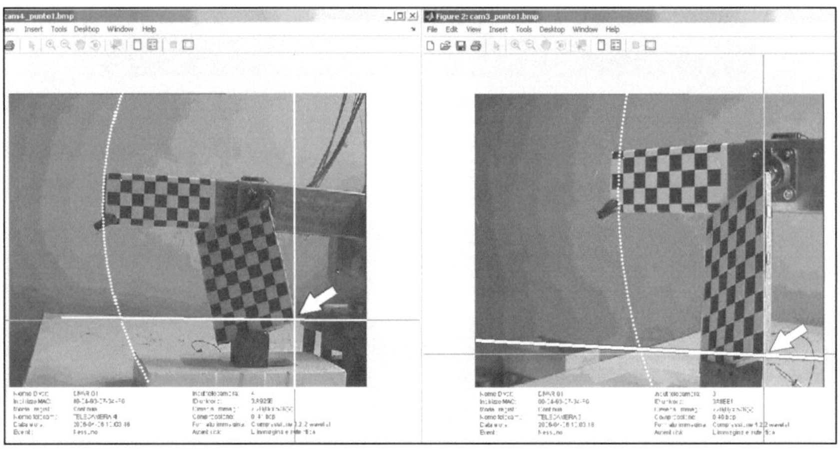

Figure 12. Point assigning by the couple of images

This procedure gives the coordinates of the selected point in the frame of the working space (world frame). Once a point has been assigned in the work space, by means of inverse kinematics it is possible to compute the joint coordinates of the robot when the robot's end-effector is in that position.
Finally the procedure permits to assign a point either as belonging to the path, or as representing an obstacle; in this last case, the path will be computed in order to avoid that point.

In figure 13 the robot arm and the work space are shown; the numbers 1, 2 and 3 represent three points of the path and the cardinals I and II represent two obstacles that are supposed to be spherical.

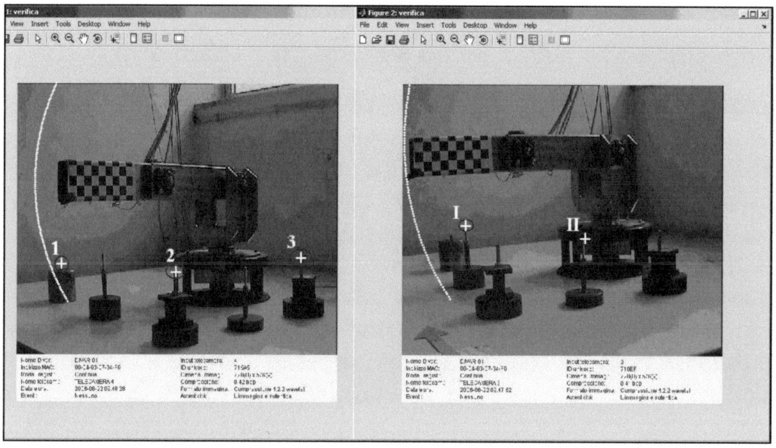

Figure 13. Path assigning

In has to be pointed out that, as previously told, to fix a point a couple of images is needed; in figure 13, for the sake of simplicity, just two images are reposted: on the left is the first image of the couple used for the points, while on the right is reported the second image of the couple for the obstacles.

The path is made up by straight segments that link the selected points (those belonging to the path). To every point that represents an obstacle, is associated the center of a sphere, the sphere radius depends by obstacle dimensions and it is chosen when the procedure starts.

If one of straight segment intersects one of this sphere, the procedure records these intersections and joints each couple of them by means of an arc of a circle. So, the path will consist in a number of straight segments and arcs of circle.

The operator has the possibility to choose the density of the segments and arcs intermediate points, the necessary time to the description of the trajectory, and the obstacles dimensions.

Figure 14. Example of path in the work space

In figure 14 the robot arm and an example of path are shown. In the same figure the points and the obstacles are, also, clearly visible. The points are marked with the same meanings used in the previous figure.

11. Solid reconstruction with a video system on a robot arm

The use of a camera in a robot application, can be performed with two types of architecture: the camera is said eye-in-hand when rigidly mounted on the robot end-effector and it is said eye to -hand when it observes the robot within its work space. These two schemes have technical differences and they can play very complementary parts. Obviously, the eye-in-hand one has a partial but precise sight of the scene whereas the eye-to-hand camera has a less precise but global sight of it.

Eye-in-hand systems are used primarily to guide robot end effectors and grippers, and to ensure that grippers properly engage the intended targets. The system can also precisely measure the distance from the end effector or gripper to a target. In a robot equipped with an eye-in-hand system, it allows positive identification of a target. In this way it is possible to use the system also to reconstruct a solid in the robot workspace, by means different camera placements and robot inverse cinematic. The next subsection will focus on one commonly used image-based reconstruction methods: *Shape From Silhouettes.*

11.1 A 3D reconstruction technique: Shape From Silhouettes and Space Carving [10, 11, 12]

Shape From Silhouettes is well-known technique for estimating 3D shape from its multiple 2D images.

Intuitively the silhouette is the profile of an object, comprehensive of its inside part. In the "Shape from Silhouette" technique silhouette is defined like a binary image, which value in a certain point (x, y) underlines if the optical ray that passes for the pixel (x, y) intersects or not the object surface in the scene. In this way, Every point of the silhouette, respectively of value "1" or "0", identifies an optical ray that intersects or not the object.

Figure 15. A computer mouse: the object acquired image (left), the computed object silhouette region (right)

To obtain object volume from silhouettes, we use the space carving technique. A 3D box is modelled to be an initial volume model that contains the object. This box is divided in discrete elements called voxels. The algorithm is performed by projecting the center of each voxel into each image plane, by means of the known intrinsic and extrinsic camera parameters (fig. 16). If the projected point is not contained in the silhouette region, the voxel is removed from the object volume model.

The accuracy of the reconstruction obtained depends on the number of images used, on the positions of each viewpoint considered, on the camera's calibration quality and on the complexity of the object shape.
Using the camera on the robot, is of great aid because, in this way, we know exactly the position of the camera reference frame in the robot work space. Therefore the camera extrinsic parameters, are known without a vision system calibration and it's easy to make an elevated number of photos.

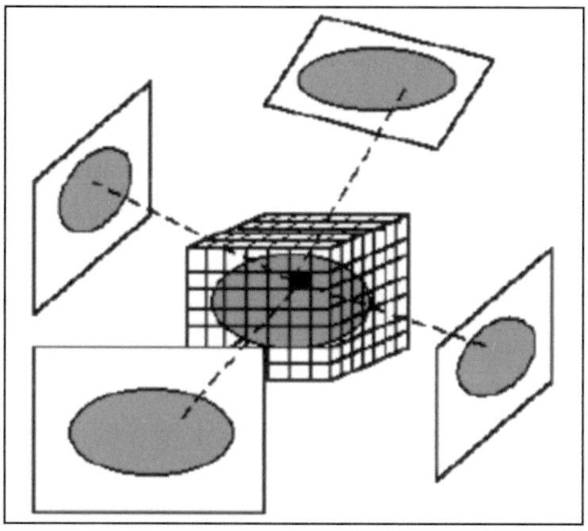

Figure 16. Space carving technique algorithm scheme

One digital camera and a robot prototype, that was designed and built at our laboratory, are used, like show in figure 17. The images have a resolution of 2592 x 1944 pixels and are saved in raw RGB format.
By means of a turntable, it is possible also to rotate the object, around a vertical axis, of a known angle. These rotations with robot movements allow to capture object images from all its sides and with different angles-shot. In this way, it is possible to use a robot with only three axis, to photograph the objects from all angles-shot.

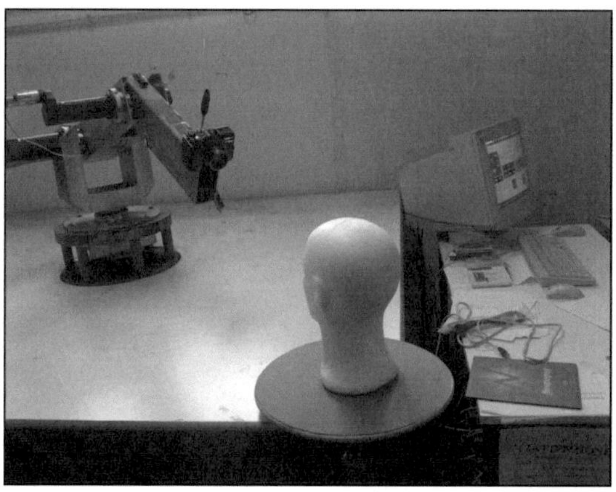

Figure 17. Acquisition system

An algorithm that use this technique was implemented; it ~~and~~ can be divided in three steps:
1. images analysis and object silhouette reconstruction;

2. calculation of the transformation matrix that permits to pass from work space coordinate to each image plane coordinate;
3. 3D-solid reconstruction.

Intersections of the optical axes of camera for each positions with horizontal reference plane of robot reference system Oxyz, are evaluated to choose object volume position. Subsequently it is possible to divide the initial volume model in a number of voxels according to the established precision. The centers of voxels are projected into each image plane by means of the pin-hole camera model. In this way it is possible to construct a matrix with the same dimension of image matrix, that has non zero-values only for volume projected voxels. The object silhouette, in the image, is represented by another matrix with non-zero values only for points of silhouette.

The elements of the product among the two matrix that have non-null value are ri-transformed in the work space and they became the centers of the voxels that must used for the following image.

This procedure is repeated for all images, to obtain the volume object in the robot workspace.

11.2 Experimental results

The reconstructions of two objects are presented to demonstrate the performance of the algorithm. As displayed in fig. 18, the test objects are a computer mouse and an mockup head.

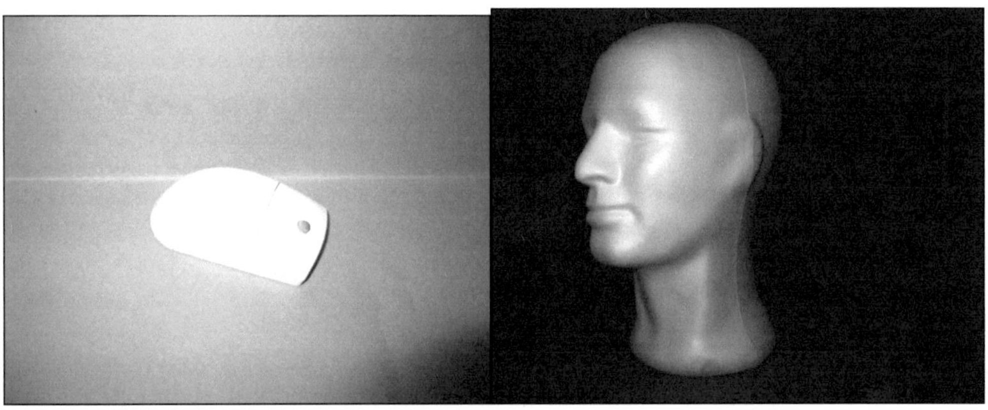

Figure 18. Test objects

Tests are carried out by varying a parameter that represents the resolution of volume.

The resolutions differ in base to the number of voxels in a fixed initial volume, for example to a resolution res = n correspond n^3 initial voxels. Assuming a initial box with sides length x y z, the tolerances corresponding to each edge are x/res, y/res, z/res.

For the mouse reconstruction, 8 photos are been used, while for the reconstruction of the head, 24 photos are been used. This is due to the greater complexity of the head shape regarding the mouse shape.

With the data of the object shape, it is possible to plan robot trajectories to reproduce the object form in any point of the robot workspace, in any position and with any scale factor.

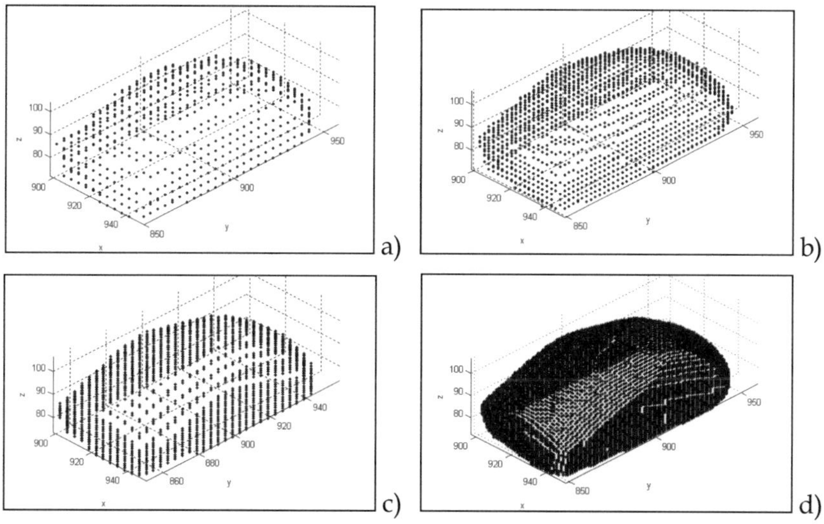

Figure 19. Reconstructed computer mouse: a) res = 50, b) res = 80, c)res=100, d) res = 150

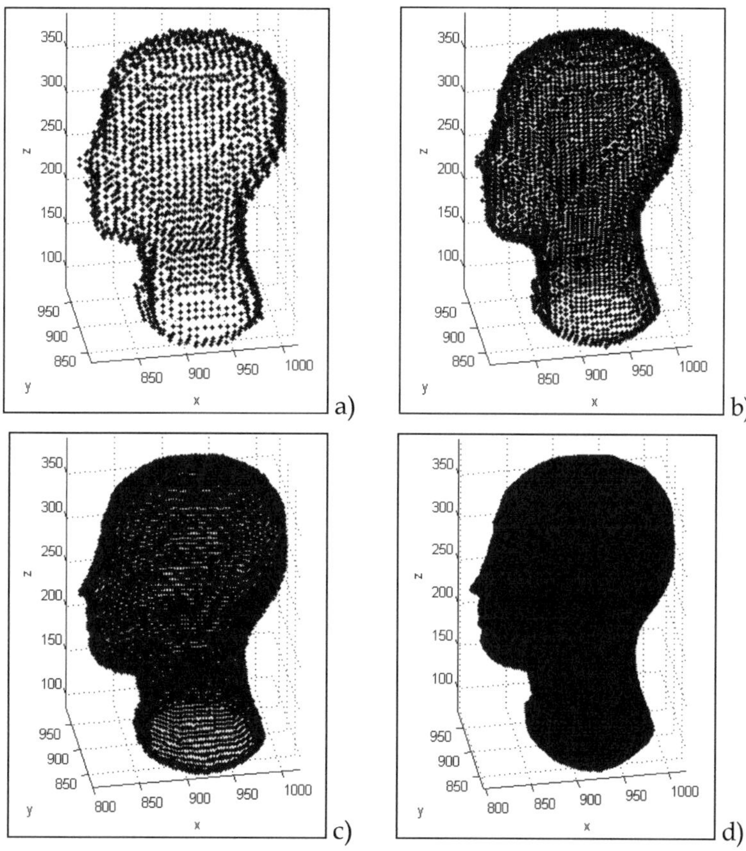

Figure 20. Reconstructed head: a) res = 50, b) res = 80, c) res = 100, d) res = 150

The simplest trajectory that can be plan with information of 3D reconstruction, is a continuous line that is bundled up around reconstructed form, passing for all characterized points. In this way a filament winding process is simulated.
An example of this kind of trajectory is shown in figure 21 for a computer mouse and for a mockup head.

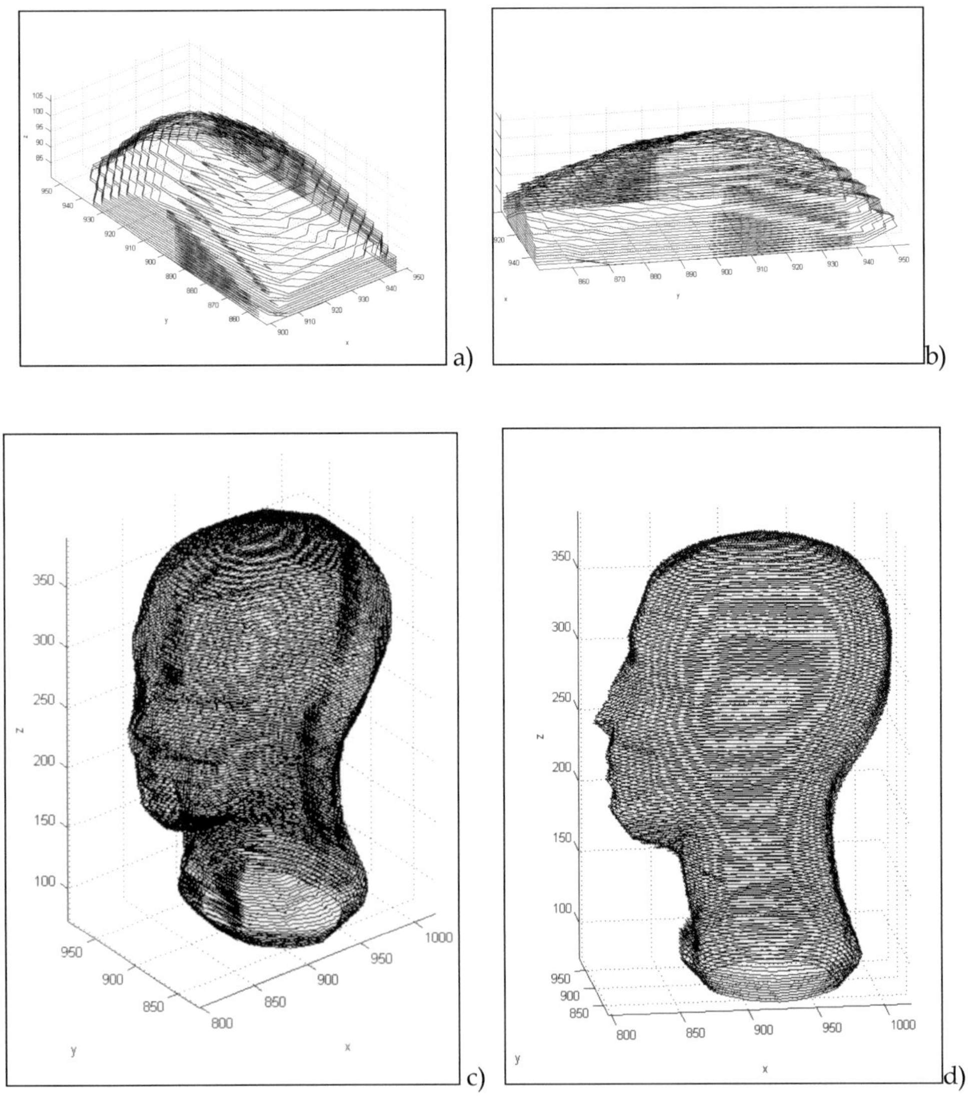

Figure 21. Robot trajectory to reproduce : a),b)computer mouse; c), d) mockup head

12. References

Niola, V.; Rossi, C. & Savino S. (2006). Perspective Transform and Vision System for Robotic Applications, *Proceedings of 5th WSEAS Int. Conf. on Signal Processing, Robotics and Automation*, February 15-17, 2006, Madrid. [1]

Niola, V.; Rossi, C. & Savino S. (2006). Modelling and Calibration of a Camera for Robot Trajectories Recording, *Proceedings of 5th WSEAS Int. Conf. on Signal Processing, Robotics and Automation*, February 15-17, 2006, Madrid. [2]

Niola, V.; Rossi, C. & Savino S. (2006). A Robot Kinematic Calibration Technique - *Proceedings of 5th WSEAS Int. Conf. on Signal Processing, Robotics and Automation*, February 15-17, 2006, Madrid. [3]

Niola, V.; Rossi, C. & Savino S. (2006). A Camera Model for Robot Trajectories Recording , Published on International review: *WSEAS Transactions on Computers,* Iusse 2, Vol.5, pp.403 - 409, February 2006. [4]

Niola, V.; Rossi, C. & Savino S. (2006). Perspective Transform in Robotic Applications, Published on International review: *WSEAS Transactions on Systems,* Iusse 4, Vol.5, pp.678 - 684, April 2006,. [5]

Niola, V.; Rossi, C. & Savino S. (2007). An Application of Vision Systems to the Path Planning of Industrial Robots, *Proceedings of BVAI 2007 2nd International Symposium on Brain, Vision and Artificial Intelligence*, vol. 1,October 10-12, 2007. [6]

Niola, V.; Pollasto, E.; Rossi, C. & Savino S. (2006). An Algorithm for Kinematics Calibration of Robot Arm, *Proceedings of RAAD'06, 15th International Workshop on Robotics in Alpe-Adria-Danube Region,* June 15-17, 2006, Balatonfured. [7]

Ciccarelli, V; D'Orsi, G.; Proni, A. & Rossi, C.(2006). Early Experimental Tests on a Vision System for Robot Mechanical Calibration, *Proceedings of RAAD'06, 15th International Workshop on Robotics in Alpe-Adria-Danube Region,* pp. 55-62, June 15-17, 2006, Balatonfured. [8]

Niola, V.; Rossi, C. & Savino S. (2007). Vision System for Industrial Robots Path Planning, *International Journal of Mechanics and Control*, pp. 35-45, ISSN: 1590-8844. [9]

Azevedo, T. C. S.; Tavares, J. M. R. S. & Vaz, M. A. P., (2007). 3D object reconstruction from uncalibrated images using a single off-the-shelf camera, *Proceedings of VIP IMAGE , Thematic conference on computational vision and medical image processing,* October 17-19, 2007. [10]

Chalidabhongse, T.H.; Yimyam, P.& Sirisomboon, P.,(2006). 2D/3D Vision-Based Mango's Feature Extraction and Sorting, *ICARCV 2006 (1-6).* [11]

Fremont, V.; Chellali, R., (2004). Turntable-Based 3D Object Reconstruction, *Proceedings of IEEE Conference on Cybernetics and Intelligent Systems,* pp. 1276-1281, Singapore, 2004. [12]

Fusiello, A., (2005). Visione Computazionale: appunti delle lezioni, Informatic Department, University of Verona, 3 March 2005. [13]

Sharma, R.; Hutchinson, S, (1994). Motion perceptibility and its application to active vision-based servo control, *Technical Report UIUC-BI AI RCV-94-05,* The Beckman Institute, Illinois University. [14]

Sharma, R., (1994). Active vision for visual servoing: a review, *IEEE Workshop on Visual Servoing: Achivement, Application and Open Problems,* May,1994. [15]

Sharma, R.; Hutchinson, S, (1995). Optimizing hand/eye configuration for visual-servo system. *IEEE International Confeence on Robotics and Automation* , pp. 172-177, 1995. [16]

Sharma, R.; Hutchinson, S, (1999). On the observability of robot motion under active camera control, *Proc. IEEE International Conference on Robotics and Automation,* May 1999, pp. 162-167. [17]

Mei, C. Camera Calibration Toolbox for Matlab, *http://www.vision.caltech.edu/bouguetj/calib_doc.* [18]

J Feddema, T. , Lee C. S. George, Mitchell O. R., (1991). Weighted selection of image features for resolved rate visual feedback control, *IEEE Trans. Robot. Automat.,* Vol. 7,, pp. 31-47. [19]

12

Multiple Object Permanence Tracking: Maintenance, Retrieval and Transformation of Dynamic Object Representations

Jun Saiki
Kyoto University
Japan

1. Introduction

Our visual world is composed of multiple dynamic objects with various visual features. For efficient interaction with the world, the visual system needs to keep binding of object features and update them as their dynamic changes. Given severe limitation of our visual short-term memory (VSTM) (Luck & Vogel, 1997; Pashler, 1988), it is a challenge to understand how the visual system deals with this binding problem in dynamic environment. In this chapter, I will review research on this issue, mainly focused on experimental studies using the paradigm called "multiple object permanence tracking" (Imaruoka et al., 2005; Saiki, 2002, 2003a, 2003b, 2007; Saiki & Miyatsuji, 2007, in press).

Transformation of object representations in dynamic environment has been investigated mainly using multiple object tracking task (MOT) (Pylyshyn & Storm, 1988; Shcoll & Pylyshyn, 1998). In MOT, a dozen of identical objects (dots) are randomly moving around on the display, and observers required to track a subset of these objects. Although research with MOT revealed various properties of object representations used by visual cognition mechanisms, the issue of binding various object features into an object representation remains unclear, because MOT only manipulates spatiotemporal location of objects, not other features. To address the issue of feature binding in dynamic environment, multiple object permanence tracking (MOPT) task used objects with different colors and shapes, and investigated how these objects' features are bound together in dynamic displays.

This chapter will describe five topics investigated with MOPT paradigm. First, how feature binding is maintained over dynamic movement of multiple objects? A series of experiments revealed that our ability of keeping binding of objects' color, shape and their spatiotemporal locations was significantly impaired when objects move (Saiki, 2003a, 2003b). Importantly, object motion was quite slow and predictable, so that the impairment was not due to failure of tracking of objects per se. Second, memory for feature binding was evaluated more strictly (Saiki & Miyatsuji, 2007). Switch detection task used in previous work showed that task performance was quite good when objects were stationary. However, simple switch detection task may overestimate our ability, and a more strict test revealed that even if objects were stationary, our ability of maintaining feature binding was much more limited than previous studies suggested. Third, is memory maintenance, or memory retrieval responsible for the performance impairment in MOPT task? To test this, I used retrieval cues in novel paradigms that directly evaluate the memory for triple conjunctions; type identification and relevant-feature switch detection, in comparison with a simple change-detection task (Saiki & Miyatsuji, in press). We found that a retrieval cue provided no benefit with the triple conjunction tasks, but significant facilitation with the change-detection task, suggesting that low capacity estimates of object file memory in VSTM reflect a limit on maintenance, not retrieval. Fourth, are these findings specific to arbitrary combination of shape and color, or more general including ordinary objects? In other words, how does prestored knowledge on color-shape binding in everyday objects affect feature binding in VSTM? To address this issue, I used everyday object such as lobster and frog, and showed that there is still significant impairment in memory for feature binding (Saiki, 2007). At the same time, there were significant differences in observer's performance. Finally, we have investigated neural correlate of feature binding in VSTM. An fMRI experiment using MOPT task revealed that in addition to frontoparietal network known to be involved in various attention related tasks, we have found significant activation of anterior prefrontal cortex, suggesting that maintenance of feature binding in visual working memory requires additional processing in anterior prefrontal cortex, which is markedly different from activation observed with the simple MOT task (Imaruoka et al., 2005).

Based on these findings, unlike the widely accepted view that VSTM has the capacity of 3-5 feature bound object representations, our ability to keep feature binding in VSTM is more limited. Relationship between MOPT experiments and other studies with various tasks, theoretical implications, and possible implications for human interface and other human factor applications will be discussed.

2. Multiple Object Permanence Tracking: Experimental Paradigm

2.1 General design

Multiple object permanence tracking (MOPT) task is conceptually a mixture of MOT and change detection tasks used in studies on VSTM. It deals with dynamic display as in MOT, but use objects defined with multiple features as in change detection tasks. Observers require to maintain feature bindings of objects, and to update as they move. The task can be decomposed into three aspects: objects to be maintained, spatiotemporal dynamics of objects, and behavioural tasks. I will summarize these aspects following the general description of stimulus configuration.

2.2 General description of stimulus configuration

Stimuli were a number of objects (usually defined by color and/or shape) configured on an imaginally circle, usually at eccentricity of 4 deg in visual angle. The objects were occluded by a gray windmill-shaped occluder, and the background was black. Objects and/or a windmill-shaped occluder smoothly rotated with constant angular velocities, so the sequence alternated visible and invisible periods regularly. Each stimulus sequence began with the visible state, followed by several alternations of visible and invisible periods. A switch event occurred at one period in the middle of the sequence (Figure 1).

2.3 Objects to be maintained

Each object was defined by color and shape. Many experiments used color manipulation alone with the same shape (disk). When shape was manipulated, either simple geometric shapes (disks, square, triangle, and pentagon) or natural objects (lobster, frog, banana, and violin) were used (Figure 2). Colors were usually four equiluminant colors. Combination of color and shape was arbitrary and randomly combined in each trial, except for the experiment in section 3.4 using natural objects. All objects in a single trial have different shape and color. The number of objects in a single trial was usually four, except for experiments in section 3.1 varying between two to six. Experiments manipulating the number of objects investigated the capacity of binding memory. A switch event (color, shape or color-and-shape) occurred at one period in the middle of the sequence.

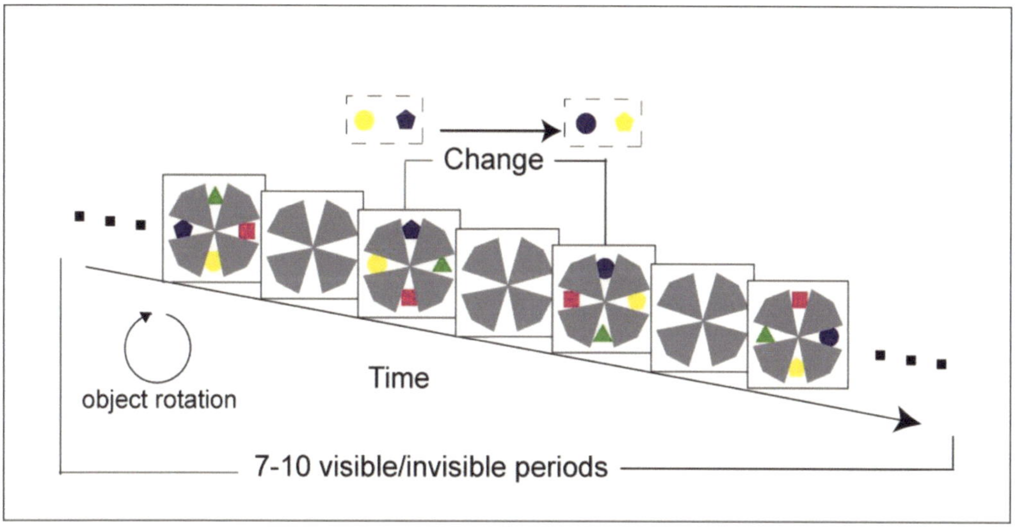

Figure 1. Schematic illustration of spatiotemporal stimulus configuration

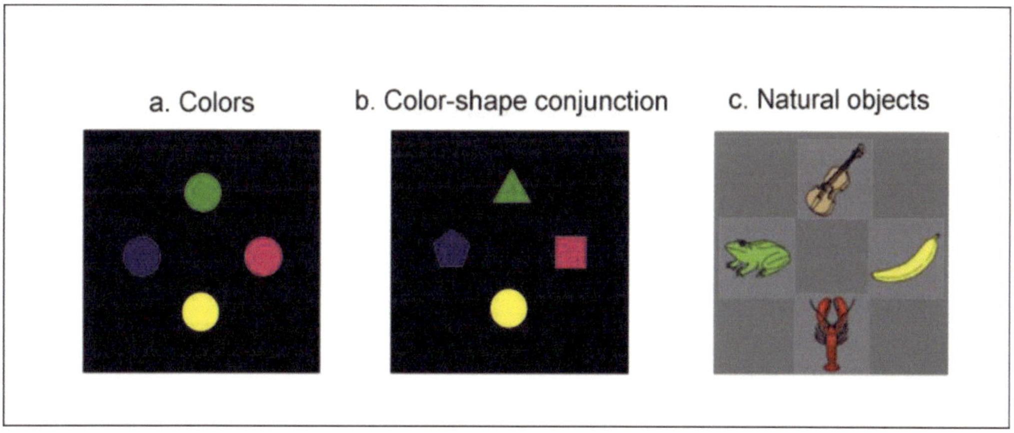

Figure 2. Sets of objects used in MOPT studies. Colors are not exactly matched to those used in experiments

2.4 Spatiotemporal dynamics of objects

Objects and/or a windmill-shaped occluder smoothly rotated with constant angular velocities, so the sequence alternated visible and invisible periods regularly. Each stimulus sequence began with the visible state, followed by several alternations of visible and invisible periods. Two rotation directions of the pattern (clockwise and counterclockwise) were used. The angular velocity of objects, from 0°/s (i.e., static) to 125°/s was manipulated by the relative motion of the objects and occluder, which kept the exposure and occlusion durations constant (Figure 3). Note that the fastest angular velocity was still much slower than the maximum velocity of approximately 360°/s in the simple location tracking task (Verstraten et al., 2000). Furthermore, regular rotation was completely predictable, unlike the standard MOT task (Pylyshyn & Storm, 1988). The occlusion duration was manipulated by the width of the occluder opening, such that the wider the opening, the longer the visible period (Figure 3).

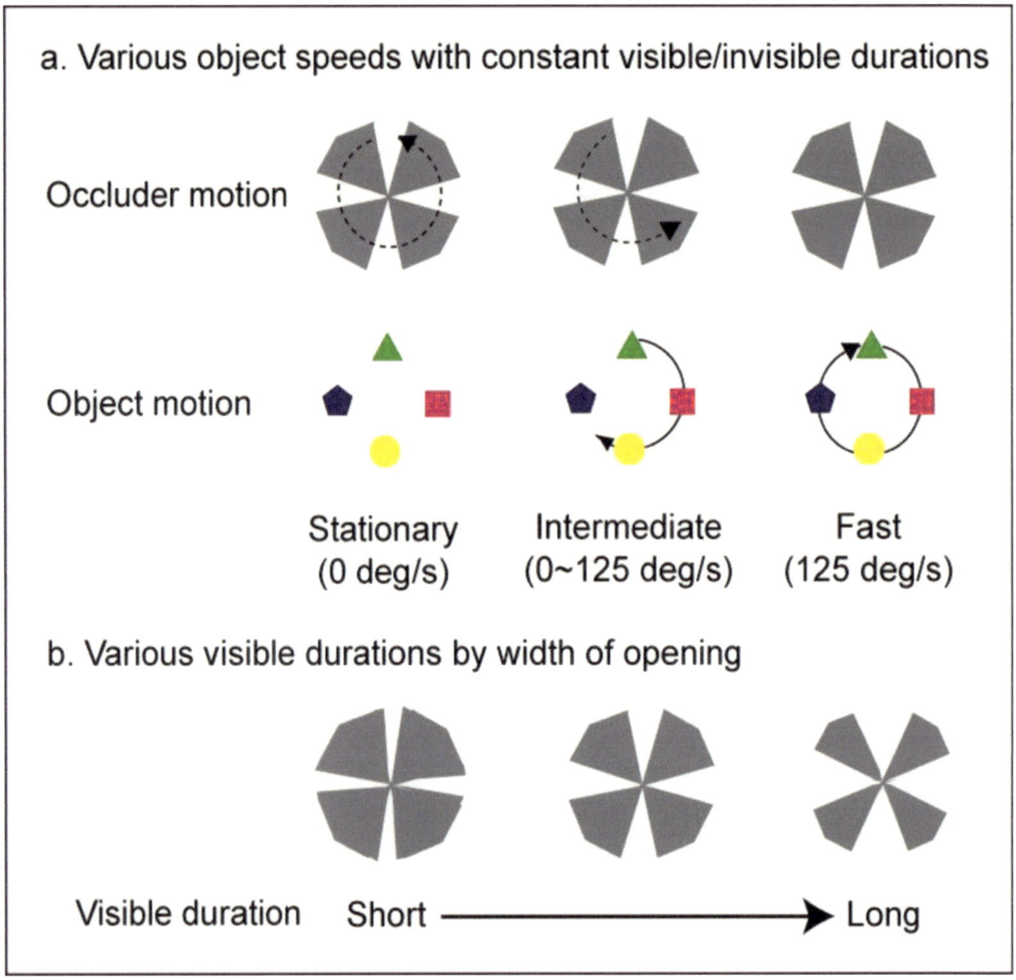

Figure 3. Illustration of spatiotemporal dynamics of objects

2.5 Behavioral task

Observers were asked to try to pay attention to the whole pattern throughout a trial, but the fixation was not monitored. They made various judgments by a key press, without correct feedback. There was no time pressure to make a response, and observers did not have to wait until the sequence ended, to make a response. To avoid verbal encoding, articulatory suppression was used. Each trial began with a beep that prompted articulatory suppression. Afterwards, the first frame of the sequence appeared on the screen and remained stationary. Five hundred ms later, the motion sequence began. Before experimental trials, observers had a block of several practice trials to familiarize themselves with the procedure.

The behavioral task is judgment about an event in the middle of MOPT sequence. When an object is defined by color and shape, four events are possible. Suppose a red square and blue circle make a change (Figure 4). The four possible change types are: no change (red square and blue circle); color change (blue square and red circle); shape change (red circle and blue square) and both change (blue circle and red square). Three different tasks were simple change detection, type identification, and relevant-feature switch detection. The simple change detection requires to judge yes when any switch occurs, which is the same as typical change detection task widely used in the literature. The type identification task requires participants to identify which event occurs in the stimulus sequence, as discrimination among four alternatives. In the relevant-feature switch detection task, the participant was instructed to monitor either color or shape, and required to judge whether the stimulus sequence included a switch event on the prespecified feature dimension. This task had only two response alternatives, as in a simple change-detection task, but required distinction between color- and shape-switch events. Figure 4 summarizes the mapping of events and responses, and I should note that the type identification and relevant-feature switch detection tasks evaluate memory for feature binding more strictly as detailed below.

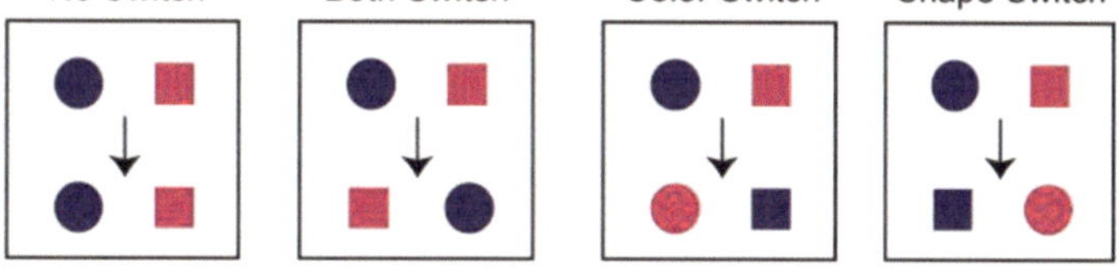

Event Type / Task	No Switch	Both Switch	Color Switch	Shape Switch
Simple Change Detection	No	Yes	Yes	Yes
Type Identification	None	Both	Color	Shape
Relevant-feature Switch Detection (color)	No	Yes	Yes	No
Relevant-feature Switch Detection (shape)	No	Yes	No	Yes

Response Mapping

Figure 4. Mapping of event types and responses in various tasks used in MOPT experiments

2.6 Specific manipulations

The basic paradigm of MOPT was modified in various ways to investigate characteristics of binding in VSTM. Besides those described above, two manipulations are worth mentioning here. One is the number of switching events, with which we investigated spontaneous strategies of selective attention. The other is cueing a target object (precue and postcue) to investigate whether performance impairment reflect memory maintenance or retrieval.

3. Studies using MOPT

3.1 Maintenance of feature binding over dynamic movement of multiple objects

The first series of experiments with MOPT (Saiki, 2003a; 2003b) investigated basic spatiotemporal characteristics of dynamic updating of multiple object representations. Saiki (2003a) primarily investigated dynamic updating of three objects with apparent motion displays. Unlike prototypical MOPT display as described in section 2, participants were shown sequences of 10 frames depicting a triangular pattern of three colored disks rotating by a certain angle per frame. The sequence was either regular clockwise or counterclockwise rotation throughout, containing one frame in which the locations of two colors were switched (color-switch), or containing one frame in which a new color was replaced with an old one (color-replacement). Participants were required to judge whether a sequence was regular or irregular without identifying its type (color-switch or color-replacement). Notice that detection of a color-switch needs memory for the conjunction of each disk's color and spatiotemporal location, whereas detection of a color-replacement does not. Thus, the performance for the color-switch condition is the critical measure of memory for the binding of color and spatiotemporal location in this paradigm. A pilot experiment with the equilateral triangle pattern rotating 60° per frame showed that color switch detection was difficult, while color replacement detection was extremely easy.

The difficulty in the color switch detection in the pilot experiment may not be due to color-location binding, but simply to failure in tracking pattern rotation. Saiki (2003a) used stimuli without such ambiguity in pattern motion, and investigated whether the difficulty in color switch detection could be overcome simply by making pattern motion unambiguous. Experiments 1 and 2 disambiguated the motion correspondence by using bilateral triangles, and smooth and continuous motion, respectively. The ambiguous condition was used as a baseline to evaluate the effect of disambiguation of motion correspondences. Overall, switch detection performance did not show any significant improvement in the unambiguous motion conditions over the ambiguous motion conditions. The difficulty in color switch detection is not due to the problem of perceiving colors with moving objects, because color replacement detection was almost perfect. Disambiguation of objects' motion by pattern configuration, smooth and continuous motion, and elimination of abrupt onset and offset is insufficient for successful color switch detection.

A second series of experiments in Saiki (2003a) investigated the effect of rotation angle on the switch detection performance. Experiment 3 showed that a reduction of the interframe rotation angle substantially improved the color switch detection performance. Within 45° interframe rotation, the hit rate for color switch was significantly better than the ambiguous baseline condition of 60° interframe rotation. Experiment 4 examined whether the effect obtained in Experiment 3 was due to the amount of spatial displacement, or the amount of angular displacement by enlarging the distances between the disks of a pattern, showing that this facilitatory effect was due to interframe rotation angle, not due to interframe spatial displacement. Experiment 5 further examined whether the effect obtained in the previous experiments was mediated by angular velocity or angular disparity by manipulating frame duration, suggesting that rotation angle, not angular velocity, determined the performance. Finally, Experiment 6 showed that the spatiotemporal predictability of locations is necessary for the facilitatory effects of reduced rotation angle. Note that these results are not simply reflecting the success or failure in object tracking, because Experiment 7 showed that object tracking was quite successful in this task setting.

A series of experiments revealed that even when the motion correspondences are unambiguous by the use of pattern configurations and continuous motion, and object tracking is successful, color switch detection performance is difficult; there was no significant improvement compared with the situations where motion correspondences were inherently ambiguous. At the same time, it has been revealed that color switch detection performance is critically dependent on the inter-frame rotation angle, and that a facilitatory effect occurred only when spatiotemporal predictability was satisfied.

As an extension of Saiki (2003a), Saiki (2003b) investigated the spatiotemporal characteristics of dynamic updating using smoothly moving multiple objects with an occluder. Objects were colored disks, and the binding of the object's color and its location should be dynamically updated. Experiment 1 investigated the effects of angular velocity of the pattern, which manipulated the objects' rotation speed with constant visible and invisible durations. Unlike Saiki (2003a) with all moving objects, this experiment parametrically varied object movement from stationary to a substantial speed (125°/s). Even within the range of successful object tracking and color perception, angular velocity strongly affected the observers' performance of color switch detection in the MOPT task, suggesting that color-location binding is quite difficult when objects are moving. The ROC analysis revealed that this effect was not due to response biases.

Experiment 2 examined the effect of occlusion duration to evaluate the "life-span" of object working memory in dynamic situations. Overall, both angular velocity and occlusion duration had significant effects on color switch detection performance, and these two factors are largely independent. The cost of object motion was significant even with a minimum occlusion period (40-ms), suggesting that object motion impairs color switch detection regardless of the length of the invisible period. The results of Experiment 2 suggest that in visual working memory, the transformation cost and retention cost, manipulated by object motion and occlusion duration, respectively, are largely independent.

Experiment 3 evaluated the "capacity" of dynamic object working memory in terms of the number of objects and the relationship between retention and processing costs. There were six objects, and observers were asked to track the color switch between target objects (2, 3, 4 or 6) prespecified at the beginning of each trial by flashing (Pylyshyn & Storm, 1988). A color switch occurred either between the target objects, or between the non-target objects, and observers were asked to ignore any color switches between non-targets. In this experiment, processing and retention costs were manipulated by angular velocity and the number of targets, respectively. Overall, the processing and retention costs were independent, and a significant effect of angular velocity was observed even in the 2- and 3-target conditions. The results of Experiments 2 and 3 showed that effects of motion were observed regardless of the retention costs, which is inconsistent with the view that motion affects general processing resource of visual working memory, and at least for the visual working memory measured by the MOPT paradigm, processing and retention are largely independent. Recently, some research on working memory has suggested the independence of processing and retention (Towse et al., 2000).

Because previous experiments investigated only color-location binding, it is unclear whether the findings reflect object level or single feature level representations. The final experiment used multidimensional objects defined by shape and color to investigate the dynamic updating of multidimensional feature binding. Objects had different shapes, as well as colors, and switch occurred with either color alone (color switch), shape alone (shape switch), or color and shape (object switch). The task was simple switch detection, and comparison of accuracy among different switch types can dissociate different hypotheses. If triple conjunction representations for objects are formed (object token hypothesis), there should be no difference among different switch types, because all these switch types involve the same amount of change in triple conjunction representations. In contrast, if a set of single conjunctions (color-location and shape-location) is formed (feature-location binding hypothesis), object switch detection will be more accurate than shape and color switches if both color-location and shape-location coding are fully available, because an object switch involves a switch of both bindings, whereas others involve only one of them. Moreover, if the availability of two types of conjunction coding is reduced due to object motion or other factors, the advantage of object switch will be reduced. Overall, results were consistent with the feature-location binding hypotheses. In the stationary conditions, object switch detection was significantly better than the color switch detection and the shape switch detection. In contrast, there was no advantage for object switch detection in the moving condition.

Our ability to maintain episodic representations of multiple objects in a completely predictable dynamic situation is limited. Objects' features are not bound together in a dynamic situation, even when their motion is quite slow and completely predictable and well within the range of ordinary object motion. This finding strongly suggests that previous findings obtained with static displays (Luck & Vogel, 1997; Vogel et al., 2001) and a dynamic multiple-object tracking task (Pylyshyn & Storm, 1988) may not reflect the function of common high level episodic representations such as object files. The dynamic maintenance of features has been used as an important hallmark of objectness in object-based attention literature (Tipper et al., 1994; Chun and Cavanagh, 1997; Valdes-Sosa et al., 1998); thus, the failure in dynamic updating of object features casts doubts on the proposal that visual working memory is object-based in a strong sense.

These results are largely consistent with recent evidence that the system of visual cognition works with much less memory than we previously believed (Ballard et al., 1997; Horowitz & Wolfe, 1998; Rensink et al., 1997). Unlike previous demonstrations, this work provides an experimental paradigm enabling parametric investigations of spatiotemporal characteristics of visual working memory, revealing some important findings. The present work has some implications for the issue of feature binding in visual cognition (Treisman, 1999). The extremely short life-span and limited capacity of memory for dynamic feature-location binding suggest that such binding is quite transient. It is well known that the binding problem is computationally quite difficult, especially in the case of multiple objects. The present findings may indicate that the visual system functions without solving a multiple-object binding problem. Instead of holding integrated representations of multiple objects, the visual system may bind perceptual features of a single object by attentional processing only when necessary (Rensink, 2000). Rensink (2000) reviewed the literature of change blindness and related phenomena, and proposed the notion of virtual representation, which provides only a limited amount of coherent structure, but provides it whenever requested, making it appear as if all the detailed, coherent structure is present simultaneously. Such representation is a "just in time" system, which is an inherently dynamic process. Although such architecture presupposes quite efficient attentional mechanisms, it has the advantage that the short life-span of feature binding avoids crosstalk among multiple binding. This simple serial binding architecture may be enough to deal with real life dynamics.

3.2 Strict evaluation of feature binding memory

In the initial studies on MOPT (Saiki, 2002, 2003a, 2003b), switch detection was markedly impaired as motion speed increased. Although performance level is rather high when objects are stationary, it is unclear how much feature bound memory can be maintained. The multidimensional MOPT experiment suggests fairly limited capacity for feature binding memory. Moreover, the results of some studies using a change detection task suggest that our capacity for object representation in visual memory is more limited than previously believed (Alvarez & Cavanagh, 2002; Bahrami, 2003; Olson & Jiang, 2002; Wheeler & Treisman, 2002; Xu, 2002). The literature is currently equivocal regarding the capacity of memory for feature binding. Saiki and Miyatsuji (2007) utilized a new experimental paradigm that appears suited for evaluating binding memory, and analyzed performances using mathematical models analogous to those used in perceptual feature binding studies.

Two necessary conditions must be met to properly evaluate the use of feature conjunctions. First, to eliminate possible contributions from simple feature information, the stimulus set should use identical sets of features in different combinations. Saiki (2002, 2003a, 2003b) and Wheeler and Treisman (2002) satisfied this condition. The second condition is the use of a task able to evaluate the representation of feature combination. One task satisfying this condition is the perceptual identification task used in perceptual feature binding. Change detection tasks used in visual memory obviously fail to satisfy this condition. Because the task is simply detecting a change, representational schemes other than feature combination, such as simple stimulus salience (Itti & Koch, 2000), can account for correct change detection.

Unlike perceptual binding, however, the simple identification task also displays problems. In visual memory, a variety of simple identification tasks tend to underestimate memory capacity, as exemplified by a classic study of the partial report paradigm by Sperling (1969). Moreover, even if subjects are simply asked to report an object with change, cognitive load in response mapping is significant, and is quite likely to affect memory performance. Furthermore, direct identification forces participants to transform visual information into verbal form, which can also compromise visual memory performance.

To avoid problems with both detection and simple identification tasks, a type identification task was devised. The type identification task requires participants to identify which event occurs in the stimulus sequence, as discrimination among four alternatives. Correct identification of change type requires memory for feature combinations. At the same time, unlike simple identification, cost in response mapping is negligible. These characteristics are crucial, particularly when using the wide varieties of colors and shapes seen in most visual memory tasks. If several colors and shapes are used, type identification based solely on salience is almost impossible, and cost in terms of response mapping in single identification becomes prohibitive. Compared with change detection tasks, the type identification task can thus extract important additional information regarding binding memory.

Using type identification with multidimensional MOPT, the role of object motion and number of switching events in binding memory for multiple objects was investigated. A unique property of the MOPT paradigm is the ability to evaluate memory for feature binding in dynamic situations. One of the hallmarks of the objectness is the maintenance of feature binding across spatiotemporal changes (i.e., motion), so the MOPT provides important information about the properties of object representations. Unlike previous studies (Saiki, 2002, 2003a, 2003b), the type identification paradigm could eliminate effects from saliency-based mechanisms, and extract the effect of feature binding more strictly. The second factor to be evaluated was the number of switches. MOPT in previous works involved two switching events in each trial, with the switched state returning to the initial state in the next occlusion period. Compared with the standard change detection task, in which only a single chance exists to detect a change, this specific manipulation may improve subject performance. This factor may be responsible for apparent discrepancies in stationary conditions between the studies by Saiki (2003a, 2003b) and Wheeler and Treisman (2002). Saiki (2003a, 2003b) reported accurate performance under stationary conditions, whereas Wheeler and Treisman (2002) found significant impairment in binding conditions. The present study compared performance in the MOPT task with two switches ("switch-back condition") and with one switch ("no-switch-back condition").

Multidimensional MOPT with the type identification task replicated the basic findings of previous MOPT experiments (Saiki, 2003a,b), in that memory for feature bindings appears severely limited. Overall, patterns of results were consistent with the view that a single switch is insufficient to use memory for binding. Lack of object motion was insufficient for the maintenance of feature bindings, as the no-switch-back condition showed significant impairment even under stationary conditions. In addition to correct type identification rates, analyses of response pattern address an important theoretical issue. Model-based analyses revealed that the number of switches affects not only accuracy, but also contingency of stimulus and response types. Error analyses suggest that people rely more on partial conjunction information (i.e., shape-location, or color-location), at the time of first switch, but at the time of second switch, they rely on triple conjunction information. Combined with the accuracy data, the results of model fitting support the interpretation that shape-color-location binding is available only when a second switch is present.

The results of Experiment 1 suggest that triple conjunction representation becomes available mainly at the time of second switch. There are at least two factors which can produce this result. First, memory representations change their format from partial-conjunction to triple-conjunction between the first and second switches. Second, the first switch functions as a cue to selectively attend to a switching object, which makes the triple-conjunction representation more accessible. To examine the effects of these two factors, Experiment 3 in Saiki and Miyatsuji (2007) introduced two manipulations. First, to investigate the transition from partial- to triple-conjunctions, we used mixed switch trials. Unlike previous experiments, where the event type of the first and second switches was the same, mixed switch trials had two different switch types, allowing us to evaluate which switch leads to observers' type identification response. Second, to investigate effects of selective attention, we introduced a condition where the first and second switches occurred with different object pairs.

When two switches occur with the same pair of stationary objects, there was a strong bias toward reporting the second switch, which is consistent with the hypothesis that triple-conjunction representation becomes available before the second switch by selectively attending to switching objects. In contrast, the significant bias toward the first switch in the different-pair stationary condition is also consistent with attentional cueing hypothesis, because if the attention is focused on the pair of first switch objects, correct type identification of the second switch is less likely than the first switch, when attention was evenly distributed among four objects. Finally, Experiment 2 in Saiki and Miyatsuji (2007) investigated whether the use of occluder significantly impaired performance in MOPT, and showed that the occluder did not have any negative effects on performance.

These results are inconsistent with the popular claim that visual working memory can hold about four objects simultaneously (Cowan, 2001; Irwin, 1992; Kahneman, et al., 1992; Luck & Vogel, 1997) even when objects are stationary. If previous works with change detection tasks reflect the use of explicit memory for feature binding, similarly accurate performances would be expected in type identification tasks. One exception in previous studies using a change detection task is Wheeler and Treisman (2002), which showed significant impairment in the change detection of feature bindings. The findings of the present study appear consistent with their data, but the mechanisms underlying performance impairment may differ. As Wheeler and Treisman used a change detection task, the saliency-based detection strategy is available. Impairment as described by Wheeler and Treisman may thus reflect a reduction to salience change in the binding condition. In MOPT with type identification, on the other hand, saliency-based identification is almost impossible, and impairment in the no-switch-back stationary condition likely reflects the limit in feature binding. This issue is discussed in the next section.

Both accuracy data and event-response contingency analyses revealed that properties of binding memory are qualitatively different between conditions involving only one switch and those presenting a second chance. One interpretation is that visual memory, similar to visual perception (Treisman & Schmidt, 1982), is structured in a feature-based fashion when multiple objects require simultaneous storage. When attention is directed to an object, feature representations are integrated to form a coherent object representation (Treisman, 1988). In other words, availability of selective attention to a particular object could result in significant changes to performance. In the no-switch-back condition with a single switch, subjects must divide their attention between all four objects, since the subject does not know which object will change. In that state, the results suggest that only partial feature binding information is available. When the first switch occurred, if the objects were stationary, subjects were likely to detect a change to one or two objects, but were unable to identify the type. Subjects then direct attention to a suspected object, and if a second switch occurred, they could identify the switch type based on selective attention. An extreme view of this account is that we can hold feature-bound object only one at a time. One remaining issue is whether selective attention affects transition from feature-based memory to object-based memory, or modulates the availability of prestored object representation.

To evaluate visual working memory for feature binding, Saiki and Miyatsuji (2007) devised a type identification paradigm, and applied it to multiple object permanence tracking task (MOPT). Compared with previous results with simple change detection, task performance was greatly reduced, suggesting that previous data reflects memory for something other than feature binding, such as stimulus salience. The number of switches facilitates performance only when objects were stationary, and the model-based analyses and mixed design experiment showed that this improvement reflects the effects of selective attention on forming or strengthening feature-bound memory representation. In contrast, when objects were moving, the effect of second switch was quite small, suggesting that either detection of the first switch, or maintenance of feature binding across occlusion is disrupted by object motion. Type identification method is a powerful tool to investigate various aspects of feature binding memory in combination with model-based analyses and various experimental procedures.

3.3 Source of performance impairment: maintenance or retrieval?

A series of experiments using MOPT (Saiki, 2002, 2003a, 2003b; Saiki & Miyatsuji, 2007) so far revealed that task performance was severely impaired even when objects are stationary. One critical problem is to evaluate whether the performance impairment reflects memory retrieval or maintenance. Saiki and Miyatsuji (in press) addressed this issue.

A deficit in a memory task may be caused by a limit in storage capacity, or by a bottleneck in memory retrieval and/or comparison between memory and perceptual representations. Some studies have suggested that low estimated capacity for feature binding memory relative to feature memory may reflect differences in memory retrieval. Wheeler and Treisman (2002) compared the single-probe paradigm, where only one object was presented in the probe display to be judged for the presence of change, with the multiple-probe paradigm, where the whole probe display needed to be compared with the initial display. They showed that the single-probe condition significantly improved performance in the binding condition compared to the multiple-probe condition. This improvement in task performance can be interpreted as a reduction of interference and/or a facilitation of memory retrieval by the single probe.

The single probe advantage in the binding condition leaves some questions open regarding the nature of representation and processing in VSTM. First, the findings of Wheeler and Treisman (2002) do not necessarily imply that memory for object files in general suffer from a retrieval bottleneck in the multiple probe condition. Wheeler and Treisman investigated simple feature conjunctions such as color-location and shape-color conjunction, so whether a single probe advantage is observed with more complex representations (triple conjunction) remains unknown. If the previous findings reflect the nature of object files in general, the single probe advantage should be observed with triple conjunction representation. Conversely, if the previous findings hold true only in certain special situations, the single probe advantage may be limited to simple conjunction representations. In Saiki and Miyatsuji (in press), retrieval cueing and memory task manipulation were combined to achieve a better understanding of the nature of binding memory.

Experiment 1 combined the type identification task and retrieval cuing using the MOPT paradigm. A cue indicating the changing object was 100% valid, and was presented either just before (precue) or after (postcue) a change occurred. If a cue is effective, the precue condition is expected to show significantly better task performance compared with the no-cue control. The critical condition was the postcue condition. Estimated capacity from behavioral data is determined by two factors: maintenance capacity and costs in memory retrieval. Because the postcue condition substantially reduces retrieval costs, estimated capacity in the postcue condition is closer to the genuine maintenance capacity than in the no-cue condition. The performance facilitation by the postcue condition thus suggests that estimated capacity in the no-cue condition suffers from retrieval costs, while the lack thereof suggests that the estimated capacity in the no-cue condition reflects genuine maintenance capacity. Also, using the moving condition of MOPT, we compared effects of retrieval cueing between spatiotemporal updating and simple maintenance of complete object files. Experiment 1 failed to obtain facilitation by the retrieval cue, suggesting that the retrieval cue benefit does not occur for triple conjunctions.

One alternative account, however, is that the complexity of the type-identification paradigm eliminated any postcue benefit. In Experiment 2, a relevant-feature switch detection task (see section 2.5) was used. This task had only two response alternatives, as in a simple change-detection task, but required distinction between color- and shape-switch events. A relevant-feature switch detection task failed to show any effect of postcue, suggesting that the results in Experiment 1 were not simply due to the complexity of response mapping. Next, to eliminate a possibility that postcue manipulation is simply not effective in MOPT task, Experiment 3 used a simple change detection task. A simple change-detection task revealed significant facilitation in the stationary condition. A retrieval cue facilitates judgment of whether any kind of change is present, but does not help identify the type of switch. The postcue paradigm can thus reveal a facilitation effect similar to that found with the single-probe paradigm of Wheeler and Treisman (2002), suggesting that postcues used in this study can effectively function as a retrieval cue. Another interesting result was the lack of postcue effects in the moving condition, suggesting that the postcue is ineffective for moving objects. This may reflect that memory retrieval and matching operation are location-based, not object-based. These results are replicated in Experiment 4 where a simple switch detection and relevant-feature switch detection tasks were directly compared with a within-subject design. Finally, Experiment 5 revealed that these findings are not reflecting overwriting effects.

Taken together, the interaction between postcue benefit and task (significant benefit with the simple change-detection and no benefit with tasks requiring triple conjunctions) suggest that retrieval cue benefit occurs only for simple feature conjunctions, and that limits in triple conjunctions primarily reflect memory maintenance. Maintenance capacity for triple conjunctions is close to the estimated capacity, that is, one or two objects, whereas, that for simple conjunctions may be larger.

The present results argue against the view that memory of feature binding is a system composed of general object file representations. General object file representations include complex representations such as triple conjunctions, and should lead to postcue benefits in all different tasks used in this work, a possibility was unsupported by the data. Unlike a previous claim by Luck and Vogel (1997) that the content of object memory, object files, is complete, regardless of the number of features, the present study suggests that the content of object files are partial by default. The present study suggests that functional properties of object files differ depending on complexity, which is related to a recent argument regarding whether complexity of objects affects the capacity of VSTM (Alvarez & Cavanagh, 2004; Awh et al., 2007).

Alvarez and Cavanagh (2004) reported that capacity estimate using a simple change-detection task is a linear function of the complexity of the object measured by the slope in a visual search task, suggesting that the complexity of objects affects the capacity of VSTM. Recently, however, Awh et al. (2007) showed some evidence that these results could be explained by difficulty of matching between memory and percept, suggesting that the capacity of VSTM is fixed regardless of object complexity, but resolution of object representations becomes degraded with increasing complexity. As far as the simple change-detection task is concerned, the results of the present study appear consistent with the argument by Awh et al. as the significant postcue benefit with simple change detection suggests that performance impairment primarily reflects memory retrieval or matching of memory and percept, and not capacity per se. In contrast, the results with tasks requiring triple conjunctions seem consistent with the argument of Alvarez and Cavanagh (2004), suggesting that impairment primarily reflects maintenance capacity. When the task requires use of triple conjunctions, the capacity of object file representation is substantially reduced.

Taken together, the idea of fixed capacity with varied resolution may hold only in the context of simple change detection, and in general, the complexity of objects may reduce the maintenance capacity of memory representation.
The effects of retrieval cue on visual short-term memory depend on task requirement. Whereas a simple change-detection task shows a facilitatory effect as seen in previous studies, tasks requiring discrimination of different feature combinations failed to show facilitation, even when task difficulty was similar to the change detection. These results suggest that retrieval cue benefit occurs in memory for simple feature conjunctions, but not for more complex representations. Limits in memory for complex object files primarily reflect maintenance capacity, whereas maintenance capacity for simple conjunctions is underestimated by a simple change-detection task due to retrieval bottleneck.

3.4 Comparison between arbitrary and knowledge-based binding

So far, all experiments investigating feature binding in visual working memory using MOPT used arbitrary color-shape combinations. However, binding of various features of natural objects are usually not arbitrary. For example, banana has often a particular shape and a yellow color. Binding in natural objects is structural in the sense that a particular combination of component features is associated with a higher level description of objects, whereas binding discussed in visual working memory lacks such a higher level unit. In other words, a problem with stimuli used in visual working memory may be the lack of such structural relations. To address this issue, an experiment was conducted to compare the effect of higher level nodes on maintenance of feature binding in visual working memory. Two specific questions are addressed:
(1) Does pre-stored knowledge about shape-color correspondence facilitate memory for feature bindings, and if so, how?
(2) Does constant mappings of shape-color correspondence within an experimental session facilitate memory for feature bindings, and if so, how?
If manipulations of (1) or (2) facilitate performance, the limited capacity for feature bindings in previous works is likely to reflect the arbitrary and independent nature of feature conjunctions used in the experiments. In contrast, if the factors above do not facilitate performance, then the capacity limit is likely to be more general.
Using the multidimensional MOPT paradigm with the type identification procedure, the roles of prestored memory representations of color-shape conjunctions in maintaining object information in visual working memory were evaluated. An experiment was conducted to investigate (1) whether known color-shape conjunctions facilitate maintenance of multiple object representations in visual working memory, (2) whether fixed color-shape conjunction facilitates maintenance of multiple object representations, and (3) whether patterns of errors demonstrate the roles of prestored conjunctions in visual working memory.
Saiki (2007) investigated whether this limitation is specific to the use of arbitrary combinations of color-shape. Two main independent variables were object type and motion type. The object types were natural when natural objects were used, geometric-constant when geometric figures were used as in previous studies, while the shape-color correspondences were fixed, and geometric-varied, which is identical to previous studies. The motion types were object motion and occluder motion. Shapes used for objects in the geometric conditions were circle, square, hexagon and triangle. Objects used in the natural condition were lobster, frog, banana, and violin, which had clear associated colors, based on

a preliminary survey. Colors were those typically associated colors: red, green, yellow, and brown, for both natural and geometric conditions. A total of four events were possible: object-switch with simultaneous switch of color and shape; color-switch alone; shape-switch alone; and no switch. Participants were asked to identify event types without feedback as to which was correct.

The results showed only a weak tendency toward performance improvement in the natural and geometric-constant conditions, and these conditions showed severe performance impairment under the moving condition. The natural and geometric-constant conditions were virtually the same in accuracy, suggesting that prestored color-shape conjunctions had limited effect on percent correct data.

However, analyses of error types demonstrated strong effects of prestored conjunction on task performance. Compared with geometric conditions, the natural condition showed significantly more errors confusing between color-switch and shape-switch, suggesting that observers were quite sensitive to detect a change in object identity, but not able to accurately identify the switch type. In the natural condition, color and shape form a unit of object identity, but to identify the switch type, its component (either color or shape) and location needs to be bound. Observers can detect the occurrence of color or shape switch when they see a green lobster, but they are not good at telling whether a red lobster changed to a green lobster (i.e., color switch), or a green frog changed to a green lobster (i.e., shape switch). In fact, they had a strong bias to judge any switch involving identity change as a color switch.

In contrast, although the error rates were about the same under the geometric-constant condition, the pattern of errors is quite different. Color and shape behave more independently, even when the conjunctions are completely fixed. Unlike the case of lobster, when a predefined red-square combination changed to a red-circle (i.e., shape-switch), errors were more likely to be an indication of no switch (i.e., overlooking the shape-switch), and in the case of feature confusion, errors occurred evenly in both directions.

Results for the natural condition support a view that visual features are first bound together to form a type representation, before further binding to a spatiotemporal location to form a token (Kanwisher, 1991). Moreover, this view holds only when type information is prestored in LTM, and without prestored types, shape-color conjunctions played no significant role.

More importantly, the availability of type information did not facilitate task performance in MOPT. Binding of type representations to their spatiotemporal location appears to be quite difficult. This raises a possibility that even the feature binding in structural descriptions may have a similar limitation. As Hummel and Biederman (1992) described, structural description is not simply a co-activation of a set of geons, but also a binding of parts with relations. Given part representation is a set of its components, it is similar to the type representation discussed here. Thus, structural description needs binding of parts (types) with spatial information, which corresponds to the binding of types with their locations in MOPT task. Thus, the formal structure has a certain level of similarity between multiple objects in the MOPT task and an object's structural description.

However, there are important differences as well. For example, parts are tightly grouped by connectedness and other grouping factors (Saiki & Hummel, 1998), but objects are completely separated in MOPT. Binding in structural description formation is limited to shape information, but shape and color (and other object features) are used in MOPT. Clearly, how these factors affect binding performance is an issue for further studies, but

Saiki (2007) shows that limits in feature binding in visual working memory are not simply an artifact of arbitrary feature combinations, and these limits may have a broader common ground including binding in object recognition.

3.5 Neural correlate of feature binding in VSTM

Although the MOPT task clarified the cognitive aspects of object representation in visual working memory, the underlying neural mechanisms remain unclear. Several neuroimaging studies have addressed either dynamic updating (Culham et al., 1998; Culham et al., 2001; Jovicich et al., 2001) or feature binding (Prabhakaran et al., 2000; Mitchell et al., 2000; Shafritz et al., 2002), but none have addressed both simultaneously. In this respect, the MOPT task provides a unique means of investigating the neural basis behind the interactions of feature binding and dynamic updating, which are a crucial part of our visual object representation.

Previous studies on dynamic updating have reported quite consistent results showing activation of the dorsal frontoparietal network involving the frontal and the parietal areas (Culham et al., 1998; Culham et al., 2001; Jovicich et al., 2001). In contrast, results from feature binding studies are less consistent, showing participation of the anterior prefrontal (Prabhakaran et al., 2000; Mitchell et al., 2000) and parietal areas (Shafritz et al., 2002; Corbetta et al., 1995; Friedman-Hill et al., 1995; Ashbridge et al., 1997), and the hippocampus (Mitchell et al., 2000). One possible reason for such discrepancies is the diversity of experimental paradigms. Importantly, most of these paradigms do not reflect feature binding in a strict sense. To investigate feature binding, standard and test stimuli should contain an identical set of features, only differing in the combination, and the task should require the use of combination information. Thus far, no clear demonstrations of neural correlates for feature bindings in memory have been presented, and exploring these with the MOPT paradigm is important.

We performed a functional magnetic resonance imaging (fMRI) experiment during the MOPT task. Sixteen observers performed two kinds of MOPT task that enabled us to compare brain activities during dynamic (object-moving) and static (object-stationary) situations under matched circumstances.

We found that the MOPT task induced not only dorsal frontoparietal activation, but also right anterior and bilateral ventral parts of frontal activation. The spatial pattern of this activation did not vary, irrespective of whether objects were in motion or stationary. This result was clearly inconsistent with a hypothesis that the MOPT task would induce only dorsal frontoparietal activation. Thus, the dorsal frontoparietal network alone cannot maintain object representations. In the ROI analyses, patterns of anterior and inferior parts of frontal activation differed from those of the dorsal frontoparietal activations. This discrepancy between two activation groups suggests that these two activation groups reflect two distinct cognitive processes. Object representation in visual working memory thus appears to be maintained by active interactions between the dorsal frontoparietal network and other frontal regions.

The present study revealed that the MOPT task induces both dorsal frontoparietal and the anterior and ventral activation of the frontal cortices. This result suggests that object representations are not contained within a single neural system such as the frontal area or dorsal frontoparietal network, but instead are represented by cooperation of distributed neural systems involving the coherency control system in the anterior frontal area and the dynamic updating system in the dorsal frontoparietal network.

However, the epoch-related design in Imaruoka et al. (2005) prevents us from further analysis, given that activities in the maintenance and change-detection periods were confounded. Recently, Takahama et al. (2005) conducted a follow-up to the Imaruoka study, using an event-related design and modifying the experimental paradigm in several points. First, with extensive practice trials before the fMRI sessions, the accuracy of behaviour data was set to be quite high, and there was no substantial difference in task difficulty across conditions. Second, visual stimuli in the maintenance period of control conditions now were exactly the same as those in the experimental conditions, so that differences in brain activity could be said to reflect top-down control of memory maintenance. Third, activities in the maintenance and change-detection periods were now decomposed by event-related design. Although still preliminary, the results were largely consistent with those of Imaruoka et al., but with some new findings. Regarding activity in posterior areas, maintenance activity showed the pattern similar to that of Imaruoka et al. (2005). By contrast, the event-related design revealed further qualifications about anterior prefrontal activity. The effect of load (moving vs. stationary) was observed during the maintenance period such that the moving condition showed stronger activation in both control and test conditions, without task effect. The effect of task (binding vs. control conditions) was instead observed during the change-detection. These data suggest that manipulation of memory representation during the maintenance period increases anterior prefrontal activity, whereas binding of color and location affects the memory retrieval and matching process. Manipulation-related activity in the anterior prefrontal area is consistent with Mohr et al. (2006), and binding-related activity at the time of change-detection appears to imply that the anterior PFC is not the storage place of feature binding, but, rather, involved in carrying out judgments based on a change in feature binding. Because all the reports of binding-related activity in the anterior PFC used epoch-related design (Imaruoka et al., 2005; Mitchell et al., 2000; Prabhakaran et al. 2000), this interpretation is consistent with those previous studies.

Taken together, studies using the MOPT paradigm support the view that maintenance and updating of feature-bound object representations cannot be carried out autonomously within the frontoparietal network. Updating of color-location binding requires activity of the anterior PFC, suggesting that the conventional MOT task is unlikely to be actually investigating the tracking of feature-bound object representations. Although memory for color-location binding cannot fully function within the frontoparietal network, there are some alternative explanations regarding the functional architecture of binding memory. First, as suggested by Wheeler and Treisman (2002), visual working memory is inherently feature-based, and memory judgment on feature conjunction, such as switch detection, is carried out by combining states of two feature-based memory systems. Alternatively, memory representations in the inferior IPS may be feature-bound, but the frontoparietal network cannot detect a change in feature combination autonomously. In other words, representations in the inferior IPS may be implicitly feature-bound, but explicit detection of change requires prefrontal activity. Recently, some studies reported that intraparietal sulcus (IPS) revealed brain activation proportional to memory load (Todd & Marois, 2004; Vogel & Machizawa, 2004; Song & Jiang, 2006; Xu & Chun, 2006). Earlier studies use simple color-location tasks (Todd & Marois, 2004; Vogel & Machizawa, 2004) and more recent ones manipulated object complexity (Xu & Chun, 2006) and the number of objects and features (Song & Jiang, 2006), showing that IPS activation is modulated by both object complexity (in particular superior IPS) and the number of features. However, whether explicit representation of complex feature conjunctions resides in IPS remains unclear. Further investigations are necessary to resolve this issue.

4. Summary and future directions

I have reviewed a series of studies using MOPT task in this chapter. In this section, I summarize the major findings and relate them in a broader context of object representations in visual cognition.

The findings from MOPT experiments can be summarized in the following way in terms of transformation, maintenance and retrieval of object representations.

(1) Transformation of object representations: Even when objects are moving slowly and in completely predictable fashion, updating object features (colors and shapes) as objects' movement is extremely costly. Extreme difficulty in feature switch detection in the moving condition reflects failure in updating feature binding, not in tracking or feature encoding alone.

(2) Maintenance of object representations: The results from the type identification and relevant-feature switch detection tasks revealed that maintenance of multiple object representations without any spatiotemporal transformation is also quite difficult. Unlike often reported capacity estimate of 3-5 objects using simple change detection tasks, the estimated capacity for complex feature conjunction representations is somewhere between 1 and 2 objects.

(3) Retrieval of object representations: Whether impairment in task performance reflects failure in memory retrieval depends on tasks. Memory evaluated by a simple change detection task suffers significant effects of retrieval bottleneck, whereas that evaluated by tasks measuring triple conjunction representations does not. This suggests that capacity estimates of 1-2 objects for complex object representations primarily reflect maintenance capacity, whereas estimates of 3-5 objects for simple conjunctions are underestimated by retrieval failures.

(4) Object representations with previous experiences: MOPT with natural objects revealed that difficulty in integrating feature and location information is not specific to arbitrary combination of features. However, the structure of memory representation is different: arbitrary objects form a set of feature-location bindings (color-location and shape-location), whereas natural objects form a type (shape-color conjunction) bound to location.

(5) Neural correlate of transformation of object representation: Although still preliminary, fMRI experiments suggest that a large network of brain areas, in particular frontoparietal network and anterior prefrontal cortex, is necessary to maintain and transform multiple object representations.

These findings suggest that although subjectively we feel that we can see multiple complex objects simultaneously, and can maintain their memory for a short period of time, it may not be the case. A strict test of object memory using MOPT paradigm shows that our capacity of visual working memory for complex multi-feature objects is surprisingly small. These findings suggest that previous findings regarding capacity of 3-5 objects may reflect partial representations of complex objects, such as just color-location or shape-location. When detailed representation of complex object is necessary, one may need to direct selective attention to the object. The reason why we do not have any serious problems in everyday life may be that selective attention mechanism is quite efficient to direct attention to an object or region which needs detailed processing just in time.

If our visual cognition system operates with minimum number of complex object representations, this becomes an important constraint in human-interface design. A situation like MOPT, color switch in the middle of object motion, rarely occurs in natural environments, but it becomes certainly possible in artificial environments, particularly computer-generated virtual environments with much less physical constraints. Thus, in dynamic control of complex systems such as driving vehicles and air-traffic control, careless design of interface may cause an accident or other serious consequences.

Are findings with MOPT paradigm specific to this paradigm? The severe limitation with complex objects is also reported studies with typical change detection tasks (for example, Xu & Chun, 2006), which is consistent with the MOPT studies. Recently, using a different experimental paradigm called spatiotemporal search, I found the results consistent with these studies (Saiki, in press).

One issue remaining unclear is the role of implicit mechanisms. All experiments with MOPT so far used an explicit task, thus even if we cannot maintain many complex object representations explicitly, they may be maintained in some implicit fashion. Indeed, object file preview effects (Kahneman et al., 1992) suggest that it may be the case. Implicit representation of feature binding and its role in visual cognition is an important future direction, which needs new ways of investigating the issue. Modification of MOPT may contribute to this line of research as well.

5. Conclusion

Multiple object permanence tracking (MOPT) task revealed that our ability of maintaining and transforming multiple representations of complex feature-bound objects is limited to handle only 1-2 objects. Often reported capacity of 3-5 objects likely reflects memory for partial representations of objects and simple cases such as just color and their locations. Also, performance in multiple object tracking (MOT) task is likely mediated by spatiotemporal indices, not by feature-bound object representations. MOPT paradigm is quite useful in investigating maintenance, retrieval and transformation of dynamic object representations with properly controlled experimental setting.

6. Acknowledgement

This work was partially supported from Grants-in-Aid (#13610084, #14019053, and #19500226) from JMEXT, the Global COE Program "Revitalizing Education for Dynamic Hearts and Minds," from JMEXT, and PRESTO from JST. I would like to think collaborators of the MOPT project, Hirofumi Miyatsuji, Toshihide Imaruoka, and Sachiko Takahama.

7. References

Alvarez, G. A. & Cavanagh, P. (2004). The capacity of visual short-term memory is set both by visual information load and by number of objects. *Psychological Science,* 15, 106-111, ISSN: 0956-7976.

Ashbridge, E.; Walsh, V. & Cowey, A. (1997). Temporal aspects of visual search studied by transcranial magnetic stimulation. *Neuropsychologia,* 35, 1121-1131, ISSN: 0028-3932.

Awh, E.; Barton, B. & Vogel, E. K. (2007). Visual working memory represents a fixed number of items regardless of complexity. *Psychological Science,* 18, 622-628, ISSN: 0956-7976.

Ballard, D. H.; Hayhoe, M. M.; Pook, P. K. & Rao, R. P. N. (1997). Deictic codes for the embodiment of cognition. *Behavioral and Brain Sciences,* 20, 723-767, ISSN: 0140-525X.

Behrami, B. (2003). Object property encoding and change blindness in multiple object tracking. *Visual Cognition,* 10, 949-963, ISSN: 1350-6285.

Chun, M. M. & Cavanagh, P. (1997). Seeing two as one: linking apparent motion and repetition blindness. *Psychological Science,* 8, 74-79, ISSN: 0956-7976.

Corbetta, M.; Shulman, G. L.; Miezin, F. M. & Petersen, S. E. (1995). Superior parietal cortex activation during spatial attention shifts and visual feature conjunction. *Science,* 270, 802-805, ISSN 0036-8075.

Cowan, N. (2001). The magical number 4 in short-term memory: A reconsideration of mental storage capacity. *Behavioral & Brain Sciences,* 24, 87-185, ISSN: 0140-525X.

Culham, J. C.; Brandt, S. A.; Cavanagh, P.; Kanwisher, N. G.; Dale, A. M. & Tootell, R. B. (1998). Cortical fMRI activation produced by attentive tracking of moving targets. *Journal of Neurophysiology,* 80, 2657-70, ISSN: 1522-1598.

Culham, J. C.; Cavanagh, P. & Kanwisher, N. G. (2001). Attention response functions: characterizing brain areas using fMRI activation during parametric variations of attentional load. *Neuron,* 32, 737-745, ISSN: 0896-6273.

Friedman-Hill, S. R.; Robertson, L. C. & Treisman, A. (1995). Parietal contributions to visual feature binding: evidence from a patient with bilateral lesions. *Science,* 269, 853-855, ISSN 0036-8075.

Horowitz, T. S. & Wolfe, J. M. (1998). Visual search has no memory. *Nature,* 394, 575-577, ISSN: 0028-0836.

Hummel, J. E. & Biederman, I. (1992). Dynamic binding in a neural network for shape recognition. *Psychological Review,* 99, 480-517, ISSN: 0033-295X.

Imaruoka T.; Saiki J. & Miyauchi S. (2005). Maintaining coherence of dynamic objects requires coordination of neural systems extended from anterior frontal to posterior parietal brain cortices. *NeuroImage* 26, 277-284, ISSN: 1053-8119.

Irwin, D. E. (1991). Information integration across saccadic eye movements. *Cognitive Psychology,* 23, 420-456, ISSN: 0010-0285.

Itti, L. & Koch, C. (2000). A saliency-based search mechanism for overt and covert shifts of visual attention. *Vision Research,* 40, 1489-1506, ISSN: 0042-6989.

Jovicich, J.; Peters, R. J.; Koch, C.; Braun, J.; Chang, L. & Ernst, T. (2001). Brain areas specific for attentional load in a motion-tracking task. *Journal of Cognitive Neuroscience,* 13, 1048-1058, ISSN: 0898-929X.

Kahneman, D.; Treisman, A. & Gibbs, B. (1992). The reviewing of object files: object-specific integration of information. *Cognitive Psychology, 24,* 175-219, ISSN: 0010-0285.

Kanwisher, N. G. (1991). Repetition blindness and illusory conjunction: Errors in binding visual types with visual tokens. *Journal of Experimental Psychology: Human Perception and Performance,* 17, 404-421, ISSN: 0096-1523.

Luck, S. J. & Vogel, E. K. (1997). The capacity of visual working memory for features and conjunctions. *Nature, 390,* 279-281, ISSN: 0028-0836.

Mitchell, K. J.; Johnson, M. K.; Raye, C. L. & D'Esposito, M. (2000). fMRI evidence of age-related hippocampal dysfunction in feature binding in working memory. *Cognitive Brain Research,* 10, 197-206, ISSN: 0926-6410.

Mohr H. M.; Goebel R. & Linden D. E. J. (2006). Content- and task-specific dissociations of frontal activity during maintenance and manipulation in visual working memory. *Journal of Neuroscience*, 26, 4465-4471, ISSN: 1529-2401.

Olson, I. R. & Jiang, Y. (2002). Is visual short-term memory object based? Rejection of the "strong-object" hypothesis. *Perception & Psychophysics*, 64, 1055-1067, ISSN: 0031-5117.

Pashler, H. (1988). Familiarity and visual change detection. *Perception and Psychophysics*, 44, 369-378, ISSN: 0031-5117.

Prabhakaran, V.; Narayanan, K.; Zhao, Z. & Gabrieli, J. D. (2000). Integration of diverse information in working memory within the frontal lobe. *Nature Neuroscience*, 3, 85-90, ISSN: 1097-6256.

Pylyshyn, Z. Q. & Storm, R. W. (1988). Tracking multiple independent targets: evidence for a parallel tracking mechanism. *Spatial Vision*, 3, 179-197, ISSN: 0169-1015.

Rensink, R. A. (2000). Seeing, sensing, and scrutinizing. *Vision Research*, 40, 1469-1487, ISSN: 0042-6989.

Rensink, R. A.; O'Regan, J. K. & Clark, J. J. (1997). To see or not to see: The need for attention to perceive changes in scenes. *Psychological Science*, 8, 368-373, ISSN: 0956-7976.

Saiki, J. (2002). Multiple-object permanence tracking: limitation in maintenance and transformation of perceptual objects. In J. Hyona, D. P. Munoz, W. Heide and R. Radach (Eds.), *The Brain's eye: neurobiological and clinical aspects of oculomotor research (Progress in Brain Research Vol. 140) (pp.133-148)*. Elsevier Science, ISBN: 0-444-51097-4, Amsterdam.

Saiki, J. (2003a). Feature binding in object-file representations of multiple moving items. *Journal of Vision*, 3, 6-21, ISSN: 1534-7362.

Saiki, J. (2003b). Spatiotemporal characteristics of dynamic feature binding in visual working memory. *Vision Research*, 43, 2107-2123, ISSN: 0042-6989.

Saiki, J. (2007). Feature binding in visual working memory. In N. Osaka, I. Rentschler, & I. Biederman (Eds.) *Object Recognition, Attention & Action (pp. 173-185)*. Springer - Verlag, ISBN 978-4-431-73018-7, Tokyo.

Saiki, J. & Hummel, J. E. (1998). Connectedness and the part-relation integration in shape perception. *Journal of Experimental Psychology: Human Perception and Performance*, 24, 227-251, ISSN: 0096-1523.

Saiki, J. & Miyatsuji, H. (2007). Feature binding in visual working memory evaluated by type identification paradigm. *Cognition. 102*, 49-83, ISSN: 0010-0277.

Saiki, J. & Miyatsuji, H. (in press). Estimated capacity of object files in visual short-term memory is not improved by retrieval cueing. *Journal of Vision*, ISSN: 1534-7362.

Saiki, J. (in press). Functional roles of memory for feature-location binding in event perception: Investigation with spatiotemporal visual search. *Visual Cognition*, ISSN: 1350-6285.

Scholl, B. J. & Pylyshyn, Z. W., (1998). Tracking multiple items through occlusion: Clues to visual objecthood. *Cognitive Psychology*, 38, 259-290, ISSN: 0010-0285.

Shafritz, K. M.; Gore, J. C. & Marois, R. (2002). The role of the parietal cortex in visual feature binding. *Proceedings of the National Academy of Sciences, U.S.A., 99*, 10917-10922, ISSN: 1091-6490.

Song, J. H. & Jiang, Y. (2006). Visual working memory for simple and complex features: an fMRI study. *NeuroImage*, 30, 963-972, ISSN: 1053-8119.

Sperling, G. (1960). The information available in brief visual presentations. *Psychological Monographs,* 74(11) [whole No. 498]), 29.

Takahama, S.; Saiki, J.; Misaki, M. & Miyauchi, S. (2005). The necessity of feature-location binding activates specific brain regions in visual working memory task: an event-related fMRI study. *Society for Neuroscience Annual Meeting Abstract.*

Tipper, S. P.; Weaver, B.; Jerreat, L. M. & Burak, A. L. (1994). Object-based and environment-based inhibition of return of visual selection. *Journal of Experimental Psychology: Human Perception and Performance,* 20, 478-499, ISSN: 0096-1523.

Todd, J. J. & Marois, R. (2004). Capacity limit of visual short-term memory in human posterior parietal cortex. *Nature,* 428, 751-754, ISSN: 0028-0836.

Towse, J. N.; Hitch, G. J. & Hutton, U. (2000). On the interpretation of working memory span in adults. *Memory and Cognition,* 28, 341-348, ISSN: 0090-502X.

Treisman, A. (1988). Features and objects: The fourteenth Bartlett memorial lecture. *Quarterly Journal of Experimental Psychology: Human Experimental Psychology,* 40A, 201-237, ISSN: 1747-0218.

Treisman, A. (1999). Solutions to the binding problem: Progress through controversy and convergence. *Neuron,* 24, 105-110, ISSN: 0896-6273.

Treisman, A. & Schmidt, H. (1982). Illusory conjunctions in the perception of objects. *Cognitive Psychology,* 14, 107-141, ISSN: 0010-0285.

Valdes-Sosa, M.; Cobo, A. & Pinilla, T. (1998). Transparent motion and object-based attention. *Cognition,* 66, B13-B23, ISSN: 0010-0277.

Verstraten, F. A. J.; Cavanagh, P. & Labianca, A. T. (2000). Limits of attentive tracking reveal temporal properties of attention. *Vision Research,* 40, 3651-3664, ISSN: 0042-6989.

Vogel, E. K. & Machizawa, M. G. (2004). Neural activity predicts individual differences in visual working memory capacity. *Nature,* 428, 748-751, ISSN: 0028-0836.

Vogel, E. K.; Woodman, G. F. & Luck, S. J. (2001). Storage of features, conjunctions and objects in visual working memory. *Journal of Experimental Psychology: Human Perception and Performance,* 27, 92-114, ISSN: 0096-1523.

Wheeler, M. E. & Treisman, A.M. (2002). Binding in short-term visual memory. *Journal of Experimental Psychology: General, 131,* 48-64, ISSN: 0096-3445.

Xu, Y. (2002). Limitations of object-based feature encoding in visual short-term memory. *Journal of Experimental Psychology: Human Perception and Performance,* 28, 458-468, ISSN: 0096-1523.

Xu, Y., & Chun, M. M. (2006). Dissociable neural mechanisms supporting visual short-term memory for objects. *Nature, 440,* 91-95, ISSN: 0028-0836.

13

Ranking and Extraction of Relevant Single Words in Text

João Ventura and Joaquim Ferreira da Silva
DI/FCT Universidade Nova de Lisboa
Portugal

1. Introduction

The extraction of keywords is currently a very important technique used in several applications, for instance, the characterization of document topics. In this case, by extracting the right keywords on a query, one could easily know what documents should be read and what documents should be put aside. However, while the automatic extraction of multiword has been an active search field by the scientific community, the automatic extraction of single words, or unigrams, has been basically ignored due to its intrinsic difficulty. Meanwhile, it is easy to demonstrate that in a process of keyword extraction, leaving unigrams out impoverishes, in a certain extent, the quality of the final result. Take the following example:

> *The budgets have deteriorate due to the action of automatic stabilisers and also because the discretionary fiscal expansionary measures of some Member-States who had no room for manouvre. In general, and despite budgetary pressures, public investment has remained static or increased slightly, except in Germany, Greece and Portugal.*

According to the previous example, one can easily identify several relevant terms. But, if in one hand, multiword terms such as "automatic stabilisers", "discretionary fiscal expansionary measures ", "budgetary pressures" and "public investment" would be easily captured by the modern multiword extractors, uniword terms like "budgets", "Member-States", "Germany", "Greece" and "Portugal" would not. However, a simple count demonstrates that in this example there are almost as many multiword as uniword terms. In fact, the relevant unigrams of a document are usually part of the important topics in it, as it may also be the relevant multiwords, and in the previous example, terms such as "Germany", "Greece" and "Portugal" should be considered extremely important because they are names of countries.

In this chapter we will look into the problematic of unigram extraction, reviewing some of the current state-of-the-art techniques and comparing its results with two metrics proposed by us. We'll also review a new technique proposed by us based on the syllable analysis that is able of improving the results in an unorthodox way. Finally, we shall present the "Islands method", a technique also proposed by us that allows one to decide about the *boolean* relevancy of a certain word.

2. Current state-of-the-art methods for unigram extraction

The current state-of-the-art approaches can be subdivided into several groups. On one side we have the linguistic approaches. These approaches are able to extract information from documents using linguistic information (morphological, syntactic or semantic) about a given text. Usually, this kind of information is obtained from the use of grammars like in (Afrin, 2001), or from annotated texts. Although there are reliable automatic techniques for text annotation or grammar building, those kinds of approaches are usually language dependent, making the generalization of such methods a very difficult aim. Other linguistic approaches, like the one used in (Heid, 2000), extracts relevant terms using regular expressions. However, in that work the author, by using 20 prefixes and 20 suffixes carefully extracted from German language shows how dependent from the language his method is.

In the same line we have the approaches based on knowledge. Those approaches are usually associated with ontologies where the main idea is to get a representative model of the specific reality of the analyzed documents. A simple example for extraction of relevant information using knowledge based approaches can be associated with the knowledge of the structure of documents to, for instance, extract keywords from the titles and abstracts of scientific documents. More complex examples, like (Gao & Zhao, 2005), are able to identify frauds on emails. However, these kinds of approaches are also quite limiting, mainly because the creation of ontologies isn't straightforward, and ontologies are something very specific to a certain subject and can't be easily generalized. For instance, in the case of keyword extraction from titles of scientific texts, one has to know exactly the structure of those documents in order to identify where the titles and abstracts are. On the other hand it's almost impossible to use those kinds of methods on documents without apparent structure.

Other authors have also tried to use Neural Networks to do unigram extraction. A Neural Network is a programming model that resembles, in a certain way, the biological neural model. Applied to information extraction, the most common application is based on a user's query answering. Made simple, a user queries a set of documents and the neural net verifies if the user query is relevant in a certain document or not. If it is, that document is retrieved and presented to the user. In (Das, 2002) a technique based on Neural Networks is presented. The basic idea is that each of the nodes (or neurons) has a user's query word associated with it. For each word on an input scientific paper, the nodes which have query words that exist on the input paper are raised to a higher level of *energy*. This process continues until the neural network stabilizes. From this, one can see which nodes have higher energy levels for that document and thus, more relevant to the query. However, also this kind of approach has problems. Neural Networks are usually slow while building because of backpropagation calculations. In this way, a neural net handling 15.000 words, the average size of a single scientific paper, or 700 distinct words would be too slow, considering you would have to create a neural network each time a user makes a query, multiplying it for the amount of documents where the user would want to search in.

Finally, following the same line as the previous ones, we also have the hybrid approaches that aim to bring the best of all the other into a single one. In (Feldman et al., 2006) the authors are using grammars in conjunction with statistical methods in order to extract information from web pages and convert them to semantic web pages. In that paper the rules of the grammar used were manually created and the probabilities used were extracted

from an annotated corpus. Also in this case there is overdependence again on something: the annotated corpus and the manual creation of the grammar.
At last, following a different line than the previous methods, we have the statistical based approaches. The main advantages in those kinds of approaches are the faster implementation and usage of the methods and the independence in relation to the language used on the texts, in relation to the structure used and to the context of the documents tested. In the next three subsections we will review three of the most known statistical approaches for information retrieval: Luhn's frequency criterion, Tf-Idf method and Zhou's & Slater method.

2.1 Luhn's frequency criterion

Luhn, in one of the first published papers concerning relevant unigram extraction techniques (Luhn, 1958), suggests a method for the classification of unigrams based on the frequency of ocurrence of terms. According to the author,

> *"… the justification for measure the relevance of a word by the frequency of ocurrence is based on the fact that a writer usually repeats some words when arguing and when elaborates certain aspects of a subject…."*

Luhn also suggested that the words with a very high frequency of ocurrence are usually considered common words and unfrequent words could be considered rare, both cases being unrelevant words. Although this approach seems quite intuitive, is not necessarily true. During our research with corpora of different languages, among the 100 more frequent words, in average, about 35% could be considered relevant. Table 1 lists some of those words:

Word	Rank	Frequency
Comission	28	1909
Member-States	38	1378
Countries	41	1219
European	55	874
Union	92	515
Europe	99	463

Table 1. Some words among the 100 more frequent ones in an English corpus

Considering the fact that in average the corpora used in our work has about 500.000 words, from which about 24.000 are distinct, one can easily understand that with this criterion possibly some or all of the words listed in table 1 would be thrown away. Luhn's criterion becomes, in this case, quite restrictive. And if we consider the fact that the words in table 1 came from European Union texts, one can see the kind of the information that would be rejected. Words like "European" and "Union" are preety descritive of the texts.
Other problem with this approach has to do with the thresholds. How can one find the threshold between very frequent words and relevant words? Or between the relevant words and rare words? Finally, Luhn considers that the relevant words are those not very frequent nor very rare. Again, this may be a problem because not all of the words between those thresholds are important. Luhn solves partially this problem using a list of common words that should be reject on the final list. But Luhn idealized its method for texts with an average

of 700 distinct words (scientific papers) and it would be impracticable to mantain a list of common words handling texts with 24.000 distinct words.

2.2 Tf-Idf

Tf-Idf, Term Frequency - Inverse Document Frequency (Salton & Buckley, 1987), is a metric for calculating the relevance of terms in documents, very used in Information Retrieval and Text-Mining. Essentially, this technique measures how important a certain word is on a document regarding other documents in the same collection. Basically, a word gets more important in a certain document the more it occurs in that document. But if that word occurs in other documents, its importance decreases. Words that are very frequent on a single document tend to be more valued than common words that occur on more documents, like articles or prepositions.

The formal procedure for the implementation of Tf-Idf changes slightly from application to application, but the most common approach was the one used in this work. Generally, the calculation of Tf-Idf is made in separate, calculating the Tf and Idf components separately, and finally multiplying both components to get the final Tf-Idf value.

Tf component (term frequency) simply measures the number of times a word occurs on a certain document. That count is then normalized to prevent word on very long documents to get higher Tf values. Equation 1 measures the probability that a term i occurs in a document j.

$$Tf_{ij} = \frac{n_{i,j}}{\sum_k n_{k,j}}, \tag{1}$$

where $n_{i,j}$ is the number of times the term i occurs in a document j and then it is divided by the total of words in document j.

Idf component measures the general relevance of a given term. Equation 2 consists in the count of the number of documents that a term t_i occurs.

$$Idf_i = \log\frac{|D|}{|\{d_j : t_i \in d_j\}|}, \tag{2}$$

where $|D|$ represents the total number of documents in the collection and $\{d_j : t_i \in d_j\}$ the number of documents where the term t_i occurs.

Tf-idf (equation 3) is then the multiplication of the two previous equations.

$$TfIdf_{i,j} = Tf_{i,j} * Idf_i. \tag{3}$$

However, we must consider that the main goal of this method is to analyze the relevance of a word in a document regarding other documents, instead of analyzing the relevance of a word in corpora. To do that, we had to change slightly the method. Basically, and because the corpora used for research were made from single documents, we've adapted the method to give a word the maximum Tf-Idf found in all methods. In this way, we can use Tf-Idf to evaluate a word's relevance on corpora.

Unfortunately, also Tf-Idf has problems. Similarly to Luhn's frequency criterion, Tf-Idf harms the very frequent relevant words because they tend to exist in almost all documents, and so, the Idf component lowers the final Tf-Idf value. On the other side, the Idf component also damages certain words by not taking into account the probabilities of

occurrence of a word in other documents. For instance, if you have three documents, and a certain word occurs 100 times in one document, and just once in the other documents, the Idf component gets equal to zero when it's pretty clear that that word is, probably, very relevant in the document where it occurs 100 times. If that same word occurs 1 or 50 times in the other two documents it's almost irrelevant to Tf-Idf, but however, occurring 1 or 50 times in those two other documents means different things about that same word.
At last, the Idf component also has the problem of benefiting rare words because if, for instance, in a document exists a unique orthographical error, it gets the maximum Idf value available.

2.3 Zhou & Slater method

Zhou & Slater method is a very recent metric proposed in (Zhou & Slater, 2003) for calculating the relevance of unigrams. It is assumed, in some way similarly with Tf-Idf and Luhn's criterion, that the relevant words can be found in certain areas of the texts either by being part of the local topics, either by being related to the local contexts, therefore forming clusters in those areas. On the other hand, common and less relevant words should occur randomly in all the text, therefore not forming significant clusters.
This technique, being an improvement and extension over the technique proposed in (Ortuño et al., 2002) measures the relevance of a word accordingly to the position of occurrence of each word in texts.
Starting with a list L_w={-1, t_1, t_2, ..., t_m, n}, where t_i represents the position of the i-th occurrence of the word w in the text and n represents the total number of words in the same text, we obtain $\hat{u}$ that is basically the average separation between successive occurrences of word w.

$$\hat{u} = \frac{n+1}{m+1}. \tag{4}$$

Next step consists in the calculation of the average separation of each occurrence of the word w, using equation 5.

$$d(t_i.) = \frac{t_{i+1} - t_{i-1}}{2}, \qquad i = 1, \ldots, m. \tag{5}$$

On equation 4 we have the average distance between all successive occurrences of word w. With equation 5 we get the local information for each point t_i, meaning that we get the average separation between each occurrence of the word w in the text.
The next step consists in the identification of the points on L_w which form part of clusters. Basically a point forms part of a cluster if its average distance $d(t_i)$ (average distance between the previous and next occurrence of the same word) is less than the average distance between occurrences ($\hat{u}$). In this way, we get $\delta(t_i)$ which, according to equation 6, identifies which points t_i belong to clusters.

$$\delta(t_i) = \begin{cases} 1, & if\ d(t_i) < \hat{u} \\ 0, & otherwise \end{cases}. \tag{6}$$

In a parallel way, using equation 7 we get $v(t_i)$ that represents the local excess of words relating position t_i. It basically consists in the normalized distance to the average value of distance.

$$v(t_i) = \frac{\hat{u} - d(t_i)}{\hat{u}}. \tag{7}$$

By equation 7, the less the value of $d(t_i)$ (or the closer the t_i points are), the bigger the value of $v(t_i)$ because, as stated before, the purpose of this technique is to value the formation of clusters.

$$\Gamma(w) = \frac{1}{m} \sum_{i=1}^{m} \delta(t_i) * v(t_i). \tag{8}$$

Therefore, starting from the list L_w={-1, t_1, t_2, ..., t_m, n}, we get the score of the word w using equation 8. Being in $\delta(t_i)$ the information about whether t_i belongs or not to a cluster, and in $v(t_i)$ the normalized distance to the average distance, $\Gamma(w)$ gets the value of $v(t_i)$ when t_i belongs to a cluster and the value of zero otherwise.

Although this is a very efficient and ingenious method, it has also the same problems as the previous ones regarding the very frequent relevant words. In a general way, all the methods that assume that relevant words occur only in certain areas of the texts suffer from that problem. Although there is a certain veracity in it, it damages the very frequent relevant words because they tend to occur allover the text and not only on local contexts. Also, by dealing exclusively with significant clusters, the relevant words with low frequency of occurrence are also very damaged by this method.

3. An alternative contribution

In this section we will present a set of innovative alternatives to the previous presented methods. We will present two new metrics recently proposed by us (Ventura & Silva, 2007) for the calculation of the relevance of unigrams, the measure Score and SPQ. We will also present a new research field based on the syllable analysis of the words and finally we will present a new unigram extractor that we've called "Islands Method".

3.1 A word about relevance

Starting with a corpus composed of several documents, one of the objectives of this work is to try to understand which words are relevant and which words are not. However, using purely statistical methods, this kind of classification isn't always straightforward or even exact because, although the notion of relevance is a concept easy to understand, normally there's no consensus about the frontier that separates relevance from non-relevance. For instance, words like "Republic" or "London" have significative relevance and words like "or" and "since" have no relevance at all, but what about words like "read", "terminate" and "next"? These kind of words are problematic because usually there's no consensus about their semantic value. So, there is a fuzzy frontier about the relevance of words. In this way, regarding the context of this work, we've decided to adopt a conservative approach and classify as relevant only those words with inquestionable semantic value.

3.2 The Score measure

One of the first steps for the extraction of relevant unigrams consists in obtaining a list ranked by the potential relevance of each of the words in a corpus. This list measures therefore the relative relevance of each word regarding other words occurring in a corpus, so, a word ranked higher in the list is considered more relevant than a word occurring in the bottom of the list. To do this we've developed a new metric where the main idea is that the relevant words usually have a special preference to relate with a small group of other words. In this way, it is possible to use a metric that measures the importance of a word in a corpus based on the study of the relation that that word has with the words that follow it. We have denominated that measure the successor's score of a word *w*, that is $Sc_{suc}(w)$.

$$Sc_{suc}(w) = \sqrt{\frac{1}{\|\gamma\|-1}\sum_{y_i\in\gamma}\left(\frac{p(w,y_i)-p(w,.)}{p(w,.)}\right)^2}. \qquad (9)$$

In equation 9, γ is the set of distinct words in the corpus and $||\gamma||$ stands for the size of that set; $p(w\ y_i)$ represents the probability of y_i to be a successor of word *w*; $p(w,.)$ gives the average probability of the successors of *w*, which is given by:

$$p(w,.) = \frac{1}{\|\gamma\|}\sum_{y_i\in\gamma} p(w,y_i) \qquad p(w,y_i) = \frac{f(w,y_i)}{N}, \qquad (10)$$

where *N* stands for the number of words occurred in the corpus and $f(w, yi)$ is the frequency of bigram (w, yi) in the same corpus. Resuming the mathematical formalism, $Sc_{suc}(w)$ in equation 9 is given by a standard deviation *normalized* by the average probability of the successors of *w*. It measures therefore the variation of the current word's preference to appear before the rest of the words in the corpus. The higher values will appear for the words that have more diversified frequencies with the words that follow it, and the lowest values will appear in the words that have less variations of frequency with words that follow it. Similarly, we measure the preference that a word has to the words that precede it using the following metric that we've denominated predecessor's score, that is $Sc_{pre}(w)$.

$$Sc_{pre}(w) = \sqrt{\frac{1}{\|\gamma\|-1}\sum_{y_i\in\gamma}\left(\frac{p(y_i,w)-p(.,w)}{p(.,w)}\right)^2}, \qquad (11)$$

where the meanings of $p(y_i,w)$ and $p(.\ ,w)$ are obvious.

So, using both equations 9 and 11 through the arithmetic average, we will obtain the metric that allows us to classify the relevance of a word based on its predecessors and successors. This metric is simply denominated $Sc(w)$.

$$Sc(w) = \frac{Sc_{pre}(w) + Sc_{suc}(w)}{2}. \qquad (12)$$

It can be seen by the previous expressions that Score measure gives better values to a word that as the tendency to attach to a restricted set of successor and predecessor words. However, it can be easily noted that this metric benefits extremely the word with the frequency of 1, because when a unigram occurs only once in a corpus, the relation with its successor and predecessor is unique, or in other words, complete. In this way, Score interprets that relation as a strong correlation, and so care must be taken to pre-process the corpus in order to remove the unigrams with frequency 1. This situation doesn't mean that frequency affects directly results; the correlation in the cases of frequency 1 is effectively high and that occurs because we're using a standard deviation. In any statistical approaches, higher frequencies represent better reliability on the results quality. For low frequencies it can be assumed that the results, whatever they are, can't be considered statistically conclusive. Table 2 shows some examples of *Sc(.)* values and ranking positions for the words of an English corpus made from documents of the European Union. It has about half million words and there are 18,172 distinct ones. We've studied the words that occur at least 3 times in the corpus. As one can see, the more common words like "the", "and" and "of" are positioned lower in the ranking while words with semantic value are positioned upper in the list.

Word	*Sc* (.)	Rank
pharmacopoeia	135.17	48
oryctolagus	134.80	64
embryonic	132.67	76
of	24.15	6627
the	19.34	6677
and	10.82	6696

Table 2. Some examples of *Sc(.)* values and ranking positions for words in an English corpus

3.3 SPQ measure

By observing some characteristics of the unigrams, it was also verified that the words considered relevant usually have some interesting characteristics about the number of predecessors and successors. For instance, with a Portuguese corpus of half million words (also from European Union documents), it could be noted that the relevant word "comissão" (commission) occurred 1.909 times in the corpus, with 41 distinct predecessors and 530 distinct successors. Also, the relevant word "Europa" (Europe) occurred 466 times in the corpus, with 29 distinct predecessors and 171 distinct successors. In both cases, most of the predecessors are articles or prepositions such as "a", "na" e "da" (the, on and of). In fact, function words (articles, prepositions, etc.) show no special preference to a small set of words: one may say that they populate the entire corpus.

The morphosyntactic sequence <article> <name> <verb> is very frequent in the case of Latin languages such as Portuguese, Spanish, Italian and French, among others. In these cases, given that there are more verbs than articles, it is natural that names have more successors than predecessors. Looking at table 3, we can find some examples of morphosyntactic sequences, and note that the list of articles is usually small while the list of verbs is more extensive.

Morphosyntactic sequences
a comissão lançou
a comissão considera
a comissão europeia
pela comissão tratada

Table 3. Example of morphosyntactic sequences in Portuguese

Following this reasoning, we have proposed another statistic metric that measures the importance of a word based on the quotient between the number of its distinct successors and the number of its distinct predecessors. We have called it *SPQ* (Successor-Predecessor Quotient).

$$SPQ(w) = \frac{Nsuc(w)}{Nant(w)}, \tag{13}$$

where *Nsuc(w)* and *Nant(w)* represent the number of distinct successors and predecessors of word *w* in the corpus.

However, although both presented metrics (Sc and SPQ) measure the relevance of words, in a language-independent basis, when we tested SPQ, the results were better for the Portuguese and Spanish corpora than for the English one. However, assuming this, it may be preferably to use this metric if one is working only with Latin languages (see results in section 4).

3.4 Syllable Analysis

Considering again table 2 in section 3.2, one can find that from those 6 words, 3 are relevant and 3 are not. It is easy to conclude that the relevant words ("pharmacopoeia", "oryctolagus" and "embryonic") are, in fact, larger than the non-relevant ("of", "the" and "and"). We could build a metric in order to favour larger words as they appear to be more relevant, but, as we will see, it is preferable to consider the number of syllables instead of the length of the words. For instance, the probability of occurrence of the definite article "the" in oral or textual speeches is identical to its Portuguese counterpart article "o". However, there is a 3-to-1 relation about the number of characters, while the number of syllables is identical in both languages (one syllable). Thus, a metric based on the length of words would value the word "the" 3 times more relevant than the word "o", which wouldn't be correct. Using a metric based on the number of syllables, that distortion would not occur.

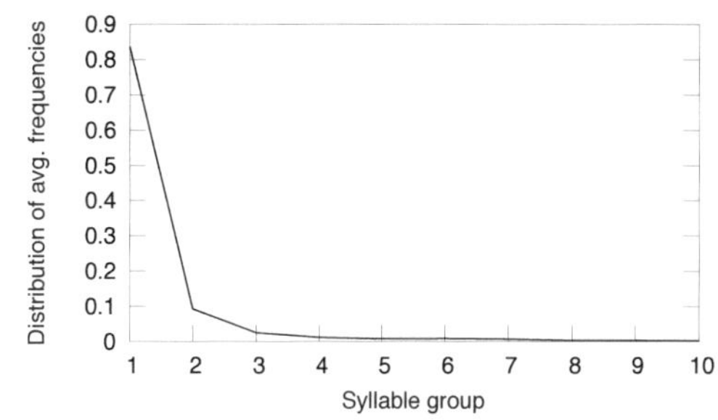

(a) Portuguese Corpus

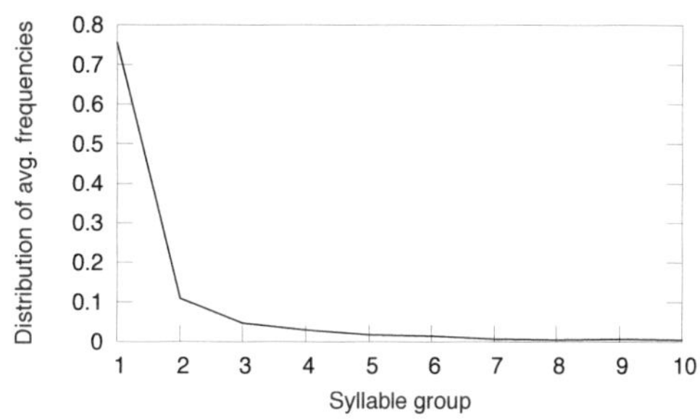

(b) English Corpus

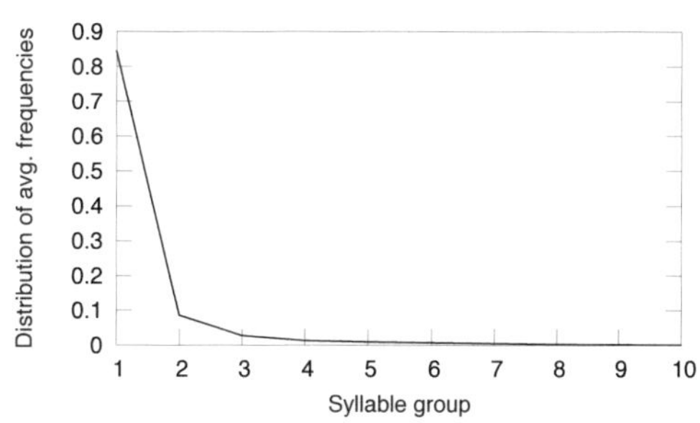

(c) Spanish Corpus

Figure 1. Normalized distribution of the average frequency of words occurrence for each syllable group, for all the three researched corpora

Figure 1 shows the distribution of the average frequency of words occurrence for each syllable group for all the corpora researched: Portuguese, Spanish and English; the values are normalized such that its sum is 1. Each one of the graphics in figure 1 represents, basically, the average frequency of occurrence of the words belonging to each syllable group, i.e., having that exact number of syllables. Looking at those graphics it is possible to see that the words with one syllable occur more frequently than the words with two syllables, followed by the words with two syllables, etc. So, the average frequency of occurrence of the words in each syllable group decreases with the increase of the number of syllables. This phenomenon is certainly related to the economy of speech. It is necessary that the words that occur more often are the ones easier to pronounce, otherwise the discourses would be too long. The words having 1 syllable are usually articles and other function words like "and", "the", "of" and "or" (in Portuguese "e", "o", "de" and "ou"); because they occur more frequently in texts, they must be easier and faster to pronounce.

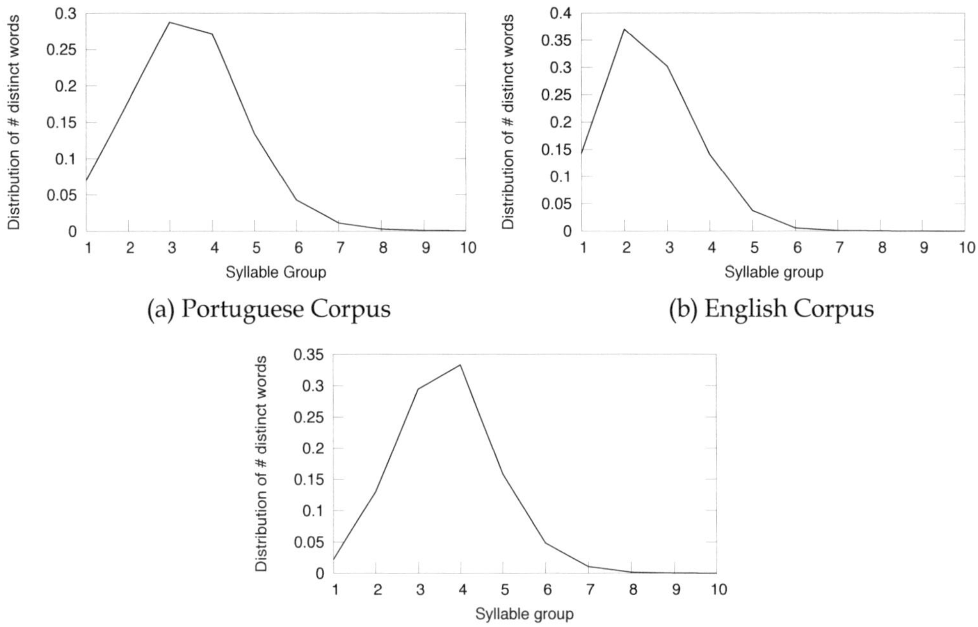

(a) Portuguese Corpus (b) English Corpus

(c) Spanish Corpus

Figure 2. Normalized distribution of the number of distinct words for each syllable group, for all the three researched corpora

Figure 2 shows the distribution of the number of distinct words for each syllable group, for the English, Portuguese and Spanish corpora; the values are normalized such that its sum is 1. The interpretation of this curve is beyond the domain of this work, but without a secure certainty, we believe that these distributions are probably connected to the number of distinct words that may be formed preferably with the least number of syllables, considering the legal sequences that may be formed in each language. In fact, the number of words that may exist with 2 or more syllables is certainly greater than the number of words with 1 syllable. In the Portuguese case, for instance, the maximum peak occurs in the 3 syllables group, while in the Spanish case the peak occurs in the 4 syllable group and the English peak in the 2 syllable group. This is probably because the Portuguese language is usually more restrictive than the English language concerning the possible number of character combinations for each syllable, needing to occupy the 3 syllables group. The same can be said regarding the Spanish corpus and the 4 syllable group. Another possible explanation for this phenomenon can be related to table 4, which shows the average number of letters of the words in each syllable group. In this way, we can see that, in average, the English words with 1 syllable have 4.7 letters while the Portuguese and Spanish words with 1 syllable have, respectively, 3.7 and 3.9 letters.

Corpus	1-S	2-S	3-S	4-S	5-S	6-S	7-S	8-S	9-S	10-S
Portuguese	3.7	5.5	7.6	9.7	11.8	14.0	16.2	18.4	21.1	27.0
English	4.7	6.8	8.9	10.8	12.9	15.5	18.8	23.3	22.0	24.0
Spanish	3.9	5.6	7.5	9.5	11.5	13.6	15.7	18.3	20.6	22.0

Table 4. Average number of letters for each syllable group for all the researched corpora

Also, according with table 4 the English language has in average more letters on the 8 first syllable groups than the other two languages. If it has more letters per syllable, it is natural that more combinations can be made with less syllables and maybe that is why the English languages reaches its peak before the other two languages. The Spanish and Portuguese languages have the same kind of graphic on the first two syllable groups and a slight inversion on the 3 and 4 syllable group which, besides language restrictions, can also be explained by the data in table 4.

Thus, figure 2 shows us that in the case of the English language (the other languages can be analysed in a similar way) there is more diversity of words with 2 syllables. In the 1-syllable group we can find, above all, function words like articles and prepositions where there is no semantic value. On the other side, very rare words, with many syllables, have semantic contents which are too specific to be considered relevant and broad simultaneously. In the case of the Portuguese and Spanish languages they have their peak respectively in the 3-syllable group and 4-syllable group. Still, both Portuguese and Spanish graphics are quite similar which reflects the fact that both languages are descendent from a common language.

Figure 3 shows us three graphics that represents the importance of each syllable group for each language. For each syllable group, importance is determined by the corresponding values used in the graphics of figure 2 (the Normalized distribution of the number of distinct words) divided by the corresponding value used in the graphics of figure 1 (Normalized distribution of the average frequency of words occurrence). If the distributions on figure 3 were used to classify words on texts, the 4 syllable group for the Portuguese and Spanish case and the 3 syllable group for the English case would be the most important group, following by the other groups accordingly to the distributions.

Although this method appears at first sight to be language dependent as it deals with very specific linguistic information, in fact it is not; that would be very disadvantageous because we want the methods to be as independent from any factors as possible . However we must mention that all the necessary information to obtain the previous distributions can be obtained directly from the research corpora. This way, if a corpus is sufficiently representative of a language, syllable distributions can be obtained, independently of the language.

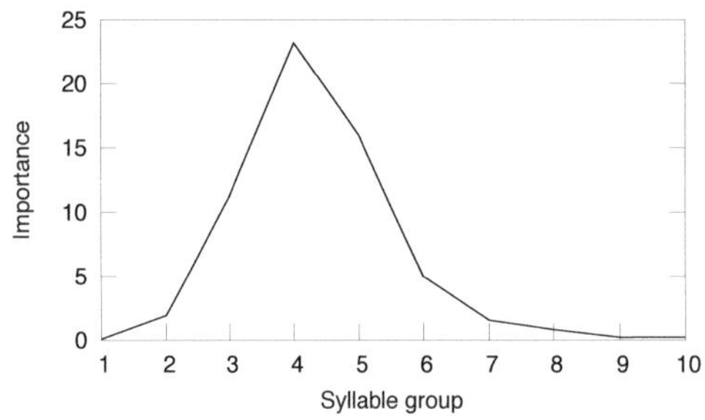

(a) Portuguese Corpus

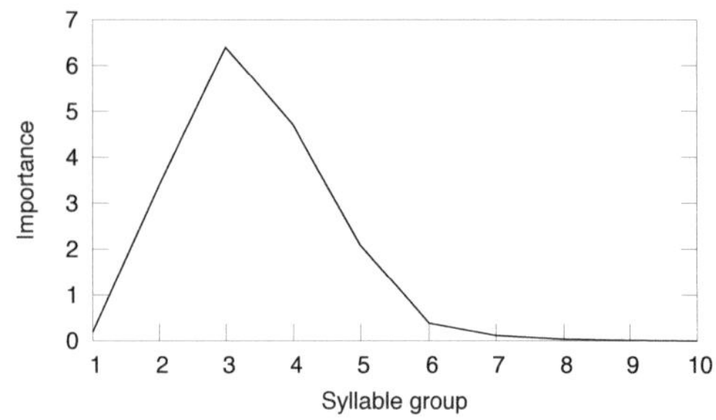

(b) English Corpus

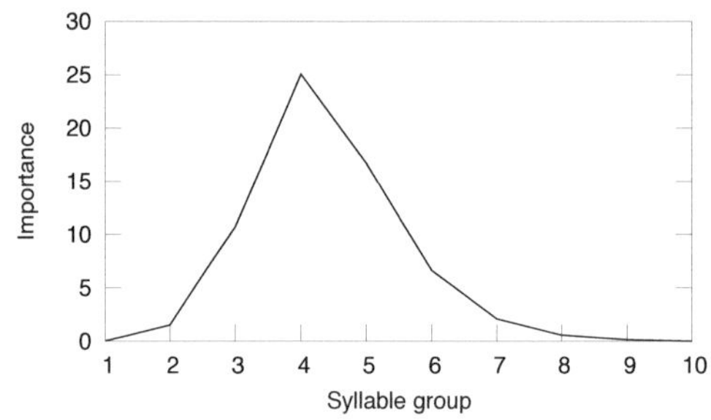

(c) Spanish Corpus

Figure 3. Importance of each syllable group, for all the three researched corpora

3.5 The Islands method – A unigram extractor

Although all the previous methods presented here (including the ones stated in section 2 – state-of-the-art techniques) are capable of identifying to a certain extent the relevant words in texts or corpora, they are, however, incapable of making decisions about the true relevance of words. The problem is that all the previous methods can only create relevance rankings, from which we can only identify, for instance, that a certain word on the top of the list must be more relevant than a word on the bottom. However, in certain situations it may be necessary to know if a given word is truly relevant (like Boolean true or false) instead of knowing that this word is more relevant than X, Y and Z. This kind of certainty is absolutely necessary for applications like Documents-ID where we desire for a set of words that truly describes a document or set of documents.

On a first analysis one could consider that all the words on top of the ranking are relevant, and that the words on the bottom are not. But this causes two kinds of problems. The first is to define the frontier that separates the relevant from the non-relevant words. Where should this frontier be? If it is too high in the list, we'd probably miss relevant words to non-relevance. If it was too low it would be the opposite. The other problem is that although the words in the ranking can be generically compared among each other, i.e, we can say that a certain word X in the top of the rank is more relevant than a certain word Y in the bottom, we can't say that Y is not relevant at all even if it is at the very bottom of the list. This is because while X has a high score of relevance and so must be very relevant in all the text, Y may be very relevant only in a local context, getting a smaller score therefore being in the final of the *general* relevance list. This can even mean that Y is truly relevant in a local context while X is not relevant in the global context!

As far as we know, there is no such method to extract relevant words on this kind of basis. We present a method that we have designated "Islands method" which allows us to extract relevant words from a text, based on a relevance ranking previously generated.
Following the same line of idea as the Score method, the main assumption of the Islands methods is that a word, to be considered relevant, must be more important than the words in its neighbourhood. This means that each word is tested in its local context, whether this context is a paragraph or even the entirety of a text. Then, recurring to the relevance rankings given by the previous methods we are able to compare the importance of all the words in a text.
In our approach we start by considering the weight that each neighbours of a word has in terms of frequency. The idea is that the more a certain word co-occurs with another, the more important that connection is. We then proceed to the calculation of a weighted average, based on the frequency of co-occurrence. Then, if a word has its score greater than 90% of the weighted average of its neighbours, we assume it as relevant. Equations 14 and 15 measure the weighted averages of, respectively, the predecessors and successors of a word.

$$Avg_{pre}(w) = \sum_{y_i \in \{predecs\ of\ w\}} p(y_i, w) * r(y_i) \quad , \tag{14}$$

$$Avg_{suc}(w) = \sum_{y_i \in \{succecs of\ w\}} p(w, y_i) * r(y_i) \quad , \tag{15}$$

where $p(y_i,w)$ means the probability of occurrence of the bigram (y_i,w) and $r(y_i)$ is the relevance value given by the generic $r(.)$ metric. The same must be considered for equation 15. Thus, accordingly to the Islands criterion, a word w is considered relevant *if and only if*:

$$r(w) \geq 0{,}9.max(Avg_{pre}(w), Avg_{suc}(w)) \, . \tag{16}$$

As it shall be presented in the next section, the results for this method are very encouraging. Words which are somehow "isolated" in terms of score in the relevance rankings in relation with its neighbours are easily considered relevant. Words that are part of relevant *n-grams* (bigrams, trigrams, and so on) aren't easily excluded because of the 90% factor on the criterion.

4. Results

In this section we present the results concerning all the previous mentioned methods and techniques including the ones stated in section 2, state-of-the-art. We will briefly describe the used corpora, as well as the criterion used to evaluate the quality of the rankings generated by the methods. Then we shall present the results concerning the unigram extractor (Islands method) and at last we shall analyse the application of the syllable method over the techniques and metrics discussed.

4.1 The test corpora

The corpora used in this work, as already mentioned, are composed of several documents extracted from the Portal for the Access to the European Union law (http://eur-lex.europa.eu/). In this site we can find an enormous repository of documents and communications of public interest in the domain of the European Union.

We have extracted documents in three different languages and created three different corpora. The Portuguese corpus is made of 43 documents, and has about half million words from which about 24.000 are distinct. The English corpus is made of 40 documents, having also about half million words, from which about 18.000 are distinct. The Spanish corpus is made of 41 documents; it has about 550.000 words, from which 22.000 are distinct.

4.2 Test sets

The test sets are subsets of the tested corpora from which certain words are classified as relevant and other as irrelevant in order to test the quality of the methods listed in this work. Table 5 lists, for convenience, the several test sets and their description.

Test Name	Description
A	100 more frequent words.
B	200 random words from the 1.000 more frequent ones.
C	300 random words from the 3.000 more frequent ones.
D	200 random words with frequency of ocurrence greater than 1.
E	Includes all the previous ones.

Table 5. List of test sets and their description

Although the "D" test set seems sufficient to evaluate the efficiency of the metrics because it uses a set of words independent from the frequency, the other tests serve to add information about the behaviour of all the metrics in specific areas of frequency. Thus, with the test set "A" we pretend to evaluate the efficiency on the very frequent words, where on the contrary to the common sense, we can find several relevant words pretty illustrative of the corpora general topics. With test sets "B" and "C" we pretend to evaluate the metrics on the intermediate areas of frequency. With test set "D" we pretend to have a broader view of the methods ignoring words of frequency 1 that are usually orthographical errors. Finally "E" test aims to evaluate the metrics in a even broader view with a higher percentage of frequent words.

4.3 Evaluation criterion for relevance rankings

As mentioned previously, when considering relevance rankings of words there is a fuzzy area of relevance where, in a certain way, the relevance of certain words may be considered dubious. We've chosen to follow a conservative approach, considering relevant only those words that are unquestionable relevant. That said, after obtaining the relevance ranks the task was to evaluate their quality. Although this seems something very simple, the fact is that we didn't find any published approach to do this. For example, on the papers we had to research, although those authors have dealt with relevance rankings, it doesn't seem they have quantified their quality results, only showing the rank position of some words. For this work, we had to create a new method to quantify the quality of a relevance ranking. It is made in the following way: first, an evaluation of a certain method has to be made. After that we have the relevance ranking ordered by score. Then the following criterion is applied: if all the words manually considered relevant are in the top of the rank, there's 100% of efficiency. On the other hand, if none is on the top of the list, we get 0% of efficiency. If, for example, we have 30 relevant words, but only 25 of them are in the 30 first positions of the ranking, we get an efficiency of $25/30 \approx 83.3\%$. In the case when the number of relevant words is greater than the number of irrelevant words, we invert the case: instead of measure the quality by the number of relevant words in the top, we find the number of irrelevant words scored low in the ranking. If all the irrelevant words are at the bottom, it means that the relevant words are in the top. For instance, with a test set of 100 words, if 90 of them are relevant and 10 irrelevant, if we only count the number of relevant words in the first 90 positions, we get efficiencies from 100% to a minimum of 89% (= 80/90). But if we invert the analysis, if we count the number of irrelevant words in the 10 bottom positions we can get efficiencies from 100% (when all the irrelevant words are in those 10 bottom positions) to 0% (when all the irrelevant words **are not** in those 10 bottom positions).

4.4 Precision and Recall for the Islands method

Precision and Recall are two statistical measures which allows to evaluate the quality of results in domains such as Information Recovery or Statistical Classification. Both these metrics deal with binary data. In this work they serve to obtain quantitative information about the quality of the unigram extractor (the Islands method). Their expressions are given in equations 17 and 18.

$$Precision = \frac{\#(relevant\_words \cap considered\_relevant)}{\#considered\_relevant} . \tag{17}$$

$$Recall = \frac{\#(relevant\_words \cap considered\_relevant)}{\#relevant\_words} , \tag{18}$$

where *relevant_words* is the set of words classified manually as relevants, *considered_relevant* is the set of words considered relevant by the unigram extractor and *#(relevant_word* ∩ *considered_relevant)* is the number of words that are relevant and were considered relevant by the extractor. Briefly, **Precision** measures the proportion of how many words considered relevant by the extractor are, in fact, really relevant, while **Recall** measures the proportion of really relevant words that were considered relevant by the extractor. For instance, if you have a test set where 100 words are really relevant and the extractor has only considered relevant one single word, if you only take the Precision measure, you'd get 100% of precision. This only means all the words considered relevant by the extractor are truly relevant. But if you'd take the value of Recall, you'd get a recall of 1%, and this would mean that although the extractor is correct in the extraction, it is pretty inefficient because only one of the 100 relevant words were considered relevant by the extractor. So, as we can see, both measures are important and inseparable.

4.5 Results

The following tables (tables 6 to 8) represent the results of quality of the several test sets presented in section 4.2, when applied to the methods presented as state-of-the-art (*Tf-Idf* and *Zhou & Slater* methods) as well as to the method proposed by us (*Score* and *SPQ*). We also present results for the syllable method isolated, i.e., as if it was a metric on its own for the evaluation of relevance, only by testing the number of syllables of each word in the test sets, getting the results accordingly to the importance of each syllable group (see figure 3). Finally we also present the results of applying the syllable method in conjunction with the other methods. The application of the syllable method to another metric is something straightforward: for each word and each *standard* metric (*Score, SPQ, Tf-Idf* and *Zhou & Slater*), we multiply the obtained score with the importance of its syllable group according to its language and the correspondent graphic on figure 3. If a word is stated in those graphics as more important because of its number of syllables, the result after multiplying benefits it. Otherwise it gets the correspondent result.

Method	Test "A"	Test "B"	Test "C"	Test "D"	Test "E"
Syllables isolated	78.6	74.0	53.8	63.1	68.6
Sc	60.7	61.0	58.3	38.5	58.1
Sc & Syllables	85.7	79.2	57.5	63.1	69.0
SPQ	71.4	63.6	65.2	38.5	63.7
SPQ & Syllables	89.3	77.9	63.6	63.1	71.3
Tf-Idf	46.4	54.5	63.6	47.7	56.8
Tf-Idf & Syllables	78.6	76.6	62.1	60.0	68.0
Zhou	25.0	58.4	66.7	35.4	58.4
Zhou & Syllables	85.7	77.9	58.3	60.0	69.3

Table 6. Quality of relevance ranking for the Portuguese corpus, including results after the syllable application; values in percentage

Method	Test "A"	Test "B"	Test "C"	Test "D"	Test "E"
Syllables isolated	73.3	65.4	60.3	69.4	66.6
Sc	56.6	48.1	48.4	47.9	49.7
Sc & Syllables	80.0	63.0	65.1	70.1	69.8
SPQ	56.7	53.1	54.0	46.5	59.1
SPQ & Syllables	73.3	65.4	68.3	70.8	71.1
Tf-Idf	56.7	61.7	59.5	68.8	65.0
Tf-Idf & Syllables	70.0	70.4	71.4	75.7	74.1
Zhou	46.7	62.7	59.5	56.3	62.0
Zhou & Syllables	80.0	69.1	69.8	72.9	72.2

Table 7. Quality of relevance ranking for the English corpus, including results after the syllable application; values in percentage

Method	Test "A"	Test "B"	Test "C"	Test "D"	Test "E"
Syllables isolated	83.8	69.3	59.5	59.2	66.9
Sc	81.1	61.4	51.4	35.5	55.0
Sc & Syllables	91.9	71.6	61.3	60.5	68.5
SPQ	64.9	61.4	50.5	36.9	55.0
SPQ & Syllables	91.9	73.9	65.8	61.9	70.4
Tf-Idf	54.1	51.1	52.3	39.5	51.8
Tf-Idf & Syllables	75.7	72.7	64.9	61.8	66.9
Zhou	51.4	52.3	52.3	42.1	56.0
Zhou & Syllables	89.2	73.9	61.3	59.2	68.5

Table 8. Quality of relevance ranking for the Spanish corpus, including results after the syllable application; values in percentage

According to the previous tables we can see that the results of almost all methods are satisfactory, with almost all results being superior to 60% (and to 80% in some cases). First of all, it should be mentioned that for the "A" test set, the one that tests the 100 more frequent words, *Tf-Idf* and *Zhou & Slater* methods are inefficient as expected. For instance, while in table 6 (Portuguese corpus) *SPQ* has values of 71.4% of quality for this test set, *Tf-Idf* and *Zhou & Slater* methods have 46.4% and 25% respectively. Second, almost all methods (excluding syllable application) start to fail in "C" and "D" test sets. This has probably to do with the fact that those test sets are made from words with lower frequency in the corpora, because although statistical methods should be frequency independent, the frequency factor for the analysis of statistical data is always present. The situation is more serious in the "D" test set which has words with lower frequency (with words having frequencies of 2) which makes *Score* and *SPQ* methods to fail with quality results below 50%.

Comparing *Score, SPQ, Tf-Idf* and *Zhou & Slater* methods directly it can be noted that in a general way, in the "C", "D" and "E" test sets they have almost the same kind of results (despite some minor exceptions). It should be noted however that for the test set "A", the metrics *Score* and *SPQ* are more efficient than the other two because *Tf-Idf* and *Zhou & Slater* methods tend to damage frequent relevant words. Also it should be noted that *SPQ* metric is, as mentioned before, more efficient in Portuguese and Spanish languages than in English.

Considering now the syllable method, it can be noted that as an isolated metric, it has good results having almost the best results when considering the other isolated methods (without syllable application). When we consider the application of the syllable method to the other methods it can be noted that it improves greatly almost all results, including the results of *Tf-Idf* and *Zhou & Slater* methods, being the most flagrant case the rise of 25% to 85.7% of the *Zhou & Slater* method in the Portuguese corpus. Also, for the "D" test set, the most problematic one, it can be noted that in average, the quality results are above 60% for the Portuguese and Spanish corpus and above 70% for the English corpus. For the "A" test set, which *Tf-Idf* and *Zhou & Slater* methods have low results, after the application of the syllable method to those metrics, we have, in average, quality values of 82% for the Portuguese and Spanish corpus and 75% for the English one.

The following tables (tables 9 to 11) present the results of Precision and Recall for the Islands method. The test set used to create the tables was the "E" test set because it is the most complete one, including all the words of the other test sets. It should be mentioned again that the Islands method aims to extract the relevant words in a *Boolean* basis, either by considering a word true or false, from the relevance rankings previously obtained by the other methods.

Method	**Precision**	**Recall**
Syllables isolated	76.4	78.1
Sc	70.6	85.8
Sc & Syllables	77.0	75.3
SPQ	75.6	64.9
SPQ & Syllables	82.0	72.1
Tf-Idf	80.0	59.5
Tf-Idf & Syllables	83.5	65.8
Zhou	70.1	79.1
Zhou & Syllables	78.9	77.4

Table 9. Precision and Recall values for the Islands method for the Portuguese corpus, including results after the syllable application; values in percentage

Method	Precision	Recall
Syllables isolated	68.2	82.2
Sc	61.1	76.8
Sc & Syllables	69.2	77.0
SPQ	63.6	48.4
SPQ & Syllables	71.6	65.7
Tf-Idf	73.6	47.1
Tf-Idf & Syllables	81.5	55.4
Zhou	66.7	75.4
Zhou & Syllables	71.5	76.8

Table 10. Precision and Recall values for the Islands method for the English corpus, including results after the syllable application; values in percentage

Method	Precision	Recall
Syllables isolated	73.5	78.2
Sc	68.3	84.4
Sc & Syllables	74.7	77.1
SPQ	70.9	65.4
SPQ & Syllables	78.5	70.2
Tf-Idf	72.5	46.6
Tf-Idf & Syllables	78.2	60.8
Zhou	66.5	75.9
Zhou & Syllables	76.6	75.9

Table 11. Precision and Recall values for the Islands method for the Spanish corpus, including results after the syllable application; values in percentage

According to the previous tables it can be noted that almost all the methods have good values of Precision and Recall which means that the Islands criterion is, in a certain way, resistant to the variations of each metric used (to create the relevance ranks). In the English case (table 10) it can be noted a situation previously stated: although *Tf-Idf* has a good result on Precision, it has, however, a low value of Recall. In this case it means that although the metric is considering as relevant words with an efficiency of 73.6%, it is only considering relevant about 47.1% of all the truly relevant words. This is due, however, not to the Islands method, but to the metric used (*tf-Idf*), otherwise all the values of Recall would be as low.

For the relevance rankings with the syllable method applied it can be seen (as in the previous tables 6 to 8) that the syllable method isolated can serve as a good relevance ranking metric to use in the Islands method, having average values of 70% for Precision and almost 80% for Recall. Also, in almost all cases Precision values rises with the application of the syllable methods to those metrics, breaking the frontier of 80% for the Portuguese corpus (and *Tf-Idf* in the English one), and reaching almost 80% in the Spanish corpus. About Recall, it changes, rising sometimes and lowering other times, but in average at about 75% in Portuguese and Spanish corpora, and slightly lower in the English corpus. In general, the syllable method is able to improve the results of the Islands method as well as the quality of the relevance rankings.

6. Conclusions

The process of extraction of relevant unigrams and *n*-grams is an area of great applicability. The most flagrant examples are associated, somehow, with the classification of documents. For instance, current search engines would benefit from having unigram and multiword extractors instead of returning results merely based on the occurrence of terms as they do nowadays. Also, applications like grouping and indexing of documents are also great candidates to benefit from this kind of extractors.

However, the extraction of unigrams has been an almost ignored area by the scientific community. As it was mentioned before, to leave out unigrams in a process of extraction impoverishes the final results. The few approaches existent today suffer, however, a few problems. Essentially, they harm severely the frequent relevant words, when they are, as seen, pretty descriptive of the general topics of texts. On the other hand, all existent approaches are only capable of creating relevance rankings, which may be restrictive for some kind of applications like the characterization of keywords of documents.

In this chapter we have presented two new metrics to evaluate words that are at the same time, language, frequency and context independent. *Score* measure is capable of improving results for very frequent words, while *SPQ*, besides that, has good results for Portuguese and Spanish (or other latin-descendent languages) documents.

About the unigram extractor also presented in this chapter (Islands method), it allows to extract, with good results of efficiency, relevant unigrams from the relevance rankings. By the fact that any relevance rank can be used, this method is then metric independent.

At last, we've presented the syllable method that can work as well as an isolated metric or with another metric. It has been seen that its results are encouraging.

Although we have encouraging results, there can be, however, some improvements or further research following the sequence of this work. There is an interest in increasing even more the efficiency of all the methods, also increasing the values of Precision and Recall of the Islands method, arrange mechanisms to associate singular and plural terms and using synonyms, and, mostly, proceed with further research in the syllable area, a very promising area.

7. References

Afrin, Taniza. (2001). Extraction of Basic Noun Phrases from Natural Language using Statistical Context-Free Grammar. *Master's Thesis.* Virginia Polytechnic Institute and State University, Blacksburg, Virginia.

Das, A.; Marko, M.; Probst, A.; Porte, M. A. & Gershenson, C. (2002). Neural Net Model for featured word extraction.

Feldman, R.; Rosenfeld, B. & Fresko, M. (2006). TEG – An hybrid approach to information extraction., In *Knowledge and Information Systems.*, Vol. 9 (1), pp. 1-18, Springer-Verlag, 0219-1377, New York, USA.

Gao, Y. & Zhao, G. (2005). *Lecture Notes in Computer Science*, Knowledge-Based Information Extraction: A case study of recognizing emails of Nigerian frauds., pp. 161-172, Springer Berlin, 978-3-540-26031-8, Heidelberg.

Heid, Ulrich. (2000). A Linguistic Bootstrapping Approach to the Extraction of Term Candidates from German Texts., Terminology, pp.161-181.

Luhn, H.P. (1958). The Automatic Creation of Literature Abstracts., *IBM Journal of Research and Development, 2.* pp. 159-165.

Ortuño, M.; Carpena, P.; Bernaola-Galván, P.; Muñoz, E. & Somoza, A.M., (2002). Keyword detection in natural languages and DNA., *Europhys.* Lett 57, pp. 759-764.

Salton, G. & McGill, M.J. (1987). Term weighting approaches in automatic text retrieval., In *Information Processing & Management.*, Vol. 24 (5), pp. 513-523, 0306-4573, Pergamon Press.

Ventura, J. & Silva, J. (2007). New Techniques for Relevant Word Ranking and Extraction. In Proceedings of *13th Portuguese Conference on Artificial Intelligence,* pp. 691-702, Springer-Verlag.

Zhou, H. & Slater, G. (2003). A Metric to Search for Relevant Words., *Physica A: Statistical Mechanics and its Applications.*, Vol. 329 (1), pp. 309-327.